PROTRACTED DISPLACEMENT IN ASIA

Law, Ethics and Governance Series

Series Editor: Charles Sampford, Director, Key Centre for Ethics, Law, Justice and Governance, Griffith University, Australia

Recent history has emphasised the potentially devastating effects of governance failures in governments, government agencies, corporations and the institutions of civil society. 'Good governance' is seen as necessary, if not crucial, for economic success and human development. Although the disciplines of law, ethics, politics, economics and management theory can provide insights into the governance of organisations, governance issues can only be dealt with by interdisciplinary studies, combining several (and sometimes all) of those disciplines. This series aims to provide such interdisciplinary studies for students, researchers and relevant practitioners.

Also in this series

Measuring Corruption
Edited by Charles Sampford, Arthur Shacklock, Carmel Connors and Fredrik Galtung
ISBN 978-0-7546-2405-9

Re-envisioning Sovereignty
The End of Westphalia?
Edited by Trudy Jacobsen, Charles Sampford and Ramesh Thakur
ISBN 978-0-7546-7260-9

Islam Beyond Conflict
Indonesian Islam and Western Political Theory
Edited by Azyumardi Azra and Wayne Hudson
ISBN 978-0-7546-7092-6

Governing the Heroin Trade
From Treaties to Treatment
Melissa Bull
ISBN 978-0-7546-7121-3

Protracted Displacement in Asia
No Place to Call Home

Edited by

HOWARD ADELMAN
Griffith University, Australia

ASHGATE

Published by

Ashgate Publishing Limited
Gower House
Croft Road
Aldershot
Hampshire GU11 3HR
England

Ashgate Publishing Company
Suite 420
101 Cherry Street
Burlington, VT 05401-4405
USA

www.ashgate.com

British Library Cataloguing in Publication Data

Protracted displacement in Asia : no place to call home. -
(Law, ethics and governance series)
1. Refugees - Asia 2. Refugees - Government policy - Asia
3. Refugees - Asia - International cooperation
I. Adelman, Howard
362.8'7

Library of Congress Cataloging-in-Publication Data

Protracted displacement in Asia : no place to call home / [edited by] Howard Adelman.
p. cm. -- (Law, ethics and governance)
Includes bibliographical references.
ISBN 978-0-7546-7238-8
1. Refugees--Asia. I. Adelman, Howard, 1938-

HV640.4.A78P76 2008
362.87095--dc22

2008023656

ISBN 978-0-7546-7238-8

Mixed Sources
Product group from well-managed forests and other controlled sources
www.fsc.org Cert no. SGS-COC-2482
© 1996 Forest Stewardship Council
FSC

Printed and bound in Great Britain by
TJ International Ltd, Padstow, Cornwall

Contents

List of Figures

List of Maps and Tables

Notes on Contributors

Howard Adelman, currently Research Professor at the Key Centre for Ethics, Law, Justice and Governance at Griffith University in Brisbane, Australia, and previously a Visiting Professor at the Woodrow Wilson School at Princeton University, was a Professor of Philosophy at York University in Toronto from 1966–2003 where he founded and was the first Director of the Centre for Refugee Studies and Editor of *Refuge* until the end of 1993. He has written or co-authored eight books and edited or co-edited 18 others. He has authored 73 articles in edited volumes, 96 articles in refereed journals, and 30 professional reports. In addition to his numerous writings on refugees, he has written articles, chapters and books on the Middle East, multiculturalism, humanitarian intervention, membership rights, ethics, early warning and conflict management. Professor Adelman is currently completing a co-authored book with Elazar Barkan entitled *Rites of Return* for Princeton University Press and a co-authored book with Charles Sampford on *Military Intervention and Non-Intervention in the Twenty-First Century: An Australian Perspective* for Routledge.

Susan Banki is a Research Fellow at the Key Centre for Ethics, Law, Justice and Governance at Griffith University. Her research interests include protracted refugee situations in Asia, refugee transnationalism, national social movements, and human security. She has authored contributions to the *Journal of Refugee Studies*, *Refuge*, *Forced Migration Review*, and UNHCR's policy evaluation unit. Her writings on Burma have appeared in *The Boston Globe* and the *Far East Economic Review* online forum.

Anita Knudsen is Research Officer at Austcare working on the Australian Research Council (ARC) linkage project in collaboration with Griffith University. She holds a Master of Applied Anthropology. Her research interests encompass political violence, armed conflict, internal displacement and civilian protection.

Hazel Lang is Senior Research Fellow at Griffith University and Honorary Associate at the Centre for Peace and Conflict Studies at Sydney University. Her research interests specialize in human security, conflict analysis, peacebuilding and displacement. She is the author of *Fear and Sanctuary: Burmese Refugees in Thailand* (Ithaca: SEAP, Cornell University, 2002) and other academic and international policy publications on displacement and security in South and Southeast Asia.

William Maley, Foundation Director of the Asia-Pacific College of Diplomacy at the Australia National University, has taught in the School of Politics, University College, University of New South Wales, Australian Defence Force Academy, and has been a Visiting Professor at the Russian Diplomatic Academy, a visiting fellow at the Centre for the Study of Public Policy at the University of Strathclyde, and a visiting research fellow in the Refugee Studies Programme at Oxford University. He is also a Barrister of the High Court of Australia, a member of the Executive Committee of the Refugee Council of Australia, and a member of the Australian Committee of the Council for Security Cooperation in the Asia Pacific (CSCAP). In 2002, he was appointed a Member of the Order of Australia (AM). He has published extensively on Afghanistan, Pakistan and East Timor, asylum seekers and refugees, security, peacebuilding and protection.

Eileen Pittaway is the Director of the Centre for Refugee Research, University of New South Wales, Sydney, Australia, and Senior Lecturer in the School of Social Work. In the past decade she has conducted research, provided training to refugees, UN and NGO staff in refugee camps and urban settings, acted as technical advisor to a number of projects, and evaluated humanitarian and development projects in Kenya, Thailand, Ethiopia, Bougainville, Egypt and Sri Lanka. She is also involved in tsunami relief projects in Sri Lanka. She has specialized in the protection of refugee women and girls and has published extensively on this issue. In 2001 Eileen was awarded a Human Rights Medal by the Australian Human Rights and Equal Opportunities Commission for her work with refugee women and children. In 2005 she was awarded a New South Wales Premier's Award for her contribution to public education regarding refugees.

Susanne Schmeidl is a Senior Researcher at the Key Centre for Ethics, Law, Justice and Governance at Griffith University in Australia and an advisor of the Tribal Liaison Office in Afghanistan. She has been a visiting fellow with the Asia-Pacific College of Diplomacy at the Australian National University (2006) and worked for nine years with Swisspeace on early warning, conflict prevention and peacebuilding and managed the Swisspeace office in Afghanistan supporting civil society development and peacebuilding. She holds an MA and PhD in Sociology from the Ohio State University (1989 and 1995) and worked at the Centre for Refugee Studies (York University, Canada) as a postdoctoral researcher (1995–1996), coordinator of the Prevention/Early Warning Unit (1996–1997), coordinator of the Interim Secretariat of the Forum on Early Warning and Early Response (1996–1997), and technical consultant for the Food and Statistics Unit of the UN High Commissioner for Refugees (1997). She has published in the areas of Afghanistan, gender, civil society, refugee migration, conflict early warning, peacebuilding and human security.

Michael G. Smith was the CEO of Austcare, an Australian non-sectarian humanitarian aid and development organization that has been active in more than

30 countries since 1967 up until the end of February 2008. He is a former Major General in the Australian Army, having served in Papua New Guinea, Cambodia, Kashmir and East Timor. With Dr Moreen Dee he is the author of (2003) *Peacekeeping in East Timor: The Path to Independence* (Boulder and London: Lynne Rienner) and 'East Timor' in William Durch (ed.) (2007) *Twenty-First Century Peace Operations* (Washington, DC: USIP and Stimson Center). He is an Adjunct Professor at Griffith University, a member of the International Advisory Board of the Asia-Pacific College of Diplomacy at the Australian National University, and a member of the Foreign Minister's National Consultative Committee on International Security Issues. Currently, Mike Smith is the Executive Director of the newly created Asia Pacific Centre for Civil-Military Coorporation.

Foreword

In 2006, I was privileged to be invited by Austcare's CEO, Michael Smith, to become their Ambassador for Protection. Austcare's vision was ambitious and exciting, and I felt compelled to accept. In my capacity as a member of parliament and international jurist, I had already visited a number of displacement camps. I remain shocked and appalled at the conditions endured by our fellow human beings. At the same time, I have been inspired by their resilience, courage and dignity to survive and hope for a better life for their children. Austcare wanted my assistance to help empower refugees and internally displaced persons (IDPs) to build their human security through the development of a practical protection programme based on action research, the mainstreaming of protection in field projects, and raising a rapid response register to quickly deploy trained protection officers to witness for and assist the displaced.

As I assumed my new Ambassadorial role, an exciting Australian Research Council (ARC) project and subject of this book, *Protracted Displacement in Asia: No Place to Call Home*, was just getting underway. This ARC project formed an important part of Austcare's protection programme because Austcare wanted to understand the protracted character of displacement in Asia, and whether practical measures might be taken to foster durable solutions and enhance the protection for the forcibly displaced. But Austcare could not do this alone! They needed research expertise and independent analysis. The resulting teaming with the Key Centre for Ethics, Governance, Law and Justice at Griffith University, and the Asia-Pacific College of Diplomacy at the Australian National University, resulted in a team whose intellectual 'whole' proved more than the sum of its parts. The ARC team was also assisted by the Centre for Refugee Research at the University of New South Wales.

In this ARC project, the five case studies of protracted displacement, and one of a potential protracted displacement, make a significant contribution to understanding the lamentable increase in such situations and the challenges in resolving them. They also demonstrate how durable solutions must be designed to fit each situation and the mixture of refugees and IDPs and suggest new thinking and innovation in lieu of accepting and condoning the 'warehousing' of people for indeterminate and lengthy periods of time.

I commend the team on the quality of their research, and look forward to working with Austcare in considering these findings and the influence they will have in shaping the agency's future research, advocacy and programming priorities.

The Hon. John Dowd, AO, QC
Austcare Ambassador for Protection and Chairperson,
Executive Committee of the International Commission of Jurists

Preface

Institutional background

The Assistant High Commissioner for Operations at the UN High Commission for Refugees (UNHCR), Ms Judy Cheng-Hopkins, noted in her address to the Annual UNHCR Consultations (2006) that she had identified protracted displacement situations as one of her key priorities. NGOs and states welcomed the emphasis, particularly the recent efforts to address two of the longest protracted displacement situations in Asia through the resettlement of Burmese refugees in Thailand and Bhutanese refugees in Nepal. She offered strong support and congratulations to the actors involved in negotiations to break the political impasse that had frozen the refugee situations in those countries for so long.[1]

The year before Cheng-Hopkins made her speech, an Australian NGO that was already assisting refugees both in Nepal and on the Thai–Burma border formed a collaboration with the Key Centre for Ethics, Law, Justice and Governance at Griffith University and with the Asia-Pacific College of Diplomacy at the Australian National University to undertake research on protracted refugees as well as internally displaced situations in Asia. Eileen Pittaway, Director of the Centre for Refugee Research, University of New South Wales, was invited to join the project as well because of her work in the region, her collaboration with UNHCR and her close working relationship with Austcare.

Austcare's concerns

Austcare, as an organization seeking to improve its understanding of the causes of and cures for protracted displacement, avoided researching so-called 'root' causes of the displacement, though it recognized that an exploration of the various historical conditions and roles of different players would be a prerequisite for grasping the circumstances behind the forced displacement. Austcare was interested in the *protracted* character of the situation much more than the violent conflict and the causes that produced the forced displacement in the first place. Given the commitment of UNHCR, and, by extension, the NGO partners that

1 Cf. 'Austcare's Report on UNHCR's Executive Committee Meeting and Annual Consultations with NGOs, Geneva, 27 September–6 October, 2006' (Austcare 2006). See also '57th Session of the Executive Committee: Report on the Annual Consultations with Non-Governmental Organizations' (UNHCR 2006).

worked with UNHCR, to finding durable solutions and not just continuing the care and maintenance of refugees and internally displaced persons (IDPs) (Chimni 1999), the key issue was why these refugee situations were allowed to continue for so long. Austcare wanted to know what more could be done to resolve situations of displacement and whether its own actions might be contributing to the protracted nature of the problem.

If the emphasis was then on the *protracted* character of refugee situations and not on the causes of forced displacement ab initio, why did Austcare choose to partner with an academic research institution? Why not undertake the research itself or simply ask a research institution with the capability and interest to undertake the research? There were many reasons. First, by becoming involved in independent research there was a greater probability that the results would be translated into actionable projects. On the other hand, by involving a research organization with expertise on refugee and IDP issues, the research was less likely to be self-serving, particularly if NGOs constituted part of the reason for refugee and IDP situations remaining protracted. Further, Austcare recognized from its own work that humanitarian service requires a professional approach. Those dedicated to humanitarian service had little time to spare for empirical research and critical self-reflection about the fundamentals underlying their activities. The demands of day-to-day crises were, and continue to be, very great. Further, Austcare acknowledged that research as well as humanitarian work required professional skills and dedication. By partnering with professional researchers, Austcare could facilitate access to the field while participating in the formulation of research questions and methods for investigation. At the same time, Austcare would have greater access to the larger network of researchers in the refugee field.

However, most of all Austcare was committed to finding a cure, and, if not a cure, a way forward for improving the lot of refugees in protracted situations, particularly in the area of enhancing protection for those refugees, and advancing the possibility of a durable solution. Austcare wanted research, but it wanted research that also focused on practical and realistic solutions. The research organization allowed Austcare to leverage the monetary allocation that it could dedicate to research by the contributions of the Australian Research Council (ARC) in order to undertake an in-depth and larger comparative research study than would have been possible on its own. By partnering with professional refugee analysts, Austcare sought to undertake action research which could be used as a catalyst for change instigated through critical reflection on the actions examined and analysed to better guide and shape Austcare's growing human security programme of 'displacement and protection'.

It is important to understand that this project was founded on the premise that it was to be an action research project that linked theory with practice. For humanitarian agencies, better theory, new paradigms and alternative frameworks are constantly needed. However, attention also needs to be paid to the relationship between these theories and the practices and events in particular contexts. Analysis has to take account of the practical realities that agencies face. As a rapidly evolving sector, trends in humanitarian thinking risk ignoring the important relationship between policy and the practices that research is intended to foster. Austcare challenges the assumption that practice is driven by policy developed without regard to research, suggesting that what makes for good policy – policy that legitimizes and mobilizes support – is research, but research that reflects realities and is grounded in practice.

The relationship between research, policy and practice is mostly understood in terms of 'divides' or 'gaps'. How do we overcome that gap? Most frequently, research for a humanitarian agency involves an evaluation of the degree to which existing policies and goals failed to be achieved and attempts to explain the shortfall. But research is not simply about evaluating the implementation of given policies and translating those policies into more effective practices. Research raises questions about the premises behind policies and practices. Often monitoring and evaluation by agencies provide a means to protect and promote policies that conceal the underlying realities and the long-term inefficacy of practice, while improving the efficacy of delivering existing services.

On the other hand, the issue is not simply a question of sound research properly applied. Researchers may become obsessed with 'root' causes that produce the displacement and focus on the causes of the violence that led to the forced displacement. Austcare was primarily concerned with treatment, with ending the protracted dimensions of refugee situations and not with the sources of conflict over which it could have little input, while recognizing its need to understand the fundamental sources of the violent conflict. The analogy is akin to searching for the discovery of insulin as Frederick Banting and Charles Best did in 1921, when they succeeded in isolating the key ingredient in the islets of Langerhans in the pancreas, even though the root causes of the 'sugar disease', diabetes, have still not been resolved over 80 years later, while its incidence has become a widespread crisis disease of modernity. One can treat problems even when one cannot explicitly define or deal with their sources.

Austcare was also always mindful that there was a third player involved in the research who provided neither research funds nor research expertise but was the most important part of the partnership – each refugee and IDP community. In the last two decades following the development of refugee studies as a research field, refugee situations have been researched and re-researched. Almost universally, refugees are tired of being probed and questioned with relatively very little to show in terms of improved conditions for themselves and improved prospects for ending their plight. For a humanitarian agency to partner with a research organization meant risking its relationship with its most important partner. For practical reasons, the displaced communities could not be involved in the research design and would be unable to implement the findings by themselves. However, if the research were not informed by the concerns and priorities of the displaced, Austcare believed that the research would risk failure. If the research design and implementation of results did not take the views of the displaced, the silent partners of the project, fully into account and ensure that their views were perceived as the most important, then those whom Austcare is dedicated to serving risked betrayal.

In one case, this involved a deliberate decision not to interview or consult with the displaced directly lest they be placed at greater risk because of the research. This limited the results, as will be discussed in the case of the Sri Lankan IDPs, but was seen as necessary under the circumstances. Instead, the research focused on a critical examination of humanitarian agencies and how they did and could serve the IDPs.

This type of partnership inevitably marries diverse representations of realities, confronting the tensions among researchers and between academic goals and the policy goals of practitioners. Further, the approach insists that theory emerges from experience and an examination of practices; theory is not to be imposed on those practices. Such research has to reflect field realities and draw on relationships across many levels, from the local, regional and transnational to the international, all of which are played out in the daily lives of refugees and IDPs. Ultimately, such research encourages critical reflection on the part of practitioners while ensuring that research communities benefit from practitioner insights. The research aims at reconciling the instrumental and critical perspectives of research.

Austcare also wanted to ensure that its staff and local partners benefited from the research and, to the extent possible, were involved in the production as well as the prospective consumption of the research results. Austcare was convinced that outputs would not have impact unless they were transformed into practitioner-orientated and accessible literature. The issue of such transformation had to be an integral part of the research process so that research also served as a capacity building process.

Research has the potential not only to reorientate practice, but it can develop evidence-based policy that mobilizes political and donor support. (Hyndman 2000) Humanitarian agencies, with access to policymakers and governments, with a visibility and influence greater than that of independent researchers, can retain and enhance support from a range of actors with different interests and agendas and maintain relationships throughout the research process to navigate the links between the wider goals of research. Most importantly, quality action research is in a better position than any other alternative research process to benefit refugees and IDPs who generously give their time and insights. Action research must rest on reciprocity, not only between the researchers and the humanitarian agency, but also between the researchers, practitioners and the forcibly displaced.

Research background

This ARC research project began against the backdrop of several researchers who had already begun to focus on protracted displacement. Jeff Crisp, in his 2001

UNHCR paper, 'Addressing Protracted Refugee Situations',[2] placed the item of protracted refugee situations on the agenda for the twenty-first century. Merrill Smith's 'Warehousing Refugees: A Denial of Rights, a Waste of Humanity', in the 2004 *World Refugee Survey* probably accelerated the new widespread focus on protracted refugee situations. The issue was on the agenda of UNHCR's Executive Committee at the 30th meeting of the Programme Standing Committee (EC/54/SC/CRP.14, 10 June 2004).

The first in-depth research projects were initiated in 2005, one by Gil Loescher and James Milner[3] in Britain, and another ARC research project led by Charles Sanford and Bill Maley, with Mike Smith of Austcare as the industrial partner. The ARC project resulted in the essays for this volume. Earlier independent and unconnected studies by Howard Adelman and Awa Abdi of Dadaab Refugee Camp in Kenya (Adelman and Abdi 2003) also helped stimulate the recognition of the need for further studies.[4] These were followed soon after by Wenona Giles' (2006) initiative at the Centre for Refugee Studies at York University in Toronto.[5]

These in-depth studies were informed by the prior work of their lead researchers. In 2004, Gil Loescher wrote a paper for UNHCR entitled 'Protracted Refugee Situations: The Search for Practical Solutions'.[6] That paper advocated a comprehensive research approach involving security and development as well as humanitarian agencies. According to Loescher's thesis, the immediate issues of violence as well as the long term plans of development had to be taken into account in resolving long-term unresolved refugee situations (Black and Koser 1999). Loescher envisioned a coordinated approach to develop a comprehensive plan of action that would involve the resolution of the conflict as well as a long range development project in which repatriation of the refugees would be one element in the three durable solutions sought for those refugees who had been living for years in a state of limbo. On 27 September 2005, Loescher gave the keynote address at UNHCR's annual consultation with NGOs.[7] He cited the June 2004 Standing Committee paper in which UNHCR pointed out that:

> protracted refugee situations stem from political impasses. They are not inevitable, but are rather the result of political action and inaction, both in the country of origin and in the country of asylum. They endure because of ongoing problems in the country of

2 See also Crisp 2002; 2003a; 2003b.

3 James Milner subsequently became a Research Fellow at the Munk Centre for International Studies at the University of Toronto. Edward Newman and Gary Troeller subsequently joined the project.

4 The Adelman study of Dadaab was conducted jointly with Awa Abdi. Cf. Adelman and Abdi (2003) and Abdi (2004). See also Abdullah (2000) for a Dadaab capacity approach as discussed in Chapter 1. Also Horst (1997); Harman (2002); HRW (2002).

5 Jennifer Hyndman of Syracuse University joined Wenona Giles on this project.

6 <http://www.org/publ/PUBL/4444/AfcbO.pdf>.

7 The presentation is available on the ICVA (the International Council of Voluntary Agencies) website <http://www.icva.ch/doc00001468.html>.

origin, and stagnate and become protracted as a result of responses to refugee inflows, typically involving restrictions on refugee movement and employment possibilities, and confinement to camps.

Loescher, joined by Milner, emphasized addressing the political issues behind the protracted nature of the conflict.[8] As Loescher concluded:

> This analysis starkly illustrates how chronic refugee situations are the combined result of unresolved political and security problems in the country of origin, the inadequate policy responses of the country of asylum, and the lack of sufficient external engagement in these situations. In fact, the prolonged presence of refugees is caused largely by both a lack of involvement by a range of peace and security actors to address the conflict or human rights violations in the country of origin and a lack of donor government involvement with the host country. Failure to address the situation in the country of origin means that the refugee cannot return home. Failure to engage with the host country reinforces the perception of refugees as a burden and a security concern, which leads to encampment and a lack of local solutions. As a result of these failures, NGOs and UNHCR are left to compensate for the inaction of those actors responsible for maintaining international peace and security. They also have been left to cope with caring for these forgotten populations and attempting to mitigate the negative implications of prolonged exile. (2005, 163)

Though the comprehensive approach involving security and development as well as humanitarian agencies focusing on the underlying political causes could be viewed as complementary to the Adelman/Abdi targeted approach (fn. 5), the latter emphasized how much could be done within the resources and mandate of the humanitarian community to seek out durable solutions even when there was no ultimate resolution to the conflict situation. The Adelman/Abdi analysis was more concerned with the options for action to end protracted refugee situations in the

8 Loescher and Milner had published ‘Protracted Refugee Situations and State and Regional Security’ that year setting out their research agenda and its significance (Loescher and Milner 2004) and together would publish a follow-up piece the next year entitled, ‘The Long Road Home: Protracted Refugee Situations in Africa’ (Loescher and Milner 2005b). In 2005, they also published their Adelphi Paper No. 375, ‘Protracted Refugee Situations: Domestic and International Security Situations’ (Loescher and Milner 2005a). Most recently, they, along with Edward Newman and Gary Troeller in 2007 published ‘Protracted Refugee Situations and the Dynamics of Peacebuilding,’ (Loescher et al. 2007). See also Betts (2006), a report on ‘The Politics, Human Rights and Security Implications of Protracted Refugee Situations’, that sought to develop a framework for comprehensive solutions as well as thematic papers, including case studies of Afghan, Somali, Southern Sudanese, Palestinian, Bhutanese and Burmese refugees. Loescher is not alone in this position. Khalid Koser, another eminent scholar of forced displacement, also argues that ‘durable solutions for the displaced are often inextricably linked to achieving peace in post-conflict settings’ (Koser 2008). However, peace in the Balkans did not lead to significant minority returns.

absence of resolving the underlying conflict and the resistance to integrating the refugees in host countries.

The two approaches did agree on some issues. Both recognized that responding to protracted refugee situations requires an understanding of the specific historical context as well as a current analysis of the situation, and the needs, desires and concerns of the refugees. Loescher stressed 'capacities' of both the countries of origin and first asylum; Adelman/Abdi recognized that their *stances* had to be taken into account. The priorities of countries of resettlement and donor countries were also important to both sets of authors.

However, each research project emphasized a different approach and different foci. While Loescher and Milner envisioned a very limited impact if discussion were restricted to the humanitarian dimensions, Adelman and Abdi believed that reliance solely on comprehensive solutions involving peaceful resolution of the violence could simply delay interim solutions that were readily available. As Adelman's studies of the Palestinian refugee situation indicate, the emphasis on a comprehensive resolution of the conflict has been an integral part of the delay in addressing the refugee situation in the interim (Adelman 1982; 1983; 1984; 1986; 1988). Adelman's (2002) other work also revealed, contrary to his own previous beliefs, that solving refugee problems was rarely if ever critical to sustaining peace agreements. Further, his studies on ethnic conflicts and return also concluded that a durable solution to protracted refugee situations in the form of return of the refugees to their original homes, except if return is facilitated by the successful use of force, was very remote and highly unlikely when the source of the violence was connected with ethnic and religious conflicts (Adelman and Barkan 2008, forthcoming).

The differences about the best approach to treating protracted displacement are not resolved by this ARC research project. However, it is important to note and clarify these differences. Loescher and Adelman have engaged in collegial discussions for almost 30 years, not only in understanding current situations and proposing solutions for the future, but in their reading and interpretation of the past. Those interpretations inform the present and allow for varied emphases in proposing longer term solutions. For Loescher and Milner (2005a), 'Increased external involvement in regions of refugee origin, comprehensive solutions to protracted refugee situations, and a more holistic approach to ensure effective refugee protection in the regions of refugee origin is not only the best way to meet the protection needs of refugees, but also is an effective way to respond to the concerns of host governments in the developing world and to address the concerns of Western states.' In contrast, Adelman's previous research and this volume suggest that although holism and situating refugees within communities of practice are prerequisites to the research, solutions to protracted refugee situations cannot wait for increased external involvement of actors in regions of origin. Indeed, such involvement is unlikely in Bhutan and Burma. Intervention complicated the problem in Sri Lanka, and has been part of the problem in both Afghanistan and Iraq. This does not mean that understanding and taking into consideration the role of such countries is not critical in relieving the protracted situation of the refugees, but that it is unlikely to come from intervention in the country of origin. A more holistic approach with respect to solutions is not only far more difficult to pull off, but this and other studies suggest that solutions to facilitate refugee repatriation are more or less futile when ethnic and religious cleansing has taken place.[9] In contrast, the Adelman/Abdi study had emphasized how much could be done within the resources and mandate of the humanitarian community to seek out durable solutions even when there was no ultimate resolution to the conflict situation. In the debate over the best and the most effective approaches,[10] without adopting a comprehensive approach to the different problems, this ARC research project looks at the efforts of humanitarian agencies on the ground. The results largely pointed to different conclusions than advocating a comprehensive holistic approach to providing solutions.

This analysis has perhaps overemphasized the differences between the Adelman and Loescher approaches. As indicated above, the approaches are more similar than different, and where different, are often complementary. Perhaps the most important of these links was not included in the list at the beginning of this comparison. This is the premise that refugee research is not a detached activity indifferent to norms and outcomes. Refugee research is propelled by an ethical imperative to improve the lives of those who have been left without the protection of a state. Though ethics propels and informs the research, it is important that those commitments do not distort the results so that we produce moral outrage as a substitute for analysis.

Overview of the volume

This research on those efforts on the ground and the multiple practices that have developed to deal with refugee and IDP situations focused on protracted displacement in the Asian region, which vies with Africa as the largest source of forced displacement. Asia is the primary humanitarian and foreign policy concern for the Australian government.

The first chapter sets out a theoretical context in conceptualizing refugees, one that is rooted in the writings of Hannah Arendt and views refugees primarily as a problem of membership in a state that protects its citizens. The other theoretical cosmopolitan perspective emphasizes refugees as universal rights holders. These

9 'Once ethnic antagonism has crossed a certain threshold of violence, maintaining the rival groups within a single polity becomes far more difficult' (Muller 2008). See also Kaufman 2007.

10 The Austcare/Griffith research team had not agreed at the beginning on the piecemeal incremental approach tailored to specific situations. Nor were researchers recruited based on an agreement on this premise. In fact, originally, at least two of the researchers explicitly advocated replicating the Loescher approach.

differences are situated within the historical development of institutions charged with dealing with refugees and the shifts over the twentieth century in how refugees were handled by the international community. The problem of protracted refugee and internally displaced situations and the different and alternative responses are then contextualized within this historical and conceptual framework.

Chapter 2 takes up the issue of the 105,000 Bhutanese refugees or Lhotshampas who have been living in seven camps in Nepal for up to 18 years. Despite 15 rounds of bilateral negotiations between Bhutan and Nepal on repatriation, not a single refugee has returned home. Recent initiatives for resettlement have come about but only after the birth and coming of age of second-generation refugee children. Further, the infusion of resettlement as a durable solution has enhanced the politicization of durable solutions amongst refugee leaders. One durable solution – the resettlement of refugees abroad – may undermine the political goals, however legitimate, of those who have been yearning for repatriation since they fled Bhutan in the early 1990s. In fact, rather than peace being a precondition for a durable solution, one type of durable solution, resettlement abroad, may even reinforce the prospect of peace, but only on terms that benefit the authoritarian political and military forces most responsible for the exodus in the first place. In Chapter 2, Susan Banki examines the durable solution discourse applied to the Bhutanese in Nepal that developed into a programme of refugee resettlement. In the aim of resolving a protracted refugee situation, the prospect of softening the policy of the Bhutan government to permit return may be undermined.

Thailand, however, is host to the largest protracted refugee situation in Southeast Asia, and prospects for a safe and sustainable repatriation remain untenable in the present context of chronic human insecurity in Burma. Over two decades have passed since the first 'semi-permanent' camps were established in Thailand. One hundred and forty-five thousand (145,000) people live in the border camps with a steady flow of arrivals continuing each month. Since 2006, resettlement as a durable solution is now firmly on the agenda, but this raised new problems. Resettlement may be interpreted as de facto condoning the Burmese junta's actions, and, to some, even justifying them. Further, there is a concern with the protection and provision of those remaining in the camps during the transition period that might stretch over many years as leaders and teachers depart for opportunities to resettle abroad. There is also the possibility of resettlement serving as a magnet to entice more of the oppressed to cross the border as well as those who wanted to take advantage of the possibility of economic improvement. In addition, there is the remainder problem – the disposition of those in the camps who do not want to resettle for various reasons. Finally, planners have to consider the potential response of unregistered refugees who live in legal limbo outside the camps.

Susan Banki and Hazel Lang examine protracted displacement on the Thai–Burmese border and the interrelated search for durable solutions in Chapter 3 of this volume. Beyond their study, however, the situation of forced displacement from Burma to Thailand and Bangladesh raises the possibility of intervening militarily to implement a presumed Responsibility to Protect (R2P) on the part of the international community. Others are more sceptical of the benefits of military intervention and are more wary of the unintended consequences that could result in protracted conflict.

While Burmese refugees along the Thai border now have a prospect of a durable solution, this is not the case for the 26,000 Rohingyas living in camps in Bangladesh who fled ethnic and religious persecution in Burma. Their numbers are multiplied many times over by the Rohingyas who live in misery as self-settled refugees among the local Bangladeshi population. They have chosen not to take shelter in the camps, in good part out of a fear of being returned forcibly (Barnett 2001; Ahmed 2003). The situation of the Rohingyas in Bangladesh includes a lack of recognition of refugee status and the threat of forcible return. In spite of dire living conditions, both in the camps and amongst the population in Bangladesh, the refugees are by and large unwilling to return to a situation at home that they regard as considerably worse than the deplorable situation in Bangladesh in which they have to live. Why has their palpable need for a durable solution been virtually ignored, though very tiny initiatives at resettlement have begun? In Chapter 4, Eileen Pittaway examines the failure of the international protection regime for the Rohingya refugees in Bangladesh, and implicitly raises the question of which refugee groups receive recognition and attention and which do not. More significantly, she questions why differential recognition takes place.

Sri Lankan IDPs offered a fourth case study for the ARC research project. Since 1983, displacement in Sri Lanka has been embedded in an intractable conflict, one where outside intervention by India with the concurrence of the Sri Lankan political authorities seems to have exacerbated the displacement problem rather than help resolve it. Many IDPs have experienced repeated and ongoing cycles of displacement while some IDPs have stayed temporarily in the same place for more than a decade. Further, the durable solutions have been thoroughly infused with political agendas. The recent deteriorating security situation in the northeast of Sri Lanka creates a particular challenge for protection approaches. It is difficult for NGO humanitarian workers to remain neutral; if they so much as appear to involve themselves with the political dimensions of the problem, they put at great risk their ability to help IDPs at all. Hazel Lang and Anita Knudsen explore the challenges and dilemmas of protection in the context of the Sri Lankan conflict-induced internal displacement in Chapter 5.

Afghan refugees at one point accounted for roughly 60 per cent of the entire world refugee population. Two-thirds of Afghans have been displaced at least once over the last 30 years so that forced displacement has become an integral feature of the Afghanistan experience. This is a case where there have been vast repatriation efforts following military intervention and the overthrow of the Taliban. Nevertheless, Afghanistan still tops the world's list of sources of forced migration and sometimes the prospects of further return do seem dependent on a final peaceful resolution, as Loescher and Milner have advocated (cited above). In the interim, neighbouring and Western countries push for return, but its character as a 'voluntary' movement is much in question. The current deteriorating security situation raises critical issues of protection and even access by humanitarian actors and, in order to be reversed, may depend not on a peace agreement but on a further and more sustained commitment of external forces. It is certainly a case where the humanitarian, political, military and development issues are all intertwined, but it is one where the repatriation may be taking place for vast numbers of refugees in spite of the lack of security because of the political positions of the adjacent host states. Chapter 6 by Susanne Schmeidl and William Maley deals with the Afghan refugee population. It is our three-for-one longest chapter because, in effect, it deals with Afghan refugees in Iran, Afghan refugees in Pakistan and the internally displaced within Afghanistan. The search for durable solutions is not only a multidimensional case, but one in which the search to resolve the problem takes place in a multi-sided and violently contested environment.

The Iraq desk-based case study in Chapter 7 examines the two million refugees and 2.2 million IDPs produced by the intervention of US-led forces in 2003 as a possible 'protracted' situation in the making even though it is too early to characterize that displaced situation as 'protracted'. Early predictions overestimated the number of Iraqi refugees;[11] ironically, the displaced population exceeded all expectations.

---

11 The original estimates were based on displacement anticipated from the initial invasion. There were predictions that the West was ill-prepared to handle the displacement. Gil Loescher had argued that planning for the inevitable refugee crisis following an attack on Iraq was woefully inadequate. Cf. Gil Loescher (2003), 'A disaster waiting to happen'. See also Helton and Loescher (2003), 'Internally Displaced Persons in Iraq: A Potential Crisis?'. Loescher had presented a paper entitled, 'War in Iraq, An Impending Refugee Crisis? Uncertain Risks, Inadequate Preparation and Coordination' to the Center for Comparative Immigration Studies at the University of California at San Diego in December of 2002 on which this op-ed piece was based. Loescher was more equivocal in the paper than in the op-ed piece by the very character of the medium and had stated that the dimension of the refugee crisis would depend on the manner and duration of the military campaign – the short, swift campaign focused on by the army resulted in little displacement. Further, Loescher had anticipated the possibility of further displacement *after* the war was over. However, he was incorrect in predicting that the overwhelming burden of the refugee crisis would fall on international agencies with little experience in the region, for the burden of the refugees has largely fallen on Syria and Jordan. In addition, in dealing with IDPs, the international agencies were not forced to deal with chemical and biological weapons as Loescher had anticipated as a possibility, one of the fictions that had propelled the march to war in the first place. Nor did Loescher anticipate that the insurgency would regard the international agencies as their enemies and bomb the UN quarters at the cost of serious injury to Loescher and the loss of the lives of his close friends and colleagues, Arthur Helton and Sergio Vieira de Mello, the UN special envoy to Iraq. However, though General Jay Garner who headed the US reconstruction effort was prepared to handle a massive refugee crisis of 150,000 to 200,000 forcibly displaced in the original effort to defeat the Iraqi army, he was actually over-prepared for the humanitarian effort at that time as there was virtually no forced displacement because the Iraqi army was defeated so quickly. The UN, in contrast, anticipated up to 600,000 displaced as a result of the original clashes with the Iraq army.

The eventual huge numbers of forcibly displaced from the insurgency and inter-religious violence were generally unanticipated.[12] Many Iraq experts had clearly adumbrated that Sunni/Shia inter-religious violence and religious cleansing was a possibility, but not one refugee scholar could predict that Paul Bremer would purge the civil service of Baathists and dissolve the Republican Guard, thereby decimating the government administration and dissolving the army, creating the basis for the insurgency and massive displacement that followed.

Given the religious cleansing that has taken place, though Sunni and Shia can return to areas where they are in the majority, the almost total expulsion of Iraq's Christian and other minorities, especially since 2006, means that the only *permanent* solution for these minorities is resettlement abroad as Chapter 7 suggests. These refugees that cannot repatriate should not be left in legal limbo in Jordan and Syria, which have been generous enough to take them in but have now effectively closed their doors and are beginning to push those who have exhausted their resources back to Iraq. While IDPs have largely resettled within Iraq in areas where their group is a majority, in the case of many of the refugees we find a probable protracted refugee situation in the making that could be prevented by a massive international resettlement movement. However, it appears that the US is currently too worried that this would be akin to the admission of failure, as in Vietnam that was also followed by a massive resettlement programme. As Adelman explains in Chapter 7, the Iraqi refugee and IDP situation is another case where the political dimensions of the conflict explain the resistance to durable solutions as well as the production of the displacement in the first place.

This brief sketch of the case studies in this ARC research project demonstrates that just as displacement takes place in politicized and militarized contexts, so do proposed solutions. Does one have to adopt a comprehensive approach integrating humanitarian, political, security and developmental dimensions in a holistic approach, or can one leave the search for an ultimate peaceful resolution and effective development programme to others and instead search for openings and opportunities to push for humanitarian solutions in the interim? That question is left to the last chapter where it is addressed by Michael Smith, who served as Chief Executive Officer of Austcare from 2002 until April of 2008. This concluding chapter summarizes a number of lessons extracted from each of the specific case studies, recognizing that sensible policies need to be extracted from in-depth studies of each situation, as well as the difficulty and dangers in trying to devise universal solutions. Nevertheless, Smith attempts to develop a set of more general lessons to suggest how humanitarian agencies can more effectively respond to protracted displacement and enhance the protection of populations living in prolonged limbo. Smith suggests that three different intertwined and overlapping

12 There were other failures to anticipate events that followed the invasion. The invading forces were totally under-prepared for the civil disorder that took place given the refusal of the Department of Defense to take into account the anticipations and preparations of the State Department for dealing with the potential for civil disorder.

dilemmas need to be mediated: (1) between state sovereignty and human security; (2) between national self-interest and universal morality; and (3) between durable solutions versus what Smith dubs 'enduring solutions' that perpetuate the plight of refugees and IDPs.

If state sovereignty continues to predominate over human security, based on the principle that individuals and communities are entitled to live in freedom from fear and freedom from want, then protracted displacement will continue. If protracted displacement continues to be perceived by states as a social and humanitarian problem to be contained and managed in order to avoid or minimize the chances of future conflict, then there is little possibility of prevention; work towards durable solutions will be marginal. If employment of the R2P doctrine to provide protection becomes feasible, given the 2005 unanimous agreement on R2P at the UN Leaders' Summit, then the possibility of prevention and mitigation may become relevant. A second tension between national self-interest and universal morality has almost always favoured the former, but Smith envisions the possibility of R2P placing national self-interest and morality on an equal footing since it is in a state's best interest to intervene to prevent or halt atrocities. Although Smith envisions R2P providing hope for the future, he recognizes that it remains an untested concept and in all likelihood may not be used to prevent or stop many situations of displacement.

Finally, Smith suggests further research on the role of camps in promoting enduring rather than durable solutions, research to uncover the conditions under which a particular humanitarian intervention is most likely to be effective, and research to determine the effectiveness of establishing regional early warning and management systems. Smith also points to the need to rethink the traditional concept of 'humanitarian space', particularly given its juxtaposition with governance and the rule of law, to rethink the traditional humanitarian principles of humanity, independence, impartiality and neutrality that have proven so difficult to apply in contested environments, and to encourage humanitarian agencies to work more collaboratively to provide better and more consistent levels of protection while developing local capacity among the displaced populations.

Howard Adelman

Bibliography

Abdi, A. (2004), 'In Limbo: Dependency, Insecurity and Identity amongst Somali Refugees in Dadaab Camps', *Refuge: Canada's Periodical on Refugees* 22: 2.

Abdullah, A. (2000), 'A Case for Refugee Technical Education', Report (Dadaab, Kenya: CARE) May.

Adelman, H. (1982), 'Politics and Refugees: The United Nations Relief and Works Agency for Palestine Refugees in the Near East', *Refuge*, May/June, I: 8.

Adelman, H. (1983), 'Palestine Refugees: Defining the Humanitarianism Problem', in *World Refugee Survey* (Washington, DC: US Committee for Refugees), 20–27.

Adelman, H. (1984), 'Palestinian Refugees and the Peace Process', in J. Stein and P. Moranz (eds), *Perspectives on Peacemaking* (London: Croon-Helm Ltd).

Adelman, H. (1986), 'Palestinian Refugees and Politics', *Middle East Focus* 9: 2.

Adelman, H. (1988), 'Palestine Refugees, Economic Integration and Durable Solutions', in A. Bramwell (ed.), *Refugees in the Age of Total War* (London: Unwin Hyman), 295–311.

Adelman, H. (2002), 'Repatriation of Refugees Following the Signing of Peace Agreements: A Comparative Study of the Aftermath of Peace in Fourteen Civil Wars', in S. Stedman et al. (eds), *Thematic Issues in Peace Agreements Following Civil Wars* (Boulder: Lynne Rienner Publishers).

Adelman, H. and Abdi, A. (2003), 'How Long is Too Long? Durable Solutions for the Dadaab Refugees', Report (Ottawa: CARE Canada).

Adelman, H. and Barkan, E. (forthcoming), *Rites of Return* (Princeton: Princeton University Press).

Ahmed, I. (2003), 'Globalization, Low-Intensity Conflict and Protracted Refugeehood: The Plight of the Stateless Rohingyas', Occasional Paper (Dhaka: Department of International Relations, University of Dhaka).

AUSTCARE (2006), 'Austcare's Report on UNHCR's Executive Committee Meeting and Annual Consultations with NGOs', 27 September–6 October 2006, Geneva, <www.crr.unsw.edu.au/documents/Austcare%20Report%20on%20UNHCR%20Excom%202006.pdf>.

Barnett, M. (2001), 'UNHCR and the Ethics of Repatriation', *Forced Migration Review* 10.

Betts, A. (2006), 'Conference Report', a Report on 'The Politics, Human Rights and Security Implications of Protracted Refugee Situations, 19–20 September, St Antony's College, Oxford University, *Journal of Refugee Studies* 19: 4, 509–14.

Black, R. and Koser, K. (eds) (1999), *The End of the Refugee Cycle? Refugee Repatriation and Reconstruction* (London: Bergahn Books).

Chimni, B.S. (1999), 'From Resettlement to Involuntary Repatriation: Towards a Critical History of Durable Solutions', New Issues in Refugee Research, UNHCR Working Paper No. 2 (Geneva: UNHCR, Evaluation and Policy Analysis Unit).

Crisp, J. (2001), 'Mind the Gap! Humanitarian Assistance, The Development Process and UNHCR', *International Migration Review* 35: 133.

Crisp, J. (2002), 'Protracted Refugee Situations: Some Frequently Asked Questions', Paper (Geneva: UNHCR, Evaluation and Policy Analysis Unit).

Crisp, J. (2003a), 'No Solution in Sight: The Problem of Protracted Refugee Situations in Africa', Working Paper No. 68 (San Diego: The Center for Comparative Immigration Studies, University of California).

Crisp, J. (2003b), 'No Solution in Sight: The Problem of Protracted Refugee Situations in Africa', New Issues in Refugee Research, UNHCR Working Paper No. 75 (Geneva: UNHCR, Evaluation and Policy Analysis Unit).
Giles, W. (2006), 'Moving Beyond Protracted Refugee Situations: Towards an Integrated Approach and Spaces of Sustainable Development and Livelihood', Paper presented to the International Association for the Study of Forced Migration (IASFM), York University, Toronto, 18–22 June. Published as Giles, W. and Moussa H. (2006), 'Responding to Protracted Refugee Situations: A Case Study,' *Refugee Studies Quarterly* 25: 2, 182–98.
Harman, D. (2002), 'In a Dire Kenyan Camp, Links to Al Qaeda: A Saudi Group Whose Funds Have Been Frozen by the US is Aiding Somali Refugees', *The Christian Science Monitor*, 18 December.
Helton, A. and Loescher, G. (2003), 'Internally Displaced Persons in Iraq: A Potential Crisis?', *Open Democracy* [website], 10 April.
Horst, C. (1997), 'Vital Links in Social Security: Somali Refugees in the Dadaab Camps, Kenya', Paper for Evaluation and Policy Analysis Unit, UNHCR, April 2001, published under same title in *Refugee Studies Quarterly* 21: 1 and 2, April 2002, 242–59.
Human Rights Watch Report (HRW 2002), 'Why Refugees Leave Kenyan Refugee Camps', <http://www.hrw.org/reports/2002/kenyaugan>.
Hyndman, J. (2000), *Managing Displacement: Refugees in the Politics of Humanitarianism*, Borderlines No. 16 (Minneapolis: University of Minnesota).
Kaufman, C. (2007), 'What Have We Learned About Ethnic Conflict? What Can We Do In Iraq?', *Harvard International Review* (Spring).
Koser, K. (2008), 'The Return of Refugees and IDPs and Sustainable Peace', Address to Brookings Institute, Washington, DC, 18 March.
Loescher, G. (2002), 'War in Iraq: an Impending Refugee Crisis? Uncertain Risks, Inadequate Preparation and Coordination', Working Paper No. 67 (San Diego: University of California, The Center for Comparative Immigration Studies) <http://repositories.cdlib.org/cgi/viewcontent.cgi?article=10>.
Loescher, G. (2003), 'A Disaster Waiting to Happen', *The Observer*, 2 February.
Loescher, G. and Milner, J. (2004), 'Protracted Refugee Situations and State and Regional Security', *Conflict, Security and Development* 4: 1, 3–20
Loescher, G. and Milner, J. (2005a), 'Protracted Refugee Situations: Domestic and International Security Situations', Adelphi Paper No. 375 (London: Taylor and Francis for the International Institute for Strategic Studies).
Loescher, G. and Milner, J. (2005b), 'The Long Road Home: Protracted Refugee Situations in Africa', *Survival: Global Politics and Strategy* 47: 2, 153–74.
Loescher, G., Milner, J., Newman, E. and Troeller, G. (2007), 'Protracted Refugee Situations and the Dynamics of Peacebuilding', *Conflict, Security and Development* 7: 3, 491–501.
Muller, J.Z. (2008), 'Us and Them', *Foreign Affairs* 87: 2, March/April, 34. See also Kaufman, C. (2007), 'What Have We Learned About Ethnic Conflict? What Can We Do In Iraq?', *Harvard International Review* (Spring).

UNHCR (2006), '57th Session of the Executive Committee: Report on the Annual Consultations with Non-Governmental Organizations', 27–29 September, Geneva: Palais des Nations, <http://www.crr.unsw.edu.au/documents/Report%20on%20the%20Annual%20Consultations%20with%20NGOs.pdf>.

Acknowledgements

The editor of this volume and the researchers acknowledge the contribution and support for the project by the Australian Research Council.

Australian Government

Australian Research Council

We also wish to acknowledge the assistance provided by Andrea Haese, Executive Officer of the Asia-Pacific College of Diplomacy, Carmel Connors, Sandra Hart and Susan Lockwood-Lee, Key Centre for Ethics, Law, Justice and Governance, Griffith University, Lauren Silver, Personal Assistant to Assistant Dean, Research Faculty of Law, Queensland University of Technology, Action Aid, Archie Law and Kate Berry as well as the programme managers and country directors at Austcare.

This research was supported under Australian Research Council's *Linkage Projects* funding scheme (project LP0668186). The views expressed herein are those of the authors and are not necessarily those of the Australian Research Council.

Erratum

Howard Adelman (ed.)
Protracted Displacement in Asia
No Place to Call Home

To Professor Charles Sampford

Director of The Institute for Ethics,
Governance and Law (IEGL)
President, International Institute for Public Ethics
Foundation Dean and Professor of Law and
Research Professor in Ethics, Griffith University
Research Professor, Queensland University of Technology

Without his initiative, organizational ability, continuing and unflagging support, inspiration and ideas, this research collaboration would not have been possible.

List of Abbreviations and Acronyms

ACF	Action Contre la Faime
AIHRC	Afghan Independent Human Rights Commission
ALNAP	Active Learning Network for Accountability and Performance in Humanitarian Action
ANA	Afghan National Army
ARC	Australian Research Council
ARCS	Afghan Red Crescent Society
AREU	Afghanistan Research and Evaluation Unit
ARV	Afghan Refugee Villages
ASEAN	Association of South East Asian Nations
ATCR	Annual Tripartite Committee on Resettlement
CARITAS	Catholic Relief Agency
CCSDPT	Committee for Co-ordination of Services to Displaced Persons in Thailand
CDA	Community Development Approach
CEWARN	Conflict Early Warning and Response Mechanism
CFA	Cease Fire Agreement
CWG	Core Working Group
DKBA	Democratic Karen Buddist Army
DP	Displaced Person
ECOSOC	Economic and Social Council
FATA	Federally Administered Tribal Areas
FIDH	La Fédération Internationale des Droits de l'Homme (International Federation for Human Rights)
GA	Government Agent
GCR2P	Global Centre for Responsibility to Protect
GK	Greater Kurdistan
GN	Grama Niladhari
GS	Grama Sevaka
HPG	Humanitarian Policy Group
HRCB	Human Rights Council of Bhutan
HRW	Human Rights Watch
IASC	Inter-Agency Standing Committee
IASFM	International Association for the Study of Forced Migration
ICRC	International Committee of the Red Cross
ICVA	International Council of Voluntary Agencies
IDP	Internally Displaced Person(s)

INGO	International Non-Government Organization
IOM	International Organization for Migration
IRIN	Integrated Regional Information Networks
IRO	International Refugee Organization
ISAF	International Security Assistance Force
ISI	Inter-Services Intelligence
JRS	Jesuit Refugee Service
JVP	Janatha Vimutkthi Peramuna
JVT	Joint Verification Team
KHRG	Karen Human Rights Group
KNLA	Karen National Liberation Army
KNM	Kurdish National Movement
KnRC	Karenni Refugee Committee
KNU	Karen National Union
KRC	Karen Refugee Committee
KRI	Kurdistan Region of Iraq
LAC	Legal Administrative Centre
LTTE	Liberation Tigers of Tamil Eelam
MOU	Memorandum of Understanding
NATO	North Atlantic Treaty Organization
NGO	Non-Government Organization
NMSP	New Mon State Party
NWFP	North West Frontier Province
OCHA	Office for the Co-ordination of Humanitarian Affairs
PRT	Provincial Reconstruction Teams
R2P	Responsibility to Protect
RTG	Royal Thai Government
RTV	Refugee Tented Villages
SAAG	South Asia Analysis Group
SLMM	Sri Lankan Monitoring Mission
SLORC	State Law and Order Restoration Council
SPDC	State Peace and Development Council
TBBC	Thailand Burma Border Consortium
TMVP	Tameleela Makkal Viduthalai Puligal (the political arm of the Karuna faction)
UDHR	Universal Declaration of Human Rights
UN	United Nations
UNAMI	United Nations Assistance Mission for Iraq
UNHCR	United Nations High Commission for Refugees
UNICEF	United Nations Children's Fund
UNSC	United Nations Security Council
USCIRF	United States Commission on International Religious Freedom
USCRI	United States Committee for Refugees and Immigrants
VMF	Voluntary Migration Forms

WFP	World Food Programme
WILPF	Women's International League for Peace and Freedom
WMD	Weapons of Mass Destruction

Chapter 1
Protracted Displacement

Howard Adelman

Protracted displacement in Asia

This book focuses on protracted refugee situations in Asia. In protracted displacement situations, no durable solution has been found ten years after that displacement took place[1] although UNHCR uses a reference point of only five years. Although it is widely believed that the largest number of those forcibly displaced are in Africa, in fact almost half of the world's population which is of concern to UNHCR are from and still reside in Asia. These include both refugees who have fled across a border and internally displaced persons (IDPs) who have been forcibly displaced within the boundaries of their own country and now number almost twice the refugee population.

Unlike refugees, internally displaced persons (IDPs) have not crossed a border and thus still have membership in a state. Of the forcibly displaced in protracted situations and who fled because of persecution or violence, IDPs usually have an advantage – they retain membership in their state and still live in a realm where the state has an obligation to ensure their protection and well-being even if the state is unable or unwilling to fulfil that obligation. When the state is the source of violence against those forced to flee or when the state is at war with a rebel group that shares the same identity as IDPs, the latter may be worse off than refugees because they are unable to access the protective mechanisms of the international community.[2] Further, a state may remove the membership of IDPs and render them stateless. If IDPs are then forcibly displaced, they become stateless persons akin to refugees, even though they never crossed a border.

Protracted displacement situations pose a problem not only because refugees and IDPs have often been confined to a camp for years and have been unable to move freely or work, but also because they challenge the implicit obligation of the UN High Commissioner for Refugees (UNHCR) and, therefore, the signatories to the Refugee Convention, to find a durable solution for refugees and IDPs (UNHCR 2002; 2004). As the chapters of this book demonstrate, refugees and IDPs in protracted situations confront us not only with their suffering but with

1 The US Committee on Refugees and Immigrants (USCRI) uses a criterion of ten years.

2 Cf. Kälin 2000 and Kälin, Cohen and Mooney 2003 for a statement of the proposed norms and principles governing conduct towards IDPs. For one example – in Angola – of whether these norms and principles are at all applied, see Jamal and Stage (2001).

our failure. The following chapters discussing the Bhutanese refugees in Nepal, Burmese refugees along the Thai–Burma border, Rohingyas in Bangladesh, IDPs in Sri Lanka, and Afghan refugees and IDPs all point to the difficulties of current situations of protracted displacement. The book also includes a chapter on the refugees produced by the Iraq war that started in 2003 in order to depict what we believe to be a protracted refugee and IDP situation in the making.

The fundamental 'problem' of refugees

'The Rights of Man, supposedly inalienable, proved to be unenforceable – even in countries whose constitutions were based on them – whenever people appeared who were no longer citizens of any sovereign state' (Arendt 1951; 2004, 372). Hannah Arendt's perspective on statelessness stands in radical contrast to the dominant current trend of trying to fit forced displacement discourse and practice into a universal human rights paradigm. According to this rights-based approach, the rights of the refugees have been abused and the most important work is to restore those rights. For Arendt, refugees could have no rights until and unless they were members of a state that recognized those persons as citizens to whom the state had an obligation. The most important objective was obtaining individual membership in a state that could protect that individual's rights, because, for Arendt, sovereignty was absolute in matters of emigration, naturalization, nationality, and expulsion.

The first copyright of Hannah Arendt's book, *The Origins of Totalitarianism*, was taken out in 1948, the same year that the Universal Declaration of Human Rights (UDHR) came into effect. Three years later, the 1951 Convention relating to the Status of Refugees (Refugee Convention) was adopted on 28 July 1951, the year Hannah Arendt's classic appeared in book stores.[3] The first preamble clause of the Refugee Convention based any rights of the refugees on the 1948 UDHR, namely that human beings shall enjoy fundamental rights and freedoms without discrimination. The second preamble clause committed the United Nations to using all its efforts 'to assure refugees the widest possible exercise of these fundamental rights and freedoms'. After the third clause expressed the need to extend those

3 Hannah Arendt completed *The Origins of Totalitarianism* in 1949, though it was not published until 1951. (See Karl Jasper's letter [#91] to her dated 4 August 1949.) Arendt complained bitterly and often to Karl Jaspers in her correspondence with him about the interminable delays and then the lack of promotion for the book. (cf. L. Kohler and H. Saner (eds) (1985), *Hannah Arendt Karl Jaspers Correspondence 1926–1969*, tr. R. and R. Kimber, New York: Harcourt Brace Jovanovich.) Chapter 5 of Part 2 on Imperialism is entitled, 'The Decline of the Nation-State and the Ends of the Rights of Man'. I have used the 1994 edition with an introduction by Samantha Powers rather than the original 1951 edition to which few contemporary readers may have access. The latest edition (2004) as well as the original were published by Schocken Books in New York.

rights in a new covenant specifically for refugees, the fourth preamble suggests the reason – to allow states to remove people it did not want: 'the grant of asylum may place unduly heavy burdens on certain countries'.[4] Burden sharing and the need for international cooperation provided the foundation of the Refugee Convention. In other words, the purpose of providing refugees with rights was NOT to enable refugees to become members of a polity that would provide for their protection, but in order for polities which had an 'excess' number of such refugees to dispose of them without abusing the basic rights of non-*refoulement* – that is, the right of refugees not to be returned to a place where they would be persecuted.[5]

The fifth preamble clause was even clearer. Refugees were not presented as a political problem needing a political solution for their lack of membership in a protecting state; rather, they were a 'social and humanitarian' problem. And why did states want to solve the problem? Not because of the refugees, but 'to prevent this problem from becoming a cause of tension between States'. On the one hand, UNHCR was set up on the basis of *individual* rights of refugees who had become a social and humanitarian rather than a political problem. On the other hand, UNHCR's creation stemmed from the need to foster burden sharing and reduce any possible tensions between *states*. As an international body, UNHCR assumed responsibility for the protection of refugees, but lacked: a police force to provide for their security; an independent source of income to provide for their welfare; and, what is most important, any ability to confer membership in a polity.

After grandfathering the meaning of the term 'refugee' to encompass previous groups of Europeans, the Convention defined a refugee as one who:

> As a result of events occurring before 1 January 1951 and owing to well-founded fear of being persecuted for reasons of race, religion, nationality, membership of a particular social group or political opinion, is outside the country of his nationality and is unable, or owing to such fear, is unwilling to avail himself of the protection of that country; or who, not having a nationality and being outside the country of his former habitual residence as a result of such events, is unable or, owing to such fear, is unwilling to return to it.

Refugees were defined as members of a state who were persecuted because they were members of specific racial, religious, national or social groups, or de facto members of a political group because they were persecuted for their opinions, usually by the state. However, although members of groups with respect to the reasons for their persecution, convention refugees were treated as individuals for purposes of determining their need for protection. Further, they were not members of groups in another sense – as the flotsam displaced by war and conflict, the major cause resulting in refugee flows. They were regarded as refugees in need of

4 This reasoning was also applied for the adoption of Nansen passports in the 1930s.

5 For a different perspective on the connection between refugees and rights, see Verdirame (1999) and Verdirame and Harrell-Bond (2000).

protection only if they had been individually targeted for persecution even if the reason for their persecution was because they were members of a certain group.

Those events that threatened their persecution had to occur before the year 1951. This was not a clause intended to cover any and all refugees produced in the future. It was intended to cover those people outside their native country who were either unable *or* unwilling to go back to that country for protection because they had a well-founded fear of persecution. In other words, these were persons that were now without a nationality because they refused to go home because they feared persecution. Being a refugee and being stateless were de facto equivalent. Classifying individuals as refugees meant that they could not be forced to go home. Displaced people who were *outside* their home states (and were not *internally* displaced), unlike refugees, could be forced to go home for they still were recognized as having a nationality with, presumably, a state that protected their rights.

Thus, signing the Refugee Convention was not a guarantee that refugee rights would always be respected in practice. Nor was the Convention even a solid foundation for protecting refugees even though countries have refined and improved their refugee asylum systems since its creation. After the promulgation of the 1967 Protocol, which expanded the temporal and geographic reach of the refugee definition, refugees still lack any guarantee that they can become members of a polity that protects their rights – the only core durable solution.

What rights are we talking about? Civil rights to practise religion, rights of free speech and free association! Refugees in this regard are protected as much or as little as anyone in a rights-based state. States have had to refine their procedures sometimes to ensure that refugee *civil* rights are protected. However, refugees do not have equal *social* rights, although their basic needs will be cared for. More importantly, refugees are not given *political* rights.

Today, the international community is expected to provide for the basic needs of refugees (Jamal 2000). Other needs, such as the right not to be persecuted, may be protected by signatory states. Practices have developed in some refugee camps that honour Convention Plus and help develop the capacities of refugees who flee war and violence. But unless they can become members of a state that provides for their protection, in the modern nation-state system, refugees have no real rights.

Hannah Arendt considered refugees a litmus test for the notion of human rights. She argued that the traditional division between statelessness, those outside their country who had no state to which they could return, and refugees, those outside their place of birth but to which they did not want to return for fear of persecution, was a distinction without an essential difference. The central issue was the fact that refugees had no rights as long as they were not members of a state. Refugees were a test of the human rights regime because they were a test of the nation-state system of which human rights were derivative. One had no rights unless one was a member of a polity that provided protection for its citizens. Arendt came to this conclusion not only as a result of her theoretical studies but because of her direct experience with Jewish refugees during and after World War II, because she experienced the dilemma of dealing with German prisoners of war from the Soviet Union who feared returning, and because she saw what happened to Germans in Eastern Europe after the war.

Even after the war, in 1947, Jewish refugees were still being kept in refugee camps. Countries in the immediate aftermath of World War II and after the Holocaust were not willing to allow them entry. Further, there had been debates in the UN, promoted by Britain and the Arab states, to define Jewish refugees as displaced persons, in which case they would and could be sent back to the countries from which they had fled or from which they had been forcibly removed. In the debates in the United Nations, the British and the Arab states lost the fight to classify the Jews as 'DPs' – displaced persons.[6] Instead, they were defined as refugees. Yet this proved problematic, because while the refugee label should have afforded them the chance to resettle, resettlement countries refused to accept them. At the same time, Britain would not allow them to go to Palestine. So in 1947, Jewish refugees remained a pariah people who, when they tried to establish a place where they could have a homeland, were thrown into camps by the British after the war, and after their people's Holocaust.

The period was also the beginning of the Cold War. After World War II, there were tens of thousands of Eastern Bloc soldiers who had been prisoners of war in Nazi Germany and did not want to be returned to Communist Europe where their

6 The Arabs did not want their territory to be used as a homeland for a nationalist movement of Zionist Jews, even if that territory had been the Jews' ancient homeland. Further, the Arabs denied that the Jews comprised a nation and that the minority indigenous Jewish population had national minority rights. They did not want their claims to be reinforced by the arrival of new immigrants from the refugee or displaced persons camps in Europe. Given the precarious hold of a weakened British Empire on its colonies, the British after World War II backed the Arab position. In 1946, the Arabs, assisted by the British, fought the pressure for entry of Jewish refugees from Europe into Palestine by two means in the international diplomatic arena. They fostered the idea of repatriation of the Jews and they tried to prevent Jewish resettlement in Palestine. The battle took place during discussions at the Economic and Social Council (ECOSOC) over the draft constitution of the International Refugee Organization (IRO). (For a more detailed account of the Arab efforts to keep the Jews from moving to Palestine via the debates over the IRO constitution and in the United Nations, cf. J. Robinson (1947), *Palestine and the United Nations*, Westport, CN: Greenwood Press, Chapter 2.) In the IRO constitution, a distinction was made between refugees – pre-or post-war victims of Nazi or fascist regimes or of racial, religious or political persecution – and displaced persons (DPs) who were displaced in the course of or after World War II. As far as the DPs were concerned, the IRO was 'to encourage and assist in every possible way the early return to their countries of origin'. If Jews were classified as DPs that classification would direct the IRO to arrange for their repatriation. To prevent resettlement in Palestine, the Arab states, backed by Britain, tried to introduce conditions before resettlement could take place, namely the consent of neighbouring countries and of the indigenous population. They also wanted the IRO to have exclusive authority to settle European refugees, largely through repatriation. They suggested that all private organizations working for resettlement transfer their assets to the IRO for that purpose.

fate was most likely to be imprisonment in the Soviet gulag because of possible contamination, cowardice or suspected treason. After all, immediately after the war some had been forcibly returned and their fate was widely known. As the distrust between the Communist states and the West grew, a debate took place among human rights advocates insisting that these individuals were also refugees and not just displaced persons because Western states that upheld human rights could not send people back who would be subjected to persecution when they returned. As the Cold War began, the West used refugees as the device to define themselves as states that protected the rights of individuals not to be *refouled*.

To add to observations about Jewish refugees and prisoners of war from the east who did not want to return, a third example is the treatment of German citizens of non-German dominated states. Hannah Arendt was a secular German and identified herself as a German all her life. After the war, at least 12 million Ouest Deutsch, Germans who had lived for generations in the lands of Eastern Europe, were forcibly removed and sent back to an impoverished and destroyed Germany (Ther and Siljak 2001).[7] It is estimated by some that at least one million of them died (Mann 2005).[8] In the immediate aftermath of World War II, states denaturalized those Germans who were born in the country that was literally the *natio*, the place of their birth. These Germans did not belong to the dominant 'nation' (where 'nation' is used in an ethnic sense) and lost their citizenship in other European countries. Unlike the Jews, however, the Germans had an internationally recognized nation-state to which they could return; they were not archetypal stateless people.

The principle of non-*refoulement*, enshrined in the Refugee Convention, stipulated that refugees could not be sent back to countries where they could be persecuted. Even so, Germans were being sent 'back' en masse to places where they had not been born because their actual birth countries now considered them an unwanted minority. While the phrase was not used at the time, ethnic cleansing was alive and well after the war, as was persecution of individuals and groups. Thus, the Refugee Convention provided that signatory states should not participate in or facilitate individual persecution, but provided no instructions on what to do about ethnic cleansing. That fundamental failure is directly connected with a build

---

7 Ther, P. and Siljak, A. (eds) (2001), from papers first presented at a Forum of the *Journal of Cold War Studies*. In particular, see M. Kramer's overview and E. Glassheim, 'The Expulsion of Germans from Czechoslovakia, 1945–46'. See also 'Perspectives on Redrawing Nations', *Journal of Postwar Studies* Summer 2003, 5: 3, 102–14; János, A. (2003), 'The Expulsion of the Germans from Hungary after World War II', in S. Vardy and T. Tooley (eds) (2003), *Ethnic Cleansing in 20th Century Europe* (New York: Columbia University Press), pp. 229–37; Kopper, C. (2003), 'The London Czech Government and the Origins of the Expulsion of the Sudenten Germans', in S. Vardy and T. Tooley, pp. 157–63; Naimark, N.M. (2002), *Fires of Hatred: Ethnic Cleansing in Twentieth-Century Europe* (Cambridge, MA: Harvard University Press).

8 Mann puts the figure at 'over two million'. For a discussion of the relationship between refugees and ethnicity, see Kagwanja (2000).

up of some groups of refugees who have lived in refugee camps for years and for whom, until very recently, no solution for their plight has been found.

Convention refugees – those who are recognized as refugees by UNHCR – who, because of a well-founded fear of persecution, flee across a border and seek relief from that persecution, are swamped by a very much larger group of people who are called humanitarian refugees. These are people who simply flee violence and war, ideological and power conflicts over resources, and any and all other forms of inhumane behaviour that force people to flee for their lives. Those who flee ethnic cleansing and even genocide are only guaranteed that they will not be forced to return.

Defining a protracted refugee situation

In a protracted refugee situation,[9] refugees are sequestered in refugee camps without rights of mobility or employment; their lives remain on hold and stagnate in a state of limbo for a long period. The refugees have few if any chances for employment and very limited opportunities to engage in commerce or trade. For many and varied reasons, one of which is often compassion fatigue, the ability to serve the basic needs of refugees gradually declines, 'consigning men, women, and children to lives unlived … beneath international standards' (Limon 2004; see also Crisp 2001; 2002b). Though the risks to their lives may be radically reduced in comparison to the situation from which they fled, their lives remain physically and psychologically insecure, oftentimes more insecure than they would be if they returned home.

The key characteristic of a protracted refugee situation is long-term confinement in a refugee camp or settlement – at least five years – from which the refugee is not free to leave. In the deliberately demeaning term adopted by the United States Committee for Refugees and Immigrants (USCRI) as a critique of the practice rather than a comment on the refugees, these refugees are 'warehoused'. Refugees in such situations live not knowing what the future will bring. Hopelessness and despair eat at their self-worth at the same time as the endlessness of the situation weakens the willingness of donor states to provide adequate supplies and services

9 A distinction must be made between protracted conflicts that continue to produce refugees over a long period, and protracted refugee situations (the subject of this book). Protracted refugee situations are often correlated with protracted conflicts, but not necessarily. Contrast Bhutan with Burma. Bhutan produced refugees who lived in camps for years without a protracted conflict. In contrast, Burma had both a protracted refugee situation in Thailand as well as a protracted conflict within Burma. In protracted refugee situations, most of those refugees around the world are confined to refugee camps in the countries of first asylum. At the same time, there may be 6.2 million refugees still awaiting the end of long lasting wars, but not all of these refugees live in protracted refugee situations. The latter number is actually about 4.5 million. So though protracted refugee situations and protracted conflicts overlap, they are not entirely congruent.

to meet the basic needs of the refugees. Living often in remote, desolate, and dangerous border areas, the refugees are subject to violence at the hands of locals and, in some cases, uncontrolled armed militias (Chen 2004; Smith 2004).[10]

Given the remote locations of many camps, the consequences of living for long periods in a confined area in this state of unending dependency in closed camps, or suffering economic exploitation in open camps, there are significant debilitating effects. 'The list of the consequences of prolonged encampment is long, and includes material deprivation, psychosocial problems, violence, sexual exploitation, exploitative employment and resort to negative coping mechanisms. As Jamal Sharif Mor described their situation, 'The consequences of having so many humans in a static state included wasted lives, squandered resources, and increased threats to security' (Mor 2004). In that same position paper, UNHCR pointed out that protracted refugee situations perpetuate poverty and 'underdevelopment' and 'can serve as incubators for future problems. Festering crises can nurture instability and conflict.' The consequences also include sexual exploitation, illegal secondary migration, tensions between the refugees and locals, and sometimes unaccountable and even exploitive camp administrations (Smith 2004).

According to the *World Refugee Survey 2004* special issue on refugee '*warehousing*', that included many of the above-cited essays, of the 11.9 million refugees worldwide in 2003, there were more than seven million refugees confined to refugee camps, segregated settlements or otherwise deprived of their rights for ten years or more. Using somewhat different criteria – five years' duration rather than ten – for the end of 2003, UNHCR provided a figure of 6.2 million refugees in 38 different mostly African countries who have lived in an ongoing refugee crisis for more than five years.[11] In fact, the average duration of refugee crises has increased from 9 to 17 years between 1993 and 2003 (UNHCR 2004). In six of these 38 countries, refugees were fully integrated economically, although the refugee situation was still extant; the refugees themselves in those six countries were not in a protracted refugee situation. The net number of refugees in a protracted refugee situation in 2003 was 4.5 million. Half were in Asia, the focus of this volume.

---

10 See also Limon 2004. USCRI categorizes Palestinian refugees as warehoused as well, although, with the very partial exception of Lebanon and Saudi Arabia, they have the *right* to work, and can own property and run businesses. With some restrictions and exceptions, they also generally enjoy the right to leave refugee camps. With the exception of one camp in Saudi Arabia, they do not live in remote, desolate and *naturally* dangerous areas. In fact, the vast majority of Palestinian refugees live in their own homeland and nascent state (Gaza or the West Bank) or are citizens of Jordan. Thus, there is a discrepancy between the core characteristics used to describe a protracted refugee situation and the groups of refugees included in the category by USCRI. (Cf. Raffonelli 2004.) For a description of an effort to end a protracted refugee situation in Africa, in this case, Côte d'Ivoire, see Kuhlman (2002).

11 Using the shorter period, this should have resulted in an even higher figure. Because the calculation excluded Palestinians, the total number was smaller.

Whatever the differences over numbers (4.5 or 7 million) or over the minimal number of years one has to be confined to a refugee camp – or even whether one has to be in refugee camp to be in a protracted refugee situation, there is general agreement on the depiction of the essential characteristics and the consequences that flow from protracted refugee situations. However, there is no agreement on either the causes or the appropriate proactive response.

With funding from the United States Bureau for Population, Refugees and Migration in 2001 to research the problem, Jeff Crisp, when he headed the Evaluation and Policy Analysis Unit of UNHCR, was part of UNHCR's latest efforts to refocus on protracted refugee situations before the issue became a cause célèbre. According to Crisp's definition, a protracted refugee was someone in exile for at least five years and *no durable solution was in sight through resettlement, local integration or repatriation* (Crisp 2002c; 2003).[12] By linking the depiction of the protracted refugee situation with a bleak if not impossible opportunity for a way out, and without detracting from Crisp's superb work as head of the UNHCR research unit, this definition of a condition without a cure either reinforced the attitude of impotence, or led for a search for mostly chimerical solutions. In 2003, Crisp modified his definition to *an absence of a durable solution* and offered an explanation. Protracted refugeehood was depicted as 'a long term refugee situation that has become a care and maintenance program with no apparent durable solution in sight, *not necessarily because one is lacking* [emphasis added], but because refugees have become marginal to major power interests'. Realpolitik, then, was offered as the explanation for the indifference.

Alternative responses to protracted refugee situations

One response to protracted refugee situations is indifference and neglect. Four other responses are identified here, all of which insist that more be done on refugees' behalf. Modern states used to put mental patients without economic means away in confined insane asylums removed from view, where they were maintained but offered little effective treatment to allow them to rejoin the rest of society. Refugees in protracted refugee situations are now subjected to similar treatment according to critics of 'warehousing'. In 2004, the international community was accused of giving up on any real effort to find a durable solution for these refugees in the foreseeable future (Smith 2004).

One response to this indifference focuses on ameliorating the situation. If refugees do not have access to long-term solutions, then authorities and donors should alleviate the camp/settlement conditions. They can ensure that aid at least meets the basic needs of the refugees. This was the tack taken in 2002 by Nathaniel Goetz, who was then Interim Director of the Forced Migration Laboratory, Center for Comparative Immigration Studies at the La Jolla campus in San Diego of the University of California (Goetz 2002a; 2002b; 2000c; 2005). Unfortunately, the

12 On local integration, see Jacobsen 2001 and Crisp 2004. See also Dick 2002.

very factors that perpetuate protracted situations are the same ones that lead to declining efforts in attempting to meet basic needs. Since the effort to improve standards does not tackle the causes, the result is a great deal of wringing of hands but little change.

A second proactive approach was adopted by UNHCR and focused on capacity-building for refugees to prepare them to lead productive lives when no solutions were found for their situation (Crisp et al. 2001). In the interim, the implementation of training and educational opportunities were supposed to serve two purposes: first, they allowed refugees to gain a minimal degree of control that, at the very least, were supposed to have an impact on the social and psychological well-being of the refugees; and second, they prepared them to get on with their lives once a solution was found. Additional development assistance was to be targeted at states hosting refugees to encourage and facilitate refugee employment. Many new worthwhile programmes were launched. However, evidence suggests that the programmes assisted only a small minority of the refugee population. Further, evidence did not establish that, when the refugees' skills were improved, they had an opportunity to utilize those skills in gainful employment. Nor did evidence indicate that the sense of self-worth improved when refugee skills were enhanced. In fact, in a study of Kakuma Camp by graduate students partaking in the Princeton Refugee Initiative (PRI) of the Woodrow Wilson School at Princeton University, refugees' sense of low self-esteem and failure was enhanced when recipients of training could not use those skills, even as skills improved (Ahlsten et al. 2005).

The third proactive response to protracted situations is a rights-based (Posner and Clancy undated; Loescher and Milner 2005) rather than a needs-based or capacity-building approach.[13] Instead of accepting the confinement of refugees to camps and restricting their right to work, instead of *merely* trying to ensure the standards in the camps meet minimum conditions for the refugees, and instead of going one step further and trying to build the capacities of those refugees, this approach envisions ensuring that countries of first asylum guarantee refugees their rights, including their rights to move and seek employment so that refugees can be *economically* integrated even if they are not *politically* integrated.

Such a position is reflected in the following depiction of a protracted refugee situation: 'Warehousing is the practice of keeping refugees in protracted situations of restricted mobility, enforced idleness, and dependency – their lives on indefinite hold – *in violation of their basic rights under the 1951 UN Refugee Convention*.' [emphasis added] (Smith 2004). As Merrill Smith wrote, 'The 1951 Refugee Convention recognizes the fundamental rights of refugees while in exile including those to work, freedom of movement and residence, own property, and receive an

13 Cf. UNHCR Pre-ExCom Consultations: 'Moving Forward: Identifying Specific Measures to End Refugee Warehousing', 29 September 2004. The NGOs critiqued UNHCR's capacity approach in favour of a rights-based approach. See also 'Protracted Refugee Situations' (UNHCR 2004).

education'. As he argues, Article 17(2)(a) of the Refugee Convention requires that states that provide asylum permit refugees to seek employment after they have been in the host country for three years. Smith argues that the key characteristic of a protracted refugee situation is not the time that people spend in camps nor their condition, but the denial of their rights.

Finally, there is a fourth proactive response to protracted refugee situations based on the analysis that the *prime* problem is not the absence of durable solutions – a premise of the other three approaches – but a systemic fault in the way refugees are treated when they flee violent wars. As many others have done, the PRI defined a protracted refugee situation by combining descriptive and interpretive causal factors, but suggested different causes. Although pointing out the failure to truly empower the refugees, the prime cause was systemic.[14] 'Protracted refugee situations are circumstances in which refugees are indefinitely accommodated in camp settings because a *political impasse as well as organizational constraints and contradictions prevent their integration, repatriation, or resettlement*' [emphasis added] (Ahlsten et al. 2005, 7). As the graduate students continued, protracted refugee situations 'are deliberate creations resulting from political interests and choices. We thus recognize protracted refugee situations as political quandaries with profound moral implications'.

The failure to pursue a permanent solution vigorously, creatively and effectively is seen to result from systemic and structural factors. The reason for that failure is not *primarily* located in donors providing insufficient aid to meet the needs of the refugees, though donors demonstrably provide inadequate resources. 'Structural and institutional barriers … effectively condemn tens of thousands of refugees to a prison' (Ahlsten et al. 2005, 5). The basic explanation is also not the failure to provide adequate assistance to build the capacities of the refugees. Nor can the responsibility be placed primarily on the countries of asylum for not allowing the refugees to have mobility, seek employment or engage in trade and business, though reversing all of these patterns would certainly benefit the refugees. The failure is located in the *way* aid is dispensed, the absence of coherent and comprehensive strategies to resolve the plight of the protracted refugee population, and, finally, the absence of innovative institutions, that can tackle the problem of protracted refugee situations in a creative way, intent on a solution to the refugee's lack of membership in a state that provides protection. The prime reason for the failure, with the stress placed on the adjective 'prime', is structural.

14 The PRI graduate students are not the first researchers to study refugee camps and discover inherent systemic factors to account for the situation. Barbara Harrell-Bond, the founding director of Oxford University's renowned Refugee Studies Centre, has repeated this theme throughout her intellectual career beginning with her first book in the 1980s. Her 2005 book, written with the legal scholar, Guglielmo Verdirame (Verdirame et al. 2005), *Janus Faced Humanitarianism*, also argues that international and humanitarian organizations are not only responsible for perpetuating problems unnecessarily, but for extensive and avoidable violations of the rights of the refugees in their care. Most recently, Harrell-Bond has combined her structural critique with a push for a human rights approach.

Just as a capacity-building approach does not rule out a needs approach, just as a rights approach does not rule out capacity-building and needs approaches, so a structural analysis and prescription for a cure does not rule out needs, capacity-building or rights approaches. In fact, the analysis argues that a systemic approach makes those other efforts more likely to succeed.

UNHCR efforts to build refugee self-reliance

On 14 December 2001 in a one-day meeting with delegations from Africa, for the first time in the new century, UNHCR beamed a spotlight on protracted refugee situations. In that meeting, UNHCR High Commissioner Ruud Lubbers solicited the support of African governments in looking for a 'new impetus' in handling refugee issues in that continent. 'We cannot go on with business as usual', Lubbers said. 'We have to speak together and see what to do about protracted refugee situations in Africa and how we can improve the protection regime.' This discussion was on the table in a context when Africa was witnessing the demise of its once vaunted openness to asylum as provided in the 1969 Organization for African Unity Convention.

Lubbers told the meeting that, *in the absence of voluntary return home*, refugees still deserve to live meaningful lives. 'We have to increase local opportunities, on top of what we are already doing, so that refugees become self-sufficient and are empowered with sufficient skills to become useful members of *local* [emphasis added] communities', he said. 'We therefore have to re-emphasize the importance of education and other self-reliance strategies.'[15] These words did not place a burden on states to fulfill refugee rights; rather, in such a capacity-building strategy, the burden primarily rested on individual refugees and aid agencies willing to assist them while lobbying host governments to relax refugee restrictions.

UNHCR adopted an 'Agenda for Protection' in December of 2002, which authorized the High Commissioner to review 'all protracted refugee situations' to promote comprehensive plans of action to develop durable solutions for refugees in such situations. In that document, UNHCR blamed political processes *both* in the producing country *and* in the country of asylum. UNHCR did not explore the possibility of a structural or systemic cause. 'They [protracted refugee situations] endure because of ongoing problems in the country of origin, and stagnate and become protracted as a result of responses to refugee inflows, typically involving restrictions on refugee movement and employment.' In other words, the cause of the refugee exodus is the country of origin; the cause of the protraction of the situation is the responsibility of the countries of asylum.

---

15 The emphasis on self-reliance was developed independently of protracted refugee situations and was rooted in a 'rights-based' community development approach in three manuals put out by UNHCR in 1996: 'Refugee Emergencies: A Community Based Approach', 'Assisting Disabled Refugees: A Community Based Approach', and 'Urban Refugees: A Community Based Approach' (all published by UNHCR, Geneva).

The Agenda for Protection had six ambitious goals, two of which were viewed as particularly applicable to protracted refugee situations, namely: more equitable burden sharing combined with capacity-building; and redoubling efforts to find durable solutions. In other words, UNHCR proposed that its traditional goals be pursued with better packaging and greater vigour. The Convention Plus (C+) strategy that revived the concept of Comprehensive Plans of Action (CPA) was one result of this effort. So was the Framework for Durable Solutions (FDS), which was proposed in May 2003 and which combined Development Assistance for Refugees (DAR), the 4Rs (Repatriation, Reintegration, Rehabilitation and Reconstruction) (cf. Black and Koser 1999), and Development through Local Integration (DLI). UNHCR offered an enriched alphabet soup, but without the coordination and integration required by a rights-based approach. The issue was whether this heady brew of letters had any effective results in fostering durable solutions.

On 10 June 2004, UNHCR issued a paper on 'Protracted Refugee Situations' to the Executive Meeting of UNHCR (EC/54/SC/CRP.14). The report, while acknowledging that camps save lives in the beginning, contended that they 'waste these same lives as the years go by'. The reason given was that camps offer only a minimum of 'care and maintenance' and physical protection. 'We have failed to offer these fellow human beings a life in dignity, or even the prospect or hope of such a life.' This is 'not an investment in the future', to quote from the paper, and 'can only ensure that such situations are perpetuated, not solved'.

What strategy did UNHCR offer in response? It pointed neither to durable solutions nor to state membership. It did point to rights, but not rights to actually *obtain* employment. UNHCR stressed a strategy that prepared refugees by training them to seek meaningful and productive employment at such time in the future when durable solutions would be available. In the interim, UNHCR would seek to enlist the cooperation of countries of asylum in providing livelihood opportunities.

> Refugee self-reliance is the key element in any strategy dealing with the effects of prolonged and stagnant exile. It is more dignified for the individual, is less costly, and is a positive factor for repatriation. Essential elements of a strategy include: (i) providing refugees with physical, legal and economic security; (ii) removing barriers to self-reliance; and (iii) creating opportunities. (UNHCR 2004)

This solution is conditional. *If* refugees are repatriated, then capacity-building would have assisted in preparing them for return. But this is clearly not a solution fostering repatriation itself. Further, there is only a passing nod to rights: the strategies are intended to ensure that 'the refugees are able to enjoy basic human rights', including those specifically mentioned in the 1951 Convention relating to the Status of Refugees. However, the solution contains no explicit discussion of the *right* to mobility and employment in the country of first asylum that was stressed in USCRI's warehousing campaign. UNHCR admits that self-reliance is often unattainable because of 'legal obstacles and restrictions on refugees' freedom of movement, employment or access to land'. UNHCR places the responsibility on host governments to lift those barriers, but does so without the fire and brimstone of USCRI, which calls such barriers illegal and a travesty, and demands, not requests or solicits, that these barriers be lifted in the name of rights guaranteed in the Convention. UNHCR effectively says we can advise but we cannot insist. For UNHCR, the issue is not insisting on rights, but removing obstacles that prevent self-reliance of the refugee so that he or she can satisfy his or her own needs. This is a capacity-based approach that is only couched in the language of rights.

The UNHCR protection approach can be illustrated through an examination of UNHCR's strategy in dealing with the Lhotshampas, the Bhutanese in Nepal. A depiction of this case study throws light on the successes as well as the limitations of the strategy. After many years, UNHCR resigned itself to dismissing repatriation as the only option (sensible as we shall see in light of the reality) and reserved its assistance in the interim to supporting self-reliance schemes for those integrating and promoting resettlement for small groups of vulnerable refugees. No consideration was given to the criticisms of its community development approach in Nepal to strengthen refugee self-reliance in a protracted refugee situation (Muggah 2003). On the positive side, Muggah found that the capacity-building programme had been very successful. The Lhotshampas had achieved a 75 per cent literacy rate and a 100 per cent school enrolment for their children. They had developed democratic institutions and displayed genuine gender equality. The refugees themselves ran a number of very successful public health programmes that had resulted in the lowest under-five malnutrition rate in Southeast Asia. UNHCR could justly be very proud of its capacity-building efforts on behalf of the just over 100,000 Bhutanese refugees in Nepal. On the negative side, neither legal nor economic integration of the refugees took place; nor was there even a hint of repatriation. As a result, psychosocial problems, particularly among the young men, were pervasive *and increasing*. Concurrently, UNHCR withdrew from efforts to cooperate with the Bhutan government. And resettlement did not seem to be an option except for a very few. What purpose would capacity-building serve if no durable solution were in the offing?

Along the Thai–Burmese border, a similar tension emerged. Since repatriation was not a prospect, UNHCR focused on capacity-building and used its best efforts to open the windows of opportunity to local integration, but with little result.[16] In

16 On 9 November 2004, Ambassador Wegger Strømmen from Norway, in addressing the 3rd Committee of the United Nations, applauded UNHCR 'for its pioneering and catalytic role in developing innovative concepts that induce the various actors to pool their efforts to the benefit of refugees, host countries and – in cases of return – countries of origin. ... Convention Plus is already a success in progress, and its 'Framework for Durable Solutions' holds great promise even for protracted refugee situations.' Other than the initiative in bringing the situation to the attention of the world, for what concrete action did Ambassador Wegger Strømmen laud UNHCR? 'Norway supports the basic idea of targeting *additional development assistance to refugees and refugee-hosting communities* [emphasis added]. Such assistance can give long-term refugees more meaningful lives by allowing them to develop their productive capacity and thus preparing them better for a

the name of promoting self-reliance of the refugees, UNHCR's alphabet soup of partnership programmes based on C+, CPA, FDS, DAR, the 4Rs, and DCI proved to be of only partial benefit to the refugees.

USCRI rights-based approach

Let me now turn to the campaign for the *rights* of warehoused refugees and their opportunity to be integrated in countries of first asylum. For the question can be asked: why conduct more research on the plight of protracted refugee populations? Solutions are needed. Solutions require developing political pressure to make countries change their policies. From this perspective, what is needed is not action research but action, action that stirs up politicians to initiate solutions, and actions to implement those solutions based on respecting the rights of refugees. Is advocacy more important for a non-government organization (NGO) than investing scarce resources in research?

In a special issue of its renowned *World Refugee Survey* on refugee warehousing of May 2004, the USCRI kicked off its campaign against refugee warehousing. The Survey reviewed the rights of refugees confined to camps and the international community's failure to guard and implement those rights. Chen, in his article in the issue, called the situation illegal, immoral and degrading. As he stated, the foundation premise of the campaign, *World Refugee Survey 2004,* is about freedom, calling upon ourselves and the international community to treat refugees as equals, giving refugees their human right to support themselves and to live normal lives in dignity. USCRI condemned the practice of refugee warehousing as legally indefensible and morally unacceptable.

Republican Senator Sam Brownback from Kansas was best known internationally to the humanitarian world for his visit to Darfur and his work in pressuring the US Congress to pass a unanimous resolution declaring the atrocities committed in Darfur as genocide. However, he also was concerned with protracted refugee situations. Prompted by USCRI, he entered into the Congressional record on 18 June 2004, in honour of coming World Refugee Day,[17] a call to end the warehousing of seven million refugees. Assistant Secretary of State Arthur E. Dewey, who directed the US Government's Bureau of Population, Refugees, and Migration, and who was a former deputy High Commissioner of UNHCR, wrote

durable solution. This approach also benefits the economy of the host countries and can play a part in poverty reduction and in meeting the Millennium Development Goals. It should therefore provide incentives for host countries to cooperate with donors and international financial institutions.' In other words, Norway was delighted by UNHCR's capacity-building policies in addressing protracted refugee situations and improving the daily lives of refugees, and relying on the *possibilities* that host countries would cooperate to ease the restrictions on refugees.

17 World Refugee Day falls on 20 June.

an op-ed piece in the *Washington Times* on 10 September 2004 calling for the 'unwarehousing' of refugees.

Soon after, on 21 September 2004, USCRI Executive Director Lavinia Limon testified before a special session on 'Refugees: Seeking Solutions to a Global Concern' of the Senate Subcommittee on Immigration, Border Security and Citizenship. Her topic was 'Ending the Practice of Refugee Warehousing', and she declared that, 'the warehousing of refugees and denial of basic human rights is wrong, both legally and morally'. How was the practice to be ended? 'UNHCR, the donor community and host governments must adopt new policies and devise new practices that prioritize refugee rights.' On 20 November 2004, Senators Sam Brownback and Edward Kennedy of Massachusetts nominated the USCRI for a Nansen medal, stating, 'The Committee is known throughout the world for its flagship campaign against refugee warehousing in recognition of the fundamental human rights enshrined in the 1951 Refugee Convention, but routinely denied throughout the world.'

On 28 September 2004, the *New York Times* published an editorial that condemned refugee warehousing that was reprinted in the *International Herald Tribune*. Not coincidentally, on the same day, the campaign was formally internationalized at the Executive Committee of UNHCR (ExCom) at its annual NGO Consultation. Not satisfied with the UNHCR position, participating NGOs passed a resolution that criticized the UNHCR position and effectively adopted USCRI's position. The Vatican joined the campaign under the urging of an old friend of refugee advocacy, Msgr. Silvano S. Tomasi, who also sat on ExCom. On 4 October 2004, the Vatican officially condemned refugee warehousing in an address to UNHCR.

On 9 November 2004, the day that Norwegian Ambassador Wegger Strømmen addressed the Third Committee of the United Nations and, on behalf of Norway, welcomed, 'the campaign launched earlier this year against the warehousing of refugees', he did so because, 'This is one way of increasing international awareness with a view to bringing this completely unacceptable situation to an end more quickly … The consequences are wasted lives, squandered resources and future problems.'

The various pressure points of the USCRI campaign described above were not just rhetorical. They delivered some results. On the same day as Wegger's speech, Prime Minister Ahmad Badawi of Malaysia announced that the Malaysian government was granting legal status to 10,000 ethnic Rohingya refugees and asylum seekers from Myanmar to enable them to enjoy freedom of movement and seek employment in Malaysia.[18]

The campaign culminated at the end of the year when, on 23 December 2004, the Tibetan Refugee Welfare Office in Nepal and the Eminent Persons Group on Refugee and Migratory Movements in South Asia in Sri Lanka issued a statement

18 See Chapter 4 for a discussion of the Rohingyas in Bangladesh and Myanmar itself for a less rosy outcome.

calling for solutions to end refugee warehousing that was endorsed by over a hundred organizations and many individuals, including refugee law scholars and human rights activists as well as four Nobel laureates, one of whom was Archbishop Desmond Tutu.

Though there were a number of problems with the USCRI approach, it was politically effective both as a public relations exercise in highlighting the issue and also possibly in using American clout to get some countries of first asylum to ease up on their restrictions on refugees living in their countries. The campaign may have been a factor that pushed the US to open up places for resettlement, though it is just as likely that the US provided those openings for strategic interests rather than to support the rights of the refugees or in response to pressure from refugee advocates.

In October 2006, the US offered to resettle 60,000 Bhutanese refugees, with Canada, Denmark, Norway, the Netherlands, New Zealand and Australia agreeing to pick up the rest who want to resettle (Asian Centre for Human Rights 2008). This initiative can be interpreted as a long awaited humanitarian gesture, as a response to an anti-warehousing campaign led by the USCRI, or as a self-interested security measure to reinforce regional security since it would undercut the human resource base for the Bhutan Communist Party (Marxist–Leninist–Maoist) (BCP) and the Bhutan Tiger Force (BTF), two armed groups intent on ensuring the return of more than 100,000 Bhutanese refugees to Bhutan (see Chapter 2 on the Bhutanese and Chapter 3 on the refugees on the Thai–Burmese border).

However, the legal and philosophical foundations of the effort were weak. One of the most fundamental weaknesses was the misinterpretation of the Refugee Convention. Article 8, for example, provides that 'Contracting states shall accord to a refugee lawfully in their territory treatment as favourable as possible, and, in any case, not less favourable than that accorded to aliens [elsewhere described as 'nationals of a foreign country'] generally in the same circumstances, as regards the right to engage on his own account in agriculture, industry, handicrafts and commerce, and to establish commercial and industrial enterprises.'

However, the norms of the Convention are, in reality, quite limited. First, the state must be a signatory to the Convention. Secondly, in signing the Convention, the signatories must not have attached any qualifications that detract from the rights provided in the Convention. Third, and most importantly, the refugees to which these rights apply are *not* humanitarian refugees but only Convention refugees, that is, those who have fled because of a well-founded fear of persecution, and not refugees who flee generalized violence, by far the greatest number of refugees in these situations. Fourth, even if the refugees are considered equivalent to Convention refugees, they are only given the same rights to work and engage in business and agriculture as those accorded foreigners – and then only if they are in 'similar circumstances'. In any case, as is well known, rights to work of foreigners are usually very restricted in most countries. In other words, even operating within the Convention's norms, it is unlikely that very many states can be induced in international law to extend such rights to refugees. USCRI was really involved in a political pressure game using the Refugee Convention as a magic wand.

There are a number of reasons why countries of first asylum are extremely reluctant to offer more rights to refugees. Four are prominent. At the meeting in Geneva with African delegations in 2001 mentioned above, government delegations pointed to rising unemployment rates in their own countries, and argued that allowing refugees to work was not an option unless 'we want to walk the path of domestic unrest'. Secondly, they argued that emphasizing local integration as a solution would serve as a disincentive for refugees to return home. Thirdly, improving opportunities to work in countries of asylum would not encourage refugee-exporting countries to look for solutions. Fourthly, offering refugees rights to work would create a magnet for more so-called refugees.

The arguments may be spurious, especially those that suggest that attitudes to violent conflict would diminish if refugees were given rights in first asylum countries, or that refugees would never opt to go home. But the fear of a backlash from the unemployed in their own countries was genuine. And the argument that loose refugee systems attract more migrants is well recognized in developed countries.

Host countries also have practical objections. As Smith makes clear, the restrictions on refugee movements in a country arise from a number of fears about competition (most admittedly counterproductive), fears of refugees as sources of instability and violence (generally but not always unfounded), and political fears of an aroused citizenry. A dominant humanitarian paradigm even plays a part in reinforcing a propensity to maintain refugees in a state of dependence, rationalized by the mandates of some agencies that play down refugee independence and empowerment.

If the essence of a rights-based approach is the appeal to an international standard and norm of treatment which every individual refugee is entitled to expect, my claim is that insofar as such a standard exists, it is too minimal to have any significant effect on finding durable solutions for protracted refugee situations. The rights approach of the USCRI may not have been well founded in international law and norms, but it may possibly have been effective in Malaysia's decision to integrate the local Rohingyas and the American initiative in agreeing to resettle Bhutanese refugees in Nepal and Burmese refugees on the Thai border. If those actions were influenced by the advocacy campaign, the appeal to rights had no more than a rhetorical effect. The actions likely took place because the political conditions were opportune in those cases for a solution to take effect.

The case of the Rafha refugee camp

I have said that the rights campaign *may* have been effective. However, since the actions were overdetermined by other factors such as strategic interests, it is difficult to assess that effectiveness. One way to test a rights approach is to examine a specific case used by a rights approach to effect change and examine whether it was successful. USCRI targeted specific states and refugee camps. One was the Rafha refugee camp in Saudi Arabia that housed 128,500 refugees, 95 per cent of them Palestinians. 5,084 were Iraqi refugees. I decided to test the rights approach by focusing on the efforts to resolve the plight of 5,000 Iraqi refugees.[19] I soon learned that there were less than 500 Iraqi refugees left in the camp when USCRI started its campaign.

As the USCRI stated in a press release dated 7 June 2004:

> None of the 483 Iraqis may live or work outside the camp, and all are denied other basic rights contained in the 1951 UN Convention and Protocol Relating to the Status of Refugees ('the Convention'), which recognizes the fundamental rights of refugees while in exile including those to work, freedom of movement and residence, and to own property. Although not a party to the Convention, Saudi Arabia's denial of rights to the Iraqis is wrong and should end.[20]

By 2005, USCRI claimed at least partial success for their campaign on behalf of the rights of the refugees:

> In late 2005, Saudi Arabia announced that the 364 Iraqis remaining in Rafha camp could leave the camp and live legally in urban areas. Previously, authorities had only permitted camp residents to visit a nearby urban center under the 'Rafha City Visits Program' and had controlled refugees' movements in and out of the camp.[21]

Was the victory in getting rights to move outside the camp and work a consequence of the USCRI campaign and, if so, was the success related to the issue of rights?

Some background is needed first. Other than the remote location and the extremes of heat and cold, compared to other refugee camps the conditions in Rafha were excellent in terms of providing for the refugees' needs. There were schools for the children, including ones for the girls, and the refugees lived in air-conditioned and heated quarters with television sets. They were fed reasonably well, had access to a hospital with 64 staff and even received a cash allowance for pocket money – 300 Saudis riyals (about US$80) every three months; women received even more – 350 riyals. The 300 jobs available in the camp were rotated among the refugees.

Nevertheless, in the summer of 2001, Rafha refugees conducted a hunger strike to protest against the miserable conditions and the hopelessness of their

---

19 In 1991, the US called upon Shiites in the south of Iraq to revolt against Saddam Hussein. Iraqi troops crushed the rebellion and 33,000 Iraqis from the Basra area in Iraq fled to Rafha in Saudi Arabia. After some initial rough treatment by Saudi authorities, the refugees were confined to Rafha camp. In the following six years, 24,264 were resettled in 22 countries (12,154 in the US) and 3,500 returned to Iraq. After 1997, this left 5,200 remaining.

20 See <http://www.refugees.org/newsroomsub.aspx?id=1032>.

21 See <http://www.refugees.org/countryreports.aspx?subm=andssm=andcid=1599>.

situation in the remote and inhospitable desert of northeastern Saudi Arabia. In Canada in July of 2001, in support of the protesting refugees, a small number of demonstrators from the Canadian Iraqi community marched in front of the offices of UNHCR in Ottawa. They wanted action to be taken to assist the Iraqi refugees marooned in Rafha.

However, Rafha camp had been virtually ignored by the international community between 1997 and 2002. When the drums of a possible invasion of Iraq grew louder and louder after the 9/11 attack, new attention focused on Rafha. UN High Commissioner, Ruud Lubbers, visited Rafha camp on 14 October 2002. At that time, Lubbers did not propose repatriation but promised to seek out opportunities for local integration and resettlement (UNHCR 2002). Saudi Arabia had actually offered to integrate up to 2,000 Iraqi refugees if the balance could be settled in Muslim countries, but the matching offers were not forthcoming at that time. In March of 2003, before the US-led invasion of Iraq in April, a riot took place in the camp in which 13 were killed, including four Saudis burnt in the arson attack on the camp facilities.[22] Following the US-led invasion and the overthrow of the Saddam Hussein regime, the UN began a programme of repatriation that returned 4,750 refugees in 2003; the first convoy transferring 240 refugees back to Iraq took place on 28 July 2003.[23] Escorted by security officials, in the eighth convoy on 8 December, 420 Iraqis were returned in air-conditioned buses with trucks carrying their belongings. On 23 May 2004, the last convoy planned to repatriate 483 Iraqis was suspended. These 483 refugees, less that ten per cent of the original remaining contingent, became the focus of the USCRI campaign. On 7 June 2004, USCRI urged Saudi Arabia to stop warehousing refugees.

Given this background, it seemed odd that the USCRI began a headstrong campaign against Saudi Arabia to stop warehousing refugees in June of 2004 (USCRI 2004). There were so few left. By then those left were virtually all Sunni rather than Shia refugees so it should not have been a surprise that by late 2005, Saudi Arabia announced that it had agreed to grant residence permits and allow the 364 remaining refugees in Rafha camp to leave the camp. Though the USCRI based its campaign on an appeal to rights, Saudi Arabia remained a country that barely recognized human rights. The polity was controlled by the Saudi royal family; the Consultative Council (*majlis al-shura*) was appointed and, in any case, had only very limited powers. There was no freedom of association and very limited freedom of self expression. The King Abdul Aziz Center for Science and Technology controlled access to the Internet. Torture was widely practised, trials were secret and those convicted were subjected to floggings, amputations

22 Even well fed and cared for refugees are susceptible to violent outbursts, especially when the situation is on the verge of change and rumours proliferate (Crisp 1999; 2000). This is very different from when militants control camps and use them as bases to continue a violent military campaign (Adelman 2002b).

23 The practice of sending refugees back in manageable waves is not just a matter of logistics. There is also a fear of potential violence upon the return of large numbers all at once. See Dirks (1995).

and beheading. Other religions were not tolerated and Shiites and Ismailis who made up one million, or six per cent, of the population of Saudi Arabia suffered from discrimination.[24] There was little likelihood that a campaign to integrate refugees based on rights would succeed. They were integrated because by 2004 there were few left and they were largely Sunni. Further, the offer to integrate them had preceded the USCRI campaign.

I suggest that given the offer of Saudi Arabia *prior* to the campaign and given its practice of demonstrating it would not be persuaded by rights campaigns, the delay in winding up the Rafha camp was possibly a result of that campaign and the refugees could have been integrated earlier. A structural analysis would have easily revealed the opportunities available that were in fact eventually taken. Though the value of USCRI's advocacy in making 'refugee warehousing' a public issue should not be undervalued, there is very little evidence that the rights campaign had any effect on the decision of the Saudis to integrate the remaining Iraqi refugees in Rafha camp.

Conclusion

The following chapters provide further, though far from comprehensive, evidence of the general truth of the importance of research and of structural analysis. Structural analysis of refugee contexts and of the positions of various stakeholders will help us locate openings and opportunities, and, in many cases, durable solutions for refugees and IDPs. Such solutions may not satisfy those who insist on refugee rights. And these solutions may also be delinked from comprehensive solutions to violent conflict or development plans that include provision for refugees and IDPs. But the emphasis should be placed on constantly and continually searching for opportunities to ensure that refugees recover or gain membership in a country that can and will provide for their protection. Improving the quality of the camps or capacity development are all well and good, but they do not get at the nub of the issue. Pressing the rights button for adjacent host states may sometimes be helpful, but in most cases is unlikely to be so. And waiting for a comprehensive plan connecting peace and development with the durable solution will, I predict, prolong refugee situations in most cases. The issue, as Hannah Arendt noted more than a half century ago, is to ensure that refugees obtain membership in a state that will protect them. Rights, development, and protection will then follow.

---

24 According to Amnesty International, in April 2000, following a protest by Ismaili Shiite Muslims in the southern province of Najran 'opposing the condition of degradation, repression and humiliation that is practiced against them and their tribesmen by Saudi authorities because of their faith', and the storming and closure of a mosque the previous December, 93 Ismailis remained imprisoned and 17 of them faced the death penalty.

Bibliography

1951 Convention Relating to the Status of Refugees, Geneva, 28 July.

1967 Protocol Relating to the Status of Refugees, New York, 31 January.

Abdi, A. (2004), 'In Limbo: Dependency, Insecurity and Identity amongst Somali Refugees in Dadaab Camps', *Refuge: Canada's Periodical on Refugees* 22: 2.

Abdullah, A. (2000), 'A Case for Refugee Technical Education', Report (Dadaab: CARE Kenya), May.

Adelman, H. (2002a), 'Repatriation of Refugees Following the Signing of Peace Agreements: A Comparative Study of the Aftermath of Peace in Fourteen Civil Wars', in S. Stedman et al. (eds), *Thematic Issues in Peace Agreements Following Civil Wars* (Boulder: Lynne Rienner Publishers).

Adelman, H. (2002b), 'Refugee Camps and Violent Conflict: The Case of Rwanda and Zaire', *Bulletin of the Atomic Scientists* 58: 6, 2.

Adelman, H. and Abdi, A. (2003), 'How Long is Too Long? Durable Solutions for the Dadaab Refugees', Report (Ottawa: CARE Canada).

Ahlsten, N., Giang, T., Hwang, T., Lam, F., Matthews, H., Ogasawa, H., Showalter, K., White, C. and Wilson, M. (2005), 'Protracted Refugee Situations: A Case Analysis of Kakuma Camp, Kenya' (Princeton: Princeton Refugee Initiative of the Woodrow Wilson School of Public and International Affairs).

Ahmed, I. (2003), 'Globalization, Low-Intensity Conflict and Protracted Refugeehood: The Plight of the Stateless Rohingyas', Occasional Paper (Dhaka: Department of International Relations, University of Dhaka).

Arendt, H. (1951, reissued 2004), *Origins of Totalitarianism* (New York: Schocken Books).

Asian Centre for Human Rights (2008), 'US Resettlement Offer For Bhutanese Refugees', Press Release, 29 February, <http://www.achrweb.org/Review/2008/208-08.html>.

Barnett, M. (2001), 'UNHCR and the Ethics of Repatriation', *Forced Migration Review* 10.

Black, R. and Koser, K. (eds) (1999), *The End of the Refugee Cycle? Refugee Repatriation and Reconstruction* (London: Bergahn Books).

Chen, G. (2004), 'A Global Campaign To End Refugee Warehousing', *World Refugee Survey 2004 – Warehousing Issue* (Washington, DC: US Committee on Refugees), 24 May, p. 21.

Chimni, B.S. (1999), 'From Resettlement to Involuntary Repatriation: Towards a Critical History of Durable Solutions', New Issues in Refugee Research, UNHCR Working Paper No. 2 (Geneva: UNHCR, Evaluation and Policy Analysis Unit).

Crisp, J. (1999), 'A State of Insecurity: The Political Economy of Violence in Refugee-Populated Areas of Kenya', New Issues in Refugee Research, UNHCR Working Paper No. 16 (Geneva: UNHCR, Evaluation and Policy Analysis Unit).

Crisp, J. (2000), 'A State of Insecurity: The Political Economy of Violence in Refugee-Populated Areas of Kenya', *African Affairs* 99.

Crisp, J. (2001), 'Mind the Gap! UNHCR, Humanitarian Assistance and the Development Process', Paper (Geneva: UNHCR Evaluation and Policy Analysis Unit), May. Also published in *International Migration Review* 35: 1, Spring, 168–91.

Crisp, J. (2002a), 'Protracted Refugee Situations: Some Frequently Asked Questions', Paper (Geneva: UNHCR, Evaluation and Policy Analysis Unit).

Crisp, J. (2002b), 'Minimum Standards and Essential Needs in a Protracted Refugee Situation. A Review of the UNHCR Programme in Kakuma, Kenya', Paper (Geneva: UNHCR, Evaluation and Policy Analysis Unit), November.

Crisp, J. (2002c), 'No Solution in Sight: The Problem of Protracted Refugee Situations in Africa', Working Paper No. 68 (San Diego: The Center for Comparative Immigration Studies, University of California).

Crisp, J. (2003), 'No Solution in Sight: The Problem of Protracted Refugee Situations in Africa', New Issues in Refugee Research, UNHCR Working Paper No. 75 (Geneva: UNHCR, Evaluation and Policy Analysis Unit).

Crisp, J. (2004), 'The Local Integration and Local Settlement of Refugees: A Conceptual and Historical Analysis', New Issues in Refugee Research, UNHCR Working Paper No. 102 (Geneva: UNHCR, Evaluation and Policy Analysis Unit).

Crisp, J., Talbot, C. and Cipollone, D.E. (eds) (2001), *Learning for a Future: Refugee Education in Developing Countries* (Geneva: UNHCR).

Dick, S. (2002), 'Responding to Protracted Refugee Situations: A Case Study of Liberian Refugees in Ghana', Report (Geneva: UNHCR, Evaluation and Policy Analysis Unit), July.

Dirks, G.E. (1995), *Population Movements and Refugee Repatriation: The Impact of Returnees on the Stability of States in Post-Conflict Situations* (Halifax: Dalhousie University).

Goetz, N. (2002a), 'Lessons from a Protracted Refugee Situation', Working Paper No. 74 (San Diego: The Center for Comparative Immigration Studies, University of California).

Goetz, N.H. (2002b), 'Evaluating International Humanitarian Action', *Journal of Refugee Studies* 15: 1, 123–5.

Goetz, N.H. (2002c), 'Refugees and the Myth of the Borderless World', *Journal of Refugee Studies* 15: 4, 429–31.

Goetz, N.H. (2005), 'Bridging the Gap: The Forced Migration Laboratory, Refugee Health, and Community-Based Solutions', *Journal of Health Care for the Poor and Underserved* 15: 2, 231–6.

Harman, D. (2002), 'In a Dire Kenyan Camp, Links to Al Qaeda: A Saudi Group whose Funds have been Frozen by the US is Aiding Somali Refugees', *The Christian Science Monitor* 18 December.

Horst, C. (1997), 'Vital Links in Social Security: Somali Refugees in the Dadaab Camps, Kenya', Paper for Evaluation and Policy Analysis Unit, UNHCR,

April 2001, published under same title in *Refugee Studies Quarterly* 21 (1 and 2), April 2002, 242–59.

Human Rights Watch (1997).

Human Rights Watch Report (HRW 2002), 'Why Refugees Leave Kenyan Refugee Camps', <http://www.hrw.org/reports/2002/kenyaugan>.

Hyndman, J. (2000), *Managing Displacement: Refugees in the Politics of Humanitarianism*, Borderlines No. 16 (Minneapolis: University of Minnesota).

Jacobsen, K. (2001), 'The Forgotten Solution: Local Integration for Refugees in Developing Countries', *New Issues in Refugee Research*, UNHCR Working Paper No. 45 (Geneva: UNHCR, Evaluation and Policy Analysis Unit).

Jamal, A. (2000), 'Minimum Standards and Essential Needs in a Protracted Refugee Situation: A Review of the UNHCR Program in Kakuma, Kenya', Paper (Geneva: UNHCR, Evaluation and Policy Analysis Unit).

Jamal, A. and Stage, O. (2001), 'UNHCR's Program for Internally Displaced Persons in Angola', Paper (Geneva: UNHCR, Evaluation and Policy Analysis Unit), May.

Kagwanja, P.M. (2000), 'Ethnicity, Gender and Violence in Kenya', *Forced Migration Review*, special issue on gender and displacement, December, 22–5.

Kälin, W. (2000), *Annotations to the Guiding Principles on Internal Displacement* (Washington, DC: American Society of International Law (ASIL)).

Kälin, W., Cohen, R. and Mooney, E. (eds) (2003), *The Guiding Principles on Internal Displacement and the Law of the South Caucasus: Georgia, Armenia, Azerbaijan* (Washington, DC: American Society of International Law (ASIL)).

Kuhlman, T. (2002), 'Responding to Protracted Refugee Situations: Liberians in Côte d'Ivoire', Paper (Geneva: UNHCR, Evaluation and Policy Analysis Unit), July.

Limon, L. (2004), 'Lives Unlived', *World Refugee Survey 2004 – Warehousing Issues* (Washington, DC: US Committee on Refugees), 24 May, p. 18.

Loescher, G. and Milner, J. (2005), 'The Long Road Home: Protracted Refugee Situations in Africa', *Survival* 47: 2, 153–72.

Mann, M. (2005), *The Dark Side of Democracy: Explaining Ethnic Cleansing* (Cambridge: Cambridge University Press).

Mor, J.S. (2004), *Refugee Reports* 25: 5, July–August, UNHCR, June.

Muggah, R. (2003), 'Hard Choices: A Critical Review of UNHCR's Community Development Approach in Nepal', *GSC Quarterly* 9, Summer.

OAU (1974), OAU Convention Governing the Aspects of Refugee Problems in Africa, 20 June.

Ojwang, A. (1995), 'Education Sector Evaluation Report', Report (Dadaab: CARE Kenya), March.

Posner, M. and Clancy, D. (undated), 'A Human Rights-Based Approach to Refugee Assistance', Human Rights First <http://www.humanrightsfirst.org/intl_refugees/regions/approach_refugess.pdf>.

Raffonelli, L. (2004), 'With Palestine, Against the Palestinians', *World Refugee Survey 2004 – Warehousing Issue* (Washington: US Committee on Refugees), 66–73.

Rutinwa, B. (2002), 'The End of Asylum? The Changing Nature of Refugee Policies in Africa', *Refugee Studies Quarterly* 21: 1 and 2.

Smith, M. (2004), 'Warehousing Refugees: A Denial of Rights, a Waste of Humanity', *World Refugee Survey 2004 – Warehousing Issue* (Washington: US Committee on Refugees), 38–56.

UNHCR (1993), 'Refugee Protection and Sexual Violence', Conclusion 73 (XLIV), UNHCR Executive Committee Conclusions.

UNHCR (2002), 'Agenda for Protection', Executive Committee of the High Commissioner's Programme, Standing Committee 24th Meeting, 26 June (EC/52/SC/CRP.9/Rev.1) (Geneva: UNHCR).

UNHCR (2004), 'Protracted Refugee Situations', Executive Committee of the High Commissioner's Programme, Standing Committee 30th Meeting, 10 June (EC/54/SC/CRP.14) (Geneva: UNHCR), available at <www.refugees.org/data/warehousing/docs/sc_prs.pdf>.

USCRI (2002), *Refugee Reports* 23: 8, November (Washington, DC: US Committee for Refugees and Immigrants).

USCRI (2004), *World Refugee Survey 2004 – Warehousing Issue* (Washington, DC: US Committee for Refugees and Immigrants).

USCRI (2004), 'USCRI Urges Saudi Arabia To Stop Warehousing Refugees', Press Release, 7 June.

Verdirame, G. (1999), 'Human Rights and Refugees: the Case of Kenya', *Journal of Refugee Studies* 12: 14, 56–7.

Verdirame, G. and Harrell-Bond, B. (2000), *Rights In Exile* (New York: Berghahn Books).

Verdirame, G. and Harrell-Bond, B.A. with Lomo, Z. and Garry, H. (2005), *Janus Faced Humanitarianism* (New York: Bergahn Books).

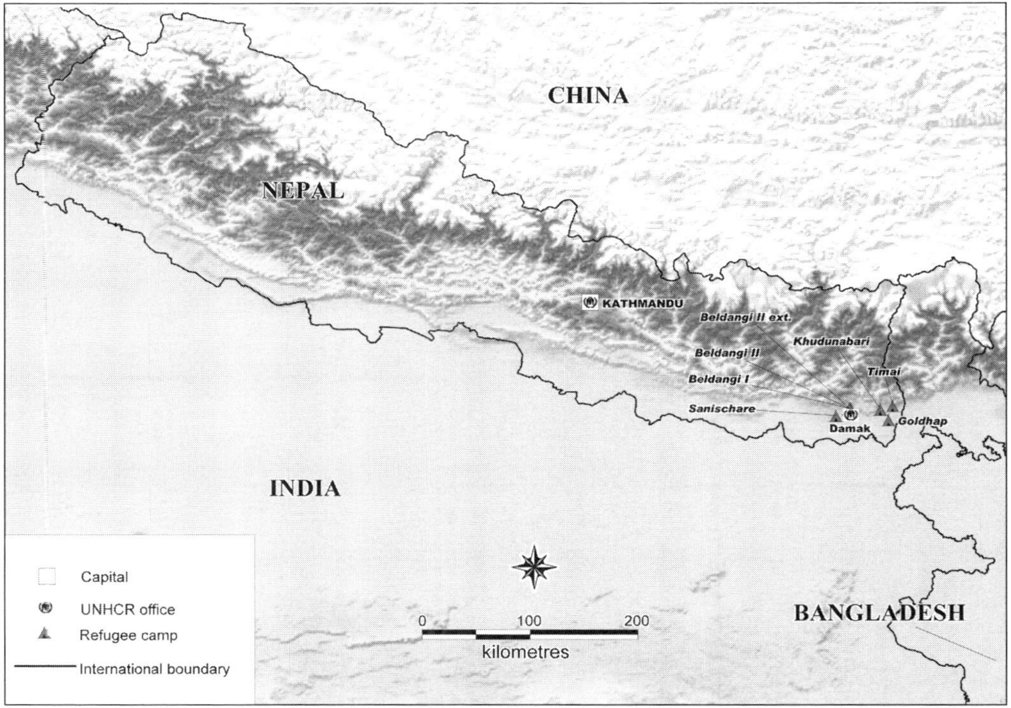

Map 2.1 Nepal
Source: UNHCR. Reprinted with permission.

Chapter 2
Resettlement of the Bhutanese from Nepal: The Durable Solution Discourse[1]

Susan Banki

Introduction

After more than 15 years of living in limbo, Bhutanese refugees living in Nepal have access to a durable solution. In early 2008, several thousand resettled in the United States, with the promise of many more to follow. Canada, Australia, and a smattering of European countries have also begun the process of registering the Bhutanese for resettlement.

For many years, the primary goal of the refugee population was to return to Bhutan. In 2000, the *Kathmandu Post* reported that even the possibility of being resettled to nearby India was rejected by refugee leaders (6 May 2000). It is not surprising, then, that the current resettlement programme has sparked debate among stakeholders and anxiety among refugees. Researchers have weighed in, considering both the benefits and shortcomings of resettlement (Hutt 2006; Charny 2007; Human Rights Watch 2007). Many refugee leaders are critical of the process[2] and those who support resettlement openly have been threatened and attacked on numerous occasions. In private, camp residents have enduring questions about what resettlement will actually mean for them and their families.[3]

Amidst the confusion about and controversy surrounding resettlement, this chapter analyses why resettlement has emerged as a prominent solution for the Bhutanese refugees in Nepal. By weaving together a historical contextual analysis with current field research, this chapter attempts to explain the resettlement trajectory for this lesser-studied population. It suggests that the policies and practices of both the home and host governments converged to thwart the return of refugees to Bhutan and discourage local integration in Nepal. At the same time, the possibility of diminishing short-term humanitarian assistance motivated the international community to find an alternative long-term durable solution. Unmet

1 The author is indebted to Robert Muggah for a careful reading and edit of this chapter.

2 See, for example, an interview by Devendra Bhattarai with refugee activist Tek Nath Rizal on *BBC Monitoring South Asia* (21 October 2006).

3 A similar anxiety about resettlement can be found on the Thai–Burmese border. See, for example, Banki and Lang (2007).

expectations about the possibility of repatriation among the refugees increased the pressure to accept *any* long-term solution, even if not the one initially desired. Against the backdrop of an international discourse centred on finding durable solutions, resettlement emerged, for better or for worse, as one way forward.

The chapter begins with an overview of the refugees in Nepal and a description of the camps as a backdrop to explain the necessity of locating durable solutions for the population. It then provides the historical and current political contexts in Bhutan and Nepal that have created and sustained the refugee situation. Turning to the role of other stakeholders, it demonstrates how host and home governments interacted with donors, the UN High Commissioner for Refugees (UNHCR) and the refugees themselves to pave the way for large-scale resettlement.

Overview of the refugee situation

Bhutan and Nepal are both land-locked kingdoms that abut the Himalayan range on their northern frontiers, separated by a small slice of India. Beginning in 1990, thousands of Bhutan's Lhotshampa population[4] – ethnic Nepalis living in Bhutan – fled the country, crossed overland through Assam, India, and arrived in Nepal. Bhutan claims that the population left willingly, or were never citizens to begin with, and has resisted the return of any Lhotshampas from Nepal. The refugees themselves – who include both educated and uneducated, and both former government officials and farmers – insist that they were forced to flee their native country because of their ethnicity, and have been pressing for their return to Bhutan for more than 15 years.

The number of refugees fleeing peaked in 1992, when as many as 600 were arriving each day, and slowed to a trickle by 1995 (Hutt 2003, 257). The presence of UNHCR began in 1991, when the government of Nepal formally requested coordination of all humanitarian relief.

4 The term 'Lhotshampa' was a term coined in the mid-1980s in order to differentiate among Bhutan's various ethnic groups (Mathew 1999). It means 'southerner' in the Dzongkha language, the language spoken by the Ngalong, the ruling elite who traditionally resided in northwestern Bhutan. The Ngalong are politically dominant but numerically in the minority in Bhutan. Along with the Sharchops, who live in eastern Bhutan, the Ngalong practise Mahayana Buddhism, while the southern-residing Lhotshampa generally practise the Hindu religion and are ethnically Nepali. The Ngalong and Sharchops are often collectively referred to as 'Drupka', although this is a misnomer, since the word means 'people who live in Bhutan' and could refer to all residents of Bhutan (HRCB 2003, 3). Population estimates in Bhutan vary widely and are politically driven, but even estimates that maximize the number of Ngalong still identify them as the least populous of Bhutan's three main ethnicities. Ngalongs account for 10–28 per cent of the population and Sharchops comprise 30–44 per cent of the population. Figures for Lhotshampa range the most widely, from 25–53 per cent of the population (Hutt 2003, 7).

Comparisons between the refugees from Bhutan and the refugees from Tibet (who arrived decades earlier and are a smaller population) living in Nepal reveal that Tibetan refugees have been able to integrate locally more easily than the Lhotshampas, despite the latter's ethnic and linguistic similarity with the local population in eastern Nepal (Subedi 2001; Banki 2004).[5] Most Lhotshampa refugees are in camps; there are an estimated 107,500 refugees in seven camps in Jhapa and Morang districts in eastern Nepal and about 10,000 outside of the camps (USCRI 2007).

Camp quality of life

The refugee camps serve the basic needs of the Lhotshampa population. Reports of malnutrition and disease outbreak were common in the first few years after the establishment of the camps, when the camps were 'plagued by measles, cholera, tuberculosis, malaria, diarrhea, beriberi and scurvy' (Proctor 1995, 1891), but since then, independent monitors have reported that conditions have improved (Ruiz and Berg 2005, 100). Today, relative to refugee camps in other countries, the Bhutanese refugee camps in Nepal are of a reasonable quality, and relative to health and education systems in rural Nepal, they are of a high quality (Muggah 2005, 156). It has even been surmised that cuts in refugee services might have emerged from a concern that the host population is faring more poorly than the refugees (Austcare 2004, 9). Nevertheless, UNHCR's *Global Appeal 2006* offers an indication of how the stress of living in limbo for such an extended period of time has been detrimental to the population:

> The protracted stay, lack of meaningful work opportunities and no apparent prospect of solutions fuel frustration and alter social and political attitudes within the refugee community. Pressure on primary health centres grows, with increased prescriptions and referrals for further treatment for an ageing and anxious population; there are more chronically ill and psychiatric patients than ever. The camp space has become overpopulated and the average area per person is sub-standard. (2005, 269)

Warehousing

Separate from the provision (or lack) of basic services, Bhutanese refugees are subject to a degree of 'warehousing', the 'indefensible practice' of depriving refugees of the rights to earn a livelihood, move freely and access justice systems (Chen 2005, 21). Legally, Bhutanese refugees are restricted in their movements and prohibited from travelling outside their camps without special permission (Ruiz and Berg 2005, 98). In practice, the government tolerates refugee movement outside the camps, although permission to exit and enter the camps can easily be

5 Recently arrived Tibetan refugees are now undergoing similar restrictions as their Lhotshampa counterparts. See, for example, USCRI 2007.

suspended, and was, in the wake of refugee protests in early 2007 (USCRI 2007). Refugees are not permitted to work legally, making the pursuit of livelihoods quite difficult, but in practice, some refugees do work as farmers and, in rare cases, as petty tradesmen (Kharat 2003, 286). Despite the fact that several NGOs offer vocational training in the camps, the skills that refugees have learned therein are of no use to help generate income, since selling these goods, even within the confines of the camp, is prohibited (Patrick 2006, 2). Highly educated refugees have also found work as teachers in schools all over Nepal, but the salaries are lower than those of daily labourers.

Protection

Related to warehousing, the lack of a legal space where refugees can move and work creates predictable protection issues. Several reports have detailed the specific risks experienced by women and children in the camps in Nepal, particularly those who leave the camps to collect firewood or attempt to earn an outside income (Giri 2005; Patrick 2006).

Women disempowered Camp registration and administration processes rely on the male head of household for identification and food distribution and hence run the risk of excluding women (Human Rights Watch 2003a). Despite ad hoc measures by UNHCR to ensure that single mothers do in fact receive rations, women, children and the elderly are more likely to fall between the cracks when there is systematic discrimination at the root of the registration system. Exploitation by aid workers, domestic violence perpetrated by male relatives in the camps and impregnation of young refugee girls by camp teachers have all been reported (Giri 2005). In 2006, there were 147 reports of gender-based violence in the camps (USCRI 2007). These problems, combined with a lack of psychosocial support on gender issues (Giri 2005), demonstrate the specific vulnerability of women in the camps. In addition, the uncertainty of refugees' final destination continues to problematize gender protection in the camp setting. 'The poor conditions in the camps combined with anxiety about the future contribute to strains and tensions that result in domestic violence and conflict in the camps' (Human Rights Watch 2007, 3).

Children affected Refugee vulnerability is often magnified in the case of children, because of their limited access to the many elements needed to afford them protection, such as basic humanitarian assistance, information and representation. Children are at particular risk of undernourishment. When food is scarce, families sometimes adopt a coping strategy of restricting the food intake of one of the younger members of the family (Lautze 1997). In the Bhutanese camps, this phenomenon is possible because rations are based on the number of individuals in a household rather than on their ages so that when children are very young, their rations yield a surplus of food for others. The optimal way to increase food intake, then, is to have a large family with many very young children (Hart 2003, 36). This creates a perverse incentive structure wherein families want more children but run into increasing difficulties in feeding them as they grow older.

As a result of undernourishment, health problems disproportionately plague the young. In early 2007, it was reported that refugee children in the Bhutanese camps were becoming infected with pneumonia and other contagious diseases at an alarming rate (JRS 2007). In protracted refugee situations, children and youths are particularly vulnerable to boredom and the lack of prospects that accompany camp life. Reports have shown that low morale and a sense of hopelessness pervade the camp atmosphere, leading to high dropout rates, even though the camp schools are of a high quality relative to Nepalese schools (Human Rights Watch 2007, 18). The aforementioned boredom and lack of alternative social structures contribute to another concern for the young – the high incidence of early marriage and pregnancy, which results in decreased educational and livelihood opportunities (Hart 2003, 36). Cramped living conditions – an average of 6.4 people live in each hut in the camps (UNHCR/WFP 2006, annex VI) – exacerbate intra-familial tensions and restlessness of the youth in particular.

Marginalization and radicalization

There is much written on how the exilic experience can radicalize refugees and migrants to become 'long-distance nationalists' in their diaspora communities (Anderson 1998; Wahlbeck 2002). There is less documentation, however, on what we might term 'short-distance nationalism' – the strategies adopted by refugees who have fled their home country but have not yet established a secure home base from which to advocate for regime change in the home country.[6] In Nepal, short-distance nationalism has manifested itself – as it often does – in young populations.

The marginalization of refugee youth in particular has consequences for the community at large, as young people channel years of boredom and frustration into violent behaviour. Of even greater concern is that the violence takes place not only because of marginalization but because of radicalization. Dhurba Rizal, a Bhutanese exile, has noted 'latent militancy' of refugee youth in the camps which stems from: an absence of strong leadership among the refugees; a lack of higher education opportunities for restless youth; a prohibition on working legally; and a temporal factor, because the Lhotshampas 'may be coming out of a stage of denial

6 For two examples of this relatively unexplored phenomenon, see Lischer (2005) and Banki (2006).

and deprivation and moving towards the next stage – of anger and frustration at their situation, which they may choose to express through militant action' (Rizal 2004, 173).

In addition, the refugee camps are in areas where Nepal's Maoist rebels operate. The attraction of the Maoists' tactics – and surely their results – has led to predictions that the youth will adopt their strategies (John 2000), and to fears that they have already started training with Maoists (SAAG 2006). Even the fear and perception of such radicalization, rather than the fact itself, has already led to tightened restrictions in the areas near the camps, making life more difficult for all camp residents (Rizal 2004).

Declining international assistance

The gravity of protection needs notwithstanding, the longevity of the Bhutanese refugee situation has inevitably led to donor fatigue. At the close of 2006, because of a lack of international donations, the World Food Programme (WFP) came dangerously close to cutting food rations that were already barely sufficient. The *Bhutan News Service* reported that stopgap funding from the US, Canada and the European Commission averted this crisis (14 February 2007). Cuts in essential services included housing materials, clothing, and vegetables and spices (Human Rights Watch 2007, 19–22). Efforts by international agencies to alleviate the effects of cuts in fuel by introducing coal briquettes have brought unintended consequences for family members, particularly for children. No longer able to rely on oil to provide reading light at night, children have been forced to limit their studying (Human Rights Watch 2007). Human Rights Watch reported that, 'the Bhutanese refugees in Nepal are trapped between their forced dependency on international assistance and the increasing reluctance of the international community to keep providing for their needs' (2007, 18–19).

Monitoring organizations have documented that the deteriorating conditions in the camps have led to depression, tension and increased agitation (Human Rights Watch 2007). Equally important is the effect that worsening conditions and decreasing international attention have on the psyche of the refugees with regard to their final destinations. Their current situation – reliance on humanitarian assistance – looks increasingly bleak. In this context, the durable solutions of repatriation to Bhutan, local integration in Nepal and resettlement to a third country are more inviting than ever.

No repatriation: Bhutan's political context

In 1961, Bhutan was called 'the world's last Shangri-la' (Karan and Jenkins 1963, 6, citing Doig 1961). For years since, it has been the darling of the international aid community. Its image is that of a benevolent Buddhist kingdom marching successfully towards modernity at its own measured pace. This munificence contrasts sharply with the story told by the country's ethnic Nepalis – the Lhotshampa people, who reside in Bhutan's south.

As is common in many situations of protracted conflict, the history of the region is a contested one. In this instance, disagreements arise not only with the flight/migration out of Bhutan in the early 1990s, but even earlier, with the migration *into* Bhutan.[7] Dissidents and government officials are at odds about when Lhotshampas arrived in Bhutan. Claims of the commencement of Lhotshampa migration to Bhutan range from the seventeenth century (Subedi 2001) to the early twentieth century (Nestroy 2004). Michael Hutt, who has written the most recent and comprehensive account of the Bhutanese Lhotshampas, argues that those who are 'still identifiably of Nepalese origin' (Hutt 2003, 32) probably arrived as agricultural labourers beginning in 1864–1865 and continued to arrive through the 1930s. Any Nepalis who arrived earlier – as Newar craftsmen from the Kathmandu valley, for example – likely assimilated centuries ago and would not today identify as Nepalese. Nevertheless, 'the psychological importance for the Lhotshampa refugees of a historical narrative in which Nepalis migrated in a 'civilizing role' to Bhutan, at a date much earlier than Bhutan's rulers now care to admit, remains significant' (Hutt 2003, 26).

The first half of the twentieth century witnessed waning British influence in the Himalayan principalities: Tibet, Nepal, Sikkim and Bhutan. Because the development of transportation and communication networks in Bhutan was so limited, ethnic groups were isolated from one another and there was little evidence of ethnic conflict even through the 1960s.[8] But in the mid-1970s, several factors converged that resulted in policies that marginalized the Lhotshampas and led to their eventual flight. These concerned a nascent fear among Bhutan's elites that their access to power was diminishing. Independence movements throughout South Asia were giving voice to people's demands for representation, and in Bhutan, elites 'failed to provide the political and social space, where multiple voices from across the country could be expressed freely and used to inform a broadly based national policy' (Rizal 2004, 158).

---

7 Disagreements about 'when our people arrived' or 'who has been here the longest' are common in conflicts that rotate around territorial claims. The importance of such claims stem from the fact that some jurisprudence relies on a particular duration of time to establish residency rights. This temporal factor is apparent in other types of laws such as those that dictate: land ownership (adverse possession); property ownership (usucaption); interpersonal status (common law marriage); and citizenship (*jus soli*).

8 Tapan Kumar Bose notes that a small political group did form in exile in 1952 in protest of Bhutan's policy of discrimination, but that in the following two decades increased political representation of the Lhotshampas led the group to abandon its calls for reform (Bose 2003, 66).

Sikkim

India's annexation of Sikkim in 1975 was the first example of regional political developments that troubled Bhutan's leaders. In that referendum, the majority of the population voted to merge with India, and Sikkim thus lost its independence. There were many ethnic Nepalis among the population who pressed for the merger, and the leadership of the two major political parties were of Nepalese origin (Gupta 1975, 786). In Bhutan's eyes, Nepalese immigration was the direct cause of the loss of independence for the indigenous Sikkimese. Likewise, the rulers of Bhutan feared that ethnic Nepalis could similarly threaten their own kingdom.

The importance of Sikkim's annexation in the Bhutanese mentality cannot be overstated. 'We live on a day-to-day basis with the fate of Sikkim', asserted one Bhutanese government official, who claimed that, at the time of Sikkim's vote, 90 per cent of the population were immigrants (Sable 2005, 22).

Today, it may seem a stretch to be sympathetic to the Bhutanese official's line of reasoning, but that is precisely because the world knows so little of Sikkim today. In the 1960s, however, Sikkim was on its way to becoming an independent nation, on a par with Bhutan, and the three kingdoms of Bhutan, Nepal and Sikkim were written about and compared on similar terms. There was even a regional term used to describe the three: 'Himalasia' (Karan and Jenkins 1963, 6).

But a narrative that describes a flood of Nepalis simply infiltrating Sikkim to take away their independence is contested by other sources. In 1971, four years before annexation, a political observer noted that the future of Sikkim rested on the shoulders of its people, but said that this could 'not be achieved as long as trained graduates do not return to take up positions in their own country' (Coelho 1970, 52), thus attributing Sikkim's problems to emigration, rather than immigration.

Dhurba Rizal further argues that the link between Nepalese immigrants and Sikkim's loss of independence is tenuous.

> Sikkim became a part of India owing to its intricate geo-political location in relation to what at the time were frayed Sino-Indian relations rather than due to the actions or support of Nepali speakers in Sikkim … The elites' strategy to play the ethnic card by pitting ethnicity against ethnicity is a response partly to their own misperception. The elites have inflated and manipulated this fear as a strategy which enables them to dominate the monarch in national decision-making. (2004, 164)

Gorkhaland

Further regional developments stirred new fears in Bhutan in 1986. The Gorkhaland National Liberation Front (GNLF), comprised of Nepali Indians, demanded a separate state of 'Gorkhaland' in West Bengal, India, and recognition of rights and language within the Indian constitution. Since their expulsion from other areas of India, anger and dissatisfaction had been growing among Nepali Indians for decades, but the GNLF's fight was the first that espoused violent means

(Hutt 2003, 194). As such, Bhutan's fears of ethnic Nepalis impinging on their sovereignty were evident, because the GNLF's tactics created fears within Bhutan that dissidents would begin using similar violent tactics (Whelpton 2005, 112).

Citizenship laws

If the political events of the day illustrated that Bhutan's leaders feared losing their power, then the policies they enacted vis-à-vis obtaining citizenship gave these fears colour and form. In 1958, before threats to elites' power emerged, Bhutan's first National Assembly passed its first Citizenship Law, granting citizenship to ethnic Nepalis living in southern Bhutan.

In 1977, after Sikkim's annexation, the Citizenship Law was amended. Previously, those married to nationals could obtain citizenship expeditiously, and marriage to a citizen made one automatically eligible. The amended law increased the time it took to obtain residence, added a linguistic and educational component and legislated that non-Bhutanese women who married Bhutanese men could not automatically obtain citizenship, although the reverse was still possible. This law was likely targeted at the Lhotshampa population since there was a common custom that men brought in wives from India and Nepal (Hutt 2003, 148).

In 1985, soon after the GNLF struggle, the Citizenship Act was amended once again. Residency requirements were made even more stringent, and citizenship by naturalization required fluency and literacy in Dzongkha, the national language (Rizal 2004, 159). Thus, the 1977 and 1985 Acts, which followed closely on the heels of political events outside of Bhutan, seemed to reverberate within the country. 'The basic regulatory trend is clear. Lhotshampas easily gained citizenship under the 1958 Act but were increasingly restricted from doing so under the 1977 and 1985 provisions' (Saul 2000, 327).

1988 census

The impact of these increasingly exclusionary laws was not tangible until the 1988 census, before which non-citizens often lived and worked in the southern regions with few problems (Hutt 2003, 149). But the 1988 census radically altered the ease with which southerners could live, work and move. Hutt points out that although

> the term 'census' has always been used by the Bhutan government … to 'identify Bhutanese nationals' … [it does] not produce the statistical profile of the population of Bhutan that one might expect from a national census. Instead, [the] main purpose is to guard against illegal immigration … 'Censuses' appear to have been conducted annually in most southern districts since 1988 but have not taken place regularly in the northern districts, except perhaps in Thimpu. (Hutt 1996, 402–403)

The 1988 census divided the southern population into seven categories, ranging from genuine Bhutanese citizens to non-nationals (Bose 2003; Hutt 2003). At the time of the census, the government did not explain what it meant for Lhotshampas to be placed in each of the categories, creating unease and unrest among the southern population (Hutt 1996, 403, citing Amnesty International 1992, 6).

Through myriad interviews with Lhotshampas who fled to Nepal in the 1990s, Hutt documents that individuals who had considered their citizenship secure in Bhutan were stymied by local officials from obtaining the proper documentation, and thus lost their rights of ownership and property. Often, members of one family were placed into five or six different categories, with the result that even those with genuine citizenship were compelled to flee with the rest of their families (2003, 152–9). Even individuals with the coveted 'genuine citizen' status sometimes had that taken away from them (Hutt 2003, Chapter 14).

Driglam Namzha

A centuries-old code of inner and outer conduct, *Driglam Namzha*, proscribes dress, greetings and aspects of public etiquette. Although *Driglam Namzha* preceded the political events of the 1970s and 1980s, it was increasingly used to promote a sense of unique Bhutanese culture, and its codes were enforced more strictly. For example, a shift in language policy in the 1970s meant that only Dzongkha was permitted in schools and offices (Rizal 2004, 156). A royal decree from the king in the 1980s further emphasized the importance of national dress.[9] Because Drupka clothing was better suited to the northern hills, rather than the tropical southern foothills, it was more burdensome for the Lhotshampas to wear it (HRCB 2003, 9).

Michael Hutt's extensive description of *Driglam Namzha* and its implementation demonstrates that the code by itself was not a exclusionary instrument, nor was it invented for the purpose of nationalism. But Hutt concedes that 'it was applied well outside the monastic and ceremonial contexts within which it originally evolved' (Hutt 2003, 170). Whether intentional or not, the implementation of *Driglam Namzha*, in conjunction with laws that began to exclude elements of the Lhotshampa population, stimulated fears among the Lhotshampas that the country in which they had been resident for decades was undergoing a process of Bhutanization (Schäppi 2005, 7).

For some, Bhutanization seemed a logical process in order to safeguard the country against outside influences (Thinley 1994). Seen from this perspective, those who left the country were not comfortable with the changes and left of their own accord. For others, the policies and practices of the 1970s and 1980s represented the beginning of Bhutan's determined efforts to expel hundreds of thousands of Lhotshampas from the country. The result, whatever the interpretation, was that,

9 The king stated in a later interview that different ethnicities were able to wear distinct styles in their own regions (Hutt 2003, 174), but there was much local abuse of the decree, and those who didn't wear the Drupka national dress were often fined or imprisoned.

beginning in 1990, Lhotshampas crossed the border into India and on to Nepal, where the refugee camps were born.

Choice versus force

Thousands of Lhotshampas who departed Bhutan in the early 1990s were required to surrender key documents to Bhutanese authorities and sign Voluntary Migration Forms (VMFs),[10] which indicated that they had left Bhutan voluntarily (Hutt 1996, 411) and amounted to an effective relinquishment of citizenship.[11] But VMFs have been employed to buttress claims by both sides. While the government of Bhutan has pointed to the VMFs to reject Lhotshampa claims of refugee status, problems associated with the VMF signing process indicate that it may not have been quite so voluntary. Some individuals didn't understand the document because it was written in the Dzongkha language (Human Rights Watch 2003a, 19) and others claim that they were coerced into signing.[12] In addition, the very existence of the forms points to the fact that its signers were at one time considered citizens (Lee 1998, 125).

Even if the Lhotshampas chose to leave of their own accord, the Bhutanese government made it difficult for the exiled ever to choose to return. Several reports show that the government instituted a transmigration programme that brought northern Bhutanese to the south to resettle on abandoned Lhotshampa land. An article from *The Economist* reported that police officers and army officials were also permitted to settle on abandoned land (25 October 2003).

Refugeehood and repatriation

As in many protracted refugee situations, the question of Lhotshampa 'refugeehood' has come to be defined in terms of the voluntary nature of flight. Bhutanese government officials refer to VMF documentation and reports by the national newspaper, *Kuensel*, to demonstrate why repatriation is not a reasonable expectation for the exiles, whom they reject as citizens. Dissidents demonstrate that the Lhotshampa population was forced to flee, not willingly, but because of a denial of education, restrictions on movement, and forced labour (HRCB 2003).

10 Also referred to as 'Voluntary Migration Certificates'.

11 Bhutanese authorities have also supplemented the VMF documentation with the argument that Bhutan's king urged people not to leave on several occasions. The most comprehensive treatment of this point, from the side of the refugees and from the side of government authorities, can be found in Hutt (2003, 222–7). Hutt notes that the king actually traveled outside the capital, Thimpu, to ask families who were planning to leave to reconsider and remain in Bhutan. But many were unconvinced, and some who remained were forcefully evicted by local authorities later.

12 Hutt provides an example of a woman who was forced to sign in order to free her son from prison (2003, 251).

Both narrations of the story demonstrate the difficulty of repatriation. Legally, it will be difficult for many refugees to prove their right to return. Politically, the Bhutanese fear that repatriation will destabilize their country. Practically, much of the Lhotshampa property and land is now in the possession of others. Given these contexts, it is evident that a durable solution based on repatriation is, at present, a closed door.

Limited local integration: Nepal's political context

Nepal is not a signatory to the UN 1951 Convention Relating to the Status of Refugees, but in the decades that Nepal has hosted refugees, its non-signatory status has not been a driving factor in its treatment of refugee populations. Historically, Nepal allowed its small Tibetan refugee population not only protection, but also freedom of movement and freedom to work. By the time the Bhutanese arrived in 1990, Tibetans still had greater freedoms, but the lax attitude toward all refugees began to tighten. Today, both sets of refugee populations face fewer freedoms. Lhotshampa refugees are primarily confined to refugee camps and some newly arrived Tibetan refugees without documentation have been detained and expelled (US State Department 2003).

Nepal's policy changes can be attributed to a convergence of many factors, including the increasing total numbers of refugees in Nepal[13] and China's growing influence (Wiencek 2005). A third factor that explains Nepal's recent actions vis-à-vis its refugee population is Nepal's fear that refugees could add fuel to the fire of the country's Maoist insurgency, the rise of which coincides with Nepal's changing policies toward refugees.

The Maoist rebellion

The origins of the Maoist rebellion in Nepal can be traced back to economic and political developments of the 1960s and 1970s when an increasingly educated public recognized that the benefits of modernization and development weren't reaching all classes of society, and political consciousness spurred opposition to the *Panchayat* system – the powerful monarchical system posing as a democracy (Hutt 2004, 3). In the decades that followed, the monarchy's efforts to stem criticism – by banning all political parties – occurred in conjunction with grave dissatisfaction among student and civil activists.

In secret, the 'chronically divided opposition', consisting of seven Communist political parties, managed to unite under the banner of the United Left Front (Mikesell 1999, 13). From February to April of 1990, the alliance staged protests, coordinated calls for action and tried to pressure foreign donors. In April 1990, the

13 Making a similar point about the size of the refugee population influencing government policy is a UNHCR report about Ghana by Shelly Dick (2002).

king agreed to legalize political parties and introduce parliamentary democracy. But triumph turned to despair as economic conditions continued to worsen and various parties manoeuvred to co-opt power. By the mid-1990s, 'the Nepali state was heading towards instability and crisis owing to unholy alliances, both in nature and purpose, that were being struck between various parliamentary parties' (Hachhethu 2004, 59).

It was in this context, in 1996, that the Communist Party of Nepal (Maoist) launched the *jan yuddha*, the 'people's war'. Responding to a decline in living standards, Nepal's Maoist leaders began with assaults on police posts in the west of the country, and spread their tactics to central regions and Kathmandu with bombings and the burning of land deeds (Thapa 2005, 131). By 2001, the insurgency had spread to nearly all of Nepal's 75 districts and affected every sector of the country (Sharma 2004, 38). The assassination of King Birendra only served to increase Maoist access to power (Hutt 2004, 8).[14]

Maoist insurgents exerted a pull on the masses for a number of reasons. First, they were vociferously opposed to the caste system and the subordination of women (Whelpton 2005, 206). Second, by establishing local courts that circumvented the corruption in the national justice system and by banning extortionist moneylending rates, they courted public favour in the desperately poor areas of Nepal (Hutt 2004, 18). Third, when the local population was not wholeheartedly supportive of their violent struggle, the Maoists cultivated fear through grassroots intelligence networks that prevented civilians from opposing them (Pettigrew 2004).[15]

More significantly for the refugee population, the Maoists were increasingly successful in recruiting from the literate but not highly educated segment of Nepal's young population.[16] Anthropological accounts of towns under Maoist rule

---

14 The assassination of King Birendra and eight members of his family in June 2001 spurred numerous rumours about palace intrigue. While a report commissioned by the new King Gyanendra charged the (now deceased) Crown Prince Dipendra with the murders because of arguments over his choice of a marriage partner, the culprit and their motivations have never been adequately explained to Nepal's general public, who suspected and continue to suspect a conspiracy (Madhavan 2005).

15 However, see Shneiderman and Turin (2004) in following paragraphs.

16 In 1996, Michael Hutt questioned the veracity of a charge that Lhotshampas who left Bhutan supported violent resistance. Hutt notes that 'it does not take into account the politically conservative nature of Nepali agriculturalists and their total dependence on land. It is unlikely that such people would give up their fields, orchards, homes and citizenship simply to express their support 'in principle' for a political movement: this is surely a weak pull factor, and stronger push factors must have been involved ... In every instance of Nepali-led political activism in recent years, whether it be the various political agitations that occurred in Nepal under the Panchayat regime (1962–1990) or the Gorkhaland movement in Darjeeling (1986–1988), the leaders have come from the educated urban class and have experienced severe difficulties in mobilizing mass support in rural areas' (1996, 410). If Hutt is correct, what is the reason for which these same Nepalis have now been motivated to pair up with the Maoists? This is a question for future research, but two possibilities

document the effective strategies that Maoist local leaders utilized in appealing to this population, and the positive results it sowed. In Dolakha district in the northeast, for example, Maoist rebels arrived in the villages and immediately bestowed respect on the villagers, asking for advice on important village matters. Rather than terrorizing the town's members, they distributed goods equally and banned the teaching of Sanskrit, all of which appealed particularly to the young (Shneiderman and Turin 2004, 92–3).

True to the movement's ideology, actions such as these cut across ethnicity, class and caste (Mikesell 1999, Chapter 12). For a marginalized population such as the Lhotshampas, whose ethnicity made them the target of expulsion from Bhutan, the attraction of the Maoist rebellion was logical. At the same time, Nepal's desire to limit Maoists' contacts with the refugee population was also understandable. With some irony, limiting Lhotshampa refugees to a camp environment has further marginalized them, making them easier targets for the Maoists. Fears brewed for years that Maoists had infiltrated the camps, and these fears were realized when recent reports confirmed camp meetings in which Maoists demonstrated the use and handling of weapons (SAAG 2006).

Bilateral action and no return: Nepal and Bhutan

If the Nepalese government has (especially recently) played the primary role in undermining the possibilities for local integration, it has, for many years, played the supporting role to Bhutan in confounding the possibilities for repatriation. Since 1993, bilateral talks at the ministerial level between the governments of Bhutan and Nepal have identified, classified and verified the Lhotshampa population in Nepal according to four categories:

1. genuine Bhutanese citizens who were forcefully expelled (who should be permitted to return to Bhutan);
2. those who had left Bhutan voluntarily (and hence, according to Bhutanese law, have sacrificed their citizenship);
3. non-Bhutanese; and
4. Bhutanese criminals.

Yet the criteria used to classify the refugees 'further complicated the negotiation process, indicating either Bhutan's unwillingness to accept all the refugees back into the country, or to [the use of] this position later as [a bargaining chip]

present themselves. First, the lengthy duration of exile has exacerbated the frustration of the Lhotshampas to the point where they will try solutions they may not have undertaken previously; and second, Nepali agriculturalists have already lost their fields and orchards; they literally have nothing to lose.

with the dissidents to squash the demands for democratic reforms' (Dhakal and Strawn 1994, 540).

The bilateral talks yielded few results until their tenth round, when, in December 2000, both countries agreed to the creation of a Joint Verification Team (JVT), comprised of representatives from both governments to verify and classify the refugees into the aforementioned four categories. The UNHCR, notably, was excluded from the process.

The results of the JVT in Khudunabari camp, the first camp to be surveyed, were announced in June 2003 to a strong outcry. Less than three per cent of the refugees were found to be forcibly evicted from Bhutan (category 1) and would as such be permitted to repatriate. The remainder of the refugees were placed into categories that might render them stateless for years. Those classified as voluntary migrants (category 2) had the possibility of returning to Bhutan and applying for citizenship like any other foreigners, for which they 'must not have acted against the king, country and people of Bhutan in any manner whatsoever' and must also prove proficiency in the Dzongkha language (Rizal 2004, 170). For refugees who have been outside of the country for more than 15 years, this burden of proof may be impossible to surmount.

One-quarter of the camp was found to be non-Bhutanese (category 3), but these results have been disputed. One woman placed in this category still possessed her citizenship card from Bhutan and reports being raped by Bhutanese soldiers in 1992 (Human Rights Watch 2003a, 25). Finally, the classification for 'criminals' (category 4) includes anyone who violates Bhutan's National Security Law of 1992, which assigns any conversation or correspondence that criticizes the king or government as a treasonable offence. Thus, 'all Bhutan's pro-democracy activists are classified under this category and will not get justice under the current regime' (Rizal 2004, 170).

The verification process itself has garnered much criticism. It was discredited as a 'flawed process' (Human Rights Watch 2003a, 22) driven by a 'nonsensical categorization scheme' (Dixit 2007). Among the problems associated with the JVT are:

- at the current pace, verification of all camps will take several years to complete, while refugees remain in the camps (Human Rights Watch 2003b, 9);
- during the verification process, women were excluded from the interviews, invalidating their personal claims of persecution and forced expulsion (Human Rights Watch 2003a, 23–5);
- the presence of Bhutanese officials on the verification team intimidated some refugees, making it difficult to assess the legitimacy of their claims (Human Rights Watch 2003a, 24); and
- the appeals process required claims to be made to the same body that offered the original decision (Rizal 2004, 170). Ninety percent of refugees in Khudunabari camp appealed the original decision (Human Rights Watch 2003b, 23, citing correspondence with the human rights organization AHURA).

Some of these concerns were considered in October 2003 when the two ministries met for their fifteenth round of talks. Progress was made and it was announced that after the visit by the JVT to the camps, repatriation of a small number of refugees would take place.

Conflicting reports record the chain of events during the visit of the JVT to Khudunabari camp, but the end result was that camp residents attacked Bhutanese members of the delegation. Whether the attacks were premeditated, as reported by the Bhutanese foreign ministry in *Kuensel Online* (24 December 2003), or whether they were, as reported by the Nepalese Foreign Ministry, spontaneous reactions to provocative statements by Bhutanese officials insisting on transit camp requirements for returning refugees and no compensation for confiscated land (Quigley 2004, 193), the attacks stalled all movement on the refugee issue. The ministerial teams have yet to meet again and not one refugee has returned to Bhutan at the time of writing.

In evaluating Nepal's role as a host government to Lhotshampa refugees, it is possible to identify three temporal phases. In the short term, Nepal rates positively. Lhotshampa refugees who were prohibited from remaining in Assam and West Bengal found immediate safety in Nepal when they arrived. They were neither expelled nor *refouled*.

In the intermediate term, Nepal's review is mixed. On the one hand, Nepal has been accused of warehousing its Bhutanese refugees, forbidding them access to secure livelihoods and sometimes restricting their freedom of movement. Local integration is officially discouraged. On the other hand, ethnic and linguistic similarity with the local population has permitted some *de facto* integration, and Bhutanese refugees are able to participate in daily labour without a fear of detention, in comparison to camps in other host countries, where leaving the camp is often the cause of arrest and/or a fine.

It is too early to judge Nepal's role as a host country in the long term, because such an assessment will require analytical hindsight of Nepal's eventual role in supporting or blocking durable solutions. Over the years, Nepal has wavered in regard to its position on repatriation for the Lhotshampas. At various points, Nepal has insisted that Bhutan should accept back the entire refugee population (Kharat 2003, 286, citing *Kuensel* 13 April 1996). On the other hand, Nepal's inability to sway Bhutan on the specifics of the JVT process has had lasting implications, because the four-part categorization scheme implicitly acknowledged that not all Lhotshampas had a rightful claim to Bhutanese citizenship (Dixit 2007).[17] In the final analysis, Nepal may have been bullied or persuaded by Bhutan to allow these categories, but its eventual acceptance of the four JVT categories may be the most prominent footprint dictating possible – and impossible – durable solutions for the Lhotshampa population.

17 Refugee activists at the time pushed for a two-category scheme (Quigley 2004, 190). Future scholarship will, it is hoped, plumb the intricacies and motivations of those first joint meetings where the four categories were developed.

Other relevant stakeholders

Thus far, this chapter has shown how deteriorating conditions in the camps began to necessitate the need for considering durable solutions rather urgently. An examination of home and host government motivations has demonstrated that the doors to repatriation and local integration are currently closed. The remainder of the chapter examines the role of additional stakeholders in obstructing the doors to repatriation and keeping the door to resettlement ajar.

India

While it is widely understood that India is the regional superpower in South Asia, neither Bhutanese nor Nepalese scholars acknowledge this openly, preferring instead to 'play down the extent to which New Delhi impinges on their national politics' (Hutt 2005, 53). But both Bhutan and Nepal are strategically linked to India.

In the case of the former, the 1949 Treaty of Friendship and Cooperation stipulated until recently that Bhutan's external relations were to be guided by advice from India and that the import of weaponry was subject to India's approval. In 2007, however, the treaty was amended to place the two countries on a more evenly balanced footing, reflecting a relationship of 'friendly cooperation.'[18] India's concurrence to the change indicates not a shift in the power dynamic, but a diplomatic nicety designed to reward Bhutan for its role in routing out anti-India insurgents in southern Bhutan (Quigley 2004, 194).[19]

In the case of Nepal, India enjoys a '*de facto* dominance' (Shah 2004, 204) that has manifested itself in: Indian support of the overthrow of the *Panchayat* regime (Rowland 1967, 146); ever-changing Indian restrictions on Nepalese imports without retribution in kind (Whelpton 2005, 230); and an active, if covert, role in supporting the Maoist rebellion (Shah 2004, 210).

On the refugee issue, India has repeatedly claimed that the issue is a bilateral one, removing itself from the public debate. But claims of neutrality notwithstanding, India's actions on several occasions show it to be more closely aligned with Bhutan.

India has used its position as the geographic middleman between Bhutan and Nepal to act as a sort of one-way swinging door. In the early 1990s it allowed refugees to depart from Bhutan before ushering them on to Nepal. But in 1996, when hundreds of refugees planned a peaceful march back to Bhutan to present the king of Bhutan with a written list of appeals concerning democracy in Bhutan,

---

18 As cited in several news sources including *Asia Times Online* (Ramachandran 2007).

19 One commentator noted that India's tacit agreement with Bhutan on the refugee issue might sour if Bhutan had refrained from helping India flush out the anti-India rebels (Rizal 2004, 165). The fact that Bhutan has cooperated with India points to the opposite probability – that India is unlikely to pressure Bhutan to budge on the Lhotshampa issue.

the Indian military arrested them and blocked their return to Bhutan (Hutt 1996, 415). In addition, India arrested, nearly extradited and has kept a tight rein on Rongthong Kuenly Dorji, a prominent opposition activist who worked closely with Lhotshampa organizations (Hutt 2005, 54).

Several commentators have noted the double standard that India applies in its relations with the two countries. India's involvement in promoting a democratic system in Nepal was not extended to Bhutan, even though Bhutan (at the time) was legally obliged to heed New Delhi's advice (Shah 2004, 201). And India's support of the Maoist rebellion is 'diametrically opposite' of the approach it takes in Bhutan, which has been to help stem rebellion as soon as it arises (Mishra 2004, 636). The advantageous treatment afforded to Bhutan in these other policy arenas indicates that India is unlikely to support repatriation.

UNHCR and the humanitarian regime

In the extensive literature on UNHCR's evolving role, one can locate three distinct elements within the agency's protection mandate. First, UNHCR *identifies* those in need of protection owing to the oft-quoted 'well-founded fear of persecution' (UN 1951). Second, in coordination with NGOs, it *assists* with the delivery of humanitarian assistance to improve the human security of the refugees. Third, through its intergovernmental make-up, it *promotes* lasting solutions to solve the problem of statelessness. In Nepal, problems associated with UNHCR's implementation of the first two processes meant that dependence on the third grew disproportionately.

UNHCR's identification process has strained its relationship with the government of Bhutan since the inception of the Lhotshampa refugee crisis. One point of contention was the *prima facie* status that UNHCR first accorded the refugee population, a designation that implicitly implicated the source country in intentional human rights violations, a suggestion at which Bhutan bristled. Bhutan also argued that because UNHCR did not begin to screen refugees until 1993, after the bulk of the Lhotshampas arrived in Nepal, the agency missed the critical opportunity to filter out those asylum seekers who were not genuine refugees. In the eyes of Bhutanese officials, this exacerbated, rather than minimized, the refugee situation (Hutt 2003, 257).

Bhutan's dissatisfaction with UNHCR's involvement critically influenced future dealings. First, Bhutan blocked UNHCR's access to the southern part of the country, making it impossible for the agency to assess whether it was safe for refugees to return there. The High Commissioner told UNHCR's Executive Committee in September 2003 that this was 'totally unacceptable' (Quigley 2004, 196). Second, UNHCR was permitted no role in the JVT process, which meant that it could not properly assess or modify the identification of those refugees who were meant to repatriate to Bhutan. As already noted, many refugees denounced the results of the JVT, and the eventual result was that no part of the repatriation process went forward.

The sudden halt of the JVT process and the perpetual postponement of refugee repatriation had lasting and significant effects on the direction of refugee destinations. From the refugee perspective, the promise of repatriation raised the hopes and expectations of the refugees that they would soon be permitted to return back to Bhutan. When the JVT process commenced, Damakant Jayshi reported that it facilitated 'return-home euphoria' amongst the refugees (*Kathmandu Post*, 31 January 2001), and when the JVT process stalled, Rakesh Chhetri, a political commentator, characterized the results as a 'betrayal of hope and dignity' for the refugees and noted that it 'brought a dead end' to refugee hopes of repatriation (*Kathmandu Post*, 26 July 2003). From this space of disappointment, it is easy to see how resettlement became a more attractive option, even for those refugees who initially wanted to return to Bhutan.

The second consequence of the abrupt about-face on possibilities for refugee repatriation was on UNHCR itself and its ability to assist with services. Having moved into the mentality of closing shop in the wake of repatriation, UNHCR and implementing organizations had to contend with budget cuts that diminished their ability to provide services adequately. Because of the protracted nature of the Bhutanese refugee situation, funding in the camps had years before moved from the emergency phase to a development-oriented approach (Muggah 2005). This meant that NGOs, who design their strategic plans some years in advance for development projects, had, in some cases, already planned exit strategies from Nepal in the wake of what was believed to be the coming repatriation process.

Austcare, for example, an Australian NGO that had been working in Nepal for some years, noted in its exit strategy that, 'Until recently, the AUSTCARE exit strategy planned to assist in the repatriation process, and was actively building [NGOs'] capacity, and the knowledge of participants (for example, through Dzongkha language and agricultural training), for the repatriation process. The plan was to assist initially with repatriation and then exit shortly thereafter' (Austcare 2004, 9).[20] When the repatriation process did not occur, Austcare scrambled to find funding to continue its project in Nepal, but was forced to pull out after another two years.[21]

Muggah notes an ironic twist in UNHCR's efforts to improve the lives of the Bhutanese refugees. By using a community development approach (CDA) in Nepal, the agency encouraged educational activities and programmes that strengthened capacity and refugee resources. This, perversely, made future cutbacks that much more difficult because the refugees by now understood some of the institutional processes driving those cuts:

20 A similar phenomenon occurred on the Thai–Burmese border, when the principal educational NGO's long-term strategy was planned with repatriation in mind. See Banki and Lang (2007).

21 Interview with Kate Glastonbury, former South Asia programme manager, Austcare. Sydney, Australia, 12 November 2007.

> Because of the shift from emergency to care and maintenance, UNHCR's programmes in Nepal have suffered budget cuts, falling from just over US$5 million in 1993 to a projected budget of US$2.8 million in 2002. As a result, UNHCR has tried to scale back its CDA activities, particularly in healthcare. This has been met with fierce resistance from a comparatively educated and rights-aware population. Predictably, dissatisfaction with the assistance provided by UNHCR and its implementing partners is growing. Many leaders of the refugee community, including university-educated refugees, are leaving the camps. (Muggah 2005, 159)

The chain of events describing humanitarian actors' presence in the camps shows how, step by step, one solution after another was blocked to the refugee population. 'The situation in the camps is not sustainable, either for the refugees who must live in the camps, or for the international community on whose continued assistance the refugees are dependent. Against this background many refugees have welcomed the US resettlement offer' (Human Rights Watch 2007, 3).

Why resettlement? US and Europe

The final section of this chapter turns to the players who have opened the resettlement door. Strategically unimportant as the Lhotshampas are in Europe, the US and Australia, it is these countries that have trodden a path in the absence of other solutions.

In the first decade of the Lhotshampa crisis, the role of Western countries in advancing durable solutions was marginal. Isolated refugees managed to make their way to the US and Europe and claim asylum there, but this was certainly not a holistic resettlement strategy. And there was very little pressure on the government of Bhutan to consider repatriation. In part, this is due to what one analyst called the 'Shangri-lazation' of the northern European countries in particular, whose view of Bhutan is rose-coloured and focuses primarily on the positive aspects of the kingdom's impressive road to development.[22]

Given the diluted interests of the West, the move toward resettlement for relatively uninvolved countries is not easily apparent. Pure realist constructions do not explain the apparent sudden impulse of several countries to accept members of this refugee population as citizens. Unlike during the Cold War, when refugees represented an instrument to delegitimize the Communist states from which they fled,[23] the Bhutanese refugees offer no such argument. One may hold up the

22 Interview with Ben Schonveld, OHCHR representative in Kathmandu. Sydney, Australia, 1 August 2007.

23 See, for example, Chimni (1998).

humanitarian basis for accepting refugees, but this does not aptly explain why *this* population, and why *now*.[24]

Two possible explanations are offered up for the current trend. First, in the US particularly – the country with the largest global resettlement quota annually by far – domestic priorities took precedence. While immigration is a heated issue for the populace, the protection of refugees is a bipartisan issue on which both parties – and the NGOs that support them – place great importance. The campaign of the US Committee for Refugees and Immigrants to end warehousing of refugees globally is just one example of the pressure brought to bear concerning the treatment of refugees internationally. But while Democrats and Republicans alike agree that refugees require fair treatment, in the wake of September 11, the US and many Western countries were reluctant to accept Middle East refugees, even though the war on terror propagated by the 'Coalition of the Willing' produced millions of them. Thus, there was a need to find refugee populations that would allow Western countries to fill their resettlement quotas without turning to those populations viewed as potentially dangerous – that is, the Middle East refugees. Thus, the US State Department's original statement to settle 'up to' 60,000 refugees in October 2006 was modified to 'more than' 60,000 refugees by November 2007, as reported in two *BBC News* articles a year apart (5 October 2006; 7 November 2007).

The second explanation points to the iterative nature of negotiating solutions for refugee populations. Governments in the UN system and UNHCR as an agency worked dynamically to aid the Bhutanese refugee population, producing an urgency that magnified the likelihood of resettlement. The interaction between donor countries (in this case, the US, Europe and Australia) and UNHCR began with an emphasis on humanitarian aid, but monetary involvement in the humanitarian sector gave way to political involvement, as financial investment appears to have spurred interest in the larger question of durable solutions. Quigley partially credits pressure from international (including European) donors with the moderate success of the bilateral talks in 2003, when Bhutan agreed in principle to allow some of the refugees to return, but he is silent on European efforts to repair the damage when the results of those talks failed after the attacks on JVT officials in Khundunabari camp (2004, 191).

The creation of the Core Working Group on Bhutanese Refugees in Nepal (CWG) – developed by government officials who focus on migration issues from Australia, Canada, Denmark, the Netherlands, New Zealand, Norway and the United States – demonstrates how donor governments became involved in locating solutions for the refugees, rather than only donating money. After the failure of the JVT, officials recognized that their humanitarian dollars were serving a population to whom no durable solution was available. The CWG thus envisioned a plan, according to the Canadian Foreign Ministry's website, to 'facilitate all forms of durable solutions' (Department of Foreign Affairs and International Trade 2007).

24 A similar question can be asked about the Burmese refugees on the Thai–Burmese border, who are also being slated for resettlement, as noted in Chapter 3.

The CWG initially prepared to pursue all durable solutions simultaneously, in the hopes that different portions of the refugee population could locally integrate, repatriate, and resettle. The emphasis on resettlement came later, when the doors to repatriation and local integration remained stubbornly closed. By then, the very creation of the CWG produced a floodgate of pressures to do something quickly to help the refugee population, leading the group, at present, to focus primarily on resettlement. This solution caught fire quickly because of the lack of any other resources to quench refugees' humanitarian need. At this point, one UNHCR official explained, 'it became a question of sequencing'.[25] That is, rather than focusing on all durable solutions simultaneously, the CWG and UNHCR started pushing resettlement first because they believe that with a significant portion of the refugee population resettled, the governments of Bhutan and Nepal may be amenable to smaller groups remaining where they are or returning home. With resettlement underway, involved parties hope to reshift their focus to press for other durable solutions.

Conclusion

It is possible to envision as a series of doors the durable solutions to which Bhutanese refugees might have access. For 17 years, refugees pushed on the repatriation and local integration doors, with little success. When the repatriation door was believed to open enough to let in a little bit of light, the pressure – from inside the refugee population and from the international community – grew to a fever pitch. When it slammed shut again, depression and anxiety skyrocketed. At the same time, a tightening of donor belts aggravated the conditions inside the camps. UNHCR and resettlement countries, swept up with the discourse of durable solutions and eager to relieve the pressure of this short-term population, opened the resettlement door.

What is behind that door – challenges or opportunities for those who resettle, stability or insecurity for those who remain – is the subject of further research. This chapter has shown that the deadlocks from the home and host governments combined with the pressure to break those deadlocks on the part of the international community facilitated the commencement and continuation of the resettlement process.[26]

25 Confidential source. Interview in Kathmandu, Nepal, 4 December 2007.

26 Recent changes in Bhutan have the potential to open the door to repatriation. In 2006, Bhutan's king abdicated the throne in favour of his son. In 2008, the first democratic elections were held in Bhutan. This may usher in possibilities for the return of the Lhotshampa refugees to Bhutan, or it may signal increasing fear on the part of Bhutanese authorities, thus continuing to shut the door on repatriation.

Bibliography

Amnesty International (1992), 'Bhutan: Human Rights Violations against the Nepali-Speaking Population in the South', Report (New York: Amnesty International), December.

Anderson, B. (1998), 'Long Distance Nationalism', in B. Anderson (ed.), *The Spectre of Comparisons: Nationalism, Southeast Asia, and the World* (London: Verso).

Austcare (2004), *AUSTCARE Exit Strategy for Micro-Skills Training Project/ BRAVVE, Nepal* (Sydney: Austcare).

Banki, S. (2004), 'Refugee Integration in the Intermediate Term: A Study of Nepal, Pakistan, and Kenya', New Issues in Refugee Research, Working Paper No. 108 (Geneva: UNHCR, Evaluation and Policy Analysis Unit).

Banki, S. (2006), 'The Triad of Transnationalism, Legal Recognition, and Local Community: Shaping Political Space for the Burmese Refugees in Japan', *Refuge* 23: 2, 36–46.

Banki, S. and Lang, H. (2007), 'Planning for the Future: The Impact of Resettlement on the Remaining Camp Population', Report (Bangkok: Committee for Coordination of Services to Displaced Persons in Thailand (CCSDPT)), July.

Bhattarai, D. (2006), 'Bhutanese Refugee Leader in Nepal says UN Conspiring to Thwart Repatriation', *BBC Monitoring South Asia*, 21 October.

Bhaumik, S. (2007), 'Bhutan Refugees are "Intimidated"', *BBC News*, 7 November.

Bhutan News Service (2007), 'US, ECHO and Canada Provide Aid to WFP', *Bhutan News Service*, 14 February.

Bose, T.K. (2003), 'Bhutan: Creating Statelessness – A Recipe for Regional Instability', in P.R.J. Chari, M. Joseph and D. Suba Chandran (eds), *Missing Boundaries: Refugees, Migrants, Stateless and Internally Displaced Persons in South Asia* (New Delhi: Manohar).

Charny, J. (2007), *Nepal: Time for Bhutanese Refugees to Choose Their Future Path* (Washington, DC: Refugees International).

Chen, G. (2005), 'A Global Campaign to End Refugee Warehousing', in M. Smith (ed.), *World Refugee Survey 2004* (Washington DC: USCRI).

Chhetri, R. (2003), 'Betrayal of Hope and Dignity', *Kathmandu Post*, 26 July.

Chimni, B.S. (1998), 'The Geopolitics of Refugee Studies: A View from the South', *Journal of Refugee Studies* 11: 4, 350–74.

Coelho, V.H. (1970), *Sikkim and Bhutan* (New Delhi: Indian Council for Cultural Relations).

Department of Foreign Affairs and International Trade (2007), 'Communique of the Core Working Group on Bhutanese Refugees in Nepal', 16 May. Foreign Affairs and International Trade Canada, Ottawa <http://www.dfait-maeci.gc.ca/canada_un/geneva/2007-05-16-en.asp>, accessed 1 November 2007.

Dhakal, D.N.S. and Strawn, C. (1994), *Bhutan: A Movement in Exile* (Jaipur: Nirala Publications).

Dick, S. (2002), *Responding to Protracted Refugee Situations: Liberians in Ghana* (Geneva: UNHCR, Evaluation and Policy Analysis Unit).

Dixit, H. (2007), 'Repatriation or Resettlement: Resolving the Lhotshampa Dilemma', *Himal Southasian*, June 2007.

Doig, D. (1961), 'Bhutan: Mountain Kingdom Between Tibet and India', *National Geographic*, September.

Economist (2003), 'In Limbo; Bhutanese Refugees', *Economist*, 25 October.

Giri, B. (2005), 'Mourning the 15th Anniversary of Crisis: The Plight of Bhutanese Refugee Women and Children', *Journal of Asian and African Studies* 40: 5, 345–69.

Gupta, R. (1975), 'Sikkim: The Merger with India', *Asian Survey* 15: 9, 786–98.

Hachhethu, K. (2004), 'The Nepali State and the Maoist Insurgency, 1996–2001', in M. Hutt (ed.), *Himalayan People's War: Nepal's Maoist Rebellion* (Bloomington: Indiana University Press).

Hart, J. (2003), *Bhutan: Conflict, Displacement, and Children* (Oxford: Refugee Studies Centre).

HRCB (2003), 'Bhutan: Political Crisis and Bhutanese Refugees', Report (Kathmandu: Human Rights Council of Bhutan (HRCB)), 25 November <bhutannewsonline.com/bhutanreport.rtf>, accessed 10 July 2007.

Human Rights Watch (2003a), 'Bhutan/Nepal: Trapped by Inequality: Bhutanese Refugee Women in Nepal', Report (New York: Human Rights Watch (HRW)), September 2003.

Human Rights Watch (2003b), 'We Don't Want to Be Refugees Again. A Human Rights Watch Briefing Paper for the Fourteenth Ministerial Joint Committee of Bhutan and Nepal' (New York: Human Rights Watch), 19 May, <http://hrw.org/backgrounder/wrd/refugees/refugees.pdf>, accessed 7 November 2007.

Human Rights Watch (2007), 'Last Hope: The Need for Durable Solutions for Bhutanese Refugees in Nepal and India', Report (New York: Human Rights Watch (HRW)), May, <http://hrw.org/reports/2007/bhutan0507/bhutan0507web.pdf>, accessed 5 November 2007.

Hutt, M. (1996), 'Ethnic Nationalism, Refugees and Bhutan', *Journal of Refugee Studies* 9: 4, 397–420.

Hutt, M. (2003), *Unbecoming Citizens: Culture, Nationhood, and the Flight of Refugees from Bhutan* (Delhi and Oxford: Oxford University Press).

Hutt, M. (2004), 'Introduction', in M. Hutt (ed.), *Himalayan People's War: Nepal's Maoist Rebellion* (Bloomington: Indiana University Press).

Hutt, M. (2005), 'The Bhutanese Refugees: Between Verification, Repatriation, and Royal Realpolitik', *Peace and Democracy in South Asia* 1: 1, 44.

Hutt, M. (2006), 'The Bhutani Refugees Should Not be Made to Wait Forever', *Nepali Times*, 8 September.

Jayshi, D. (2001), 'Return-home Euphoria Peaks Among Refugees', *Kathmandu Post*, 31 January.

John, A. (2000), *Potential for Militancy among Bhutanese Refugee Youth* (Colombo: Regional Center for Strategic Studies).

JRS (2007), 'Nepal: Poor Housing Causes Illness Among Refugee Children', Jesuit Refugee Service (JRS), 17 January <http://www.jesref.org/news/index.php?lang=esandsid=1607>, accessed 11 November 2007.

Karan, P.P. and Jenkins, W.M.J. (1963), *Himalayan Kingdoms: Bhutan, Sikkim, and Nepal* (Princeton: D. Van Nostrand).

Kathmandu Post (2000), 'Bhutanese Refugees Worried Over Resettlement Scheme', *Kathmandu Post*, 6 May.

Kharat, R.S. (2003), 'Bhutanese Refugees in Nepal: Survival and Prospects', *Economic and Political Weekly*, 25 January.

Kuensel Online (2003), 'Bhutanese JVT Officials Attacked in Jhapa', *Kuensel Online*, 23 December.

Lautze, S. (1997), *Saving Lives and Livelihoods: The Fundamentals of a Livelihoods Strategy* (Medford, MA: Feinstein International Famine Center).

Lawson, A. (2006), 'Breakthrough for Bhutan Refugees?', *BBC News*, 5 October.

Lee, T.L. (1998), 'Refugees from Bhutan: Nationality, Statelessness, and the Right to Return', *International Journal of Refugee Law* 10: 1/2, 118–55.

Lischer, S.K. (2005), *Dangerous Sanctuaries: Refugee Camps, Civil War, and the Dilemmas of Humanitarian Aid* (Ithaca: Cornell University Press).

Madhavan, G. (2005), 'Nepal: Turmoil Reloaded', Paper No. 1240 for South Asia Analysis Group (SAAG), 2 February, available at <http://www.southasiaanalysis.org/papers13/paper1240.html>, accessed 7 July 2008.

Mathew, J.C. (1999), *Ethnic Conflict in Bhutan* (New Delhi: Nirala Publications).

Mikesell, S.L. (1999), *Class, State, and Struggle in Nepal: Writings 1989–1995* (New Delhi: Manohar).

Mishra, R. (2004), 'India's Role in Nepal's Maoist Insurgency', *Asian Survey* 44: 5, 627–46.

Muggah, R. (2005), 'Distinguishing Means and Ends: The Counterintuitive Effects of UNHCR's Community Development Approach in Nepal', *Journal of Refugee Studies* 18: 2, 151–63.

Nestroy, H. (2004), 'Bhutan: The Himalayan Buddhist Kingdom', *Asian Affairs* 35: 3, 338–52.

Patrick, E. (2006), *The Perils of Direct Provision: UNHCR's Response to the Fuel Needs of Bhutanese Refugees in Nepal* (New York: Women's Commission for Refugee Women and Children).

Pettigrew, J. (2004), 'Living between the Maoists and the Army in Rural Nepal', in M. Hutt (ed.), *Himalayan People's War: Nepal's Maoist Rebellion* (Bloomington: Indiana University Press).

Proctor, M.H. (1995), 'Human Rights Violations among Bhutanese Refugees (Letter from Jhapa and Morang)', *Journal of the American Medical Association* 274: 23, 1891–2.

Quigley, J. (2004), 'Bhutanese Refugees in Nepal: What Role Now for the European Union and the United Nations High Commission for Refugees?', *Contemporary South Asia* 13: 2, 187.

Ramachandran, S. (2007), 'India, Bhutan: No More Unequal Treaties', *Asia Times Online*, 17 January.

Rizal, D. (2004), 'The Unknown Refugee Crisis: Expulsion of the Ethnic Lhotsampa from Bhutan', *Asian Ethnicity* 5: 2, 151–177.

Rowland, J. (1967), *A History of Sino-Indian Relations; Hostile Co-existence* (Princeton, NJ: Van Nostrand).

Ruiz, H.A. and Berg, M. (2005), 'Unending Limbo: Warehousing Bhutanese Refugees in Nepal', in M. Smith (ed.), *World Refugee Survey 2004* (Washington, DC: US Committee for Refugees and Immigrants).

SAAG (2006), 'Bhutan: Refugee Issue – Stalemate continues – Update No. 55', *South Asia Analysis Group (SAAG)* [website], 25 July, <http://www.saag.org/notes4/note322.html>, accessed 5 November 2007.

Sable, J. (2005), 'Reconciling Culture, Security and Development in Bhutan', unpublished MA thesis (Medford, MA: Department of International Relations, Tufts University), 84.

Saul, B. (2000), 'Cultural Nationalism, Self-Determination and Human Rights in Bhutan', *International Journal of Refugee Law* 12: 3, 321–53.

Schäppi, D. (2005), *Cultural Plurality, National Identity and Consensus in Bhutan* (Zurich: Center for Comparative and International Studies).

Shah, S. (2004), 'A Himalayan Red Herring? Maoist Revolution in the Shadow of the Legacy Raj', in M. Hutt (ed.), *Himalayan People's War: Nepal's Maoist Rebellion* (Bloomington: Indiana University Press).

Sharma, S. (2004), 'The Maoist Movement: An Evolutionary Perspective', in M. Hutt (ed.), *Himalayan People's War: Nepal's Maoist Rebellion* (Bloomington: Indiana University Press).

Shneiderman, S. and Turin, M. (2004), 'The Path to *Jan Sarkar* in Dolakha District: Towards an Ethnography of the Maoist Movement', in M. Hutt (ed.), *Himalayan People's War: Nepal's Maoist Rebellion* (Bloomington: Indiana University Press).

Subedi, B.P. (2001), 'The Problem of Bhutanese Refugees and Comparison with Tibetan Refugees in Nepal', *Contributions to Nepalese Studies* 28: 1, 71–93.

Thapa, M. (2005), *Forget Kathmandu: An Elegy for Democracy (*New Delhi and New York: Penguin, Viking).

Thinley, J.Y. (1994), 'Bhutan: A Kingdom Besieged', in M. Hutt (ed.), *Bhutan: Perspectives on Conflict* (Gartmore, UK: Kiscadale Publications).

UN (1951), Convention Relating to the Status of Refugees (Geneva: UN).

UNHCR (2005), *UNHCR Global Appeal 2006* (Geneva: UNHCR).

UNHCR/WFP (2006), 'Report of UNHCR/WFP Joint Assessment Mission: Assistance to Bhutanese Refugees in Nepal' (Kathmandu: UNHCR/WFP), May–June 2006.

US State Department (2003), 'Nepal: Expulsion of Tibetan Refugees', press statement, *US Department of State* [website], 2 June, <http://www.state.gov/r/pa/prs/ps/2003/21136.htm>, accessed 11 November 2007.

USCRI (2007), *World Refugee Survey 2006* (Washington, DC: US Committee for Refugees and Immigrants).
Wahlbeck, O. (2002), 'The Concept of Diaspora as an Analytical Tool in the Study of Refugee Communities', *Journal of Ethnic and Migration Studies* 28: 2, 221–39.
Whelpton, J. (2005), *A History of Nepal* (Cambridge and New York: Cambridge University Press).
Wiencek, D.G. (2005), 'China's Geopolitical Maneuvering in the Himalayas', *Asian Research* [website], 5 July, <http://www.asianresearch.org/articles/2649.html>, accessed 25 October 2007.

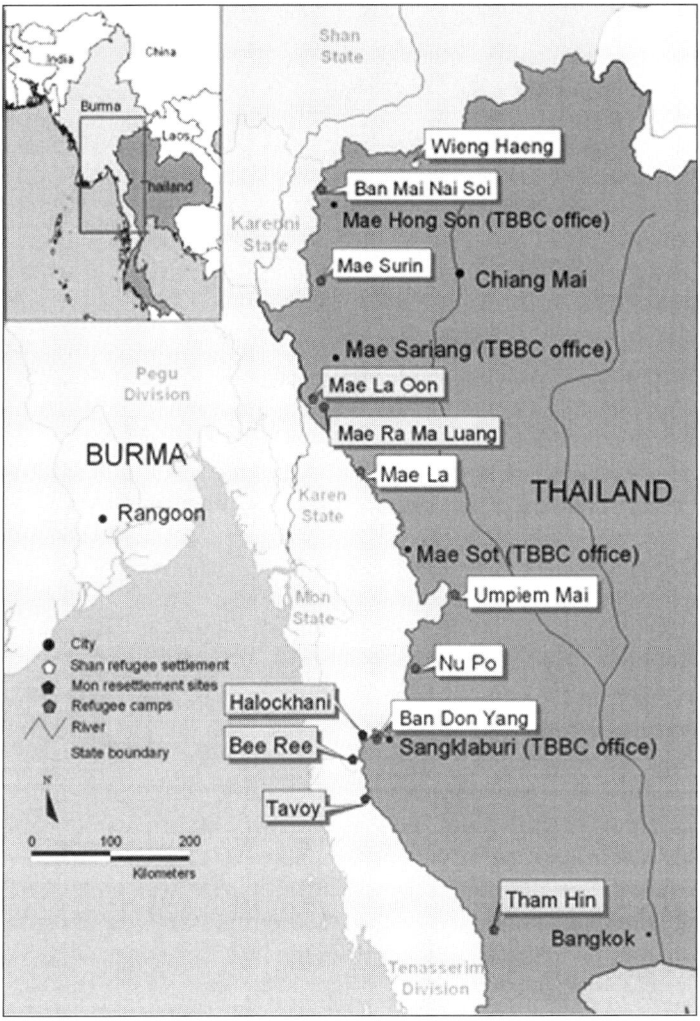

Map 3.1 Thai-Burmese border

Source: Reproduced with the kind permission of the Thailand Burma Border Consortium.

Chapter 3
Protracted Displacement on the Thai–Burmese Border: The Interrelated Search for Durable Solutions

Susan Banki and Hazel Lang

Introduction

Protracted conflict in Burma (Myanmar)[1] has produced a mix of groups of displaced on the Thai–Burmese border: refugees and internally displaced persons, in-camp and outside-camp populations, and recognized refugees and undocumented migrants. Some 145,000 recognized refugees in the main nine camps abutting the border represent the largest protracted refugee situation in East Asia, and a long-standing predicament given the establishment of the camps in 1984. Until recently, it appeared that the refugees would be indefinitely 'warehoused', with little or no prospect for permanent and durable solutions to their plight. A new large-scale multilateral resettlement programme has, however, changed this situation dramatically, as tens of thousands of refugees apply for resettlement. Hundreds of thousands of other civilians from Burma also live precariously in Thailand outside of camps, including over 250,000 displaced ethnic Shans who have entered Thailand since 1996 and as many as 1.5 million or more documented and undocumented migrant workers of many ethnicities. The number of internally displaced persons (IDPs) in the eastern border regions within Burma number approximately 500,000.

While examinations of the protracted refugee situation on the Thai–Burmese border have focused predominantly on a subset of the displaced community – either undocumented migrants or refugees, for example – there is value in analysing the

1 In July 1989, the regime changed the name of the country from Burma to Myanmar, along with the names of several other large cities and administrative divisions. (For example, Rangoon became Yangon.) The UN and many governments (including the states of the Association of Southeast Asian Nations) recognize these name changes, but some countries (including the US and Australia) still refer to the country as Burma. Whether to call the country 'Burma' or 'Myanmar' frequently provokes controversy. While the government claims it has simply reinstated the original transliterations for the country, its political opponents regard the name change as illegitimate. This chapter retains 'Burma' as the more familiar form for referring to the country.

displaced population as a single entity with separate but interrelated parts. This chapter demonstrates the extent to which the circumstances, needs and actions of one group of displaced interrelate with those of the others, particularly concerning durable solutions. It begins by demonstrating how the conflict has shaped different portions of the displaced population, from independence to the present. It then turns to an overview of the situation of Burma's displaced populations today. An examination of various stakeholders follows, charting their responses to and policies concerning the treatment of the displaced. Because of its recent position as the primary solution for Burmese refugees today, much of the examination focuses on resettlement's impact on other populations. Given the way in which these populations are shown to affect one another, the chapter concludes by questioning the utility of classifying displaced populations by their destinations, as is primarily done by the international refugee regime.

Review of the conflict

Burma's independence from Britain in 1948 ushered in a decade of tumultuous democracy, followed by two coups and the rise of an authoritarian military regime, most recently calling itself the State Peace and Development Council (SPDC). In 1988, a pro-democracy uprising led to a fierce crackdown by the armed forces (the *tatmadaw* in the Burmese language), which has 'created a choke hold on power unrivalled in the world' (Callahan 2004, 207). The results of the subsequent 1990 elections were never heeded, and the leader of the victorious party, Aung San Suu Kyi, was placed under house arrest, where she has remained for 13 of the past 17 years. The *Human Security Report 2005* lists Burma as the world's most conflict-prone country (Human Security Centre 2005, 27). Indeed, Burma's protracted and seemingly intractable conflict in its periphery qualifies among the longest running in the world today.

The historical and political underpinnings of violent conflict in Burma have been described comprehensively elsewhere. The vestiges of colonial administration (Lang 2002, 25), economic mismanagement, a lack of trained Burmese professionals in government (Fink 2001, 23), an inability to address issues of representation among peoples with great ethnic diversity (Smith 1999, 324) and contingent events outside of Burma (Callahan 2004) all offer plausible explanations of why the country remains steeped in conflict and stagnation six decades after independence. Of particular relevance to this study is the ethnic context and the way that ethnicity has informed the flow of refugees into Thailand.

Ethnicity in Burma: Geography and history

As elsewhere, Burma's physical geography plays a role in maintaining and sustaining cleavages between the powerholders and the marginalized. The ethnic geography of modern Burma is generally described as having a Burman-dominated, central heartland surrounded by a horseshoe-shaped ring of mountain ranges peopled by over one hundred ethnic sub-groups from four main Tibeto-Burman, Karen, Mon-Khmer and Shan (Tai) linguistic groupings. Three great rivers – the Irrawaddy, the Salween and the Mekong – have carved not only deep valleys into the landscape, but shaped highly localized specific linguistic and cultural practices among Burma's residents. Non-Burman ethnic minorities make up between one-third and one-half of Burma's ethnically diverse population and the border areas constitute some 40 per cent of Burma's land mass.[2]

Throughout its short history, myriad ethnic groups struggling for varying degrees of autonomy and independence in Burma have set the stage for the protracted conflict that has followed. While historically the military has held a firm grip on power in the central heartland, in the border areas insurgencies have abounded. Defection of ethnic Karen units from the Burma Army began almost immediately after independence from Britain in 1948, and was followed by rebellion from other ethnic groups such as the Karenni, Mons, Pao and Kachin. In the northwest in Arakan, 'the level of insurgency never really subsided since the end of the Second World War' (Smith 1999, 28).

Bertil Lintner has conducted extensive research on the numerous rebel armies and anti-government groups in Burma, not only pre-1988, but also thereafter (Lintner 1999, Appendix 3). His exhaustive survey includes more than one hundred groups, some of which only functioned for a few years, while others have continually confronted the government. Some groups divided into smaller factions, others merged together; others formed loose alliances or became part of umbrella organizations. The earliest was founded in 1939 (the Communist Party of Burma), but most came into being in the 1940s, 1950s and 1960s. Several emerged after 1988, and, given the propensity of these groups to reshuffle and rename themselves with great frequency, new groups (or the same rebels under a different acronym) continue to form. Over the years, these groups have ranged in size from 50 members to more than 20,000.

The response of the *tatmadaw* to insurgents has been the *Pya Ley Pya* or 'Four Cuts' strategy, officially endorsed in 1968 and still in operation today. Designed to suppress internal insurgency by cutting the insurgents off from their support system, the strategy translates as 'denying water to the fish' and is targeted at cutting off civilian support systems in ethnic areas by denying food, funds, intelligence and recruits to opposition forces (Lang 2002, 37–42).

---

2 Martin Smith notes that population figures in Burma are highly contested, but he suggests that the Burman ethnic population is probably about two-thirds of the population, including assimilated Mons and Karen in Lower Burma (1999, 27–31). The Karen Human Rights Group (KHRG), however, asserts that many ethnic minorities have Burmanized names (to avoid official discrimination) but should not be counted among the Burman majority. KHRG estimates that the Burman population is about one-half of the total population (see the KHRG website, at <http://www.khrg.org/background_on_burma.html>, accessed 29 September 2007).

Over time, the Four Cuts strategy has forced more and more civilians to flee their homes, as insurgency and counterinsurgency warfare effectively blurs the boundary between combatants and non-combatants. Insurgency (in the form of guerrilla struggle) relies on a civilian support base, and the distinction between civilians and non-civilians becomes muddled because they share geographic and social spaces. Thus, the Four Cuts strategy not only affects the combatants but strikes at the heart of the civilian population, which has suffered the brunt of the conflict (Lang 2002, Chapter 3). The refugees and other civilians internally displaced in this war are fleeing insurgency and counter-insurgency, as well as wider conditions of human insecurity created by extensive militarization and chronic underdevelopment.

Eastern Burma and the border with Thailand

The southern half of Burma's eastern border abuts Thailand, with four ethnic states and an administrative division directly adjoining Thailand's western border. In each, state–minority relationships remain politically unresolved. The following paragraphs offer a basic contextualization of the primary ethnic groups that operate along the Thai–Burmese border and the related displacement of many of their members.

The ethnic Karen are perhaps Burma's best known ethnic minority group and have been conducting an armed struggle since 1949, shortly after Burma's independence. The Karen dream is embodied in the term *Kawthoolei* – a 'land without evil' – which represents the dream of an independent Karen state. The Karen have their own political administration and army which operate in rebel-held territory, respectively called the Karen National Union (KNU) and the Karen National Liberation Army (KNLA), the senior leadership of which is Christian-dominated, while the rank-and-file are primarily Buddhist. This political–religious difference has been aptly exploited by Burma's government, which has used the pro-government Democratic Karen Buddhist Army (DKBA, a breakaway faction of the KNU, which mutinied in late 1994, with the support of the *tatmadaw*) as a proxy for its own ends (Ball and Lang 2001).

Karen State shares a long border with Thailand, and the Karen people in Burma are ethnic brethren with the Thai Karen across the border. Physical proximity and ethnic similarity both account for long-standing seasonal migration patterns between Karen State in Burma and the western portion of Thailand that preceded the demarcation of the border. In 1984, however, large numbers of Burmese Karen crossed into Thailand, and, unlike in previous years, remained permanently. This represented Thailand's first Burmese refugees, and these settlements eventually grew into what is now a population of over 140,000 people registered in the camps, comprised mostly of ethnic Karen.[3]

3 The refugee camps also house a small number of urban political refugees, who are generally of Burman ethnicity or Burmanized Karen.

Karenni State sits just north of Karen State, and its shared border with Thailand is only about one-third the length of Karen State. The Karenni refugees arrived in Thailand starting in 1989, fleeing military incursions and human rights in their areas from the *tatmadaw* (Demusz 1998). While ethnically a sub-group of the Karen, the Karenni differentiate themselves from the Karen in two ways. First, the ethnic Karenni do not have hill-tribe cousins in northern Thailand as the Karen do. Therefore, the possibility of quietly integrating among the local population (as numerous Karen have) is not an option for the Karenni. Second, the Karenni independence struggle was characterized to a large extent by infighting and disunity. During the 1950s, the Karenni joined with other ethnic groups in order to fight the central government, but amongst themselves they were sorely divided on religious and ideological issues (Smith 1999). Of approximately 200,000 ethnic Karenni, over 20,000 are now in refugee camps in Thailand (TBBC 2006) and they primarily occupy two camps in the north where the camp committee is comprised of Karenni leaders.

Further south, before a ceasefire was concluded with Rangoon in 1995, the Mon insurgency led by the New Mon State Party (NMSP) was concentrated in areas of Mon State and Tenasserim Division in southeastern Burma. As with the other main ethnic insurgencies, Mon armed insurrection began in the newly independent Burma as early as March 1948. The Mons once flourished as a great Indianized civilization of Southeast Asia, with influence and kingdoms extending at times from present day Lower Burma to Thailand and the western borders of Cambodia, before the rise of the Thai and Burmese states. But since 1757, the fluctuating fortunes of the Mon kingdoms came to an end and the Mon population was concentrated in Lower Burma, along the shore of the Gulf of Martaban, in the northern portion of the Tenasserim panhandle. At Burma's independence in 1948, the political and cultural aspirations of the Mons were not addressed and protracted armed conflict ensued.

The Mon refugee camps on the Thai border were established in 1990, following the capture by the Burma Army of NMSP and KNU strongholds. The Mon camps in Thailand experienced numerous relocations by the local authorities and were finally moved across the border and out of Thailand in 1996. However although the military ceasefire brought respite from fear and flight from direct hostilities, it did not engender the confidence of the refugees in the form of a durable solution. Instead, the transfer of the camps effectively represented a conversion of the displaced Mons from refugees into IDPs. The conditions in the ceasefire areas remain insecure and heavily militarized accompanying the expansion of the Burmese military into formerly contested regions. The internally displaced population has remained constant since the involuntary repatriation in 1996, and stands at 11,713 according to data from the Thailand Burma Border Consortium (TBBC) (2007). One veteran Mon relief worker estimates that overall 80 per cent of the Mon displaced population remains in the camps, another ten per cent stay as IDPs within the Mon region (particularly those areas impacted by Mon splinter groups or close to KNU areas) and that ten per cent have moved in Thailand.[4]

Shan State abuts the northeastern border of Thailand, with a similar topography that has encouraged centuries of trade routes. The Shan people are ethnically and linguistically similar to their northern Thai counterparts, so much so that an alternate name for the Shan is 'Tai'. Throughout British rule and up to independence, the ethnic Shans had a highly structured social order consisting of feudal princes (*saophas*) and their subjects, for whom representative democracy and the sharing of power were new, but not unattractive concepts (Yawnghwe and Alagappa 1995). The first president of the Union of Burma was a Shan prince, but as a figurehead with little power, he had no ability to successfully incorporate Shan autonomy into the workings of the new state.

In response to a tightening of power by the central government, the Shans drifted into several armies to maintain control of their trade routes, battling the *tatmadaw* and each other for the right to manoeuvre the regional supplies of opium, which helped them to fuel further battles (Smith 1999, 387). The more violent the government's response, the more civilians were affected by the conflict. Seasonal migration patterns began to look starkly different in 1996, when the government began building the first of many dams in Shan State. Forced relocations from these areas began immediately thereafter (Human Rights Documentation Unit 2007, 40). Thus large numbers of Shans began to enter Thailand on a permanent basis after 1996, where their pre-existing trade routes paved a well-trodden path to facilitate a smoothly functioning migrant network, and the best developed in Thailand among all of Burma's ethnicities (Grundy-Warr and Wong 2002, 108).

Other groups of refugees – such as the Kachin, the Chin and the Lahu – have small populations residing in Thailand. A smattering live in the camps and others have tried to fade into obscurity into the towns. Their desires for autonomy and independence roughly reflect those of Burma's other ethnic groups in Thailand. Their position as refugees, if recognized at all, is negligible.

A larger portion of Burma's forced migrant population in Thailand is constituted by migrants, rather than refugees. Differentiating the former from the latter, however, is an inherently problematic effort, because it seeks to separate those fleeing from political persecution from those fleeing economic hardship, two phenomena that are often intertwined. Refugees fleeing persecution are technically under the protection of the 1951 Convention Relating to the Status of Refugees, whereas economic migrants, no matter how desperate, are not identified as such. The literature on the migration–asylum nexus has demonstrated that this division is more of a continuum than a dichotomy (Van Hear 1998; Crisp and Dessalegne 2002; Castles and Van Hear 2005), evidence that supports the case of Burmese migrants, between one and two million of whom have crossed the border into Thailand for work. Their situation may be classified as primarily economic, but influenced by underlying political factors. Alternatively, they may have fled for

4 Personal communication, Chiang Mai, 27 October 2007.

political reasons, but have chosen to remain as undocumented migrants because they fear not receiving refugee status. Government policies have deprived migrants of their livelihoods in towns, villages and major cities in Burma and while they may come to Thailand to work, they are increasingly likely to bring their families and attempt a more permanent move.

Recent events

An exploration of recent events in Burma demonstrates why the displacement situation comes from a combination of 'push' and 'pull' factors. In so-called 'low-intensity' warfare situations, the causes of displacement are multiple and people flee the direct and indirect impacts of armed conflict and militarization. Displacement is caused not only by direct armed hostilities and assaults on the civilian population (for instance, raiding villages, seizure of livestock and other property, interrogation, etc.), but also by requisition of civilian forced labour (to carry ammunitions or for use on military projects), a stream of coercive financial demands ('taxes' and 'fees', extortion, etc.), confiscation of land and forced relocation of villages.

These phenomena are all actively occurring in Burma today. On the border, Burma's human rights abuses are legion and well documented. Forced labour, portering and military conscription occur systematically, and labourers are often put to work building dams that will destroy their future livelihoods (Karen Rivers Watch 2004, 30). Extra-judicial summary and arbitrary executions are common. A partial list of incidents in 2006 listed over 50 victims of execution (Human Rights Documentation Unit 2006, Chapter 2). The Assistance Association for Political Prisoners (Burma) reports that there are more than 1,200 political prisoners in detention in Burma today and that severe conditions have caused 'many deaths ... from severe torture, inadequate medical treatment and even wrong injections'.[5]

In October 2004, the purge of Burmese General Khin Nyint precipitated a severe and far reaching crackdown against all his former associates (military intelligence, political, business, charities). As a result of the purge, SPDC junta Chairman, Senior General Than Shwe and his army hardliner faction (the combat wing of the military) now dominate the military hierarchy. In November 2005, the SPDC moved its capital to Naypyidaw (or Pyinmana), located some 350 kilometres north of Rangoon, prompting speculation about reasons for this 'bunkering down'. Since the building of the new capital at Naypyidaw the Burma Army has conducted some of its most severe military operations against the border insurgencies (especially in the eastern border region) in a decade. The military has deployed a disproportionate number of its frontline troops in the eastern borderlands where it has waged continuous counter-insurgency offensives – predominantly in the form

5 See Assistance Association for Political Prisoners (Burma) website at <www.aappb.org> (last accessed 27 September 2007).

of search and destroy operations – against the Karen, Karenni and Shan armed groups. The consequences for civilians in the affected areas have been continuing dislocation and deprivation of livelihoods and security.

In September 2007, Burma experienced the most significant outbreak of political unrest in the almost two decades since the 1988 uprising, when tens of thousands of people – led by saffron-robed monks chanting the *metta sutta* (Buddhist discourse on loving-kindness) – took to the streets of cities and towns all around the country to protest against the regime. The protests were precipitated by sudden 100–500 per cent fuel price rises that pushed an already impecunious population to the brink of poverty. The protests, which included both monks and courageous political actors (including members of the '88 Generation'), were met with a heavily armed brutal crackdown. The army's subsequent stampede on Buddhist monasteries in a deeply devout Buddhist country was incomprehensible to many, and the international outcry was such that interest in the failed 'saffron revolution' was so great it pushed the news from Iraq off the front pages of international newspapers for the first time since the 2003 invasion (Lintner 2007, 39). Long-time Burma observers and activists believe that though the uprising may have failed on this occasion, further protests are inevitable and the bloodshed and violence has further intensified anti-regime sentiment within and outside the country.

Overview of the displacement situation

In the camps

Since the first semi-permanent camps were established in 1984, Thailand has hosted a steadily growing displaced population. In late 2007, the total registered population was comprised of over 153,000 people living in 13 main camps along the border (nine on the Thai side), with 62 per cent from Karen State, 13 per cent from Karenni State, 9 per cent from Tenasserim Division, 5 per cent from Mon State (the Mons were involuntarily returned to the Burmese side of the border following the ceasefire in 1995) and the remaining percentage from other states and divisions in Burma.[6]

There has been extensive research conducted on life in the refugee camps on the Thai–Burmese border (for example, Normand 1990; Demusz 1998; Beyrer 1999; Caouette et al. 2000; Eltom 2000). Because of their longevity and because of tight administrative structures that the Karen were able to bring from the local governments inside Karen State, the camps have been run with relative efficiency and success under the auspices of the Karen Refugee Committee (KRC). Camp committees are well organized and include sub-committees that tackle issues such

6 The Thailand Burma Border Consortium (TBBC) updates refugee figures periodically on its website. See <http: www.tbbc.org> for the most recent figures.

as security, health, education and logistics. The refugees themselves monitor, audit and distribute the supplies and food that make their way into the camp (TBBC 2004). The Karenni Refugee Committee (KnRC) developed in a similar fashion, from the leadership of the administration in Karenni State. Demusz observes about the Karenni a point that is relevant for the Karen as well: both ethnic groups initially received funding from their respective local administrations from inside Burma, but as time passed, 'the amount of aid necessary has increased in proportion to length of their stay' (Demusz 1998, 235).

As the duration of time and needs of the camps increased, so did the involvement of international organizations and research about the border. Access to the camps – or at least the towns near the camps – was relatively easy, and Bangkok's infrastructure encouraged many players to descend on this refugee situation. As a result, even more research has been conducted and more organizations have made their homes there. This phenomenon has spawned a host of new initiatives and trial programmes in the camps, along with the monitoring of several human rights groups, such as Human Rights Watch, Amnesty International and UNHCR's own evaluation unit (Human Rights Watch 1998; Amnesty International 2005; UNHCR 2006a). The plethora of assessments in the camps has advantages and disadvantages. On the one hand, the camps on the border were the recipients of some of the most inventive new global initiatives addressing refugee problems. For example, the creation of Legal Administration Centres (LACs) emerged from findings that there was limited or no access to reasonable justice systems in the camps. Victims of rape, for example, could neither rely on camp committees nor on the Thai justice system to seek protection (UNHCR 2006a). On the other hand, the LACs have been controversial because refugee groups argue that they take valuable resources away from other programmes (Cho 2007). The fungibility of humanitarian aid comes into question here; when aid organizations design their field strategies based on the programmes that donors currently consider attractive, then they can do more harm than good (Duffield 1993).

The ability of the camp population to obtain other freedoms – working and moving outside the camps, for example – varies considerably depending on the current political situation, the particular camp and the individual refugee him or herself. Over time, a trend has emerged: refugees in camps are far more restricted than they were years ago. The warehousing of the Burmese camp refugee population has, at its core, several related factors, including: the Royal Thai Government's (RTG) growing wariness of hosting refugee populations for decades (Human Rights Watch 2004); increased cooperation between the RTG and the Burmese government on trans-border issues (Caouette et al. 2000); and the extended role of the UNHCR with respect to the border camps since the late 1990s (Banki 2004).

Outside the camps

Thousands more displaced people survive outside the camp structure, notably some 200,000–250,000 displaced ethnic Shans, fleeing violence and forced relocation, residing mainly in Thailand's northern provinces since 1996. The Shans have not been permitted to establish their own camps in Thailand, with the exception of a small population living in Wieng Heng in Chiang Mai province, most of whom arrived in 2002, fleeing human rights abuses near their homes (TBBC 2006).

There is another settlement at Doi Tailang for Shan refugees that is neither acknowledged by the RTG nor serviced by the many aforementioned humanitarian organizations that work elsewhere on the border. The settlement is estimated to house as many as 15,000 Shan refugees, up from 250 in the year 2000. The Shans in this settlement are without documentation and risk deportation and arrest, but they continue to move and work in the area. The settlement has very basic medical care and education (Human Rights Documentation Unit 2007).

Other than Wieng Heng and Doi Tailang, the Burmese Shans are mostly engaged in irregular employment at the lowest rungs of the labour market in the agricultural, tourism and construction industries. The fact that they can blend in with the northern Thai people is crucial, since remaining invisible is important for this self-settled population. But when the economy suffers, so does the fate of the Shan migrants. After years of relatively little scrutiny, thousands of Shans were deported in 1997 during the economic crisis in Thailand, where these 'fugitives from ethnic terror in Shan state were expected to be thankful for this capricious hospitality' (Marshall 2002, 172).

Thus, while the Shans are not restricted to camps, they face insecurity as well as the risk of impoverishment. As the Human Rights Documentation Unit notes,

> Because of the large numbers of Shan labourers in Thailand, the government has put a blanket label on all Shan people in the country, regardless of how or why they crossed the border. As a result it is extremely difficult for aid organizations to provide legitimate aid to the group and their access to health care and educational opportunities is limited. (2007, 708)

Internally displaced persons

The problem of IDPs has continued to plague Burma's eastern border region, presenting possibly the most difficult, as well as invisible and difficult to access, challenge of human insecurity and protection. A major report released in October 2007 on internal displacement in eastern Burma estimated the number of conflict-induced IDPs at around 500,000 (TBBC 2007). These IDPs have been forced to leave their homes over the past decade and have not been able to reintegrate into any society.

Comprehensive documentation on the plight of IDPs in Burma is a relatively new research arena. Recently, IDPs have been the subject of growing attention, as evidenced by studies commissioned by the TBBC (noted above, publicly available), the local NGO Backpack Health Worker Team (Backpack Health Worker Team 2006) and UN agencies in Burma and Thailand (not publicly available), seeking to document the nature and scale of the problem.[7] In addition to the more familiar category of conflict-induced internal displacement, recent work has sought to identify different types of IDPs that take into account other forms of displacement connected with militarization and poor governance. It is possible to identify a three-part typology of internal displacement based on underlying causes. These are: (1) armed conflict-induced displacement (TBBC has collected considerable quantitative data on this category of IDPs); (2) state–society conflict-induced displacement ('post-armed conflict'/military occupation/state-sponsored 'development' activities); and (3) livelihood vulnerability-induced displacement (or 'distress migration').[8] This typology, like the migration–asylum nexus, should not be viewed as discrete elements but rather as features on a continuum.

IDPs in Burma are found in four state and non-state 'governable spaces'.[9] These are: (1) relocation sites (including consolidated villages under direct Burma Army control); (2) ceasefire areas where ethnic groups are supposed to have some autonomy and protection from *tatmadaw* attack; (3) mixed administration areas (or brown areas, disputed by both sides, so that people live part time under opposition and part time under government forces' control); and (4) 'free fire' zones (black areas, effectively controlled and administered by the opposition and therefore most dangerous for civilians who are collectively regarded as insurgent sympathizers).[10] The presence in 2007 of 295,000 IDPs found in the ceasefire areas administered by the opposition ethnic forces (TBBC 2007, 25) shows that the displacement cycle does not end with (military) ceasefires, because people continue to experience the impacts of militarization and human insecurity. International humanitarian agencies are increasingly working to identify delivery mechanisms to IDPs in complex and risky environments through in-country (from within Burma) and cross-border (from Thailand) access points. It is estimated that approximately 100,000 IDPs live in areas of current conflict where only cross-border aid can reach them; some 200,000–250,000 live in areas only accessible by groups providing assistance from inside the country; and a further 100,000–150,000 live in areas where it may be possible for both cross-border and in-country groups to reach them (House of Commons International Development Committee 2007, 5–6).

---

7 For further background, see also a new report by Refugees International (2006).

8 Personal communication with Ashley South, Burma/Myanmar Update Conference, Singapore, 18 July 2006.

9 Term used by Ken MacLean, 'Communities of Interpretation', International Burma Studies Conference, Singapore, 14 July 2006.

10 While this typology is important to understand the specific causes and results of internal displacement, it has been recognized as a 'largely theoretical exercise' because it is often difficult to distinguish one IDP group from another (TBBC 2007, 13).

Key stakeholders

This section sketches the key characteristics and interests held by the range of stakeholders and their relationships with refugees and migrants. The analysis demonstrates that stakeholder interests are neither aligned with one another nor are their policies consistent across the groups of displaced. This results in circumstances under which the pursuit of durable solutions for one group does not necessarily result in long-term solutions, leaving us to explore different threads of the question: 'durable solutions for whom?'

Government of Burma

The Burmese government (SPDC) has perpetrated five decades of violence as a means to solve Burma's internal crises, generating extensive militarization and displacement. In human security terms, in Burma the state is more a security threat than a security guardian.[11] Burma's priorities indicate a politicization of the refugee issue that, at present, repudiates any chances for a repatriation process. Similarly, displaced populations within Burma have neither the opportunity to return to their original homes nor the likelihood of remaining safe where they are.

The fleeing of a country's nationals can be damaging to the government's legitimacy – the existence of refugee camps provides a visible reminder of the precarious situation inside the country. Indeed, displaced persons and refugees who have fled from Burma are often used as the basis for demonstrating the wholly rotten core of Burma's government (for example, Myint 2003). Due to the arcane nature of the SPDC regime, accurate or authoritative information on the repatriation question is difficult to obtain. The SPDC has hitherto been unwilling to acknowledge responsibility for the refugees encamped along the Thai border. The only movement has come from bilateral agreements with the Thai government on the migrant issue (see following section).

According to senior Thai military sources, the SPDC has been unwilling to meaningfully discuss the matter of repatriation with its Thai counterparts. Further, at the biannual Regional Border Committee meetings between the two militaries, the official Burmese response has stipulated that it can only accept back 'Myanmar citizens', which represents a serious problem when a high proportion of the displaced people do not possess this documentation (Lang 2001, 7).

In practice, it is unlikely that the Burmese regime will want to take back refugees until it has secured ceasefire surrenders (on its own terms) and/or complete control over the minority military forces and their border territories. Because the aim of the government's counter-insurgency strategy is to undermine and eliminate the civilian support base for the insurgents, it is unlikely that it will accept back people about whom it is suspicious (Lang 2001, 7).

11 For further details, see Lang (2007).

Within Burma, the humanitarian situation has grown increasingly desperate, particularly since power shuffling in the junta in October 2004 led to an even more hardliner government. The SPDC has increased its restrictions on international agencies operating in the country. This applies particularly to the eastern border regions, where dramatic interventions forced the closure of all field offices of the International Committee of the Red Cross (ICRC) in November 2006. In its December 2006 briefing, 'Myanmar: New Threats to Humanitarian Aid', the International Crisis Group describes access and assistance in the conflict-affected areas along the Thai border as a 'critical gap' (2006, 4). This further exemplifies the fact that neither camp residents nor migrants are free to return to Burma. Quite the opposite is occurring, in fact. The TBBC notes that while the total estimated number of IDPs has decreased in the past five years, this is not because the situation has improved in ceasefire areas, but partially because flight into Thailand has increased (TBBC 2007, 26). But, problematically, when such flight is seen only through the lens of resettlement, it is assumed to be a 'pull factor' and the 'push factors' of human rights violations are overlooked. The consequences to the entire displaced population are significant.

Royal Thai Government (RTG)[12]

Since the late 1990s, the RTG and international agencies have broached the topic of repatriation when discussing the plight of Burmese refugees. Thailand does not want to remain an indefinite host, its own security long troubled by instability and human insecurity in Burma. NGOs and refugee advocates have periodically expressed fear that Thailand might one day send back the refugees precipitously and/or involuntarily. Thai civilian and military officials (including those friendly with the Burmese regime) at the highest levels have recognized that a safe and voluntary repatriation is possible only when conditions of peace and security allow, and Royal Thai Army officers have noted that Thailand will not push displaced persons back until conditions are acceptable to the key parties. Other Thai agencies, including the Ministry of Interior and Ministry of Foreign

12 The RTG is neither a signatory to the 1951 Convention on Refugees nor to its companion 1967 Protocol, and under national law, asylum seekers in Thailand are technically illegal immigrants. In strictly legal terms, legal refugee protection, and even the terminology 'refugee' does not exist. Since the late 1990s, the official parlance of Thai policy has been expressed in terms of 'displaced persons fleeing fighting' rather than 'refugees'. In practice – and with Cabinet consent – the Burmese in the border camps are recognized as a group with real claims to asylum. The general policy approach from Bangkok has been to 'accept and assist the displaced persons on a humanitarian basis', a policy that provides for 'temporary shelter'. On the matter of a future repatriation, the Thai position also holds that before it is possible to return the displaced persons it is necessary to communicate with the government of Burma and be sure that it is willing to cooperate (Lang 2001, 3, 6).

Affairs, are also actively contemplating the conditions for future repatriation but analogously acknowledge the obstacles (Lang 2001, 6).

Over the past couple of years, there has been a significant shift in policy away from a 'care and maintenance' model on the part of the Thai government. In officially recognizing the Burmese refugees as being part of a protracted refugee situation, the RTG has permitted fairly dramatic changes within a very short space of time.[13]

The key changes included: (1) establishing procedures and greater responsibility on the part of Thai local authorities for reception, status determination and camp registration; (2) the acknowledgement of resettlement as a viable solution for the refugees (UNHCR 2005); and (3) the in-principle green light in terms of granting opportunities and skills to refugees in vocational training, education (including Thai language), access to income generation inside the camps and employment opportunities outside the camps.[14] With respect to this latter initiative, the RTG has shown a mix of willingness and obdurateness in nurturing refugees' skills as a way of facilitating durable solutions in the longer term. English language classes, for example, are permitted in the camps, but foreigners are not permitted to be the teachers, thus draining the camp community of teachers skilled in other subjects as they are relied upon to teach English. Initiatives to make higher education available to a select number of refugees are also moving forward slowly; at the time of this writing, fewer than twenty individuals had been given permission to study at a university in Thailand.[15]

The shift in RTG policy that allowed resettlement to occur was not a foregone conclusion. Initially, the RTG was reluctant to issue exit visas to refugees, without which they would not be able to resettle. This points to a frustrating paradox: the RTG neither wanted the camp refugees to remain in the camps nor wanted to grant them permission to leave. More recently, the RTG has become actively involved in the resettlement process, refusing to issue permits only rarely and participating in registration and verification of the camp population.[16]

RTG policies concerning the non-camp Burmese population are linked to the economy, and by association, to decisions made by the Ministry of Labour. Thailand signed joint agreements with the governments of Burma, Cambodia and Laos to regularize its Burmese migrant population. Under these agreements, migrant workers in Thailand are required to register for work permits, after which the RTG sends the records to each of the home governments to confirm applicants' citizenship. The home country is then responsible for issuing travel documents (Arnold 2004). This trend toward controlling and regulating a part of the economy

13 Personal communication, Jack Dunford, Geneva, 27 September 2006.

14 Ibid.

15 Minutes from CCSDPT monthly meeting, 14 March 2007. Restricted Circulation.

16 There is considerable controversy about the role of the Thai military in determining which camp residents are considered genuine refugees and thus 'deserving' of resettlement. See, Banki and Lang (2007, 55).

that once worked smoothly in the shadows has already impacted the non-camp population. Burmese migrants are hard-hit by such an initiative, because as the Thai–Burmese agreement is concretized, illegal Burmese are neither able to enter Thailand easily nor remain safely.

In January 2006, 109 formerly stateless ethnic Shans were granted Thai citizenship. The first recognition of its kind, the treatment of this group could indicate a critical trend towards RTG acknowledgement of refugee status from all ethnicities of the Burmese population. Thailand's Department of Provincial Administration formally granted citizenship and Thai identification cards to 1,109 immigrants and members of 'hill tribe' communities (Human Rights Documentation Unit 2007).

The RTG has no specific policies concerning IDPs in Burma, but ongoing and improving relations with Burma serve to disempower this already extremely vulnerable population. The forced repatriation of the Mons in 1996 provides one example (see Lang 2002, Chapter 5). The transfer of the displaced Mons from the Thai to the Burmese side of the border followed a set of political pressures coming from parties in Thailand who were increasingly aligned with the Burmese. Pressure on the ethnic insurgent NMSP to negotiate a ceasefire stemmed from its own dwindling resources and the opportunity to participate in the development of a pipeline from which the NMSP could garner resources, demonstrating that the Mon refugees were simply pawns in both larger and localized political–military developments in the Thai–Burmese borderlands. While the ceasefire between the NMSP and the Burmese government remains in place, the formation of splinter factions opposed to the ceasefire has meant that sporadic conflict continues outside the narrow jurisdiction of the ceasefire territories, and access to humanitarian aid remains nearly impossible, particularly since the ICRC closed its office in the state capital, Moulmein, in 2007 (TBBC 2007, 40). The record of bilateral agreement between Thailand and Burma on this issue does not present as a durable solution for the Mon refugees, but rather a lesson to avoid in future scenarios.

UNHCR

By its definition and mandate, UNHCR is only responsible for those Burmese in Thailand who stake a claim on refugee status. Thus, its role is centred on solutions for the camp population, with only tangential treatment of other displaced populations.

Since the formal agreement in 1998 to enhance UNHCR's role on the Burmese border for the first time, the agency has expanded its activities and its mandate on the border. The agreement between the RTG and UNHCR for an operational role arose out of both the deteriorating borderlands' environment in the mid-1990s and Thailand's desire to work towards the resolution of what had become a long-term, protracted refugee problem. There was also recognition that the issue was becoming more difficult to deal with informally and that a spontaneous and speedy return of the displaced persons could no longer be contemplated.

Today, Thailand is regarded by UNHCR as a model for partnerships to strengthen protection capacity between NGOs and the agency.[17] After becoming operational in 1999, UNHCR began a major registration exercise, in conjunction with the Ministry of Interior. In addition to recording the bio-data of each household member, the exercise also aimed to record demographic information such as the refugees' places of origin within Burma by township district. The agency also worked with Thai authorities to formalize refugee admission procedures. Provincial Admissions Boards (PABs) were established in the border provinces, which functioned until 2003, and then, after an impasse, recommenced in 2005 (UNHCR 2005, 1).

In Burma itself, UNHCR came to an ad hoc agreement with the government to establish a roving presence in Karen State, Mon State and Tenasserim Division in order to assess the conditions in anticipation of a future repatriation once conditions allow. However, in practice, access has been limited by precarious political and military circumstances (including ongoing fighting between the KNU and *tatmadaw* and the relocation of the capital to Pyinmana), widespread anti-personnel landmines and unexploded ordnance and difficult topography. The border areas lack rural infrastructure of all kinds and communities remain extremely vulnerable. The agency concludes that 'the situation on the Myanmar–Thailand border is not conducive for refugees and IDPs to return in safety and dignity' (UNHCR 2006b, 4).

Resettlement With repatriation looking bleak, UNHCR – along with other stakeholders – has focused its resources into registering, screening and processing refugees for resettlement. From 2005, when resettlement opened up as an option for residents in the border camps, through to the end of 2007, over 63,000 refugees have been referred to the UNHCR for resettlement consideration; about 27,000 have been accepted and by October 2007 over 22,000 had departed from Thailand.[18] This represents a significant portion of the registered population and the trend is expected to continue at a similar annual rate until the camp population dwindles to a smaller size. It is impossible to say how small that number will be, and any predictions are likely to stimulate impassioned debate from both those who want to remain in Thailand and those who want to resettle to third countries.

Resettlement presents those individuals and families selected with an exciting – though oftentimes daunting – opportunity to put an end to a life in limbo. Until recently, refugees held a long-standing dream of returning home, and their leaders' struggle for independence, starting as early as 1947, is not easily forgotten. Many of the people in the camps have been closely associated with that struggle for decades, and their role as political constituents of the KNU also makes resettlement a sensitive issue in terms of the political and ethnic politics

17 Janet Lim, Director of the Bureau for Asia and the Pacific, UNHCR, speaking at UNHCR's Annual Consultations with NGOs (Pre-ExCom), Geneva, 27 September 2006.

18 Email correspondence with UNHCR Bangkok, 15 January 2007.

of the border insurgencies because the camp residents comprise an important component of the political constituency originating from opposition-held areas. But resettlement also has the potential to play a positive role in opening up possibilities to improve local conditions for the remaining refugees, such as in the areas of education and livelihoods. This concept, termed by the UNHCR as the 'strategic use of resettlement', implies that the careful application of resettlement to some portions of the population will unlock pathways for other refugees to access the other durable solutions of local integration and repatriation (van Selm 2004). As already noted, the latter is not an option for refugees from Burma at present. And while in principle Thailand is open to allowing some members of the refugee population to locally integrate, the achievement of improved local conditions for the remaining population is yet to be realized in practice.

The immediate effects of this new large-scale multilateral resettlement programme on the remaining camp population have thus far presented several problematic consequences, at least in the short and intermediate term. First, the skilled and educated leaders of the camps have resettled in far higher proportions than the remainder of the population, depleting the camps of medics, teachers and experienced administrators. While NGOs and UNHCR are working together to ensure the continuation of quality services in the camps, this has proved a challenge. Second, as some refugees prepare to depart from Thailand – going for medical checks and participating in cultural preparation courses – the morale of some remaining camp members reveals a mix of depression and anger for those rejected, anxiety for those who are still waiting to hear the final decision and confusion for those who have not yet decided what they want to do (Banki and Lang 2007).

Camp resettlement indirectly affects other displaced populations. The effect of resettlement on the migrant population is as yet unclear. The impact of the aforementioned bilateral labour agreement is likely to be the primary driver of treatment of the migrant population, as Burmese migrants find it increasingly difficult to find work in the informal sector. But this challenge is made more strenuous when the RTG commands army personnel to remain alert for illegal migratory movement, and in the wake of resettlement, this is exactly what has occurred. Travel from place to place (and thus, the ability to reside and work) is severely difficult when checkpoints dot the entrances and exits to northern towns and cities. More restrictions on illegal migrants translate into greater possibilities for exploitation, and despite years of advocacy on the part of labour organizations in Thailand and the efforts of the Thai government to regularize the migrant population, exploitation continues.[19]

Internally displaced populations are affected as well. Resource inflow into the camps has always served as a way to unofficially deliver additional and needed resources across the border into Burma. Rice, medicines and other provisions make their way to those populations that have no other way to access aid. But because of

19 See the Migrant Assistance Programme at <http://www.map.org>.

declining human and financial resources in the camps today, it is difficult to share those resources with the internally displaced. This leads to a potential chain effect wherein the increased vulnerability of the IDP population makes them more likely to flee to Thailand. However, as noted earlier, the subject of access and delivery of aid to the internally displaced in eastern Burma has emerged as a serious issue for policy and operational discussion by international humanitarian actors and is currently the subject of study by the TBBC, UN agencies and donors. At the same time, precisely because of the fear of the 'pull factor' associated with resettlement, the RTG is trying to prevent the entrance into Thailand of people from Burma.[20]

The primary focus of resettlement countries' efforts is providing protection to the refugees through citizenship in their respective countries. Variance in acceptance rates has caused some accusations of 'cherry-picking', in which some resettlement countries choose only the best educated or most talented. Other countries have slowed the process with cumbersome acceptance procedures. Resettlement countries can and do continue to serve as donors to the remaining programmes on the Thai–Burmese border but over time it is expected that these donations will decrease; whether or not NGOs will be successful in transferring donations to other displaced groups in Thailand remains to be seen.

NGOs

While some organizations have been involved on the border since the establishment of the first semi-permanent camps in 1984, in recent years many have begun to work with migrant and displaced populations. In general, involvement with one group of displaced generally engenders involvement with others, even if tangentially. For example, while the Migrant Assistance Programme works primarily with migrants, it also holds women's workshops that target female camp refugees. The International Rescue Committee now serves both camp refugees and migrant workers. World Education provides an interesting example of an NGO whose target population has changed in step with the changing migration environment. World Education began by providing educational services to Indochinese refugees on the Thai–Cambodian border, working only with those who were to be resettled to the US. In the aftermath of the Burmese refugee flight, they became operational in the refugee camps on the Thai–Burmese border where they provided different modes of teacher training. As migrant populations – and the presence of migrant children in particular – grew, there was an increased need for educating this group, and World Education now works primarily with the migrant population.

The role of NGOs in dictating the treatment of displaced populations should be relatively straightforward, yet a ballooning literature reveals that institutional

20 Until large-scale resettlement was underway in 2007, there was not a single quarter in the preceding seven years in which a reduction of the flow of refugees (estimated at some 200 a month) occurred. Personal communication, Desmond Ball, Chiang Mai, October 2007.

survival, fights over donor resources and grabs at media attention can undermine even the most well-meaning humanitarian aid organizations (de Waal 1997; Omaar and de Waal 1994). In the context of the Thai–Burmese border, several trends emerge in relation to the various displaced groups and their relationships with NGOs.

NGOs are necessarily beholden to their donors. Resettlement represents a significant future reduction in the need for aid, and NGOs focused entirely on the refugee population will certainly find their budgets cut in the long term, even if the short-term needs of the refugee population are high. At the same time, because NGOs have developed their resources for specific ethnic populations – by translating books into the Karen language, for example, or creating specific monitoring mechanisms to assist the ethnic border populations – it will in some instances be difficult for NGOs to immediately target non-camp populations. In the short term, some NGOs have already started to focus on refugees who do not plan to resettle. In this regard, lobbying the RTG has become a more prominent NGO activity, as international agencies push for greater local integration in terms of work, schools and residence.[21] In the wake of resettlement, it is hoped that the remaining (and much smaller) refugee population will have the opportunity to remain in Thailand and gain, if not permanent legal status, some basis under which they could be at least temporarily protected. Work with the internally displaced remains a grave challenge because of the problems of access and delivery mechanisms for humanitarian aid in the context of the intransigence of the Burmese government.

Refugees and migrants

In the past, the agenda of the refugee representatives was for change and a durable peace permitting repatriation. This agenda, as mentioned above, has been closely linked to the status of the political–military struggles across the border. In many cases the representatives of the refugees are closely associated with, if not members of, ethnic insurgent organizations. Not only are refugee committees reliant on the opposition armies for information; their work is fundamentally entwined with the circumstances and dynamics of the wider military and political context. Also, refugees have generally fled those regions previously under the control and *de facto* administration of the insurgent organizations and are by implication identified with the insurgencies.

Yet the views of the refugee representatives are not always simply synonymous with their armed ethnic organization counterparts.[22] Traditionally there are problems of representation within the indigenous refugee committees, such as the

21 At the CCSDPT monthly meetings, NGOs frequently refer to the work entailed by conversing with various Thai ministries on topics of refugee education and migrant labour. Internal monthly documents.

22 See Lang (2001, 10–11).

lack of women's participation within the key decision-making processes. With present military developments in Burma, and especially in the border regions, it is important to be aware of whose voices are presented as the refugees' representatives and the particular agendas underpinning those voices. Field research has revealed that the majority of refugees, above all else, would prefer to return to Burma under safe conditions (Banki and Lang 2007). Barring that, their choices centre on where they might be able to carve a manageable life for themselves and their children. The fear of a new country, new language and new culture has discouraged some families from applying for resettlement, while others have some access to land and documentation in Thailand and prefer to remain. Migrants' choices are more restricted; given the worsening economic conditions in Burma, it can be surmised that their primary interest is to find safe work in factories, fields, or families in Thailand. For the internally displaced, if they are free to move at all, they face the difficult decision as to whether they should risk the journey to Thailand or remain where they are.

Conclusion

After more than two decades of protracted displacement from Burma, and with the prospect for durable solutions a seemingly distant dream for so long, resettlement has started to play an important part in addressing the prolonged limbo of encampment for a significant portion of the registered camp residents. There has been no possibility for a sustainable return of the refugees, given the conditions of chronic human insecurity in their homelands. Local integration in the form of legal status and residency rights also remains off the agenda for the majority of the Burmese in Thailand. The positive openings arising from 'the strategic use of resettlement', particularly as these relate to improving local conditions in Thailand, are on the agenda as the RTG contemplates the future of this protracted refugee population within its territory. Meanwhile, all stakeholders struggle to cope with, and find creative solutions to, the impact of resettlement on the remaining population in the short and intermediate term. Whilst resettlement provides people with hope for a new life abroad it does not contribute to enduring solutions in the form of a permanent resolution of the underlying causes of displacement; nor does resettlement connect with the wider conditions of insecurity, underdevelopment and impoverishment driving tens of thousands of Burmese nationals from their homeland in search of work in Thailand and neighbouring countries; and it does not relate to the predicament of the internally displaced who are also the sources of future refugee flows.

Every month hundreds of new arrivals cross the Thai border escaping the situation in Burma. This chapter has shown that the pursuit of solutions – any solutions, whether these be short-term or durable – for the displaced populations are linked into the underlying political and economic context within and among stakeholders. It is thus important to avoid isolating the categories of refugees, IDPs and migrants from a wider, more comprehensive analysis in pursuit of enduring solutions to the plight of forced migrants from Burma.

Bibliography

Amnesty International (2005), 'Thailand: The Plight of Burmese Migrant Workers', Report (London: Amnesty International).

Arnold, D. (2004), *The Situation of Burmese Migrant Workers in Mae Sot, Thailand* (Hong Kong: Southeast Asia Research Centre (SEARC)).

Backpack Health Worker Team (2006), 'Chronic Emergency: Health and Human Rights in Eastern Burma', Special Report (Mae Sot, Thailand: Backpack Health Worker Team).

Ball, D. and Lang, H. (2001), 'Factionalism and Insurgent Organisations in the Thai–Burma Borderlands', Working Paper No. 356 (Canberra: Strategic and Defence Studies Centre, Research School of Pacific and Asian Studies, Australian National University).

Banki, S. (2004), 'Refugee Integration in the Intermediate term: A Study of Nepal, Pakistan, and Kenya', New Issues in Refugee Research, Working Paper No. 108 (Geneva: UNHCR, Evaluation and Policy Analysis Unit).

Banki, S. and Lang, H. (2007), 'Planning for the Future: The Impact of Resettlement on the Remaining Camp Population', Report (Bangkok: Committee for Coordination of Services to Displaced Persons in Thailand (CCSDPT)).

Beyrer, C. (1999), 'The Health and Humanitarian Situation of Burmese Populations Along the Thai–Burmese Border', *Burma Debate* 6: 3, 4–13.

Callahan, M.P. (2004), *Making Enemies*: *War and State Building in Burma* (Singapore: National University of Singapore Press).

Caouette, T., Archavanitkul, K. and Pyne, H.H. (2000), *Sexuality, Reproductive Health and Violence*: *Experiences of Migrants from Burma in Thailand* (Bangkok: Institute for Population and Social Research, Mahidol University).

Castles, S. and Van Hear, N. (2005), 'The Migration–Asylum Nexus: Definitions and Dimensions', Paper presented at the Ninth International Conference of the International Association for the Study of Forced Migration, São Paulo, Brazil.

Cho, V. (2007), 'New IRC Funding Proposal Draws Fire from Local Aid Groups', *The Irrawaddy*, 10 July.

Crisp, J. and Dessalegne, D. (2002), 'Refugee Protection and Migration Management: The Challenge for UNHCR', New Issues in Refugee Research, Working Paper No. 64 (Geneva: UNHCR, Evaluation and Policy Analysis Unit).

Demusz, K. (1998), 'From Relief to Development: Negotiating the Continuum on the Thai–Burmese Border', *Journal of Refugee Studies* 11: 3, 231–44.

Duffield, M. (1993), 'NGOs, Disaster Relief and Asset Transfer in the Horn: Political Survival in a Permanent Emergency', *Development and Change* 24, 131–57.

Eltom, A.A. (2000), 'Joint Assessment of Burmese Migrants' Health in Thailand', Report (Geneva: International Organization for Migration (IOM)).

Fink, C. (2001), *Living Silence: Burma Under Military Rule* (New York: Zed Books).

Grundy-Warr, C. and Wong, E. (2002), 'Geographies of Displacement: The Karenni and the Shan Across the Myanmar–Thailand Border', *Singapore Journal of Tropical Geography* 23: 1, 93–122.

House of Commons International Development Committee (2007), 'DIFID Assistance to Burmese Internally Displaced People and Refugees on the Thai–Burma Border: Responses to the Committee's Tenth Report of Session 2006–07' (London: House of Commons International Development Committee).

Human Rights Documentation Unit (2006), *Human Rights Yearbook Burma 2005* (Mae Sot, Thailand: Human Rights Documentation Unit (HRDU)).

Human Rights Documentation Unit (2007), *Human Rights Yearbook Burma 2006* (Mae Sot, Thailand: Human Rights Documentation Unit (HRDU)).

Human Rights Watch (1998), 'Unwanted and Unprotected: Burmese Refugees in Thailand', Report (New York: Human Rights Watch (HRW)).

Human Rights Watch (2004), 'Out of Sight, Out of Mind: Thai Policy Toward Burmese Refugees', Report (New York: Human Rights Watch (HRW)).

Human Security Centre (2005), *Human Security Report 2005* (New York: Oxford University Press).

International Crisis Group (ICG) (2006), 'Myanmar: New Threats to Humanitarian Aid', Policy Briefing Paper (Brussels: International Crisis Group (ICG)).

Karen Rivers Watch (2004), *Damming at Gunpoint: Burma Army Atrocities Pave the Way for Salween Dams in Karen State* (Kawthoolei: Karen Rivers Watch).

Lang, H. (2001), 'The Repatriation Predicament of Burmese Refugees in Thailand: A Preliminary Analysis', New Issues in Refugee Research, Working Paper No. 46 (Geneva: UNHCR, Evaluation and Policy Analysis Unit).

Lang, H. (2002), *Fear and Sanctuary: Burmese Refugees in Thailand* (Ithaca, NY: Southeast Asia Program, Cornell University).

Lang, H. (2007), '"Freedom from Fear": Conflict, Displacement and Human Security in Burma (Myanmar)', in A. Burke and M. McDonald (eds), *Critical Security in the Asia Pacific* (Manchester: Manchester University Press).

Lintner, B. (1999), *Burma in Revolt: Opium and Insurgency Since 1948* (Chiang Mai: Silkworm Books).

Lintner, B. (2007), 'Tales from the Land in Between', *The Irrawaddy*, 1 November.

Marshall, A. (2002), *The Trouser People* (New York: Counterpoint).

Myint, S. (2003), *Burma File: A Question of Democracy* (New Delhi: India Research Press).

Normand, R. (1990), 'Refugee Voices: Inside Site 2', *Journal of Refugee Studies* 3: 2, 155–62.

Omaar, R. and de Waal, A. (1994), 'Humanitarianism Unbound? Current Dilemmas Facing Multi-Mandate Relief Operations in Political Emergencies', African Rights Discussion Paper No. 5 (London: African Rights).

Refugees International (2006), *Ending the Waiting Game: Strategies for Responding to Internally Displaced People in Burma* (Washington DC: Refugees International).

Selm, J. van (2004), 'The Strategic Use of Resettlement: Changing the Face of Protection?', *Refuge* 22: 1, 39–48.

Smith, M. (1999), *Burma: Insurgency and the Politics of Ethnicity* (London: Zed Books).

TBBC (2004), *Between Worlds: Twenty Years on the Border* (Bangkok: TBBC).

TBBC (2006), *Program Report for January–June 2006* (Bangkok: TBBC).

TBBC (2007), *2007 Survey: Internal Displacement in Eastern Burma* (Bangkok: TBBC).

UNHCR (2005), 'Thailand' in *UNHCR Global Report 2005* (Geneva: UNHCR).

UNHCR (2006a), 'Analysis of Gaps in Refugee Protection Capacity: Thailand', Report (Geneva: UNHCR).

UNHCR (2006b), 'Country Operations Plan: Myanmar 2006' (Geneva: UNHCR).

Van Hear, N. (1998), *New Diasporas: The Mass Exodus, Dispersal and Regrouping of Migrant Communities* (Seattle: University of Washington Press).

Waal, A. de (1997), *Famine Crimes: Politics and the Disaster Relief Industry in Africa* (Bloomington: Indiana University Press).

Yawnghwe, C.T. and Alagappa, M. (1995), 'Burma: The Depoliticization of the Political', in B.M. Koppel (ed.), *Political Legitimacy in Southeast Asia: The Quest for Moral Authority* (Stanford, CA: Stanford University Press).

Chapter 4
The Rohingya Refugees in Bangladesh: A Failure of the International Protection Regime

Eileen Pittaway

> We are like deer caught between two tigers.
>
> In 30 years in the field, I have never before been in an established camp where the fear was so palpable and pervasive and where malnutrition and poverty was so rife. Corruption, rape, sexual abuse, abductions, trafficking, organized prostitution, including of children, ration fraud and a systematized regime of terror has left a population of at least 26,000 refugees in a state of trauma and with little or no hope for the future. I have never seen so many 'sexualized' children. Deaths from malnutrition and untreated medical conditions are common. These refugees have been living in the camps for up to 15 years. (Pittaway 2007)

Introduction

The Rohingya population from Rakhine State in Burma, currently living near the city of Cox's Bazar in Bangladesh, on the Bay of Bengal just north of the Burmese border, are both stateless and refugees. They are persecuted in their identified homeland and denied adequate protection in the host country to which they have fled. To date, the international community has been unwilling and unable to offer an effective solution to their predicament. In this chapter, the nexus between statelessness and refugee status and the consequences of a protection vacuum for these refugees is examined. The inadequacy of the three most commonly accepted durable solutions[1] to address these issues is explored, in particular the way in which recurrent waves of forced repatriation have exacerbated the problems of the Rohingyas.

There are currently an estimated 26,000 Rohingya recognized as 'prima facie' refugees by the United Nations High Commissioner for Refugees (UNHCR) sheltering in two camps controlled by the Bangladeshi government at Nayapara

---

1 The three durable solutions are voluntary repatriation to the home country, local integration in the country of first asylum and resettlement in a third country (UNHCR 2006).

and Kutupalong. An additional 7,000 refugees live nearby in Teknaf 'makeshift' camp. It is also estimated that between 100,000 and 200,000 unregistered Rohingya refugees live outside camps in the local area. They are not recognized as refugees and are often labelled as economic or illegal migrants. In March 2007, a community consultation was held with refugees as part of UNHCR's strategy to address the protection failures in the camps and ensure refugee input into the provision of durable solutions for the Rohingya population (UNHCR 2007b).[2] It was already acknowledged that the conditions in the camps are some of the worst in the world.

Method

The consultation ran for two weeks and involved 120 refugees (50 per cent male, 50 per cent female) in four groups, including detailed interviews with over 80 refugees. It was conducted with interpreters who received training in the methods to be used. Following an introduction to human rights and gender analysis, refugees were invited to share their experiences and concerns within this framework. A technique called storyboarding (Wallace 1997) was also used; refugees worked in small groups to draw six pictures based on the discussions of the stories that they had shared. The pictures depicted:

1. a particular human rights abuse, or problem that they identified as endemic in the community;
2. the impact of this abuse on individuals, families and communities;
3. what the refugees wanted done about this particular problem;
4. the people and organizations who could assist in implementing solutions;
5. what the community was already doing to address the problem and what assistance they need to build their capacity to address it more effectively;
6. what they would like the outcome to be.

2 The consultation was led by the author, Eileen Pittaway, from the Centre for Refugee Research (CRR) at the University of New South Wales, Australia. Team members included staff from UNHCR Geneva, UNHCR Bangladesh, representatives from the Victorian Foundation for Survivors of Torture, Australia, Austcare, an Australian non-government organization (NGO) and Amnesty International Australia. The consultation was part of the implementation of the UNHCR Executive Committee's 'Conclusion on Women and Girls at Risk' (UNHCR 2006) and field tested an assessment methodology for the early identification of those persons most at risk and traumatized in refugee communities, particularly women and girls (Pittaway and Bartolomei 2005). The consultations were held in an extremely difficult political climate, at a time when UNHCR was negotiating with an interim government in constant threat of military uprising and insurgency.

The groups then presented the completed storyboards to the larger group. They were encouraged by skilled facilitators to discuss what was happening in the pictures and, with their permission, their stories and the discussion were fully documented.

The result of this process was a rich situational analysis. Not only did the refugees share their experiences, they also identified problems, trends and ongoing human rights abuses. They analysed the impact of these on the community and they shared potential solutions. They used their local knowledge and experience to identify who could help and how solutions could best be achieved. Finally, they explored what help they would need to enable them to be more active in addressing the problems themselves. The refugees were informed that the consultation team had no power to implement any of their suggestions, or to offer aid or advocacy on behalf of individual refugees. Despite this, refugees involved in this process spoke of the value of being consulted. Women and girls commented that no one had ever '*allowed*' them to talk about rape and sexual abuse before. Men spoke of how powerless they feel in the face of violence against their families. *This challenged conventional wisdom that refugees are 'ashamed' to discuss these issues.*

The verbatim documentation was analysed and a comprehensive report containing the refugee's storyboards and a DVD were produced from this consultation (UNHCR 2006). All refugee quotes and stories in this chapter come from that report.[3] The results revealed that conditions in the camp were even worse than had been previously detailed. The entire refugee population is traumatized and lives in constant fear. Refugees do not receive the minimum services promised under the umbrella of 'International Protection' as described in the various Conventions, Conclusions and UNHCR Standard Operating Procedures.

3 The Consultations were covered by UNSW and UNHCR ethics procedures based on the notion of informed consent. It must be noted that CRR has grave concerns over the meaning of 'informed consent' in situations such as these, when the power balance is so much in favour of the researchers (Mackenzie et al. 2007). A confidentiality agreement was written in both English and Bangladeshi. It was read to the participants by the interpreters as many participants were functionally illiterate. A full hour was spent with the participants explaining the procedure, and ensuring that they knew that at any time they had the right to withdraw or to retract information they had given. All participants either signed the paper or put their mark on the agreement. They were informed that neither their images, nor their personal stories would be used in a way that could identify them, even if they did give permission. The researchers themselves signed an additional agreement to this effect, which they left with the refugees. To ensure that individuals were not identified, small details were altered in the case studies in the reports, and faces were pixellated in the DVD made of the consultations.

The creation of statelessness – the history of the Rohingya diaspora

The problems of the Rohingya refugees in Bangladesh are not new. Their history reveals a population who have suffered from waves of persecution and forced migration at the hands of successive regimes, both within Burma[4] and without. They have become pawns in the game of colonial and post-colonial politics and are stateless because of a history over which they had little control.

Originally from the mainly Muslim kingdom of Arakan, in 1784 the Rohingyas were conquered and incorporated into the majority Buddhist kingdom of Burma. At that time many Rohingya refugees fled to an area now called Cox's Bazar,[5] in the British controlled colony of East Bengal. Some merged into the community, which was possible because the Rohingyas are culturally and linguistically similar to the local Chittagonian people and share a strong Muslim faith (UNHCR 2007a).

The British colonized Burma following a series of invasions during the 1800s. It was administered as a province of India and the British frequently moved populations between East Bengal and Burma to suit their labour needs. Many of the Rohingyas who had fled to Bangladesh took the opportunity to return to their former homes. At that time, this movement of populations was considered to be an internal movement. However, the current Burmese government considers that the migration that took place during this period was illegal and has refused citizenship to the majority of the Rohingyas who reside in Burma or who have sought to return (Human Rights Watch 2000).

In 1942, Japanese forces invaded Burma and Britain retreated, causing many Rohingyas to cross the border again into East Bengal. The Muslims from Bangladesh were promised that if they supported the British they would be given their own national area, but the British later reneged on that promise. This further exacerbated the tensions between the majority Buddhist Burman people, the Muslim Rohingyas and the Arkanese Muslims who had stayed in Burma (Silverstein 1980).

Burma became independent in 1948 and tensions between the government and the Rohingyas grew. There was a move to have all Muslims living in Burma integrated into East Pakistan, but this was rejected both by the Rohingya people themselves and the new government of East Pakistan. The Burmese government continued to treat the Rohingyas who remained in Burma as illegal immigrants, while those who returned were treated as illegal Pakistani immigrants. The Rohingya people suffered from extreme persecution; their properties and land

---

4 At the request of the refugees, we are using 'Burma' to describe their homeland, rather than 'Myanmar' which is the name nominated by the current Military Regime. Refugees from all ethnic groups in exile refuse to acknowledge the name imposed by a dictatorship which has forced them to flee their homes.

5 Cox's Bazar is now part of Bangladesh. Following the Partition of India in 1947, Bangladesh was known as East Pakistan, until gaining independence in 1971. Prior to that it was know as the British Colony of East Bengal, which was part of the Indian Empire.

were confiscated; they were denied the right to citizenship and prohibited from military service and participation in the civil service.

In 1962, the Burma Socialist party seized power and dismantled Rohingya social and political organizations. In 1977, the military registered all citizens prior to a national census in order to screen out those they deemed foreigners. It was a time of extreme violence, which included widespread killings, rape, and the destruction of mosques. By 1978, more than 200,000 Rohingyas had fled to Bangladesh (formerly East Pakistan). The Burmese authorities claimed that this flight proved that Rohingyas knew they had no legal status in Burma. The Bangladeshi government was forced to request assistance from the United Nations in order to deal with the huge influx of refugees and 13 refugee camps were established along the border (Silverstein 1980). The government declared that it would not accept the Rohingyas as citizens nor would it allow them to stay in Bangladesh as refugees. Recognition as refugees would give the Rohingyas a status and the right to protection measures that the government did not wish to acknowledge. The government immediately began discussions with the Burmese military to enforce a programme of repatriation of the Rohingyas to Burma. At first, the Burmese military refused to cooperate, as their position was that the refugees were not citizens of Burma. It was only when the United Nations threatened to withdraw foreign aid from Burma that they reluctantly allowed the refugees to repatriate. However, many refugees did not wish to return because they knew they were returning to conditions of brutality, confiscated land and lack of citizenship (Lambrecht 1995).

In response to this refusal to return, the Bangladeshi government restricted food rations and conditions in the camps declined dramatically. Refugees reported beatings and killings and the withdrawal of all basic services. This forced the Rohingyas once again to flee for their lives. In Burma, the persecution continued with the introduction of the 'Four Cuts' strategy, which denied people from several ethnic minorities access to land, food, shelter and security. This again caused a mass exodus in the early 1990s when 250,000 Rohingyas crossed the border to Bangladesh. On this occasion, anticipating that this was a short-term crisis, the Bangladeshi government was, at first, welcoming to the refugees (Barnett 2000).

UNHCR and international relief agencies opened 21 camps in the vicinity of Cox's Bazar to accommodate these refugees (UNHCR 2007b). However, once it became apparent that the crisis would be of longer term, the Bangladeshi government declared that it would not allow the refugees to stay, citing the economic cost to a country that was one of the poorest in the world. They again refused to allow any form of local integration and stated that the Rohingyas would be repatriated as soon as possible. The repatriation, which began in 1992 in collusion with the State Law Order Restoration Council (SLORC) in Burma, was, in fact, a major programme of *refoulement*,[6] condemned by human rights groups around the

6 Refoulement: 'No contracting state shall expel or return (refouler) a refugee in any manner whatsoever to the frontiers of territories where his life or freedom would be

world (Amnesty International 2004). UNHCR attempted to monitor the returns, but withdrew its support from the programme in December 1992 when it became clear that coercion was being used. UNHCR next signed a formal memorandum of understanding (MOU) with the Bangladeshi government to assist in a monitored process of repatriation and in May 1993 began to interview refugees individually in order to ensure that the authorities were respecting the principle of voluntary return. One survey revealed that only 30 per cent of the Rohingyas wished to repatriate; however, the Bangladeshi government insisted that all of the Rohingyas should return by the end of the year (Human Rights Watch 2000). A second review of refugees claimed that the majority wished to return, but this is generally thought to be an invalid claim as the refugees were given inadequate information and were threatened with violence if they did not cooperate (Barnett 2000).

In 1994 and 1995, UNHCR again signed MOUs with the Bangladeshi government and cooperated with the repatriation, while simultaneously attempting to work with the Burmese regime in order to ensure that there would be safety for the refugees upon their return. However, this was very problematic, as UNHCR representatives were not permitted to travel to states within Burma without prior clearance from the Burmese junta. The regime also failed to provide commitments that it would recognize the rights of the Rohingyas to Burmese citizenship. At this time, Human Rights Watch and other NGOs expressed concern at the process of repatriation and the accuracy of the information provided to the refugees by UNHCR. They noted that the push for repatriation could not be blamed on financial pressure, as the UNHCR budget for the Rohingya operation had a substantial surplus at that time (Barnett 2000). Despite these concerns, between 1993 and 1997 some 230,000 refugees where forcibly returned to Burma. The horror of this forced repatriation has never been fully acknowledged by the international community, which failed to respond both at the time and subsequently.

For the refugees who participated in the March 2007 consultations, memory of the forced repatriation and knowledge of the continuing persecution in Burma was overwhelming and generated fear which affected all aspects of their daily lives. This was particularly true for those who knew themselves to be on a UNHCR list of those eligible for repatriation:

> I was 27 years old, a widow. My husband was taken as a forced labourer and they broke his back and he died. The Buddhist people supported by the military came and raped all the women. My house was next to a Buddhist village and next to a military barrack. One day six soldiers came to my house and took my 17-year-old niece and raped her for hours; I was forced to watch. When they had finished, she was beaten unconscious and completely covered in blood. We tried to carry her to the hospital, but when we got 50 yards from the house the military saw us and made us go back. We were not allowed to leave the house for over a month. I tried to nurse her without any medical attention,

threatened on account of his race, religion or nationality, membership of a particular social group or political opinion' (Article 33 (1) 1951 Refugee Convention).

> but on the 29th day she died. We were watched the whole time and it took me two more months to escape with my children. My nephew, the brother of my niece, was so ashamed that he had not protected her that he tried to kill himself. We had to help him too. (UNHCR 2007b)

A further source of fear was of the *process* of repatriation, which some people had experienced multiple times. Refugees described being held in custody prior to deportation and being subjected to torture and violence. One woman described how, while they were in custody, her husband was tortured by having logs rolled up and down over his body. Her baby was thrown to the floor and she was raped. After being held in captivity for 25 days, she tried to drown herself in the river. Men and children were made to walk in figures of eight in the hot sun until they fainted. Families were separated and left behind. Many refugees showed the scars on their bodies from being beaten by the authorities during forced repatriation (UNHCR 2007b).

In July 1997, the Burmese government advised that it would accept no more returnees from the end of that year. The Bangladeshi authorities responded by accelerating their push to make all refugees repatriate to Burma. This was done with great brutality, causing fear and despair to the refugees in the two remaining camps, Nayapara and Kutupalong. There was an uprising, as the refugees seized control of the camps in a desperate effort to remain in Bangladesh. Despite the very poor conditions, they knew that they were safer there than returning to the persecution in Burma. This situation lasted for a year and, during that time, repatriation ceased. However, in 1998 the Bangladeshi authorities moved into the camps to restore order. Many refugees were arrested, beaten and thrown into jail. There were reports of systematic mass rapes and the looting of homes (Pittaway 2007). UNHCR intervened and brokered a fragile peace agreement. Later that year, under pressure from the Bangladeshi government, the Burmese junta agreed to allow repatriation. However, the process put in place between the two governments was so unwieldy that even those who wished to be repatriated could not be returned (Barnett 2000). In the years since 1998, the Rohingya refugees have become one of the groups of 'forgotten refugees'. Geographically and politically isolated, they have become one more of the protracted refugee populations, a 'residual caseload' with no foreseeable solution (Human Rights Watch 2007).

The current situation of the refugees

> What is your life like in the camp? A woman replied 'Do you know about hell? This place is not hell. It is worse than hell.' (UNHCR 2007b)

The Cox's Bazar area is designated a [dangerous] security 'Phase 1' posting for UN staff, which means that among other security measures, UNHCR vehicles are not allowed on the road after dark. They have only a restricted MOU with the government of Bangladesh and are only allowed in the camps from 9am to 5pm from Monday to Friday, leaving refugees effectively without protection for 16 hours each day and at weekends. In the two weeks that the author was in the camps, the team was involved in two serious security incidents. There is still fear and resentment from the refugees towards UNHCR for the role they played in the 1992/3 repatriations. This is particularly problematic, as some of the members of the local UNHCR staff who took part in the repatriation exercise are still employed in the camps in a protection capacity.

Major concerns voiced by refugees in consultations were the constant violence, exploitation and total lack of safety they were experiencing in Bangladesh, exacerbated by corruption. Sexual and gender-based violence was endemic and this had a horrendous impact not only on the women and girl victims, but also on their families and the wider community. Inadequate nutrition, poor health, the absence of minimal and accessible health services, no education for the young people past primary grades, and the impact of the living conditions on family life were all discussed at length.

Corruption colours every aspect of the refugees' lives and prevents them from achieving any level of safety, security or peace. A tightly organized crime ring that controls the camps is supported by a totally corrupt system in Bangladesh. Government officials, police, military, some local villagers and the refugee 'leaders' appointed by the government, '*Majhees*' – they are all part of this ring. They organize trafficking, ration scams and control the lives of the people. Everything from marriage, divorce, registration, family books, food rations and going to school, to leaving the camps to find work, or visit relatives in jails outside the camp, appears to carry a price whether financial or in kind (UNHCR 2007b). Failure to pay bribes can result in false accusations, imprisonment and physical violence. Females also fear sexual violence. The *Majhees* have become very important and powerful in the camps and with their close family members play an important role in supporting the corrupt authorities. This situation has left the refugees with no means to appeal against the violence, exploitation and extortion that shape their lives. They told researchers that if it became known that they were reporting corruption to UNHCR, this act would place them in danger of more violence and false accusations.

In the first few days in the camp, the consultation team often heard the words 'false accusation'. It took a while to uncover the importance of the term, which has a special meaning in the context of the crime ring and the corruption of police, prison officers, court officials and the Bangladeshi legal system. We were told numerous stories of refugees being falsely accused of crimes such as theft, of hoarding explosives (which were sometimes planted in their homes), or murder. Once accused, the refugees, both male and female, are taken to the local police station where they are routinely beaten (tortured) and women are often raped. They are then taken to the jail in Cox's Bazar, where they are held for indefinite periods. It can take years for a case to go before the court. The jail was built for 800 and currently holds 3,600 (UNHCR 2007a). Prisoners have to pay bribes to be able to lie down and sleep. They have to provide their own medicine, have only one meal a day and bathe once a month. UNHCR confirmed that these accounts are true and they have a Protection Officer working with refugees currently held in jail. In the mean time, while the men are in jail, women are left without protection and in danger in the camp. Men's names are removed from the ration books. Even when they are released, it can take months to have them reinstated, leaving the families with even less food. While a first hearing can sound like a relatively minor punishment, in reality it represents a major human rights abuse.

Another term, which had much deeper meaning than at first understood, was that of 'Family Books'. The Family Books are the only documents which the refugees have that can validate their existence in the camp. It is the ration book, the document which determines the amount of food and non-food items each family will receive and without which the family cannot access medical attention. It is the only document that validates their status as refugees. The books are all years old, many of them falling to pieces. Whole extended families are recorded in one flimsy exercise book. As new family members are born, or arrive in the camp from Burma, they have to be added to the family book before rations or services can be provided for them. This process can take months. Refugees were punished by corrupt authorities by having names crossed out from Family Books. These books are the most valuable item the refugees own, the only thing with which they can use to barter.

Sexual and gender-based violence

Sexual and gender-based violence is endemic in the camps. Women and girls as young as nine years old are routinely abducted by local villagers and forced into so-called marriages only to be returned to the camps when they become pregnant. There were reports of young girls and young women being abducted and trafficked into the sex market in nearby Cox's Bazar and Chittagong and of organized child prostitution within the camp. Women described their fear of going to the latrines and of having to collect firewood or green leaves for food in the local forest:

> She was 11 years old when she was raped. Now that this has happened everybody knows so no one wants to marry her. What will happen to her in the future? When she came back from the forest after the rape she didn't get any medical attention. (UNHCR 2007b)

Men talked of how the police, military and local villagers come to the sheds at night to take their daughters and wives for sex. If the husbands or fathers try to prevent the women from being taken away, they are beaten up, falsely accused and imprisoned. They described how they organize themselves into groups and take shifts to watch over the sheds to try to protect the women:

> My 14-year-old granddaughter is very beautiful so I keep her hidden in the shed [accommodation block] most of the time. I am terrified that she will be abducted and raped if she goes out into the villages or the police see her … I am also terrified my daughter-in-law will be raped; my son is in jail and I try to keep her in the shed too. (UNHCR 2007b)

An older woman described how some of the girls try to abort the babies of rape and that some girls die. Husbands of young women who are abducted and raped frequently refuse to have them back when they are returned. The Imam will sometimes arrange a marriage for a girl who has been abducted and is pregnant. These marriages are to older men and the girl becomes the second or third wife. The men accept these girls because they are then added to their Family Book bringing additional resources. Many women described the horrendous domestic violence and abuse experienced by the young girls forced into these marriages. Having survived abduction and rape, they are then condemned to a life of domestic violence and alienation.

The impact on family life is profound. Both men and women described the grief of forced separation, the loss of loved ones and the inability to function as family units in the horrendous conditions. Overcrowded conditions in the camp make normal family life impossible and domestic violence is a major problem. Mothers talked about the daily struggle to provide adequate nourishment for their children. Traditional parenting and the practice of many of the cultural ceremonies are not allowed, and parents are powerless to protect their children. Young people are drifting away from the authority of the parents and elders and from the influence of religion into an aimless and antisocial lifestyle.

Health concerns

Refugees reported significant health problems in the camp, both physical and mental. There is insufficient food with a very limited water supply and very poor living conditions:

> It's really crowded and we cannot move. There is smoke in the sheds, because we have to cook inside when it's the rainy season. We get a lot of diseases, the children get sick, water supply is totally insufficient and we get it only in the morning and only two buckets. (UNHCR 2007b)

Tuberculosis is prevalent as are stomach complaints, skin diseases, respiratory problems, high fever, poor eyesight, dental problems and the physical manifestations of rape and torture. Many refugees have disabilities that make living conditions even more difficult for their families. There are complaints about the doctors who are described as rude, disrespectful and corrupt. There are no home visits, making access to the doctors by those who are extremely ill or disabled impossible. Prescription medicines are very rare and refugees described selling their rations and mortgaging their Family Books in order to buy medicines or medical treatment outside the camps. The act of going outside the camps to obtain these medicines also puts them in danger. One woman with a disabled daughter cried as she described the pressure put on her by her husband and other family members to let the child die.

All refugees reported psychosocial health problems such as tension-related aches and pains, headaches, stomach problems and an inability to sleep due to constantly being on the alert for danger. Depression and suicidal tendencies were discussed and refugees shared their deep concern for the mental health of their children who grow up familiar with the violence of armed conflict, rape and seeing their parents beaten.

Inadequate nutrition

> I dream of eating a whole fish!! (UNHCR 2007b)

Refugees identified the inadequate food rations as a major cause of the health problems and expressed their deep frustration at the inability to work to provide additional food for their families. Even those who risk moving outside the camp to work in the local community face exploitation and danger. They are paid less than the local labourers and are constantly threatened with false accusations and violence. They have to pay bribes to the police and military at the gates to leave and return to the camp. After 15 years of eating rice and lentils, they described how husbands and wives fought over food and how they occasionally sold rations in order to purchase food items such as fish, vegetables, onions and garlic. They reported having to sell part of their food rations to purchase basic items such as skin oil, medicines, sanitary napkins and kerosene. Many women told how by the end of the fortnightly ration period, no matter how hard they try, there is little food left. They often spent two or three days each fortnight feeding their children if possible, but eating no food themselves:

> A young mother who has suffered multiple losses came into the camp with her young son two years ago and they are therefore unregistered … The father was killed in Burma, her mother and sister both died in Bangladesh ... At 14 she married a man aged 25 who protected her. When their son was one month old her husband went fishing and never returned. The mother and child lived with the husband's relatives but it was a very abusive situation … Fundamental rights to food, clothing and shelter for herself and her child are denied because of her unregistered status and she has to beg … She feels great distress that she cannot adequately feed her young son and finds it unbearable when her son cries at night because of hunger pains. She also faces constant threats of sexual exploitation, violence and harassment … She is extremely vulnerable … and suffers significant psychological distress because of their situation. Protecting her son is all that keeps her alive. (UNHCR 2007b)

Education

Parents regarded education as critical, the only way forward for their children if they are ever to have a future. Education in the camps is very basic and only offered to primary level. The students sit at crude wooden benches in overcrowded huts without electricity. Books are scarce and only three subjects are taught. The teachers have often only received basic education themselves. Some attempts have been made by older educated refugees to run private classes for the older children. This was forbidden by the authorities and both the students and teachers were fined, beaten or imprisoned if they were discovered. Parents commented that it was difficult for the children to study when they were constantly hungry. There is no lighting for the children to study at night. There are limited play areas for the children; authorities have banned the children from playing organized games. UNHCR has recently formed youth groups to try and address some of these problems. The *Majhees* have done everything in their power to close down these groups and stop the young people attending.

Livelihoods

A major focus of UNHCR is that of self-help and self-sustainability. This is based on the obvious need to break the cycle of dependency resulting from 15 years of incarceration and the lack of adequate resources to meet refugee needs. However, it ignores the fact that the cumulative effect of violent persecution, flight and survival in horrendous camp conditions has seriously impacted on the capacity of some refugees to achieve this goal. Until the refugees have some measure of security, permission to work and to travel outside the camps, as well as recognition of and response to the trauma they have endured, self-sustainability is a chimera.

The only NGO working in the camp provides 'self-sufficiency' programmes that need to be significantly restructured. It was stated that women are being trained in the production of soap and that this was a major step towards self-sustainability and capacity-building (UNHCR 2007a). In fact, only a small group of women were employed at any given time in the soap-making workshop. They were paid by being given a small number of bars of soap either for their own use or to sell. After three months, they were dismissed and a new group of women came in. There was no facility for those women already trained to undertake soap making on their own behalf. The NGO receives funding for the distribution of soap around the camp. Despite this, the women were never paid in cash for their labour. A similar situation occurred in the tailoring workshop. Women were trained to make dresses or clothes for their children. The length of training was very short and the skills imparted inadequate to allow the women to earn a living, and there was no ongoing access to the necessary equipment.

The 'makeshift camp'

Outside the two official camps, forced evictions of unregistered refugees in the district have led to the establishment of a makeshift camp, which is situated on a small stretch of flood-prone land between the river and a main road. The overcrowded camp houses 7,000 people. The homes are hovels, intersected by open sewers with few latrines or bathing facilities. There is no food distribution and little clean drinking water. Health problems are endemic. The men commonly leave, seeking work in other areas. The women have to beg or engage in survival sex to keep their families alive (Medecins Sans Frontieres 2007). There are reports that girls as young as nine years can be seen working as prostitutes, serving lorry drivers and workers from the nearby port (Pittaway 2007). The provisional Bangladeshi government has recently agreed to resettle this community on government land, which will provide a more sanitary environment for the refugees.

The knowledge and impact of statelessness

It was clear from the consultations that statelessness[7] was a major issue for all of the refugees. They fully understood the position they were in and saw little hope for the future as long as they were denied recourse to the protection and security that accompanies citizenship. 'In Burma the military regime tells us we have no rights and no place. In Bangladesh the government tells as we have no rights and no place' (UNHCR 2007b). In talking about their lives, they frequently used metaphors such as 'we are caught between two tigers', 'as a Rohingya, I am caught between a crocodile and a snake' (UNHCR 2007b). Many of the older women said 'we have no soil beneath our feet. We belong nowhere' (UNHCR 2007b). They constantly asked for a safe place to live, in Bangladesh or elsewhere and many saw resettlement as the only hope left. They discussed the psychological implications of being unable to plan a future for themselves and for their children. The combination of statelessness and the apparent lack of recognition of their refugee status by the international community has left them feeling powerless and helpless. While they themselves, UNHCR and many in the international community regard the Rohingyas as refugees, and since the governments of neither Burma nor Bangladesh regard them as citizens of their respective countries, they are essentially stateless. Until this situation is resolved, it is difficult to see how their status as refugees can be addressed.

Since 1950, the UNHCR mandate has been expanded by the UN General Assembly to protect people not formerly covered by the 1951 Refugee Convention or 1967 Protocol. It now includes stateless persons and 'persons with respect to

7 'A stateless person is someone who is not considered to be a national by any State under the operation of its law. He or she may be, but is not necessarily a refugee' (UNHCR 2001).

whom concerned states do not recognize that they have a responsibility under any of the refugee instruments' (UNHCR 2001, 22). Despite this, statelessness remains one of the critical challenges facing refugees and countries of asylum today (UNHCR 2006). Bridging the protection gap that exists in situations where there is disagreement among states and UNHCR regarding the status of particular groups is crucial for their safety (UNHCR 2001).

Durable solutions

Repatriation or refoulement?

Since 1978, repatriation has been the major solution proposed for the Rohingyas by the Bangladeshi government and UNHCR. However, the majority of the Rohingyas have resisted this move. The nature of the voluntariness of the repatriation is a major point of contention and a barrier to identifying solutions to the current situation. Voluntariness is not mentioned in the Refugee Convention, which discusses instead the principle of 'safe return', implying that returnees will be protected by the state (Goodwin-Gill 1996). Some scholars have argued that 'once a receiving state determines that protection in the country of origin is viable, it is entitled to withdraw refugee status' (Hathaway 1997 cited in Chimni 1999). The notions of subjective and objective assessment of 'safe return' have become central to the argument. Chimni (1999) argues that one of the most important principles of voluntary repatriation and non-*refoulement* is that 'refugees cannot be returned against their will to a home country that in their *subjective* assessment has not appreciably changed for the better' [emphasis added]. UNHCR insists that decisions must be made based on *objective* facts. However, it can be argued that the very determination by UNHCR and states of what is 'objective' is in fact a subjective interpretation to suit their current actions (Ighodaro 2002). Chimni argues that this 'objectivism' disenfranchises the refugee voice in decision making about whether or not it is safe to return home. Through their communication networks, refugees often have more credible evidence of the situation in their homelands than do the authorities. It would be difficult for the government of Bangladesh or UNHCR to argue that 'safe return' had ever been established for the Rohingyas when all credible evidence points to the opposite (UNHCR 2007c). Since UNHCR, as the mandated agency of the international community, has granted the Rohingyas the status of 'prima facie' refugees, it is hard to argue that what has happened to this population over the years is not in fact *refoulement*.

The actions of UNHCR in this particular case have to be understood in light of the repatriation culture that developed in that organization in the 1990s. In his comprehensive critique of the role of UNHCR in the repatriation of refugees, Michael Barnett explores the factors underlying this culture (Barnett 2000). They include the surge of refugees seeking asylum, particularly in poor and undeveloped countries, the increasing reluctance of developed countries to accept new waves of refugees and the fall in financial support to enable developing countries to support refugees (Chimni 1998). It was claimed that in many cases, situations in the camps were worse than those in the home country and therefore repatriation was in the best interest of the refugees. Another argument favouring repatriation was the untested assumption that all refugees wish to return home. 'Protection' equated with returning refugees to their home countries as quickly as possible, even if that occurred under less than ideal circumstances. Harrell-Bond and other leading researchers spoke out strongly about the lack of research to test these assumptions (Harrell-Bond 1989). Many refugees did and do wish to return to a *safe* homeland, but very few wish to return to the persecution from which they have fled. UNHCR claimed that given the circumstances in Bangladesh, they had a moral obligation to ensure that repatriation did as little harm as possible, even if doing so meant involving itself in forced repatriation (Barnett 2000). They distanced themselves by naming it as 'imposed return' (Chimni 1999, 63).

Currently, UNHCR has acknowledged that return is not a viable option for the Rohingya refugees (UNHCR 2007c). Reports by Amnesty International (2004) and stories of persecution of Rohingyas in Burma as late as 2007 present credible evidence that refugees who are forcibly returned to Burma will find their life and freedom threatened. However, under pressure from both the Bangladeshi and the Burmese governments, UNHCR is still exploring the possibility of future repatriation. Many refugees do not understand the political positioning of UNHCR and see their continued consideration of repatriation as an act of betrayal (Pittaway 2007).

Resettlement

The psychological consequences of pre-arrival experiences of ongoing threats and lack of safety are apparent in all refugees. Resettlement has come to be seen as the only way in which they can regain a meaningful life. One older woman said:

> If you cannot take us away from here to a place of safety, you had better bomb the camps and kill us all. I am not saying this because I am mad. I am saying this because our lives have been so terrible. I do not want my grandchildren to have lives like this. (UNHCR 2007b)

Until 2006, resettlement was not considered to be an option for the Rohingya refugees in Bangladesh. The government refused permission for refugee travel and countries offering programmes of resettlement showed no active interest in accepting this caseload. However, UNHCR has instigated a programme of resettlement for the most vulnerable cases. As of May 2007, Canada had accepted 23 Rohingya refugees with the potential of accepting 200 more. New Zealand had agreed to take 50 people, and the UK had expressed interest in this population.

Sadly, the selection criteria of those countries resettling refugees from Bangladesh would appear to focus on those most likely to integrate easily into the host communities, rather than those in greatest need. There are concerns about the more intensive on-arrival needs and the poor integration of refugees from protracted refugee situations and the potential cost to the host communities (ATCR 2007). The poor health status, low levels of education and trauma experienced by this population make it unlikely that they will easily fit 'integration criteria'. The notion that the application of integration criteria can accurately predict the ability of refugees to settle in a developed country is another untested assumption dictating the fate of many refugees. It reflects current trends in all refugee situations and seriously challenges the philosophy of the resettlement programme as a durable solution available for the most vulnerable.

It is also feared that the international backlash against groups suspected of being fundamentalist Muslims will prevent some countries from even considering this caseload for resettlement. The author has recently been at several undocumented meetings with UNHCR and governments where the preference for non-Muslim refugees was discussed. Refugees from Southeast Asia are seen to be easier to integrate, in particular the mainly Christian refugees from the Karen and Karenni camps in Thailand. The Thai government initially agreed to a programme of resettlement as a way of clearing the camps on their borders. Even if resettlement countries do become more open to receiving Rohingya refugees, Bangladesh has expressed its concern that the resettlement programme would act as a 'pull factor' for new waves of refugees.

UNHCR is endeavouring to address these problems and to persuade countries to offer resettlement to the most vulnerable of these refugees who have no other durable solution available to them. Even if the Rohingya resettlement programme becomes viable, it still has to be seen in the context of the overall UNHCR resettlement programme. UNHCR targets for the resettlement of people from protracted refugee situations in 2008 stand at 156,000, with only 95,000 places committed by resettling countries and doubts expressed about whether they can all be processed within the resource constraints experienced by the agency (ATCR 2007). There is a long list of refugee populations included in this target and the Rohingya will, at most, only be allocated a small number of places.

Other governments in the region are reluctant to become involved in the debate around the Rohingya refugees. They are afraid of secondary movement to their territory and do not wish to accept any additional refugee caseload. There has also been reluctance from regional powers to criticize the human rights record of the Burmese regime, as they do not wish to jeopardize trade with this resource-rich country. Rohingya refugees do, however, flee to other countries, including India, the Gulf States, Japan, Pakistan, Saudi Arabia, Thailand and the United Arab Emirates. This movement is often facilitated by criminal gangs who charge exorbitant fees, leaving the refugees vulnerable to abuse and exploitation. Many states deny admission to the Rohingyas and some have engaged in systematic *refoulement* to avoid creating pull factors to their countries (UNHCR 2007a). There is a significant movement of Rohingyas from Bangladesh to Malaysia, with many reports of refugees drowning when inadequate small boats are wrecked.

The Malaysian government is unwilling to accept these arrivals, who again find themselves in very difficult circumstances as unregistered refugees. Movement to a third country either by resettlement or as a secondary movement will not provide a durable solution to the majority of the Rohingya in Bangladesh.

Local integration

'Local integration' is a legal, economic and political process by which refugees progressively become members of the host society (UNHCR 2001). The government of Bangladesh continues to reject local integration as a durable solution for the Rohingya refugees, leaving UNHCR with very limited options. There have been strong criticisms of the actions taken by UNHCR in the past in relation to the Rohingya refugees.

Caught in the culture of repatriation and faced with two apparently intransigent governments, UNHCR sought to engage in a 'harm minimization strategy'. However, at the current time, while still working to influence the Burmese regime to allow full and proper repatriation, UNHCR has acknowledged that it is not possible for the Rohingyas to return home. UNHCR has instead focused on alternative solutions for the short and medium term and the current situation in Bangladesh has provided a window of opportunity for this to occur. The previous government insisted that repatriation was the only solution. The interim government, which took power in 2006 on a platform of anti-corruption, has shown itself willing to consider the humanitarian plight of the refugees. It is believed that the opposition party is also willing to take a more soft line approach to the issue. UNHCR is therefore working to use this opportunity to improve the situation of the refugees while, at the same time, contributing to the development of the local area, as an acknowledgement of the concerns of the Bangladeshi government. The result of the promised election in 2008 will have a major impact on the future of the Rohingya populations.

The current team of UNHCR personnel working in Bangladesh is taking very positive steps to address these challenges, with the full support of UNHCR Geneva.

Their focus has shifted from limited 'care and maintenance' towards permanent solutions. They have adopted the model of short-, medium- and long-term strategies discussed by Milner:

> Short term solutions are designed to address specific challenges and impasses, medium term solutions consider the three durable solutions, while longer term solutions engage with peace and security, development and humanitarian actors to formulate and implement comprehensive solutions. (Milner 2007)

In 2006 and 2007, UNHCR conducted two participatory community consultations and published two significant and extremely honest reports about the situation in Kutupalong and Nayapara camps, the refugees in Tek Naf and the unregistered refugees in and around Cox's Bazar (UNHCR 2007c). Short-term solutions include an agreement between the government and UNHCR to gradually abolish the *Majhee* system and replace it with an elected group of elders to ensure effective representation for the protection of the refugees. Inroads are being made into addressing corruption and refugees are now receiving their full food rations. The government has also consented to allow NGOs back into the camps and UNHCR is forging partnerships to provide critical services for the refugees. They have also negotiated to improve the delivery of education in the camps and taken steps to increase the protection of the refugees from violence. UNHCR Geneva has commissioned research into the condition of the unregistered refugees.

For the medium term, UNHCR is addressing the challenges with a great deal of creativity and has devised a strategy that will assist not only the refugees in the camps, but also the local population. UNHCR Bangladesh is committed to working in partnership with international NGOs, civil society and the UN in-country team in an assertive programme of development to benefit all of the people in the Cox's Bazar area. A new inter-agency community-based programme is being developed to provide livelihoods and community structures in the region. By enhancing the capacities of local communities as a whole, it is hoped that the self-settled Rohingya will have increased opportunities to achieve self-sufficiency. UNHCR Geneva has targeted Bangladesh as a priority area in the *Global Appeal 2008–2009*. The key targets for this period include improved accommodation, better access to education, improved sanitation and health care, increased capacity for self-sustainability, assistance for urban refugees and the establishment of a refugee institution in Bangladesh. Pressure will continue to be exerted on the government of Bangladesh to ratify the Refugee Convention and Protocol (UNHCR 2007c).

In looking forward to a longer-term solution, the prospect that democracy will be reinstated in Burma and that the Rohingyas will be safe to return home in the foreseeable future seems extremely unlikely. If this does not occur, the international community could consider using internationally brokered Security Council Resolutions, and Conventions other than the Refugee Conventions to seek solutions to the problems of the Rohingyas. UN Security Council Resolution 1325 (UNSC 2000) was developed to address the protection needs of refugee women and girls in situations of conflict and refugee camps and to facilitate their participation in the peace process. There are many women in the camps in Bangladesh who are competent to take their place in decision making for the future of their community.

If the military junta in Burma continues to be intractable in persecuting ethnic minorities in Burma, the international community could consider the potential of UN Security Council Resolution 1674 (UNSC1674), a reaffirmation of the 'Responsibility to Protect' (R2P) populations who suffer from extreme human rights abuses and lack of protection from their own governments (UNSC 2006). R2P asserts that, 'when a state is unwilling or unable to protect its citizens from genocide, war crimes, ethnic cleansing and crimes against humanity, it is the responsibility of the international community to not only react, but to prevent conflict and rebuild the afflicted region' ('"The Responsibility to Protect", International Commission on Intervention and State Sovereignty', December 2001). In January 2007, a draft resolution was presented to the UN Security Council by the United Kingdom and the United States evoking UNSC1674 in relation to Burma. Amongst other things, it called for the Burmese government to cease all attacks on ethnic minorities, including rape, and to offer unhindered access to humanitarian organizations. China and Russia voted against the resolution, China stating that Burma did not pose a threat to international peace and security in the region. However, this was contested by members of the Association of South East Asian Nations (ASEAN) who expressed dissatisfaction with the slow pace of reforms in Burma (Thompson 2007).

It must be noted however, that the threshold for engagement for R2P is that a state is 'unwilling or unable' to protect its *citizens* from crimes against humanity. However, the current regime appears to deny that the Rohingyas are citizens of Burma (HRW 1993; Lambrecht 1995; AI 1997; HRW/Asia and RI August 1997, 9). This is despite ample evidence that the Rohingyas were established in the area they claim as home since the early twelfth century (Human Rights Watch 2000). A complicating factor is that there is tension, dating back to the time of the British withdrawal from Burma, between the Rohingyas and the Arakanese Muslim population who stayed in Burma and who do not support the Rohingya claim to citizenship of Burma. The junta has further exploited the division between the Muslim minority groups by redistributing some of the land confiscated from the Rohingyas to the Arakanese.

Thus the position of the Rohingyas is unique among the 12 other ethnic groups targeted for persecution by the Burmese regime, many of whom have sought refuge on the Thai–Burma border. The regime is not denying the citizenship of these other ethnic groups; they are not deemed 'stateless'. As argued above, until the Burmese regime is willing to accept that the Rohingyas are in fact citizens of Burma, R2P will not help their case. In order to resolve this impasse, the international community will need to address this instance of statelessness. 'The 1954 Convention Relating to the Status of Stateless Persons aims to regulate and improve the status of stateless persons and to ensure they can access fundamental rights and freedoms without discrimination.' Additionally, 'The 1961 Convention on The Reduction of Statelessness covers such issues as the granting of nationality and the loss or renunciation of nationality' (UNHCR 2001, 25). These conventions were developed to ensure that governments do not withdraw or withhold the benefits of citizenship from populations who have a genuine claim on that country. Bangladesh and Burma should be encouraged by UN member states to sign and ratify these conventions and implement the provisions contained within them. *This action could then provide a climate in which the Rohingyas could voluntarily return to their homeland, and if the persecution continued, would allow the Security Council to evoke R2P.*

Conclusion

The complexity of this case highlights problems inherent in the implementation of durable solutions for refugee communities. It illustrates the political contingencies intrinsic in the execution of international law, even when the interpretation of the law would appear to be straightforward. It highlights the need for all countries to sign the Refugee Convention and Protocols, to adopt national refugee legislation that conforms to international law and standards and to adhere to the measures contained in the UNHCR Convention Plus and the UNHCR 'Conclusions', which assist governments in the interpretation of the Convention. The absence of any system of refugee determination in Bangladesh has placed the burden on an already overstretched UNHCR in spite of the 1967 Declaration on Territorial Asylum, which states clearly that it is the responsibility of the country of asylum to evaluate a person's asylum claim. Given the historical and political dimensions to the problems of the Rohingya refugees in Bangladesh, it would appear that the current strategies suggested by UNHCR present the most realistic and potentially achievable solutions. The support of the international community, donor countries, international NGOs, the Bangladeshi government and civil society within Bangladesh will all be necessary for the success of these strategies and an end to the enduring indigence and danger confronting the Rohingyas.

Acknowledgements

We thank all of the refugees who courageously shared their histories, hopes and dreams to make this chapter possible. They did so knowing it was likely to put them at further risk. Thanks to Emma Beacham who co-authored the initial report from the consultation and to Judi Tucker, Nghia Nguyen-Le, Emma Pittaway and Geraldine Doney for their constructive comments.

Bibliography

Amnesty International (1997), 'Rohingyas – The Search for Safety', Issues Paper (London: Amnesty International), September.

Amnesty International (2004), 'Myanmar, The Rohingya Minority: Fundamental Rights Denied', available at <http://www.amnesty.org/en/alfresco_asset/a9a272d9-a48a-11dc-bac9-0158df32ab50/asa160052004en.html>.

ATCR (2007), 'Meeting Notes', Annual Tripartite Committee on Resettlement (Geneva: UNHCR).

Barnett, M. (2000), 'UNHCR and Involuntary Repatriation: Environmental Developments, the Repatriation Culture and the Rohingya Refugees', Working Papers, 41st Annual Convention of the International Studies Association, available at <http://www.ciaonet.org/isa/bam01/>, 1–21.

Chimni, B.S. (1998), 'The Geopolitics of Refugee Studies: A View from the South', *Journal of Refugee Studies* 11: 4, 350–74.

Chimni, B.S. (1999), 'From Resettlement to Repatriation: Towards a Critical History of Durable Solutions to Refugee Problems', in M. Barnett (ed.), 'UNHCR and Involuntary Repatriation: Environmental Developments, the Repatriation Culture and the Rohingya Refugees', New Issues in Refugee Research, UNHCR Working Paper No. 2 (Geneva: UNHCR, Evaluation and Policy Analysis Unit), 1–21, available at <http://www.ciaonet.org/isa/bam01/>.

Goodwin-Gill, G.S. (1996), *The Refugee in International Law*, 2nd edn (Oxford: Clarendon Press), 275–6.

Harrell-Bond, B. (1989), 'Repatriation: Under What Conditions is it the Most Desirable Solution for Refugees?', *African Studies Review* 32, 41–69.

Hathaway, J.C. (1997), 'The Meaning of Repatriation', *International Journal of Refugee Law* 9: 4, 551–8.

Human Rights Watch (1993), 'Bangladesh: Abuse of Burmese Refugees from Arakan', *HRW Journal* 5: 17, 9 October.

Human Rights Watch (1996), 'Burma: The Rohingyan Muslims Ending a Cycle of Violence?', 8–9 September.

Human Rights Watch (1996), 'The Rohingya Muslims: Ending a Cycle of Exodus?', Historical Background Paper, 8: 9, 16–21.

Human Rights Watch (Asia) and Refugees International (1997), 'Rohingya Refugees in Bangladesh: The Search for a Lasting Solution', *HRW Journal* 9: 7, August.

Human Rights Watch (2000), 'Historical Background', in 'Burmese Refugees in Bangladesh', Report available at <http://www.hrw.org/reports/2000/burma/burm005-01.htm>.

Human Rights Watch (2007), 'Rohingya Refugees from Burma', Press release, 22 May.

Ighodaro, M.E. (2002), 'A Critical Anti-Racist Interrogation of Voluntary/Forces Repatriation Theory: The Intersections of African Refugees' Dilemma', *Refuge* 21: 1, 49–60.

Lambrecht, C. (1995), *The Return of the Rohingya Refugees to Burma: Voluntary Repatriation or Refoulement?* (Washington, DC: US Committee for Refugees and Immigrants), 8.

Landreg, K. (1998). 'The Future of Refugee Protection,' *Journal of Refugee Studies* 11: 4, 416–32.

Mackenzie, C., McDowell, C. and Pittaway, E. (2007), 'Beyond "Do No Harm": The Challenge of Constructing Ethical Relationships', *Journal of Refugee Studies* 20: 2, 299–319.

Medecins Sans Frontieres (2007), 'Nowhere to Go: Rohingya Refugees in Bangladesh', available at <http://www.doctorswithoutborders.org/news/2007/08-31-2007.cfm>.

Pittaway, E. (2007), 'Field Notes, UNHCR Mission to Cox's Bazar', Unpublished.

Pittaway, E. and Bartolomei, L. (2005) 'Woman to Woman: A Gender Sensitive Response to Tsunami Affected Women', Training Report (January), available at <http://www.crr.unsw.edu.au>, accessed 17 May 2006.

Reid, A. (1994), 'Repatriation of Arkanese Muslims from Bangladesh to Burma, 1978–79: Arranged Reversal of the Flow of an Ethnic Minority', Paper presented to the 4th International Research and Advisory Panel Conference, University of Oxford, 13–21.

Silverstein, J. (1980), *Burmese Politics: The Dilemma of National Unity* (New Brunswick, NJ: Rutgers University Press), 50–51.

Thompson, J. (2007), *World Council of Churches Australia Refugee Sunday Education Kit* (Sydney: WCCA).

UNHCR (1997), *The State of the World's Refugees: A Humanitarian Agenda* (Oxford: Oxford University Press), 147.

UNHCR (2001), *Refugee Protection: A Guide to International Refugee Law (Handbook for Parliamentarians)* (Geneva, UNHCR).

UNHCR (2006), 'Conclusion on Women and Girls at Risk', Document No. 105 (LVII), available at <http://www.unhcr.org/excom/EXCOM/45339d922.html>.

UNHCR (2007a), 'Bangladesh: Analysis of Gaps in the Protection of Rohingya Refugees', UNHCR Report, 8–38.

UNHCR (2007b), 'Refugee Consultations: Bangladesh', Report (UNHCR, Foundation House, Victoria, and Centre for Refugee Research, UNSW), March.

UNHCR (2007c), 'Bangladesh', in *UNHCR Global Appeal 2008–2009*, available at <http://www.unhcr.org/publ/PUBL/474ac8da11.pdf>.

UNHCR News Stories (2005), 'Rohingya Refugees Living in Tough Conditions in Bangladesh Camps', UNHCR, available at <http://www.unhcr.org/news/NEWS/43316f084.html>.

UNSC (2000), United Nations Security Council Resolution 1325 (2000), available at <http://daccessdds.un.org/doc/UNDOC/GEN/N00/720/18/PDF/N0072018.pdf?OpenElement>, accessed 14 July 2008.

UNSC (2006), Resolution 1674, available at <http://domino.un.org/UNISPAl.NSF/361eea1cc08301c485256cf600606959/e529762befa456f8852571610045ebef!OpenDocument>, accessed 14 July 2008.

Wallace, M. (1997), 'The Story of Storyboarding – Part 2 Displayed Thinking', available at <http://www.llrx.com/columns/guide6.htm>, posted June 1997, archived July 1997.

WILPF (2008), 'United Nations Security Council Resolution 1325 on Women, Peace and Security (RES/1325)', available at <http://www.peacewomen.org/un/sc/1325.html>, accessed 14 July 2008.

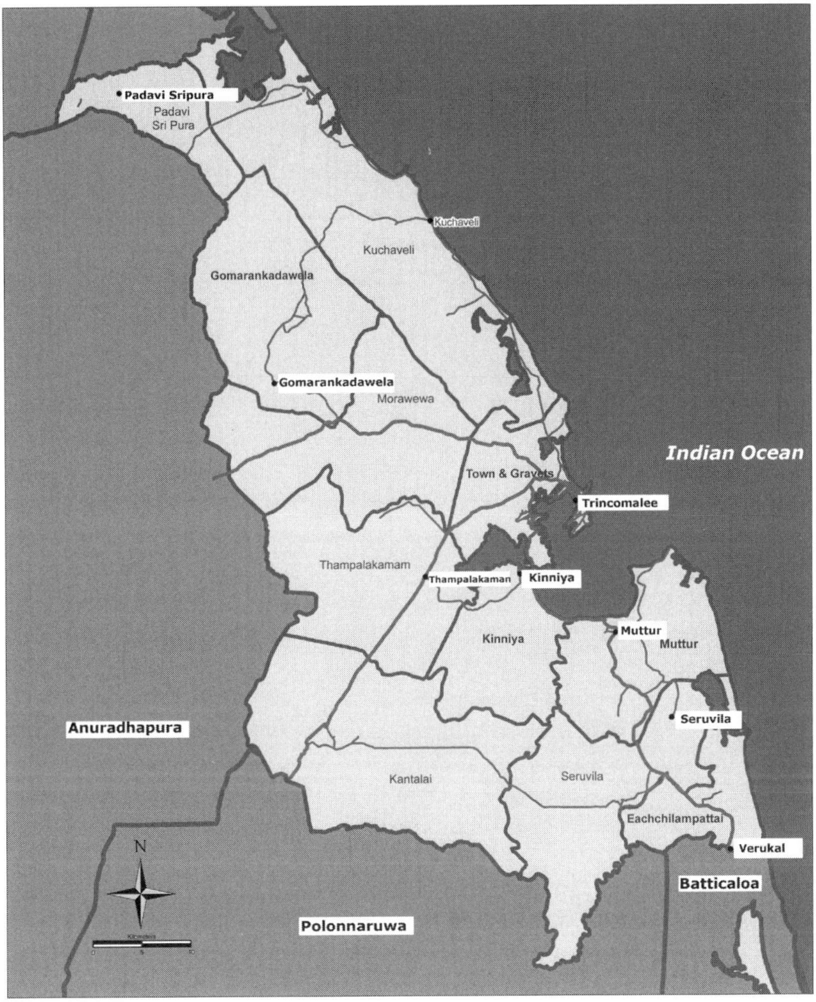

Map 5.1 Sri Lanka

Source: The UN Office for the Coordination of Humanitarian Affairs (UNOCHA), 2007.

Chapter 5

Sri Lanka's Conflict-Induced Internal Displacement: Challenges and Dilemmas of Protection for Humanitarian Agencies in Trincomalee[1]

Hazel Lang and Anita Knudsen

Introduction

This chapter diverges from the focus on refugees examined in the previous chapters to scrutinize in some detail the particular challenges presented in a protracted case of internal displacement. Refugees, by definition, have crossed an international border and are, therefore, entitled to international protection. Internally displaced persons (IDPs), that is, those who have been forcibly displaced within national borders, remain in closer proximity to the conflict and the causes of their displacement. In their flight, instead of escaping the violence and finding a place of safety, IDPs remain part of the protracted conflict. Humanitarian agencies seeking to assist and protect civilians displaced within a state and otherwise rendered insecure by prolonged, sometimes pulsating, civil war are confronted with challenges deeply connected with the political problems underpinning the conflict. Agencies are compelled to grapple with dilemmas and challenges about how to engage in the most skilful and effective way in a risky and difficult environment. A politicized context is not the exception but the rule. The findings of field research detailed in this chapter are necessarily context specific but some of the issues and their implications have wider resonance with challenges and lessons for other difficult politicized protection crises and humanitarian operational environments.

Internal displacement in protracted crises

Particular attention to the issue of 'protracted IDPs situations' is a new area of policy discussion and has been the subject of relatively little analysis and action to date (Brookings-Bern 2007b). However, the majority of IDPs in the world today

1 We are grateful for the generosity and assistance provided to us in Trincomalee by Austcare's partners in the field . We wish to extend our appreciation to respondents in agencies working on the ground who kindly gave us their time and reflections.

find themselves in a protracted state of limbo. Further, the problem is a large-scale one with two to three times more IDPs than refugees living in protracted situations (Brookings-Bern 2007b, 1, 39).

As with refugees, protection for IDPs ultimately entails ensuring a durable solution to their plight (Brookings-Bern 2007a, 1). The question of when displacement ends, however, is not always clearly identifiable as cessation is 'contingent upon a change in the factual situation of displacement' (Brookings-Bern, 2007a 17). The Guiding Principles on Internal Displacement deliberately do not contain a cessation clause for this reason, though Principles 28 and 29 do spell out conditions for voluntary return in safety and dignity to place of origin, resettlement and reintegration (UN-OCHA, 1998). 'Resettlement', as it is termed by the Guiding Principles, means local integration in the areas in which IDPs initially take refuge or relocation to another part of the country (IASC 2007b, 2). In developing a framework for durable solutions for IDPs, the Brookings-Bern Project on Internal Displacement defines a durable solution as 'no more displacement-specific needs and vulnerabilities' (2007a, 14), although 'this does not mean that they may not continue to have a need for protection and assistance, but their needs would be no different from other similarly situated citizens' (2007a, 8). As Jeff Crisp notes, because conflict-induced IDPs remain citizens of the country in which they are living, solutions – at least theoretically – 'must be grounded in State responsibility even if whether or not the government is part of the cause of the displacement' (Brookings-Bern 2007b, 7). National responsibility for protection and solutions is particularly difficult when the state is unable or unwilling to protect its citizens and is itself a source of human insecurity. In its own interests, a government may claim an end to the existence of IDPs in an effort to create an image of normalcy or to distract international scrutiny (IASC 2007b, 1).

Protracted internal displacement crises leave people exposed to risks and threats to their security and livelihoods over a prolonged period of time. The achievement of protection and solutions is always politically contingent – solutions may be elusive for IDPs due to threats, risks and vulnerabilities that continue to persist following a putative or politically fragile effort to resolve a crisis. Internal displacement in Sri Lanka is one such case in which protracted war, political violence and polarization of society along ethno-political lines has produced protracted, multiple, fluid and hidden forms of displacement and has generated chronic human insecurity including the breakdown of trust and protection at the community level. This examination of humanitarian agency approaches to protection with respect to internal displacement in Sri Lanka as a protracted condition is divided into four main sections – origins and underpinnings of the ethnic conflict; analytical approaches to protection and the context of insecurity and displacement in Trincomalee; the specific protection challenges confronting humanitarian agencies operating in this difficult environment; and finally, the lessons and creative strategies crafted by agencies to negotiate these challenges.

The 'incurable habit of war' in Sri Lanka

Uyangoda (2007, 4) explains that the parties to Sri Lanka's ethnic conflict 'have the incurable habit of returning to war'. By way of background, this section briefly sketches the origins and phases of the war, key stakeholders and ethnic groups, and the consequences in terms of mass displacement of affected civilians. The origins of ethnic conflict in Sri Lanka stem from Tamil minority perceptions of discrimination by an ethnocratic state – with antecedents in colonial administration and augmented since independence in 1948 (Saravanamuttu 2004, 124) – and from perceptions of Sinhalese-dominated governments which 'created the impression that the Sinhalese were the discriminated and threatened group' (Schrijvers 1999, 310).

In 1956, accompanying a rise in Sinhala-Buddhist nationalism, the first major discriminatory legislation in the form of the Sinhala Only Act was passed, making Sinhala the sole official language. This policy triggered the first inter-ethnic riots since independence followed by a further series of deadlier riots in 1958, 1978 and 1981 (Schrijvers 1999, 310; DeVotta 2007, 77). The 1983 anti-Tamil riots ignited full-scale armed conflict in the country, and a dynamic 'conflict-sustaining trajectory' (Uyangoda 2007, viii) has prevailed ever since. In 1983, security forces simply stood by and watched without intervening in the ethnic clashes between Tamil militants and Sinhalese mobs. Militant Tamil groups, which were previously relatively marginal, gained new recruits, with the LTTE eventually becoming the predominant force led by the LTTE's then young militant leader Vellupillai Prabhakaran. Indian military engagement in Sri Lanka's conflict through a peacekeeping force (the Indian Peace Keeping Force, IPKF) despatched to the northeast of the island in 1987–1989 further fuelled Sinhalese nationalist fear of Indian annexation (Uyangoda 2007, 21).[2] The years 1989–1990 are widely recalled as years of terror in Sri Lanka, with government forces fighting revolts on two fronts – against the radical nationalist Janatha Vimutkthi Peramuna (JVP) in the south and the LTTE in the north and east (ICG 2006, 4).

Sri Lanka has experienced a 'long drawn out life cycle of ethnic war' (Uyangoda, 2007, vii) spanning over the past 25 years. The armed conflict between the LTTE and the government of Sri Lanka has generally been divided into three different phases of Eelaam War I, II and III (Schrijvers, 1999, 310–11; Sorensen 2001, 14). Eelaam War I, from 1983–1990, was a period marked by confrontations between army forces and Tamil militants which featured violent internal power struggles among various Tamil organizations but resulted in the LTTE becoming dominant as the voice for Tamil Eelaam. After the IPKF withdrew from Sri Lanka in 1990, the LTTE took control of the Tamil population in the north, and started

2 A coalition of Sinhalese nationalist forces (led by the radical nationalist Janatha Vimutkthi Peramuna, JVP) emerged to resist Indian political mediation and a devolution initiative on the grounds that it viewed the initiative as seeking the territorial division of the country on behalf of the Tamil minority (Uyangoda 2007, 21).

the second Eelaam War (1990–1994) with the government. Further, in an act of 'ethnic cleansing' in October 1990, the LTTE expelled the total population of some 75,000 Muslims from the Northern Province within 48 hours (Brun 2003, 384). The northern Muslims have since lived as IDPs in Puttalam, and prospects for return are extremely weak (Brun 2003, 384). Eelaam War III broke out in 1995, following failure of the government-initiated peace negotiations with the LTTE in late 1994 and August 1995. The government then adopted a 'war for peace' approach, combining large-scale, high-intensity military assault on the LTTE and political appeals to the Tamil people (rejected by the LTTE). In December 1995, the government captured the Jaffna peninsula, which had been the LTTE's military and political headquarters, at which time the LTTE retreated to the jungles of the Vanni region, south of Jaffna (Uyangoda 2007, 22).

The three main ethnic groups are the Sinhalese (mostly Buddhist, 74 per cent), the Tamils (mostly Hindu, 18 per cent) and the Muslims (Tamil-speaking, seven per cent). The Tamils comprise two very different communities – the 'Sri Lanka' Tamils (69 per cent) mainly from the north and east and the 'Indian' or 'plantation' Tamils who are descendants of a plantation workforce brought in by the British from Tamil Nadu in southern India in the nineteenth century. Within Tamil communities, there are also divisions along lines of caste, class and regional affiliations (important differences, for example, between the Tamils from the north and the east) (Schrijvers 1999, 310; ICG, 2006). Further, political divisions are sharply drawn between LTTE and anti-LTTE Tamil groups; it is well known that 'LTTE attempts to coopt or physically liquidate its opponents within the Tamil community date back to the 1980s' (ICG 2006, 13). Many Tamils, however, have little sympathy for militant groups, government or anti-government (ICG 2006, 14). The LTTE itself suffered a split in March 2004 when its eastern commander ('Colonel Karuna') broke away and began collaborating with elements of the Sri Lankan military, moving into areas of former LTTE control.[3] Divisions within the Sinhalese political community are formalized in the parties and the extreme ethnocentric views have played their part in mobilizing against devolution of power to the Tamils and in the failure of the main parties to agree even on a limited peace agenda (ICG 2006, 15; DeVotta 2007, 24).[4]

The Sinhalese-Tamil dimension of the conflict in Sri Lanka has overshadowed the significance of Muslim minority aspirations (Uyangoda 2007, 26–7). In the Northern and Eastern Provinces, Tamil and Muslim communities have lived side by side, but the ethnic war has radically altered the coexistence between the two

3 In 2007, the Tamil Makkal Viduthalai Puligal (TMVP) was formed as the political arm of the 'Karuna' faction. The group, 'now led by the ex-Colonel Karuna's former deputy, Pillayan, continues to rule Batticaloa and other parts of the east through terror and crime, with tacit police, military and Colombo approval. Still seen by the government and military as useful to block a Tiger re-emergence in the east, its reign of abductions, child recruitment, robberies and repression of dissent is extensively documented' (ICG 2008, 12).

4 Also note that the Sri Lankan military is 98 per cent Sinhalese (DeVotta 2007, viii).

communities through the use of violence by Tamil armed groups against Muslim civilians, particularly in the Eastern Province; the deliberate policy of Sinhalese political leaders of 'divide and rule' in the Eastern Province; and 'competition for land and economic opportunities between the two communities in conditions of war, particularly in situations where population displacement occurred due to violence' (Uyangoda 2007, 27). Muslims are seven to eight per cent of the national population, but make up more than one-third of the inhabitants of the Eastern Province.

Uyangoda (2007, 1–2) argues that the puzzle of Sri Lanka's ethnic conflict between the government and the LTTE is embedded in 'the non-negotiability of the vital question of state power' and 'protracted war has redefined the core issue of state power as one without negotiable options'. He concludes that Sri Lanka's ethnic war is propelled by two contradictory and mutually exclusive state-formation agendas and war machines, one linked to the state's 'reasserting majority nationalism' and one linked to the 'state-seeking minority nationalism spearheaded by the LTTE' (2007, 45). The LTTE claims it is a national liberation movement for a Tamil Eelam (Tamil homeland) in response to institutionalized racism and violence against the Tamil people by a Sinhala-dominated state. It views a separate Tamil state as the only solution to the Tamils' problems.[5]

The post-2002 Cease-Fire Agreement (CFA) period of 'No War/No Peace' allowed 'both parties to go through the motions of peace talks while exploring military options', descending into low intensity conflict and into open undeclared war in the east in particular (Centre for Policy Alternatives 2006, 11–12). Uyangoda (2007, 1) notes how 'Sri Lanka's ethnic conflict seems to have found a new vitality toward remilitarization after four years of a ceasefire agreement, one year of peace negotiations, and the unprecedented humanitarian disaster of the tsunami which struck Sinhalese, Tamil and Muslim communities in almost equal measure.'

The February 2002 CFA between the government and the LTTE completely collapsed in January 2006.[6] It is estimated that some 5,000 people (troops and civilians) have been killed since the beginning of 2006 (ICG 2008, 9). The situation descended into open war in 2006, particularly in the east. The intensification of hostilities led to a serious humanitarian crisis, violations of human rights, and large-scale displacement of over 290,000 IDPs (ICG 2007b, 7–8). Over 16,000 refugees left for South India, adding to the existing caseload of over 60,000

5 The international intelligence and security community today assesses the LTTE as 'one of the world's most effective terrorist organisations'. It is the only organization to have assassinated two heads of government and developed a sea arm capable of countering a conventional navy; it also maintains considerable capabilities for conventional war and possesses a dedicated suicide squad (Jane's Security News 2007). However, the LTTE is more than an armed militant group – it controls territory and administers a civilian population (Uyangoda 2007, 40).

6 In January 2008, the government announced its withdrawal from the Norwegian-brokered ceasefire.

in Tamil Nadu. In September 2007, the total number of IDPs stood at 503,000 (UNHCR 2007, 237). Armed conflict and human rights violations have led to displacement of all communities in Sri Lanka, both in LTTE (called 'uncleared' areas by the government) and government-controlled areas (including so-called 'cleared' areas).

The death and displacement toll of the war in Sri Lanka has been extensive. The civil war has killed more than 70,000 people (DeVotta 2007, 77). As the International Crisis Group (2006, 23) notes, Sri Lankan civilians, caught between LTTE oppression and security force brutality, bear the brunt of the violence. The displacement crisis in Sri Lanka has fluctuated with the vicissitudes of war, generating between 500,000 and one million IDPs of the total population of some 20 million. Though the war has displaced people from all three communities, it is estimated that Tamils make up around 80 per cent of all IDPs in Sri Lanka, and in the late 1990s the diaspora of Sri Lankan Tamils in the west was estimated to be some 800,000 people (Schrijvers 1999, 309). The role the diaspora plays in financing the Tamil separatist struggle led by the LTTE is well known.[7]

According to the United Nations High Commissioner for Refugees (UNHCR),[8] IDPs in the Sri Lankan context have three theoretical options for durable solutions: (1) returning to their place of origin (if and when it is safe); (2) local integration into the host community; or (3) resettlement elsewhere in the country (UNHCR 2006, 11). But of course 'durable solutions', including sustainable return, are problematic in an intractable conflict. Many who have been returned to their original areas had to flee again due to renewed conflict and insecurity. Return is thus always plagued with the risk of renewed displacement, so that return is hardly 'durable'. The following sections contextualize the key features of displacement in the east, with particular reference to Trincomalee.

Protection and protracted conflict in Trincomalee, approach and context

Progressive thinking on protracted internal displacement situations[9] suggests a definition focused on the absence or failure of solutions rather than the duration or scale of displacement. In the course of this research, it became apparent that multiple cycles of displacement in Trincomalee compound the protracted

7 For an examination of methods of funds generation of the LTTE, see Jayasekara (2007).

8 The UNHCR has been in Sri Lanka since 1987. Its original mandate was to facilitate the repatriation of some 100,000 Sri Lanka refugees from India. When the civil conflict intensified in the early 1990s, generating further widespread displacement, UNHCR extended its mandate to protection and assistance of IDPs, and remains the designated lead agency for IDPs in Sri Lanka (UNHCR 2007).

9 See UNHCR and Brookings-Bern Project on Internal Displacement, 'Expert Seminar on Protracted IDP Situations' (2007b).

condition of insecurity and belie a narrower or static definition of protracted displacement.[10]

Humanitarian protection means engaging directly with an understanding of the behaviour of actors and dynamics of the conflict. As Mahony (2006) suggests, protection relies on a precise analysis of the specific situation. Sri Lanka demonstrates many of the archetypal characteristics of a difficult and unaccommodating protection environment: high levels of insecurity for humanitarian workers,[11] a politicized humanitarian agenda and unpredictable levels of humanitarian access. Exploring operational perspectives on the challenges of humanitarian protection in politicized and militarized environments is necessary to ensure that research on protracted IDP situations reflects the ground realities.[12] In what follows, we outline our approach to humanitarian protection; sketch the protection landscape of Trincomalee and the nature of human insecurity; and then consider in some detail field perspectives on the challenges of humanitarian protection, lessons learnt from operating in a protracted conflict setting and creative strategies to negotiate these challenges.

Defining humanitarian protection

Sri Lanka is an arena in which the Guiding Principles on Internal Displacement are violated throughout all phases of displacement. Displacement is used as a tool or even a method of combat by warring parties. Approaches to displacement, protection, and 'durable solutions', therefore, need to be understood in relation to the political-military contours of the conflict. The case study draws on approaches that conceptualize humanitarian protection focused on 'civilian security' (Darcy 2007).

10 The standard definition of a protracted refugee situation used by the UNHCR – as 'one in which refugees find themselves in a long-lasting and intractable state of limbo' (UNHCR 2000, 106), drawing on the basic measure of refugee populations of 25,000 and greater who have been exiled for five years or more – does not resonate in most protracted IDP contexts. However, Loescher and Milner's (2005, 14) critique of this definition with respect to refugees – that is, protracted refugee situations 'include chronic, unresolved and recurring refugee problems, not only static refugee populations' – also applies in cases of protracted internal displacement. This definition allows for an understanding of protracted displacement to take account of repeated cycles of internal displacement.

11 Sri Lanka is regarded as among the most dangerous places in the world for aid workers. Sir John Holmes, UN Secretary General for Humanitarian Affairs, described the gunning down on 6 August 2006 of 17 Action Contre la Faime (ACF) employees in Muttur town (Trincomalee district) as the 'single worst crime committed against humanitarian workers in recent history' (IRIN 2007).

12 This is not the first exploration of challenges and dilemmas of humanitarian protection. Humanitarian Policy Group (HPG) has been developing a body of work on the protection of civilians entitled 'Protection in Practice' which examines current practice in humanitarian protection. See for example, <http://www.odi.org.uk/hpg/meetings/genevaroundtable_meetingreport.pdf>.

The objective of humanitarian protection strategies and activities 'is to minimize threats of violence, coercion and deprivation, as well as enhancing opportunities to obtain security. The achievement of civilian security, or at least the reduction in insecurity, thus lies at the heart of protection' (Pantuliano and O'Callaghan 2006, 6). Protection encompasses physical and legal protection; primary responsibility for protection rests with the government, though international humanitarian law (IHL) imposes duties on all the parties to the conflict.[13]

Protection and security for civilians involve three different actors: the authorities (governments, authorities and other bodies in control of a given territory, including armed groups and international forces); affected individuals and communities; and humanitarian agencies. The ICRC-devised egg model[14] emphasizes diversity and cooperation in the protection system, and how agencies can complement one another in their work with authorities, people at risk, civil society and each other. As Slim and Bonwick (2005, 44–5) note, programming diversity can be a 'protection multiplier':

> A concerted effort by all agencies to use their different mandates, expertise, resources and networks to meet commonly identified protection needs and desired outcomes for threatened populations can dramatically increase the likelihood of protection being realized. Complementarity does not mean every agency doing the same thing. Instead, it involves each agency doing what it does best and what it is best placed to do.

The limits of humanitarian agencies as protection actors are of course widely recognized, as noted by the ICRC: 'Humanitarian endeavors … can never be a substitute for political action' (Aeschlimann 2005, 25). Humanitarian agencies can, however, support affected populations to avoid and resist threats through:

- Humanitarian presence, witnessing, accompaniment, monitoring, etc., consciously used to inhibit abusive behaviour (Slim and Bonwick 2005, 91). The Centre for Humanitarian Dialogue's 'Proactive Presence' guide identifies three ways that field presence contributes to protection of civilians: deterrence (constraining abusers), encouragement (supporting

13 The Active Learning Network for Accountability and Performance in Humanitarian Action (ALNAP) defines protection to encompass safety, dignity, integrity, empowerment and rights, in accordance with human rights, humanitarian and refugee law (Slim and Bonwick 2005, 30–33). We maintained a broad perspective on protection in our approach to protection in field interviews to encompass the varying mandates and perceptions of different agencies.

14 The 'egg model' spans three interdependent, complementary spheres of action (Slim and Bonwick 2005, 42): responsive (immediate or urgent activities aimed to stop, prevent or alleviate the immediate/worst effects of the abuses); remedial (restorative action to assist people to recover while they live with the effects of abuses); and environment-building (supporting political, social, cultural and institutional norms that prevent or limit violations or abuse).

people to protect themselves) and influence (supporting reformers and changing societal attitudes) (Mahony 2006).[15]

- Protection-focused programming (assessing, designing, implementing, and monitoring programmes) takes two forms: first, activities or interventions aimed at specific protection objectives or outcomes;[16] and, second, 'mainstreaming' or integrating protection into humanitarian programmes[17] (protection-sensitive assistance to build a protective environment).
- Protection through advocacy – influencing responsible authorities (government, as well as de facto authorities) to ensure respect for norms, rights and duties of international law.

The protection landscape, Trincomalee district

Trincomalee district is situated in the northernmost part of the Eastern Province of Sri Lanka. At face value, the scale and frequency of displacement in Trincomalee has been comparatively lower than that which occurred in northern Sri Lanka.[18] However, the Eastern Province has been an unstable and continually contested area throughout the war and is considered pivotal to Sri Lanka's future. The district is of strategic importance to the Sri Lankan government and the LTTE. Trincomalee harbour is the world's second deepest harbour, of geopolitical and economic importance to both parties. It is also of particular nationalistic importance to the LTTE, which envisages Trincomalee as the capital of Tamil Eelaam. The strategic importance of the district bears significant implications for the insecurity of civilians in a context of intractable conflict.

Over the past 25 years, Trincomalee has experienced a complex process of 'mixing' and 'unmixing' of people (Rajasingham-Senanayake 2002, 60). The multi-ethnic composition of Trincomalee is unique in Sri Lanka. Unlike the mono-ethnic north, today Trincomalee has fairly equal proportions of Muslims, Sinhalese and Tamils.[19] As McGilvray (2001) shows, Trincomalee has experienced decades

15 Mahony's manual (2006, 13) describes proactive presence as 'actions and strategies that deter or dissuade against abuses, persuade abusers to behave differently, strengthen or expand civilian capacity for self-protection, and foster institutional reform'.

16 For an outline of a risk-based model of protection in humanitarian programming, see Slim and Bonwick (2005), 51–5.

17 Programming is also informed by the 'Do No Harm' (DNH) approach that recognizes that good intentions do not necessarily result in good outcomes. DNH seeks to analyse the impact of assistance on conflict.

18 The conflict zone in Sri Lanka is customarily divided into the three areas: the Vanni – mostly controlled by the LTTE; Jaffna, and the border areas south of Vanni – areas which the government has regained and which it calls 'cleared' areas; and the contested areas of Trincomalee, Batticaloa and Ampara in the east which have been declared 'cleared' by the government since July 2007.

19 A reason for the unique ethnic composition was the state sponsored irrigation, and Sinhalese settlement schemes that began in the 1940s (Peebles 1990); a process that

of demographic manipulation. More recently, the introduction of 'buffer zones' in post-tsunami 2005, a 'Special Economic Zone' in 2007 and the High Security Zones has spawned allegations of Sinhalese 'colonization' in government land use, development and settlement policy (Hyndman 2007; Rampton 2007).

Trincomalee has experienced a high level of political violence that is expressed in suspicion and mistrust between different ethnic groups of the population.[20] The defection of 'Colonel Karuna' from the LTTE in 2004 generated intra-ethnic tensions felt at the community level,[21] and the renewed war in 2006 exacerbated tensions between eastern Tamils and Muslims (ICG 2007a). The politicization of ethnicity and violence has polarized communities and produced a volatility that contains features unique to the east of the country.[22] Causes and solutions are localized in the eastern context and within its sub-regions; protection problems therefore contain specific geopolitical and community sub-dynamics and require a locally contextualized understanding.

Trincomalee district has undergone waves of displacement since the 1980s, and again in 2006 became a main site of displacement in Sri Lanka. In April 2006, a bombing in Trincomalee town triggered communal violence and displacement; later in April mass displacement in LTTE-controlled areas in Muttur and Eachchilampattu divisions resulted from government military operations, especially around Sampur. In August 2006, the government launched a military offensive in response to the LTTE shutting the sluice gates in the Serunwara area. The LTTE launched a counteroffensive, seizing control over parts of Muttur, and provoking massive retaliation by government forces. The civilian population of Muttur and its locality fled en masse within the district and into neighbouring Batticaloa.[23]

In July 2007, the government officially declared the Eastern Province under its control ('cleared' of the LTTE) and ready for development, but influential agencies (such as the ICRC and the SLMM) still consider the region a conflict area. As noted above, political underpinnings of Sri Lanka's 'conflict-sustaining trajectory' (Uyangoda 2007, viii) ensure that peace remains a distant prospect overall. In the context of an enduring capacity for war, people have experienced repeated displacement for over two decades. Experiences of multiple cycles of displacement over this protracted period have perpetuated a state of uncertainty, impermanency

radically altered the political demographics of Trincomalee. Previously the east coast was a region composed of two historically interlinked, but contentious communities, the Tamils and the Muslims. Both Tamil-speaking, they have a long history of conflict and coexistence (McGilvray 1999; 2001).

20 For an overview of ethnicized community relations in eastern Sri Lanka, see Foundation for Coexistence (2004).

21 For an overview of the causes and dynamics of the Karuna defection, see Philipson and Thangarajah (2005).

22 For a full account of eastern dynamics, see Philipson and Thangarajah (2005).

23 For a detailed chronological account, see IASC (2007a, 39–52).

and insecurity.[24] Attention therefore needs to be directed to understanding the sources of civilian insecurity and the most effective responses available to support protection and human security at the community level.

Risks, threats and vulnerabilities are pervasive and intricately part of every aspect of people's lives: 'the environment is such that we [agencies] can't avoid protection [in our work]'.[25] The conflict-related displacement landscape is marked by forced displacement, restrictions on freedom of movement and forced returns and relocations (IASC 2007a). Protection concerns also include extreme human rights abuses such as disappearances, abductions for ransom, extra-judicial killings, forced recruitment (including of children), arrests and detentions, 'round-ups' by 'masked men', extortion and wider insecurities connected to the loss of livelihoods and the impacts of militarization.

The vivid unknown: Human insecurity

Civilians are not collateral damage in this war, but are often deliberately targeted as part of the military strategy of parties to the conflict (state, armed non-state and paramilitary actors). The scale and intensity of military operations in 2006, including aerial bombing and shelling (use of 'multi-barrels') targeting civilian areas, has compounded returnees' sense of insecurity in this phase. The shift in military–political balance to the government in return areas formerly controlled by the LTTE has also shaped civilians' perceptions of their ability to flee: 'we are surrounded in this place'.[26] Also, as noted by the ICRC,[27] military structures (such as army camps and buffer zones) in Sri Lanka are in close proximity to civilians. The militarization of return areas as well as past experiences of retaliatory attacks undermine prospects for sustainable return, 'when we get back [return] the military will look at us. If something happens the military will shoot'.[28] People's sense of security is also influenced by specific local factors such as the behaviour of local military authorities, the proximity of their homes to contested areas (for example, jungle, sea coast, etc.), and events occurring in neighbouring villages.

People expressed a pervasive sense of insecurity in their lives and prospects for their future, 'we don't have hope [for the security of our future] at all. We don't dare to develop hope'.[29] Active hostilities may have ceased for the time being and people have returned home, but people do not feel secure. They are not sure when the conflict might reignite and when they will need to run again. An imminent sense of a renewed conflict marks their return.

---

24 Focus group discussions, Trincomalee, October 2007.
25 Interview, Trincomalee, 8 October 2007.
26 Household visit, Eachchilampattu DS Division, 12 October 2007.
27 Interview, Trincomalee, 9 October 2007.
28 Interview, Kiliveddi Transit Camp, 12 October 2007.
29 Household visit, Eachchilampattu DS Division, 12 October 2007.

For those who have returned, they prefer to be back in their own villages but noted that political divisions and mistrust are being played out at the community level – 'before one and two were there, now there is one, two, three and four'.[30] Political factionalism is producing and reproducing threats and vulnerabilities. Political factions in the Tamil community, for example, have led to a breakdown in the collective coping mechanisms used by communities in the past, so that now, 'We can't even trust the next door neighbour. We don't know who's coming and for what reason'.[31] Political violence is played out at the personal and family level, such as with abductions out of personal vengeance.[32] Returnees from the 2006 conflict expressed renewed and intensified forms of suspicion, mistrust and divisions resulting from their experiences of violence and displacement.[33] The present political violence is described by a local commentator as the most serious she has known. The next section explores implications for agencies working in this intractable conflict environment, with multiple cycles of displacement and continuing insecurity.

Protection challenges for agencies

In eastern Sri Lanka, humanitarian protection confronts the highly militarized, politicized arena and/or the denial of access in some areas. It is an environment in which all political actors (state, non-state, paramilitary) are perpetrators of violence and insecurity, and international principles and rules for the protection of conflict-affected civilians and IDPs are not respected. Agencies therefore confront 'strategic risks'[34] and operational dilemmas in their protection work. In general, agencies working in the context of *internal displacement* are often constrained by the policies, actions or inactions of governments. Governments have the primary responsibility for the protection of IDPs and affected civilians, but too frequently they fail to protect and/or are sources of insecurity. International humanitarian law obliges all parties to distinguish between the civilian population and combatants at all times. In Sri Lanka, the failure of the government to protect civilians constrains and frustrates humanitarian actors working in the midst of the conflict-affected environment.

---

30 Interview, household visit, Trincomalee, 12 October 2007.

31 Interview, household visit, Trincomalee, 12 October 2007.

32 CBO focus group discussion, 4 October 2007, and confidential interview 16 October 2007.

33 Returnees from Eachchilampattu believe that their homes had been looted by neighbouring Muslim communities facilitated by the army. The Karuna faction is still relatively young in the area; however, communities are aware that they are particularly vulnerable when power and control are disputed in their area. As the social fabric of the community shatters, 'protection' afforded by supporting the Karuna faction becomes a survival technique.

34 For a general overview of strategic risks see Slim and Bonwick (2005, 46–7).

The key operational challenges for humanitarian agencies relate to negotiating the politically sensitive relationships with the government, dealing with a militarized and deeply divided environment, and internal factors influencing how agencies approach their work. The sections below outline these challenges, but first several introductory points need to be established. 'Agencies' is the vernacular catch-all term, but for the purposes of disaggregating agencies' perspectives we have broadly categorized international and local agencies as (1) international agencies encompassing the UN agencies, the International Committee for the Red Cross (ICRC)[35] and international non-governmental organizations (international agencies include protection mandated[36] and non-protection mandated agencies);[37] and (2) local agencies encompassing local non-governmental organizations and community-based organizations.[38]

Enduring dilemmas, working with the government

International agencies are primarily concerned with the *conditions* under which the war is played out, though some agencies reflected on how the provision of humanitarian assistance has been used to propagate political agendas. Some international agencies have become concerned about the government's exploitation of the 'No War No Peace' period for the militarization of 'liberated' regions and the securitization of development. Both governmental objectives were pursued by instigating rapid returns that did not meet internationally agreed benchmarks for conditions and processes of return.

Agencies risk instrumentalization of assistance by government for political purposes. Working with the government can present agencies with the dilemma of how to do their work without the 'risk of implementing a plan that is not a humanitarian plan'.[39] Agencies identified the need to avoid the risk of incorporating assistance into a plan that legitimizes forced return or that contributes to neglect or abuse of a population. One area is the instrumentalization of return (termed

35 It should be noted that the ICRC's mission – defined in the 1949 Geneva Conventions and their 1977 Additional Protocols and in the 1986 Statutes of the International Movement of the Red Cross and Red Crescent – is 'to protect the lives and dignity of victims of war and internal violence and to provide them with assistance' and 'to prevent human suffering by promoting and strengthening humanitarian law and universal humanitarian principles'. Protection is therefore of primary concern to the International Committee of the Red Cross (ICRC). However, ICRC is under no obligation to coordinate with other agencies.

36 Agencies charged by states to lead on a particular aspect of humanitarian protection. For an overview of protection responsibilities and protection mandates see Slim and Bonwick (2005, 36–8).

37 Humanitarian NGOs offering humanitarian action in support of protection, that is, agencies that recognize the importance of linking protection of, and assistance to, people affected by conflict.

38 NGOs are registered through a national secretariat in Sri Lanka.

39 Interview, UN agency, Trincomalee, 17 October 2007.

'resettlement' by the Sri Lankan government) by the military for political purposes. For example, according to some international agencies, rapid (mass) return occurred in order to consolidate the government's military campaign by bringing back civilians into an area at risk of incursions by the LTTE. Rather than an agenda for sustainable return, 'to the government, return means surveillance and [military] security'.[40] Return of the people enables the government to more tightly control and scrutinize the population through screening and identification of people formerly living in LTTE areas.[41] Agencies grapple with how to engage with militarized return.[42] As another international agency head put it, 'on the one hand we are working with the state as a real partner but at the end of the day when you need real commitment they have their own political and military agenda'.[43]

Agencies noted political interference in their humanitarian work plans, described by one observer as 'à la carte humanitarianism'[44] or a situation in which the government picks and chooses activities according to its own agenda. For example, agencies' access has improved in resettlement areas in Eachchilampattu where the government is keen to reconstruct the area.[45] Agencies noted that the high regulation of agencies impinges on their independence.[46]

Agencies are contending with a politically confronting environment where protection work is considered highly sensitive because it is negatively perceived as challenging the agendas of political and military actors. International and especially local agencies noted that 'you can't be outspoken on protection'. It is not possible to use the 'P-word' (protection) openly. Or as one veteran of a CBO (community-based organization) responded: 'Your subject of protection is a dangerous one'.[47] Protection work can risk jeopardizing agencies' relationships

40 Interview, UN agency, Trincomalee, 10 October 2007.

41 New, duplicate identification cards in Sinhala language have been issued to returnees from formerly LTTE-administered areas, labelling people with 'red letters'. Mobile phone coverage is blocked in the return areas of Eachchilampattu further impinging on agencies' security, constraining involvement in and approaches to the area. The Sri Lankan Army has established camps in return areas to create 'buffer zones'.

42 Agencies were unclear about the return and rehabilitation process as the government did not provide a resettlement (that is, return) plan. Agencies were initially unable to access return areas in Eachchilampattu and Vakarai.

43 Interview, INGO, Trincomalee, 10 October 2007.

44 Interview, UN agency, Trincomalee, 10 October, 2007.

45 The government has launched a 'Recovery and Rebuilding' process of the 'Sun Rising Region'. In July 2007, the Eastern Province military commander notified local civil administrators that his office would have final say on the selection of humanitarian agencies that would be invited to work in return (formerly LTTE) areas (ICG 2008, 18). For an overview of securitized development in eastern Sri Lanka, see Rampton (2007).

46 The government has issued 'Guidelines for NGOs/INGOs in their Dos and Dont's' which stipulates that agencies should 'not waste time and resources' on 'awareness programs'. Interview, UN agency, Trincomalee, 10 October 2007.

47 Interview, Trincomalee, 10 October 2007.

with the authorities due to the uncomfortable exposure of the government's failure to protect its people and the political reality underpinning the causes of protection problems. Agencies in this environment need to consider the political consequences of undertaking protection work and risk of 'protection backlash' (provoking the ire of the authorities).[48]

Protection work also exposes local staff to risks of threats from various armed actors (such as the Tameleela Makkal Viduthalai Puligal, TMVP, the political arm of the Karuna faction) that perceive their involvement as biased or interfering.[49] There is reluctance on the part of local agencies to work on protection-related issues due to concern for the security of their staff. Similarly, international agencies weigh decisions against the potential cost to staff, programmes and communities.

The political sensitivities of the environment mean that some agencies compromise their principles[50] in order to remain operational. Agencies find themselves balancing the need to stay operational with negotiating the political agenda of the government. Further, international agencies do not take a strong principled position on situations from the outset of engagement leading to erosion of humanitarian principles and a breakdown of collective action of agencies. Despite the endorsement of the Saving Lives Together framework (IASC 2006),[51] there remains limited collective action and solidarity.[52] Agencies will lobby for parties to adhere to humanitarian principles but proceed to work within the prevailing conditions.[53] Even advocacy in the form of quiet diplomacy with government authorities may amount to 'lipstick service to our principles'.[54] Failure of principled action inadvertently contributes to legitimizing actions that contravene the Guiding Principles on Internal Displacement.

Agencies noted that the government may perceive their work as biased in favour of one population (notably the Tamils, who have been disproportionately affected by displacement). This apparent bias can result in the erosion of perceived

48 Interview, Trincomalee, 10 October 2007.

49 The TMVP is widely regarded as a proxy to the government. The strengthening of TMVP has created political and criminal obstacles for agencies to negotiate. The TMVP are considered less disciplined than the LTTE and are viewed by some as a criminal group rather than a political movement.

50 Interview, UN agency, Trincomalee, 10 October 2007. Principles refer to adhering to agencies' mandates and to supporting and promoting the Guiding Principles on Internal Displacement.

51 Saving Lives Together was prepared by a sub-working group of the IASC Task Force on Collaborative Approaches to Security led by InterAction and UNICEF, 17 November 2006.

52 Interview, UN agency, Trincomalee, 10 October 2007.

53 This has been seen, for instance, in a reticence to be associated with building alternative housing for returnees whose homes are occupied by the army. Whilst working towards humanitarian goals, that is, the need to provide shelter, this action has the potential to assist in the consolidation of military objectives.

54 Interview, INGO, Trincomalee, 17 October 2007.

neutrality; in the eyes of the government, 'to assist people is a political statement'.[55] There are entrenched perceptions held by Sinhalese nationalists, the government and armed forces of NGOs as 'criminals', spoilers, wrongdoers.[56]

Coordination with the government has been problematic. Agencies must deal with a centralized administration dominated by military interests.[57] Agencies are constrained in their planning by ad hoc and inconsistent government decision-making processes, including a lack of consultation regarding a consolidated resettlement and rehabilitation plan. For many humanitarian agencies, coordination with civil administrators charged with military objectives is deeply problematic as it can result in the compromise of principles of independence. Further, agencies contend with different models of the state in different regions and sub-regions. Civil administration decisions are connected to the larger military campaigns of the Sri Lanka Army and LTTE. For example, negotiations at the Grama Sevaka (GS) and Grama Niladhari (GN) level can boomerang at the level of the Government Agent (GA) as military priorities take precedence.[58] This endemic feature of the protection environment creates certain requirements in agencies' initial engagement in order to understand power structures and to set objectives.

Wider contours of the operational environment

Agencies are limited in their capability to contribute to the protection and security of conflict-affected IDPs and civilians due to features inherent in the militarized environment that impact access, presence, monitoring and reporting. Agencies are constrained by limited access determined by government as well as their own security guidelines (which, for example, require them to return to base by sunset). Within UN agencies, for example, it is a requirement that local staff be accompanied by international counterparts on fieldwork, placing a strain on resources available for field presence. Local agencies and communities are calling for presence,[59] yet international agencies are constrained by the dangers and risks of the operational environment (in addition to their own mandates) to maintain humanitarian presence in affected areas.[60] For local agencies and staff, access and security conditions are also garmented in fear and mistrust between ethnic groups.

55 Interview, INGO, Trincomalee, 17 October 2007.

56 Interview, INGO, Trincomalee, 11 October 2007. Refer to DeVotta (2007, 33) for a comprehensive view of antagonistic attitudes towards NGOs.

57 The most powerful civil administrator of the region, the Government Agent (GA), is a former Major General.

58 Interview, UN agency, Trincomalee, 8 October, 2007.

59 Local agencies view presence at the field level as a preventative mechanism that will deter perpetrators, but also provide reporting leverage and empowerment for communities.

60 Many human rights violations occur in the night and this is an aspect of protection that is not addressed in the current responses by international agencies (with the exception of the work of the Non-Violent Peace Force).

Precise reporting and referrals are also limited as the process presents risks for victims and witnesses. People fear to speak out and report on protection incidents due to the risks of retaliation by parties identified as perpetrators. CBOs, too, are reluctant to report protection incidents because of lack of witness protection and risk of revenge and intimidation of their own staff. This limits specific case reporting. Humanitarian agencies have put together a referral mechanism for protection cases in Trincomalee which details how agencies can refer protection cases that they come across in their daily work, and explains the mandates of protection agencies. However, in practice the timely action necessary for effective reporting and follow-up of cases is not always delivered. Agencies are often unable to verify information due to the communities' fears and/or lack of access to cooperative authorities to cross-check details of cases. Further, some local NGOs and CBOs are insufficiently informed of international agencies' mandates, scope of action and the establishment of a referral mechanism. Lack of communication and clarity between international and local humanitarian agencies also hampers local agencies from utilizing the referral system.

Internal views

Institutional challenges, such as diverse attitudes and awareness of protection, rigid views of institutional mandates and lack of experienced personnel pose challenges for agencies. Some international agencies are blinded by their own mandates – they may be 'pushing their own agenda, [which] means missing the bigger picture'; or they may concentrate on 'the small things we have in front of us' rather than take a longer-term view.[61]

Agencies have different understandings of humanitarian protection. 'Protection' in the context of Trincomalee is largely understood in terms of basic physical security and the need to ensure safety. Particularly for local agencies, the protection agenda is limited to a concern with physical security, that is, 'hardcore' protection issues of abductions and killings. For local agencies there is an uncertainty about the scope of *how* internationals protect civilians, and *what* the international protection agenda is. Some non-mandated protection agencies work well with mandated agencies (for example, utilizing the referral mechanism) and approach their work with a protection-sensitive orientation. Other non-mandated agencies understand protection as requiring a specialist mandate, 'we are not a protection agency'.[62] Rather than working with a wider understanding of protection-sensitive programming, protection is seen as the responsibility of a particular set of humanitarian agencies charged with protection mandates or offering expertise in protection.

Most non-mandated agencies do not have systematic approaches to protection-sensitive programming but depend on local staff to identify protection issues in

61 Interviews, INGO, Trincomalee, 10 and 17 October 2007.

62 Interviews, INGOs Trincomalee, 9, 10 and 11 October 2007.

their programme design and the varying capacity of international staff to consider security issues in programme development. Largely, non-mandated agencies did not view technical interventions as an opportunity to provide protection nor did they approach protection as intrinsic to assistance. Uncooperative relationships between the government and NGOs have hampered NGOs' influence. Non-mandated agencies have limited bargaining power and frequently no political leverage or relevance to the authorities. Non-mandated agencies rely heavily on protection-mandated agencies (in the form of the ICRC, the UN and the former SLMM) to access government authorities and advocate on issues. Non-mandated agencies are reliant on the lead agency (the UNHCR) to take a principled stance as an authoritative voice and representative of humanitarian interests. However, a major weakness in responding to internal displacement has been the absence of clear operational accountability and leadership in key sectors impacting on the efficacy of common goals and collective action.

Agencies noted internal constraints of donor timetables, headquarter requirements and support as constraining flexibility, creativity and responsiveness. The pulsating nature of the war (alternating flares between the north and east coast) means agencies' resources and high-capacity personnel are often reallocated to the new emergency areas, reducing investment in and commitment to the ongoing protection crisis in comparatively 'stabilized' areas. In some cases, non-mandated protection agencies expressed a lack of headquarter support for protection activities due to the perception that protection advocacy is too politically risky in terms of jeopardizing established relationships at the Colombo level. Mandated agencies noted that they are reliant on Colombo to be a vocal advocate of their recommendations.

Cooperation and coordination between international agencies depend heavily on personalities. Good collaboration relies not on the organization but on particular persons within an organization. Protection agendas are driven more by personalities and the confidence and knowledge of individuals on the ground than by an institutional system-wide agenda. Ensuring that agencies sustain coordinated engagement is an 'ongoing battle'.[63] Coordination and engagement with local agencies has been limited due to constraints of a weak civil society, security risks to nationals posed in a politicized environment and the limited investment of international agencies in utilization and building of local capacity.

Agencies responding to the tsunami and development actors were not prepared for or skilled in operating in a complex, conflict-affected environment of intractable war: 'here, there is a lack of interest in protection. People start thinking things are normal when they are not'.[64] Or as another agency put it, 'considering what's going on, there are not many agencies really getting it'.[65]

63 Interview, Trincomalee, 10 October 2007.

64 Interview, UN agency and INGO, Trincomalee, 10 and 17 October 2007.

65 Interview, UN agency, Trincomalee, 10 October 2007.

Lessons and creative strategies of agencies

Protection responses and strategies to avoid and resist threats to the security of affected populations relate to all areas of protection work – presence, protection-sensitive programming and advocacy. They encompass the immediate and long-term complementary spheres of the 'egg model'.[66] Clearly, there are different agencies, with different organizational structures and mandates. However, it is useful to distil lessons out of the various perspectives. Trincomalee illustrates how the politicization of humanitarian protection by all parties to the conflict requires agencies to develop context-specific, creative approaches to their work. Overwhelmingly, agencies reflected on the need to develop humanitarian action that is informed by a political understanding of the context and to consistently take a principled and protection-sensitive approach.

Agencies have been limited in the extent to which they can counter the risk of instrumentalizing assistance for political purposes. However, there has been a concerted effort to build productive relationships with the high-level administrators (especially the powerful Government Agent), which has given agencies greater negotiation space and the possibility for influence. For example, recent efforts to consult with the Government Agent on humanitarian plans prior to public coordination meetings between government and humanitarian agencies have improved government–agency relationships.

For non-mandated agencies, it is particularly important to maintain a low profile in the way they do their protection work. Agencies have had to avoid publicly using the 'protection' label but rather focus on building a protection-sensitive orientation into their work. In this environment, protection is as much an orientation as a set of activities. Long-term engagement with Sri Lanka has enabled agencies to decipher and utilize non-controversial entry points (such as activities involving women and children) that are perceived as less 'political'. As the local conflict dynamics are in flux, agencies need to remain vigilant regarding how communities and the authorities perceive their protection work.

For the protection-mandated agencies, it is important to work transparently and confidently according to the principles of the agency and to ensure the government is held accountable for its responsibilities. At present, a lack of communities' confidence and trust in the government has resulted in reliance on international agencies (such as UNICEF and ICRC) rather than the state (including the police) which in turn contributes to the stagnation of the existing system. It is therefore important to build government accountability and capacity.

'Stick to principles!'[67] Agencies have principles and privileges and they need to use them. An important lesson revealed was that agencies should maintain principled action from the outset of their engagement with the authorities. As this chapter has

66 The three spheres of action are responsive, remedial and environment-building (Slim and Bonwick 2005, 42). See this chapter.

67 Interview, Trincomalee, 10 October 2007.

shown, the failure of principled action inadvertently contributes to legitimizing actions that contravene the Guiding Principles on Internal Displacement and the breakdown of collective action by agencies. This applies to the larger and UN protection-mandated agencies in particular, as these are the agencies with access and influence. As one key respondent noted, taking a principled stand should mean that protection-mandated agencies 'don't get intimidated [by the authorities] and do it anyway'.[68] In other words, agencies should be consistent in their application of principles.

Agencies have addressed the government's perceptions of bias by actively communicating with the relevant authorities to demonstrate commitment to a balanced approach with all three communities. Agencies also are engaging with IDPs in conjunction with host communities to ensure that agencies do not fuel mistrust and resistance between and among communities.

Effective communication and coordination is essential. If agencies are well coordinated, this enables a 'protection multiplier' effect, bringing together agencies with their different mandates, expertise, resources and networks to meet commonly identified protection needs. Further, non-mandated international agencies are utilizing the Trincomalee referral system for protection cases (reporting of abductions, killings, etc.) to benefit from the access and influence that mandated agencies possess.

In the absence of international presence, some international agencies have developed their approach to build community networks and capacity, for example, community-based child protection systems are supported in collaboration with the relevant government agencies. Strengthening community protection capacity is particularly important in an environment in which political divisions are manifesting at the community level and are breaking down traditional community/collective coping mechanisms. Agencies are realizing the inherent value of engaging at the community level and utilizing community capital as an entry point for engagement.

Local agencies are calling for international agencies to support the mobilization of local agencies' capacity-building and to pursue long-term environment building approaches. In the current phase of return and rehabilitation, local agencies see an urgent need for international agencies to support local agencies to create attitudinal change in divided communities. Local agencies highlighted the challenges of engaging in a context of 'generalized' violence and understanding the meaning of violence in a Sri Lankan context, '[international] agencies don't see the Sinhala-Tamil dynamic as reproducing violence; they do not understand spirals of personalized violence'.[69] Protection-sensitive programming should closely consider linkages with peacebuilding in a context of protracted conflict.

There is a vital space for protection and human security at a very local level. Building community resilience to safeguard against the breakdown in community

68 Interview, Trincomalee, 10 October 2007.

69 Interview, Local NGO, Trincomalee, 17 October 2007.

protection strategies is necessary in the context of political factionalism and fractured communities. Creating shared mechanisms and interests between and within communities should be incorporated into approaches to build opportunities for resilience in divided communities. Agencies have an opportune moment to incorporate preventative action and contingency planning in the reconstruction of return areas, for example, creating shared community facilities to build trust. Further, the 'Recovery and Rebuilding' phase of the conflict provides an inlet for packaging programmes in economic objectives, such as creating joint or mixed livelihood programmes between different communities as a protection mechanism to prevent inter-ethnic and intra-ethnic violence. Threats need to be analysed at a village level. Agencies are realizing that taking a longer-term commitment to particular villages rather than pursuing available spaces (such as priority areas for the government) for intervention enables agencies to more effectively understand the threats, vulnerabilities and capacities of communities to build locally resonant approaches. Partnership with CBOs ensures genuine commitment to the community: 'they [CBOs] are not part of the local NGO industry game, they will not leave'.[70] However, international agencies need to remain aware of the potential politicization of local agencies in the ethnicized and politically fractured environment.

Often perceived success can be divorced from the realities of engaging with civilian insecurities. Agency pressure to demonstrate success to donors prevents agencies from approaching protection as a *process*. Longer-term engagement is necessary to address entrenched features of the protection environment to support attitudinal change: 'it is difficult to influence behaviour; it takes time'.[71] A commitment to capacity-building by local authorities and humanitarian agencies is essential. As one international agency reflected, 'Consider us [international agencies] short term, consider them [local agencies] long term'.[72] Local agencies want stronger and genuine partnerships: 'we expect mutual partners; not only funds, not only an outsider observing everything'.[73] International agencies must communicate clearly their role and limitations in order to ensure accurate expectations and facilitate greater collaboration between international and local protection actors. Most crucially, internal displacement in Sri Lanka exists in the broader context of a protracted condition of insecurity. The failure of *lasting* solutions in the absence of a transformative peace process requires humanitarian agencies to understand the discreet phases of renewed displacement against a backdrop of the longer-term, unresolved nature of the conflict that continues to (re)produce insecurities.

70 Interview, INGO, Trincomalee, 16 October 2007.

71 Interview, local agency, Trincomalee, 17 October 2007.

72 Interview, UN agency, Trincomalee, 10 October 2007.

73 Interview, Trincomalee, 17 October 2007.

Bibliography

Aeschlimann, A. (2005), 'Protection of IDPs: An ICRC View', *Forced Migration Review*, Supplement, October.

Brookings-Bern Project on Internal Displacement (2007a), *When Displacement Ends: A Framework for Durable Solutions* (Washington DC: Brookings Institution).

Brookings-Bern Project on Internal Displacement (2007b), 'Expert Seminar on Protracted IDP Situations', Geneva, 21–22 June, available at <http://www.brookings.edu/events/2007/0621_displacement.aspx>.

Brun, C. (2003), 'Local Citizens or Internally Displaced Persons? Dilemmas of Long Term Displacement in Sri Lanka', *Journal of Refugee Studies* 16: 4, 376–97.

Centre for Policy Alternatives (2006), *War, Peace and Governance in Sri Lanka: Overview and Trends 2006* (Colombo: Centre for Policy Alternatives).

Darcy, J. (2007), 'Political and Humanitarian Perspectives on the Protection of Civilians', paper prepared for HPG Geneva Roundtable on Protection, 22 January, available at <http://www.odi.org.uk/hpg/meetings/protection_conceptsnote.pdf>, accessed 24 September 2007.

DeVotta, N. (2007), 'Sinhalese Buddhist Nationalist Ideology: Implications for Politics and Conflict Resolution in Sri Lanka', *Policy Studies* 40.

Foundation for Coexistence (2004), 'Ethnic Relations and Human Security in Eastern Sri Lanka', Report (Washington: Asia Foundation).

Goodhand, J. and Lewer, N. (1999), 'Sri Lanka, NGOs and Peace-Building in Complex Emergencies', *Third World Quarterly* 20: 1, 69–87.

Hyndman, J. (2007), 'The Securitization of Fear in Post-Tsunami Sri Lanka', *Annals of the Association of American Geographers* 97: 2, 361–72.

Inter-Agency Standing Committee (IASC) (2006), 'Task Force on Collaborative Approaches to Security, Saving Lives Together: A Framework for Improving Security Arrangements Among IGOs, NGOs and UN in the Field', prepared by a sub-working group of the IASC Task Force (led by InterAction and UNICEF).

Inter-Agency Standing Committee (IASC) (2007a), 'Conflict-Related Internal Displacement in Sri Lanka: A Study on Forced Displacement, Freedom of Movement, Return and Relocation', Report covering April 2006–April 2007 and Addendum covering April–July 2007.

Inter-Agency Standing Committee (IASC) (2007b), 'Benchmarks for Durable Solutions for Internally Displaced Persons' (Washington, DC: Brookings Institution).

International Crisis Group (2006), 'Sri Lanka: The Failure of the Peace Process', Crisis Group Asia Report No. 124, 28 November.

International Crisis Group (2007a), 'Sri Lanka: Muslims Caught in the Crossfire', Asia Report No. 134, 29 May.

International Crisis Group (2007b), 'Sri Lanka's Human Rights Crisis', Crisis Group Asia Report No. 135, 14 June.

International Crisis Group (2008), 'Sri Lanka's Return to War: Limiting the Damage', Crisis Group Asia Report No. 146, 20 February.

IRIN (2007), 'Sri Lanka, UN Urges Investigations of Deaths and More Security for Aid Workers', UN Office for the Coordination of Humanitarian Affairs, 7 August, available at <http://irinnews.org/PrintReport.aspx?ReportId=73621>, accessed 7 December 2007.

Jane's Security News (2007), 'Group Profile: Liberation Tigers of Tamil Eelaam (LTTE)', 27 March 2007, available at <http://www.janes.com/security/international_security/new/jwit/jwit070327_1_n_shtml>, accessed 14 November 2007.

Jayasekara, S. (2007), 'LTTE Fundraising and Money Transfer Operations', Unpublished Paper presented at the International Conference on Countering Terrorism in Colombo, 18–20 October 2007.

Loescher, G. and Milner, J. (2005), 'Protracted Refugee Situations: Domestic and International Security Implications', Adelphi Paper 375 (London: International Institute for Strategic Studies).

Macrae, J. and Harmer, A. (2004), 'Beyond the Continuum: An Overview of the Changing Role of Aid Policy in Protracted Crises', HPG Report 18 (London: Humanitarian Policy Group, Overseas Development Institute).

Mahoney, L. (2006), *Proactive Presence: Field Strategies for Civilian Protection* (Geneva: Centre for Humanitarian Dialogue).

McGilvray, D. (1999), 'Tamils and Muslims in the Shadow of War: Schisms or Continuity?', in S. Gamage and I.B. Watson (eds), *Conflict and Community in Contemporary Sri Lanka: 'Pearl of the East' or 'Island of Tears'?* (New Delhi: Sage), 217–28.

McGilvray, D. (2001), 'Tamil and Muslim Identities in the East' in *A History of Ethnic Conflict in Sri Lanka, Recollection, Reinterpretation and Reconciliation*, Marga Monograph Series No. 24 (Colombo: Marga Institute).

Pantuliano, S. and O'Callaghan, S. (2006), 'The 'Protection Crisis': A Review of Field-based Strategies for Humanitarian Protection in Darfur', Humanitarian Policy Group (HPG) Discussion Paper (London: Humanitarian Policy Group, Overseas Development Institute).

Peebles, P. (1990), 'Colonisation and Ethnic Conflict in the Dry Zone of Sri Lanka', *The Journal of Asian Studies* 49: 1, 30–55.

Philipson, E. and Thangarajah, Y. (2005), *The Politics of The North-East. Part of the Sri Lanka Strategic Conflict Assessment 2005*, Vol. 4, Six Part Series (Colombo: Asia Foundation).

Rajasingham-Senanayake, D. (2002), 'Identity on the Borderline: Modernity, New Ethnicities and the Unmaking of Multiculturalism in Sri Lanka', in N. Silva (ed.), *The Hybrid Island* (London: Zed Books).

Rampton, D. (2007), 'Development, Humanitarianism and the Spectre of Colonization in the Eastern Province', Paper for International Seminar,

Humanitarian Action in the 'Undeclared War' in Sri Lanka, Geneva, 22 September.

Saravanamuttu, P. (2004), 'Governance in Plural Societies, Sri Lanka', in R. Thakur and E. Newman (eds), *Broadening Asia's Security Discourse and Agenda: Political, Social, and Environmental Perspectives* (Tokyo: United Nations University Press).

Schrijvers, J. (1999), 'Fighters, Victims and Survivors: Constructions of Ethnicity, Gender and Refugeeness among Tamils in Sri Lanka', *Journal of Refugee Studies* 12: 3, 307–33.

Slim, H. and Bonwick, A. (2005), *Protection. An ALNAP Guide for Humanitarian Agencies, Active Learning Network for Accountability and Performance in Humanitarian Action* (London: ALNAP).

Sorensen, B.R. (2001), 'Sri Lanka: Developing New Livelihoods in the Shadow of War. Displaced, Relocated and Resettled Muslims', in M. Vincent and B.R. Sorensen (eds), *Caught Between Borders: Response Strategies to the Internally Displaced* (London: Pluto Press and Norwegian Refugee Council).

UN Security Council (2007), 'Report of the Secretary General on the Protection of Civilians in Armed Conflict', S/2007/643, 28 October.

UNHCR (2000), *The State of the World's Refugees* (New York: Oxford University Press).

UNHCR (2006), Internally Displaced Person (IDPs) Working Group, 2006 Workplan and Supporting Documents (unpublished, Colombo), May.

UNHCR (2007), 'Sri Lanka', in *UNHCR Global Appeal 2008–2009*, available at <http://www.unhcr.org/publ/PUBL/474ac8dc0.pdf>, accessed 21 February 2008.

United Nations Office for the Coordination of Humanitarian Aid (UN-OCHA) (1998), 'Guiding Principles on Internal Displacement', available at <http://www.reliefweb.int/ocha_ol/pub/idp_gp/idp.html>.

Uyangoda, J. (2007), 'Ethnic Conflict in Sri Lanka: Changing Dynamics', *Policy Studies* 32.

Chapter 6

The Case of the Afghan Refugee Population: Finding Durable Solutions in Contested Transitions

Susanne Schmeidl and William Maley[1]

Introduction

After 30 years of turbulence and vast repatriation efforts, Afghanistan still tops the world's list of sources of forced migration. At the height of the refugee crisis, Afghans accounted for roughly 60 per cent of the entire world refugee population. Mobility has become not only a key livelihood and survival strategy for many Afghans, but an integral part of their lives. Possibly two out of three Afghans have been displaced at least once; families have scattered across countries and continents.

After an overview of the political/military context and resultant displacement, this chapter traces the current situation of return in a country undergoing a political transition. In addition to the two neighbouring countries of Iran and Pakistan, Western countries also push for 'voluntary' return in response to domestic concerns regarding asylum seekers, and as a sign that all is not yet lost in Afghanistan. The use of 'voluntary' in this context, however, is problematic, especially when the bulk of the remaining refugees have lived most of their lives in exile and many have never set foot in their home country. Many returnees are caught in makeshift camps, squatter settlements, or ad hoc accommodation and they face renewed internal displacements due to insurgency violence, landlessness or natural disasters such as floods. Failures of physical, economic, social and political reconstruction, unfortunately, do not provide fertile ground for resolving the Afghan refugee situation any time soon. The current deteriorating security situation in Afghanistan, coupled with insufficient humanitarian access to vast parts of the country for the United Nations High Commissioner for Refugees (UNHCR) and other international actors, raises concerns about protection. If the situation spins further out of control, the country will be faced with yet another wave of forced migration.

1 The authors would like to thank Alessandro Monsutti, Pierre Centlivres, Micheline Centlivres-Demont, Salvatore Lombardo, Ewen McLeod, Ceri Oeppen and Zuzanna Olszewska for helpful comments on this chapter.

We will examine the sustainability of 'voluntary return' as a preferred durable solution for Afghan refugee communities against the backdrop of national and regional political and security considerations. Increasingly, Afghan refugees have become a political football for the regional powers; the two major host countries (Pakistan and Iran) have made the return of Afghan refugees part of their regional as well as international policies. The transitional nature of the Afghan refugee situation, in the end, may show that voluntary return is anything but a durable solution at this juncture and that 'sustainability' may not equate to returning to places of origin, highlighting the need to begin exploring alternatives for much of the remaining refugee population. Sustainability of return needs careful consideration in light of the limited absorptive capacity of Afghanistan.

Overview of the context

Demographics and division

Presently, the Afghan population is estimated at something over 20 million, but no comprehensive population census has ever been carried out (with the last one in 1979 still being the most accurate one). The population is segmented on ethnic, sectarian, geographical, occupational, and life-experience lines. Ethnographers have identified more than 50 ethnic groups (Orywal 1986; Jawad 1992; Schetter 2003) but there are four dominant ones: ethnic Pashtuns (40 per cent), Tajiks (25 per cent), and Hazara and Uzbeks tied for third place (9 per cent each). Within these ethnic groups there are further divisions. Pashtuns are divided into two big tribal confederations (Ghilzai and Durrani) with additional tribal sub-divisions (Glatzer 1998; 2001; 2002). The majority languages are Pashtu and Dari (Afghan Persian), but many minority languages also prevail.

While almost all Afghans are Muslim, the population reflects the familiar Sunni–Shiite division, with around 80 per cent Sunni and the rest Shia (Hazara are mostly Shia). Within these groups there are significant further branches, such as 'Twelvers' (also the dominant sect in Iran) and Ismailis among the Shia. In addition, ideological or attitudinal differences exist, notably between intellectual and 'village' Islam (Saikal and Maley 1991).

There was, and still is, also a very noteworthy difference in orientation between rural dwellers and the residents of cities: the lives of the former tended to revolve around cyclical forms of economic activity associated with agriculture or pastoralism, while the latter were more likely to be involved in secondary or tertiary industries, or to be employees of state bureaucracies. There are also Kuchi (nomadic pastoralists of Afghanistan) who may total anywhere from 600,000 to 2.5 million.[2] The Afghan wars, but also years of drought, diverted the rural and

2 According to a 2005 *National Multi Sectoral Assessment on Kuchi* conducted by the Ministry of Rural Rehabilitation and Development in close collaboration with the Ministry

nomadic populations towards semi-urban and sedentary lifestyles both in refugee camps and later, upon return home.

Historical background

In April 1978, a Communist coup led to a major slide to war; the situation was further aggravated by the Soviet invasion of Afghanistan in December 1979. By the beginning of the 1990s there were an estimated 6.2 million Afghans living as refugees outside the borders of their homeland (Colville 1997) out of a pre-war population estimated at just over 13 million (Eighmy 1990, 10). This refugee population was not created by steady accretion but paralleled the phases of conflict (Goodson 1998). Though some Afghans became refugees prior to the Soviet invasion in 1979, millions moved to Pakistan subsequently. As large numbers returned following the collapse of the Communist regime in April 1992, still others fled Kabul as rival *Mujahideen* factions bombarded the city. The emergence of the Taliban from 1994 created new incentives for flight, while others returned hoping for an end to arbitrary and fragmented rule (see Figure 6.1). The overthrow of the Taliban in late 2001 led to some additional forced migration, more than offset in 2002 when nearly two million refugees returned home (UNHCR 2007b).

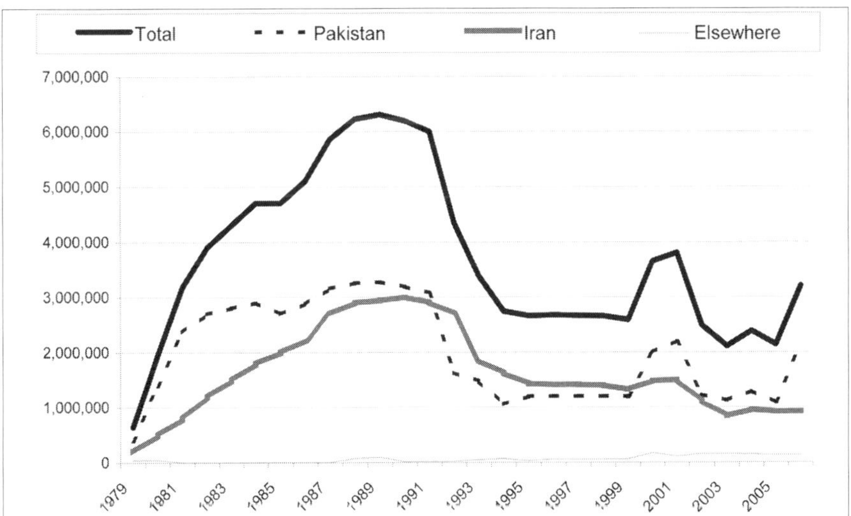

Figure 6.1 Afghan refugee population, 1979–2006
Source: UNHCR (Statistics of Population of Concern, various years).

of Frontiers and Tribal Affairs and the Central Statistics Office, a total of 2,426,304 Kuchi were identified, with the following breakdown: long-range migratory Kuchi (52 per cent), short-range migratory Kuchi (33 per cent) and settled Kuchi (15 per cent).

Displacement over time has varied in its precise form and character. Many Afghans have been internally displaced, some on numerous occasions. Others became refugees in neighbouring states, in some cases as refugees *sur place* (that is, they became refugees when they were outside Afghanistan), especially in Iran, and on other occasions as either 'anticipatory' refugees who fled in the early stages of upheaval with some resources or 'acute' refugees who left with little forewarning, mainly for Pakistan, and able to take only a few possessions (Kunz 1973). Smaller numbers moved on to countries of resettlement, adding substantially to the Afghan émigré communities in the United States, Germany, Australia, India, and the Russian Federation. With the passage of time, the consolidation of Afghan communities abroad, family reunification and marriage have led to new patterns of 'chain migration'. During the late 1990s, as the Taliban movement expanded in Afghanistan, some Afghans used smuggling networks to move abroad, fearing that adjacent countries would be increasingly inhospitable (Maley 2001).

Not all flows were necessarily driven purely by 'push factors'. Some Afghan communities had strong traditions of mobility to access labour markets in nearby states (Hanifi 2000; Monsutti 2005). For others, the flight of the Prophet Muhammad from Mecca to Medina in 622 CE, known as the *Hijra*, provided religious backing for flight in face of threats; indeed, the word *muhajirin*, commonly used amongst Muslims as a label for refugees, derives from the same Arabic root as the word *hijra* itself, and imports a rich range of positive connotations that the English word 'refugee' does not (Centlivres and Centlivres-Demont 1988c; Shahrani 1995). While reasons for flight were extremely complex (Guillo et al. 1983), and survey evidence points to a range of specific factors triggering or underpinning refugee movements (Connor 1987), the main cause of the Afghan refugee outflow in the 1980s was fear of physical insecurity. The bulk of movements to Pakistan (Sliwinski 1989a) came from Afghan provinces near the Durand Line (the boundary separating Pakistan from Afghanistan drawn by Sir Mortimer Durand in 1893, that divided the Pashtuns between the two territories) as the USSR sought by force to secure their clients from the threat of resistance coming from *Mujahideen* fighters operating from refugee camps in Pakistan. Figures on mortality in Afghanistan during the period of Soviet occupation underscore the rationality of flight as a strategy, as unnatural deaths in Afghanistan between 1978 and 1987 amounted to 876,825, or on average over 240 every day throughout the decade (Khalidi 1991).

Regional political and security dimensions

In the complex regional geopolitical situation, refugee populations serve as tools of neighbouring power interests. Pakistan, which after 1979 became the host for the largest single population of Afghan refugees, historically had an extremely tense relationship with Afghanistan (Grare 2003). Prior to the 1947 partition of India, the Afghan government helped foster claims of a right to 'self-determination' for Pashtuns in India under the rubric of a demand for a distinct unit to be called

'Pashtunistan'. Afghanistan was the one state to vote against the admission of Pakistan to the United Nations. From the 1940s to the 1970s, the issue flared from time to time, leading to a severing of diplomatic relations between Pakistan and Afghanistan between 1961 and 1963 (Maley 2002, 68–9; see also Qassem 2007).

The April 1978 coup d'etat, internal strife, and the subsequent Soviet invasion to shore up Communist rule under a reliable puppet triggered a deep chill in East–West relations (Westad 2005, 299–330) and provided Pakistan with an unprecedented opportunity 'to reshape its strategic environment' and become 'a frontline state, placed for the first time in its history at the top of America's strategic regional priorities' (Grare 2003, 67). Afghanistan became the site of the biggest proxy war between East and West in the last decade of the Cold War, with Pakistan facilitating financial support to the Afghan resistance. The historic 'Pashtunistan' dispute strongly disposed Pakistan to support more religiously radical Afghan resistance groups, seen as less likely to revive a territorial–nationalist dispute in the future.

Pakistan's involvement in supporting radical groups was somewhat blunted by the events of 11 September 2001, but not eliminated. Sanctuaries in Pakistan continue to sustain an active 'neo-Taliban' movement responsible for insurgency in southern Afghanistan. Indeed, in August 2007, Pakistani President Musharraf, speaking in Kabul, stated that 'The problem that you have in your region is because support is provided from our side' (Maley 2007, 5).

While this positioned Pakistan as a proactive regional actor in Afghanistan, other regional states had interests as well. Iran assumed a certain 'protective responsibility' with respect to Afghanistan's Shiite Muslim minority. In turn, fear that Afghanistan could fall under Iranian influence led states such as Saudi Arabia to support Sunni Muslim groups based in Pakistan. Individual Saudis, such as Osama Bin Laden, made their way to Peshawar in Pakistan where they supported Arab volunteers associated with radical Sunni resistance groups (Rubin 1997). Thus, Afghanistan became a theatre in which diverse rivalries – initially between the Soviet Union and its opponents, and then between states reflecting different strands of Islamic thinking – were played out.

War also distorted traditional lifestyles. Afghans inhabit simultaneously a multiplicity of social worlds, and circumstances may well influence which of these worlds is most powerful in shaping their responses to particular situations. Further, the importance of specific social cleavages is not fixed but variable, and this has particular pertinence to the prospects of securing durable solutions to refugee problems. For example, in regions in which ethnic differences were not exceedingly salient, recruitment practices of *Mujahideen* factions (and later the Taliban) along ethnic (and also tribal) lines escalated latent group tensions into conflicts or created new ones altogether. While Afghanistan has not experienced mass ethnic conflict, there have been some grim specific episodes that have left their mark on the psyches of different refugee groups. The Taliban, overwhelmingly from the Pashtun ethnic group, engaged in a number of massacres of ethnic Hazaras, who were not only distinctive in their physical appearance, but also largely Shia and thus exposed to charges of heresy from more extreme Taliban circles. On the other hand, Pashtuns from the north, descendants of settlers relocated there in the late nineteenth century (Tapper 1983), faced harassment and forced expulsion during the short rule of the *Mujahideen* government (1992–1996) when the Uzbek warlord Abdul Rashid Dostum controlled much of the region. This continued after 2001 when evidence surfaced that these Pashtuns fell victim to revenge attacks from victims of the Taliban, who saw them as having been complicit in earlier Taliban domination out of ethnic solidarity (International Crisis Group 2003).

Socio-economic and resource contexts

Afghanistan has long been one of the poorest countries in the world, and across a whole range of socio-economic indicators such as income per capita, life expectancy at birth, and maternal mortality, its performance is little short of catastrophic (Maley 2006, 79). Strong norms of reciprocity and social solidarity have historically helped to circumvent major crises such as widespread famine (except in the early 1970s), but the livelihoods of many Afghans are under constant pressure. Day-to-day survival depends on engaging in a multiplicity of economic activities, and occasional borrowing. Large numbers of Afghans have no defensible legal title to their ‘property’, and are unable to use it as collateral for borrowing; thus, much of the country’s wealth cannot be used to facilitate productive investment. Furthermore, the turmoil of the last 30 years has led to serious deterioration in infrastructure and capital, loss of skills, and major damage to the state’s capacity to enforce contracts.

Although the Afghan economy has never ‘collapsed’, the disruptions since 1978 have handicapped significant elements of the economy with little in the way of a banking system, increasing the significance of *hawala* informal money transfers (Monsutti 2005); poor infrastructure (creating local autarkies with consequent loss of potential gains from access to wider regional markets); and illegal opium crops. Afghanistan may be, or become, a ‘narco-state’ as the world’s largest opium producer (8,200 tons in 2007), reflecting a range of ‘opium economies’ with differing incentive structures at work (UNODC 2007). This requires a range of nuanced responses that take into account local specificities (Mansfield 2007).

Given the fragility of the Afghan economy as well as deteriorating security, the Afghan government has recently discouraged further repatriation, fearing disastrous consequences on top of Kabul’s enormously swollen population of over four million (one of the fastest-growing conurbations in the world). This has undermined the January 2006 Afghanistan Compact’s provisions for refugee repatriation, and raises the question of just how sustainable ‘return’ is likely to be.

Stakeholder analysis – roles, interests and approach

Stakeholders include the diverse Afghan refugees who are active agents in shaping their futures, the United Nations High Commissioner for Refugees (UNHCR) involved in refugee assistance and return, the two main countries hosting major Afghan refugee populations – Iran and Pakistan, and international actors with regional interests.

Support for Afghan refugees from Western countries, especially the US, was largely driven by a Cold War mentality of curbing Soviet expansion in line with the Carter Doctrine in the early 1980s and a much more forceful Reagan Doctrine in the mid-1980s, pursuant to which the US wanted to maintain a dominant position in the Persian Gulf region (Schöch 2008). Donor fatigue began to set in after the Soviet Union withdrew from Afghanistan in 1989 and the Cold War ended. Following the emergence of the Taliban, which the US initially tolerated, the US relinquished its weighty position in the region for a period of time (Gutman 2008), which it came to regret given its weak position when the 9/11 attacks occurred. The great interest of the US in Afghanistan was subsequently revived, and prompted the invasion by Coalition Forces (under US leadership) to overthrow the Taliban for having hosted *al-Qaeda* (Schmeidl 2007). Since its 'war on terrorism' started, the US has seen Afghanistan, and especially Pakistan, as major allies.

After the Bonn Agreement in December 2001, the International Security Assistance Force (ISAF), with 26 contributing nations in Afghanistan, entered the arena but was initially blocked from expanding beyond Kabul. The US introduced Provincial Reconstruction Teams (PRTs) at the end of 2002 to add a reconstruction element to the war on terrorism (Stapleton 2007a), and ISAF was put under NATO command and coordination in August 2003. There are currently 25 PRTs in Afghanistan, 11 led by the US (the largest donor country) and others led by various contributing nations (Maley 2006).

Refugee organizations

Afghan refugees have had dynamic social and political lives, albeit constrained by the unnatural milieu of the refugee camps in Pakistan, by broader resource scarcities, and by particular problems for women refugees (Dupree 1992; Centlivres-Demont 1993). Far from camps constituting an apolitical humanitarian space (Baitenmann 1990), they became important venues for political interests, where different Afghan actors struggled to achieve superordinate positions, and for nurturing 'refugee warriors'. The overall political agenda was displacing the Soviet Union and its Afghan Communist surrogates from positions of power (Centlivres and Centlivres-Demont 1988a; Terry 2002, 55–82; Lischer 2005, 44–72).

Refugee organizations mirrored Afghan traditional society where each village or community (*qaum*) usually had either appointed (*malek*) or inherited (*khan*) traditional leaderships that represent their *quams* to outsiders and the central government. Due to disruptions during displacement and enlistment of some leaders by the *Mujahideen*, new leaders, *rupiah maleks*, emerged who grew powerful mainly through controlling aid and the distribution of food (Centlivres and Centlivres-Demont 1988a; Centlivres and Centlivres-Demont 1988b; Centlivres 1993). *Maleks* were chosen by communities living in the refugee camps in part for their organizational and linguistic skills – such as speaking Urdu or English (Centlivres 1993, 28). Another tradition-oriented refugee organization revolved around conflict resolution through appointed committees of influential individuals (Centlivres 1993, 28) that mimicked the traditional conflict resolution mechanism of a *jirga* or *shura* in Afghanistan. If conflict involved outsiders, new leaders with technical and linguistic skills were called to the job.

Refugees in Pakistan were required to register with one of the seven Sunni *Mujahideen* parties which Pakistani authorities sanctioned (Schöch 2008). Thus, political parties of the Afghan resistance (Centlivres 1993) served as intermediaries in dealing with the refugees, mirroring the role of Afghan government officials such as the *arbab*, especially in dealing with Pakistani officials or in helping refugees secure access to official government relief. As a direct result, resistance parties were legitimized through 'enforced' support. Furthermore, several refugee camps were under the control of commanders of the Afghan resistance:

> A good example was the Jalozai camp, near Peshawar which was established in 1980–81 … by … Abdul Rasoul Sayyaf, the leader of the Ittihad-i Islami (Islamic Unity) Party … [and] became an important *mujaheddin* training camp, with arms and ammunition depots; barracks and family quarters; a medical college and hospital; schools and *madrassas*; and an office of Pakistan's Inter-Services Intelligence (ISI). (Turton and Marsden 2002, 11)

Not all refugee villages, however, were like this; others mainly functioned as safe havens for the families of the *Mujahideen* fighters.

Afghan non-governmental organizations (NGOs) provided another form of refugee organization for middle class urban refugees willing neither to join *Mujahideen* factions nor emigrate to the West and became an alternative way to channel assistance to the refugee community, especially in the areas of health and education, sometimes responding more to donor than to community needs (Azarbaijani-Moghaddam 2002). As with the *Mujahideen* parties, humanitarian assistance mixed with political goals.

Countries of asylum

Iran 'Although Iran was a signatory to both the Refugee Convention and its subsequent protocol, it chose to give Afghans the status of *mohajerin*, or people who seek exile for religious reasons' (Turton and Marsden 2002, 14). Many refugees were actually guest workers whose status changed to that of refugees *sur place* as a result of the Soviet invasion of Afghanistan. Furthermore, arriving refugees were only housed for short periods in transit camps before moving into wider society. Absorption into local labour markets was facilitated by the sharing of the Persian language between the hosts and the bulk of the refugees in Iran. While these factors may have contributed to Iran receiving less attention than Pakistan, the most important reason for sidelining Iran may have been its regional and international politics and standing. Shortly after the start of the Afghan crisis, the 1979 Iranian revolution brought an Islamic radical regime to power, and with it, Iran fell out of favour with Western countries, particularly the US (Benard and Khalilzad 1984). Thus, even though Iran hosted nearly as many Afghan refugees as Pakistan, and 'Afghan refugees in Iran comprised one of the world's largest refugee populations', it did so largely without international assistance (UNHCR 2000, 117). The same year as the 1979 Iranian revolution, Iran also witnessed the US hostage crisis. The 'resulting tensions in the relationship between Iran and the West probably explain why Iran did not, at least initially, seek international assistance in dealing with the influx of refugees' (Turton and Marsden 2002, 11). Under pressure from Shiite refugees from Iraq, Iran did request assistance from UNHCR in 1980 (UNHCR 2000). However, 'International assistance to Iran was not forthcoming … and UNHCR wrestled with the disparity between the international response to the refugee crises in Pakistan and Iran' (UNHCR 2000). According to UNHCR (2000), Pakistan received in excess of US$1 billion over the course of 20 years (1979–1997) while Iran had to be content with a mere US$150 million (UNHCR 2000, 118).

Wilkinson (1997, 15) observed that 'until now, Iran has been fiercely proud of its ability to handle the refugee influx and consequently has limited both the international and NGO presence in the country'. However, impatient with the duration of displacement due to lack of improvement in Afghanistan, from 1997 the Iranian government 'refused to register new arrivals from Afghanistan, and the police have stepped up their random questioning of Afghans in the street', considering most Afghans as illegal immigrants (Turton and Marsden 2002, 15). Furthermore, in response to US pressure over Iran's uranium enrichment programme, some circles in Iran may wish to stir up trouble in Afghanistan in order to send a message to Washington of the risks of pushing Iran too far.

These all may be contributing factors for Iran's pursuing a policy of forced return. Since April 2007, the Iranian government has moved actively to expel Afghans who lack formal papers permitting them to reside in Iran. Many are now housed in IDP camps near Herat, and some reports suggest that their ranks comprise a significant number of ethnic Pashtuns, whose anger at their precipitate expulsion from Iran has been a recruiting boon for the Taliban movement in the hitherto relatively stable area of western Afghanistan. According to a recent IRIN (2008) report, Iran deported some 360,000 Afghans in 2007, including during the worst winter the region has seen in years (IRIN, 17 February 2008).[3] Even though 'the majority of deportees were single males, the humanitarian situation of over 4,500 affected families made it a politically sensitive issue in Afghanistan' (UNHCR 2007c, 257).

Pakistan Even though Pakistan is not a party to the 1951 *Convention Relating to the Status of Refugees* or its 1967 *Protocol*, in recognition of its role as host for millions of refugees, Pakistan is nonetheless a member of the Executive Committee of the Office of the United Nations High Commissioner for Refugees.[4] Although Pakistan proved notably hospitable in a macrocosmic sense, accommodating refugee numbers on a scale that puts to shame wealthier countries seeking to block the arrival of far smaller numbers of forced migrants, at the microcosmic level, the refugees found themselves acutely vulnerable to harassment by both Pakistani and Afghan forces. Refugee camps offered a difficult environment where women faced constraints they had not had to endure in Afghanistan (Boesen 1988; Dupree 1992; Centlivres-Demont 1993), where many petty irritants blighted refugees' daily lives (Saikal and Maley 1986), and where the milieu offered easy access for those seeking to mobilize and utilize a socially dislocated generation of young men ripe for recruitment (Maley 1998).

Pakistan's policy towards Afghan refugees needs to be seen in its historical and geopolitical setting, both vis-à-vis India, and also Afghanistan itself, possibly linked to Pakistan's political quest for 'strategic depth' in the region (see Rubin et al. 2001, 7). Initially, Afghan refugees were a means for Pakistan to become an important player in the region as the middleman between international assistance and the refugees. This helped legitimize the position of General Zia-ul-Haq, Pakistan's ruler from 1977 to 1988, who had been marginalized due to his seizing power and hanging his predecessor, Zulfikar Ali Bhutto (Grare 2003, 78). In essence, the more Afghan refugees Pakistan hosted, the more generous was the assistance from outsiders, and the more powerful Pakistan would become. Grare (2003, 68) labelled this behaviour 'calculated kindness'. By supporting refugee warrior communities (first the *Mujahideen* parties and later the Taliban), Pakistan could play a crucial role in determining who was to rule Afghanistan. In order to counterbalance India's power, Pakistan has always tried to create a friendly Islamic regime in Afghanistan. Pakistan's move to control the refugee camps through the flow of humanitarian assistance, however, was also linked to a fear that the refugees could become a geopolitical threat, mainly by awakening the old Pashtunistan question and thus creating unrest in Pakistan. At the same time, Pakistan could mend a previous breakdown in political relations with Afghanistan (Grare 2003, 65–66).

---

3 'Afghanistan mass deportation from Iran may cause crisis, official warns', 17 February 2008 (IRIN), available at <http://www.irinnews.org:80/Report.aspx?ReportId=76790>, accessed 21 May 2008.

4 <http://www.unhcr.org/excom/40111aab4.html>, accessed 29 February 2008.

During the war against the Soviet-backed Afghan government, there was an overlap between the agendas of the Afghan parties and their Pakistani hosts, although the Pakistanis tended to support religious radicals rather than more secularized nationalists and royalists from within the refugee ranks (Hussain 2005). With the collapse of the Communist regime in April 1992, some parties shifted the focus of their activities back to Afghanistan, while others saw their support bases erode. Nevertheless, refugee populations have remained significant recruiting grounds for the radical *Hezb-e Islami* ('Islamic Party') led by Gulbuddin Hekmatyar, for the Taliban in the mid-1990s, and for the current 'neo-Taliban' movement. The Taliban was not a traditional force, but emerged from a generation of refugees that neither knew their homeland nor peace (Rashid 2000, 32), and, like the *Mujahideen* parties before, also benefited directly from the patronage of Pakistan's Inter-Services Intelligence directorate (ISI).

Despite its assistance to Afghan *Mujahideen* parties, Pakistan was keen on calling the refugee camps Afghan refugee villages (ARV) in order to avoid the connotation of camps being linked to some form of military training. For the same reasons Pakistan discouraged actual training of the *Mujahideen* fighters in the camps (even so some did occur) so that it could 'deny any involvement in the war' (Grare 2003, 71). The relationship between Pakistan and the Afghan insurgency was akin to 'holding a tiger by its tail' with the risk of getting savaged when letting go. The recent displacements of Pakistanis into the eastern provinces of Afghanistan due to insecurity in the Federally Administered Tribal Areas (FATA) are a worrying step in this direction.

Even though the reception of Afghan refugees in Pakistan was initially very generous, the honeymoon slowly came to an end in the 1990s when it became apparent that there was no swift resolution in prospect for the refugee population's problems (Schmeidl 2002). The growing discontent with Afghan refugees can be attributed to several factors linked to the relative size of the refugee population, the duration of displacement, and national and regional political developments. First, the sheer size and length of displacement meant that many Afghan refugees outstayed the traditional religious and tribal hospitality of Muslim countries (Rogers 1987; Centlivres and Centlivres-Demont 1988b). The longer refugees stayed, the greater the environmental impact (in the form, for example, of deforestation around camps) and the higher the stress on Pakistan's infrastructure and resources such as schools, hospitals, land, and water (Grare 2003, 63–4). According to Centlivres (1993, 33), the Pakistani government and population held Afghan refugees accountable for ecological disturbances, rising prices, spreading diseases, and stress on the demographic balance.

Second, initial massive international assistance turned into donor fatigue shortly after the Cold War incentive to finance the *Mujahideen* resistance fighters vanished with the withdrawal of Soviet forces from Afghanistan in 1989. Assistance to Afghan refugees began to decline in the 1990s and only picked up again at the end of 2001 when, with the fall of the Taliban regime, massive repatriation was anticipated (Margesson 2007). Turton and Marsden (2002, 15) consider the aid decline 'perhaps the most important reasons for the change in attitude' by the government of Pakistan towards Afghan refugees, as it meant a burden shifting from rich Western states onto its own shoulders.

A third factor was resource competition between refugees and the host population (over water, firewood and employment). As Afghan refugees initially received international assistance, many low-skilled Pakistani labourers were resentful that Afghans benefited from the international humanitarian sector while seemingly draining scarce Pakistani economic resources at the same time. This was especially felt in the North West Frontier Province (NWFP), near the border between Afghanistan and Pakistan, where Afghan refugees were concentrated.[5]

Later on, issues of insecurity were added to this long list, such as 'Peshawar's and other cities' growing social ills, including crime, the widespread availability of weapons, drug abuse, prostitution, and the decline in the Pakistan economy' (Ruiz 2001, 4; see also Cheema 1988; Grare 2003). Indeed, Afghan refugees did move frequently between Pakistan and Afghanistan with Pashtuns in particular continuing traditional trade networks, and the *Mujahideen* resistance fighters and later also the Taliban constituting a refugee warrior community that operated out of refugee camps. Furthermore, 'the war in Afghanistan introduced massive quantities of small arms into Pakistan and provided capital for investment in smuggling' (Rubin et al. 2001, 9). More recently, when the Pakistani government increasingly came under international pressure over the growing insurgency in Afghanistan, it was easy for the Pakistani government to make refugees the scapegoats for Pakistan's internal trouble and its own failure to curb the growth of fundamentalism within its borders, as well as to cover up for its own contribution to the problem through its continuing to support the Taliban. While contemporary insurgency fighters in Afghanistan have links to some refugee camps in Pakistan (such as the Chaghi and Gerdi Zangal camps in Baluchistan), blaming an entire refugee population is far-fetched, especially as camp closures so far have not lead to a reduction of instability in Pakistan or in insurgency activity in Afghanistan. Both have likely increased in the past year despite camp closures. The December 2007 assassination of former Pakistani Prime Minister Benazir Bhutto that plunged Pakistan into an internal turmoil unfortunately contributed further to the negative trend of scapegoating refugees.

5 Afghan refugees, who had initially lived mainly in the rural area of the NWFP, began to move into the urban areas of Peshawar (creating an entire suburb – Hayatabad – of Afghan refugees), but also Islamabad and the economic centre of Karachi in the south of Pakistan. This made Karachi and Peshawar the cities with the largest Pashtun populations outside Afghanistan (Rubin 2000; Ruiz 2001). While they boosted the economy by opening small businesses and becoming a source of cheap labour (Ruiz 2001, 4), many Pakistanis blamed the refugees for driving up the price of rental accommodation (Cheema 1988). In 1985, one in every six people in the NWFP was an Afghan refugee (Centlivres and Centlivres-Demont 1988b, 72).

All this influenced Pakistan's new stringent policy of 'voluntary' return of Afghan refugees, mainly via the forced closure of refugee camps, starting in 2004 with camps in South Waziristan. The goal, which was not achieved, was to close all camps by late 2007. UNHCR appealed to the Pakistani government not to close refugee camps before mid-2008 in order to avoid a humanitarian crisis in Afghanistan. This may harden Pakistan's negative policy toward Afghan refugees. However, the aftermath of the February 2008 Pakistani elections may also possibly preoccupy the Pakistani government to the extent that the repatriation programme may be less forcefully pursued. Regardless of the roles Pakistan's various regimes had in creating and supporting the Taliban, the US chose to stand behind Pakistan's policies, including those of scapegoating refugees for allegedly contributing to insecurity and terrorism. Recent events in Pakistan, however, have shaken US strategic thinking.

The United Nations High Commissioner for Refugees

UNHCR entered the picture after Pakistan called for assistance in 1979. (In Iran, UNHCR was not permitted to work until 1983.) It opened its first permanent office in Peshawar in 1980 (Grare 2003, 73) and five years later in Iran (Abbasi-Shavazi and Glazebrook 2006). As aid was administered through the government of Pakistan, UNHCR was never able to act in a fully independent manner. Similarly, in Iran, UNHCR's access was initially limited to specific settlements only. Nevertheless, despite a more limited role in Iran, the UNHCR role was less politicized there than in Pakistan.

A major point of contention between UNHCR and the government of Pakistan was an early and ongoing disagreement over how to determine refugee status, as Pakistan took registration through a *Mujahideen* party as the basis for providing government assistance (Schöch 2008). This created ongoing tensions between UNHCR, Pakistan and the Afghan *Mujahideen* parties, with UNHCR generally losing out (Grare 2003, 74). A second problem was the channelling of aid via middlemen in refugee camps (see our earlier discussion) handing control over camps to the resistance factions that, in effect, militarized the 'refugee camps' (Turton and Marsden 2002, 11). Loescher observed that 'UNHCR and the World Food Program had no way of ensuring that food went exclusively to non-combatants' (Loescher 1993, 88–9). Donors looked the other way when the Pakistani intelligence service operated in refugee camps and controlled international assistance funds (see Zolberg et al. 1989; Rashid 2000; Turton and Marsden 2002). This went as far as refugee villages boasting 'tanks and heavy artillery' (UNHCR 2000, 248).

Terry (2002, 55) criticizes the absence of 'debate concerning the ethical issues … or the implications for the safety of the refugees' regarding such an acceptance by the aid community that refugee camps were used by resistance fighters. Schöch (2008) argues that UNHCR was caught in a 'typical humanitarian dilemma' forcing it to accept 'infringement' of its principles in order to continue its work and provide assistance to refugees. It appears that this may have set a precedent for how host (but also donor) countries thought they could influence UNHCR's action and assistance in the region, as currently UNHCR seems caught in a very similar dilemma to that which existed 20 years ago – having to compromise principles to continue receiving assistance to aid Afghan refugees. The only difference may be that, with the current repatriation programme, UNHCR found itself 'alone on the dance floor' and unable to forge timely and effective partnerships with development organizations to ensure the successful 'reintegration' of refugees (Turton and Marsden 2002, 36; see also UNHCR 2006c):

> Recognizing that tensions would eventually emerge over the scope and duration of the agreements on voluntary repatriation, [UNHCR] launched a policy initiative in mid-2003 to explore more comprehensive approaches. While supporting voluntary return as the preferred durable solution, it argued that a purely humanitarian and refugee-oriented perspective would be insufficient to address the more complex challenges of development, poverty, migration and demography that have emerged.

Afghanistan currently is the second largest operation for UNHCR after Chad, and certainly the biggest in the Asia Pacific, even bigger than Iraq. In the Global Appeal for 2008–2009, the main focus is still on repatriation of refugees, but emphasis is also given to dealing with the IDP problem inside Afghanistan. This is reflected in the distribution of funds shown in Table 6.1, with more monies going to Afghanistan than to Iran and Pakistan even though they continue to host the bulk of the remaining refugee populations. This is despite UNHCR's recognizing that the 'deterioration in the security situation over the last two years, compounded by the increase in poppy cultivation, threatens to overshadow the progress that has been made' – although it does recognize that 'maintaining the momentum of the voluntary repatriation programme and ensuring sustainable reintegration will likely pose even greater challenges in the years to come' (UNHCR 2007a, 256). Already in 2004, UNHCR acknowledged that 'challenges in Afghanistan are such that even an extension of existing arrangements for repatriation *sine die* may resolve neither the immediate tensions between the rate of return and absorption capacity inside Afghanistan, nor provide a definitive solution' (UNHCR 2004a, 2). As such, UNHCR considers that 'natural repatriation' has come to a halt, with future returns likely to respond mainly to push factors.[6]

6 Email exchange with UNHCR official in Afghanistan, 27 January 2008.

Table 6.1 UNHCR Global Appeal 2008–2009: South-West Asia (USD)

	2008	2009	Total
Afghanistan	$49,871,900	$50,595,410	$100,467,310
Pakistan	$18,374,173	$18,884,942	$37,259,115
Iran	$12,376,669	$12,273,117	$24,649,786
Regional	$120,000	$412,962	$532,962
Total	**$80,742,742**	**$82,166,431**	**$162,909,173**

Source: UNHCR Global Appeal 2007a.

There was early concern 'that large numbers of returns to a situation in which these returns cannot be sustained will be detrimental both to the safety and human rights of returnees as well as to the long-term reconstruction of Afghanistan' (Amnesty International 2003, 6). Still, donor fatigue and host country pressure, coupled with seeing large-scale repatriation 'as a way of boosting the legitimacy of a fledgling state apparatus, struggling to exert its authority in a situation where power is still contested', may have forced UNHCR in 2002 to embrace return as a preferred durable solution for Afghan refugees despite a recognition that repatriation aid was 'in the best interests neither of the majority of its intended beneficiaries nor of the long term reconstruction of Afghanistan' (Turton and Marsden 2002, 35, 56). UNHCR let its concerns be known by only '*facilitating*' and not '*promoting*' return to Afghanistan (Amnesty International 2003). Yet such a distinction may be difficult to uphold in a context where both host countries (Iran and Pakistan) forcefully promote refugee return while the remaining refugees have no strong desire to return.

Even before the assassination of Benazir Bhutto, UNHCR was struggling for humanitarian space in Afghanistan, and was not optimistic that it would have much political space to manoeuvre in Pakistan for the next three to five years.[7] With the assassination, this period of uncertainty may prove to be even longer. One could argue that UNHCR is merely trying to sit out a difficult political situation, especially in Pakistan. On the one hand, UNHCR opposes Pakistan's policy orientation on 'principled protection and practical grounds'; on the other hand, it seeks positive opportunities on which it can build, hoping that powerful international actors will pick up and support its concerns.[8] A UNHCR official in Afghanistan described their current work mainly as reactive, struggling to put out one fire after the other.[9]

This, however, may force UNHCR to go along with the political games played by both Iran and Pakistan, possibly becoming hostage to them or even an

7 Interview with UNHCR official, Kabul, Afghanistan, 11 November 2007.

8 Interview with UNHCR official, Kabul, Afghanistan, 11 November 2007 and follow-up commentary via email 16 February 2008.

9 Interview with UNHCR official, Kabul, Afghanistan, 11 November 2007.

accomplice to a repatriation scheme. Repatriation is questionable from a protection stance as well as from the perspective of sustainability and stability in Afghanistan. In 2004, Pakistan's forced closure of refugee camps in South Waziristan caught UNHCR off balance,[10] resulting in a situation where expulsion was accepted as 'voluntary return' in order that UNHCR could assist the refugees.[11] As a pragmatic approach seems to prevail, UNHCR may already have compromised its principles of protection by putting regional politics ahead of the rights and needs of refugees (something acknowledged by UNHCR officials on the ground).

All this clearly highlights the difficulty faced by an operational organization that has to stand for the rights of refugees while still having to function effectively on the ground (see Maley 2003). One has to understand that UNHCR, like the UN in general, is largely an organization influenced, at the very least, by the wishes and priorities of states, particularly donor and host states. Earlier in the history of the Afghan refugee crisis, it struggled to obtain funds for those displaced to Iran and encountered political obstacles. UNHCR once again seems caught in a difficult position where especially the US seems to be putting pressure on the organization to go along with Pakistan's repatriation programme.[12] This said, Turton and Marsden (2002, 56) find that 'UNHCR may have more leverage than it appears to think', especially with the growing humanitarianism and focus on responsibility to protect among Western states. Furthermore, Loescher (2001, 350) has argued that while state interests have shaped UNHCR as it is at the mercy of donor funds, it has never been fully a 'passive mechanism of states'.

The current situation of refugees and IDPs

Overview of the refugee population

According to the *UNHCR Global Appeal 2008–2009*, there are currently still three million Afghan refugees in exile, with two-thirds residing in Pakistan (2.1 million) and one-third in the Islamic Republic of Iran (915,000) (UNHCR 2007a, 257). This statistic already exposes the difficulty of 'sustainable return' to Afghanistan. Despite over five million reported or recorded returnees, the remaining refugee population seemed to remain stable or perhaps increased. Retrospectively, this led UNHCR to adjust the initial refugee population to 8 million, about 2 million

10 Information provided by email by UNHCR official in Afghanistan, 16 February 2008.

11 Discussions with UNHCR officials in 2004 when Pakistan closed refugee camps in South Waziristan and forced the residents over the border into the province of Paktika. While UNHCR assumed that return was forced, it went along with the official Pakistani policy that return was voluntary in order to be able to assist the refugees.

12 Interview with UNHCR official, Kabul, Afghanistan, 11 November 2007. It is important to note the strong alliance between Pakistan and the US.

higher than estimates in the past. While some ostensible 'growth' of a refugee population can be attributed to fertility and an inclusion of previously unregistered refugees (Kronenfeld 2008), a greater proportion was linked to the 'so-called "recycling" problem' – return and re-entrance into Pakistan or Iran in order to benefit more than once from return assistance packages (Turton and Marsden 2002, 20).[13] The practice of recycling by refugees here may seem less surprising – as it occurred during previous repatriation schemes (Centlivres 1993) – than UNHCR's readjusting their figures to such a high level, accepting refugee figures at face value rather than questioning them.

Afghan refugee populations outside Iran and Pakistan are much smaller, with over half residing in Europe (mainly in Germany, the Netherlands, the United Kingdom and Denmark, but also smaller countries such as Switzerland and Austria) and the other half in Australia and New Zealand, North America (USA and Canada), Russia, Central Asia, and India. According to Orywal (1993–94), for example, at the end of 1992 there were already more than 40,000 Afghans living in Germany. Early migration was largely limited to the wealthier and more highly educated urban population – many of whom had previous links to Western countries through having studied there (Boesen 1988; Centlivres and Centlivres-Demont 2000). Later on, family reunification schemes, but also smuggling and individual asylum applications, and to a lesser degree resettlement (see later discussion), completed the picture. Labour migrants are also mixed in with the refugees, showing the complexity of the situation. Nowadays, there are many Afghan migrant workers to be found in the Gulf States. Statistics are difficult to interpret, as Afghans in these countries are a mix of those who have been granted asylum and/or citizenship, and asylum seekers. According to UNHCR (2005b):

> since 1994, when the Taliban first emerged, some 238,000 Afghans have sought asylum in industrialized countries outside the region. Germany has received 50,000 since 1994. The next largest recipient is the Netherlands, which has received 36,000 in the same period, followed by the UK with 34,000, Austria with 31,500, Hungary with 13,500, and Denmark with 11,500.

The current figure for Afghan asylum seekers with pending status claims is 14,974 (UNHCR 2006b).[14]

---

13 In a recent registration process of Afghan refugees in Pakistan, however, only 5.4 percent of all remaining refugees admitted to having gone to Afghanistan and returned (Government of Pakistan 2007, 14).

14 In addition to Europe, North America (the USA and Canada) hosts about 27,000 Afghan refugees, with over half residing in Canada (UNHCR 2007b, i). Australia hosts some 7,000 Afghan refugees. The figure in India is disputed, and lies between 8,000–30,000 Afghan refugees, mainly of Hindu/Sikh origin. There are about 6,000 left in Central Asia (mainly Uzbekistan, Tajikistan, Turkmenistan and Kyrgyzstan), with a majority having served in the former Communist government or having fled more recent sectarian violence,

Afghan refugees in Pakistan

As noted earlier, Pakistan is not a party to the 1951 Refugee Convention (or related 1967 Protocol), and thus 'the 1946 Foreigners Act (amended 2000) remained the only law applying to refugees and asylum seekers even though it recognized no distinction between them and other foreigners'.[15] This provided Pakistan with some leverage in dealing with the refugees on its own terms, rather than having to adhere to international standards. Only in January 2007 did the Pakistani government register refugees in such a way as finally to give them a legal status for residing in Pakistan (UNHCR 2007a, 257).[16]

Initially, the bulk of Afghan refugees in Pakistan were housed in what were first called Refugee Tented Villages (RTVs) and then so-called Afghan Refugee Villages (ARVs) as with the passage of time they acquired a more permanent appearance and mud-brick structures replaced tents. Unlike other refugee situations, UNHCR was able to set up 345 official ARVs where the majority of refugees lived (Centlivres 1993, 14; UNHCR 2000, 116). According to Colville (1997), these refugee villages 'were not closed off from the outside world' and Afghan refugees 'were allowed to move freely ... [in order] to find work and set up businesses' (Colville 1997, 4). Some refugees, often those supported by funds from relatives abroad, moved to urban centres, especially Peshawar city, Rawalpindi, and Karachi, and prior to repatriation efforts, refugees living outside camps made up a majority of the remaining refugee population: 1.7 million out of 3.05 million (Collective for Social Science Research 2006, 3), many of them having acquired Pakistani IDP cards. By the time of the registration exercise of the government of Pakistan in 2007, this figure had moved closer together for the remaining population, with 55 per cent of all refugees living outside camps (1.2 million) and 45 per cent inside camps (976,605), suggesting a higher trend of repatriation among the non-camp population.[17]

Registered refugees in camps could access basic support supplied through the Commissionerate of Afghan Refugees of the North West Frontier Province,

---

therefore being unable to return, see IRIN (2003), 'Turkmenistan: Afghan refugees want third-country resettlement', 30 July 2003, available at <http://www.irinnews.org/report.aspx?reportid=20566>, accessed 4 January 2008, and IRIN (2004), 'Tajikistan: Focus on Afghan refugees', 16 February 2004, available at <http://www.irinnews.org/report.aspx?reportid=40399>, accessed 4 January 2008.

15 <http://www.refugees.org/countryreports.aspx?id=2013>, accessed 24 January 2008.

16 'The registration exercise … resulted in the issuance of Proof of Registration (PoR) documentation valid until 2009 to 2.15 million Afghans' (UNHCR 2007a, 257).

17 The majority of Afghan refugees in Pakistan live in two provinces bordering Afghanistan where the refugee camps are also located: the North West Frontier Province (NWFP, 64 per cent) and Balochistan (Quetta, 21 per cent). The rest lives in the urban centres of Punjab (Islamabad, 9 per cent) and Sindh (Karachi, 4 per cent). Currently, Afghans constitute six percent of NWFP's population, 5.9 per cent in Balochistan and 3.4 per cent in Islamabad (see Government of Pakistan 2007).

Balochistan, and Islamabad. While reports surfaced in the 1980s of multiple registrations that could have artificially inflated refugee numbers, to some extent this problem was offset by a countervailing phenomenon, namely the presence of unregistered refugees, including urban dwellers (see Farr 1985, 104–5; Dupree 1987; 1988). As a UNHCR (2007b, i) source put it, 'Before March 2005, ascertaining the number of Afghan refugees living in Pakistan was always at best a calculated guess'. In early 2005 (25 February–11 March), three years after massive repatriation to Afghanistan had begun, the Pakistani government, assisted by UNHCR, finally conducted the first ever census of Afghans who had arrived in Pakistan over the previous 25 years, leading to a subsequent registration process.[18] This prompted UNHCR to adjust its refugee figures from previous years as the census came up with three million Afghan refugees residing in Pakistan. As UNHCR figures were just shy of 1 million in 2004, an adjustment of close to 2 million had to be made (see UNHCR 2006a, 8).[19]

Information from the registration process reveals that the remaining Afghan refugee population in Pakistan mainly consists of young individuals whose families arrived in the country at the onset of the conflict in Afghanistan, with 77 per cent having arrived by the end of 1988 and 50 per cent in 1979–1980 alone (Government of Pakistan 2007, 13). A majority of the Afghan refugees who now remain in Pakistan were either born in exile (with 13 per cent being under the age of five, and 55 per cent 17 years or younger) or spent most of their lives there, thus having no experience of living in their 'home' country. This is also reflected in that about two-thirds of all refugees are single (66 per cent) and only 33 per cent are married (Government of Pakistan 2007, 11). Out of the 46.8 per cent women refugees, four per cent are single heads of households while 96 per cent are considered female dependents. Overall there are more male than female refugees 'across all age brackets' (Government of Pakistan 2007, 8).

The education level of remaining Afghan refugees is also very low with 71 per cent reporting no formal education (Government of Pakistan 2007, 8). Only 20 per cent of all refugees participate actively in the labour market, with 71 per cent having no effective monthly income, and 89 per cent reporting no skills (Government of Pakistan 2007, 8). Over half of all refugee households obtained their livelihoods from daily labour. Lack of skills makes return difficult and reduces the refugees'

18 Participation was mandatory for all Afghans who arrived in Pakistan after 1 December 1979, the month in which Soviet troops invaded Afghanistan and triggered a mass exodus of refugees to Pakistan and Iran. Only those who were included in the census would be eligible to be included in a registration, which was to provide some form of identification.

19 Earlier estimates never accounted for the increase of refugees from births and never captured out-of-camp populations living in cities, or the recycling of returnees (see Kronenfeld 2008). The US Committee for Refugees estimates that there are 2.4 million Afghan refugees in Pakistan, even though only 2.15 million were given registration cards: <http://www.refugees.org/countryreports.aspx?id=2013>, accessed 24 January 2008.

prospects of finding an adequate livelihood upon return (UNHCR 2004a). Because Afghan refugees in Pakistan came disproportionately from provinces in the south and east of the country, Pashtuns made up an overwhelming majority of the refugee population, well over 80 per cent (Sliwinski 1989b) and 93 per cent of the camp population (Government of Pakistan 2007, see Figure 6.2).

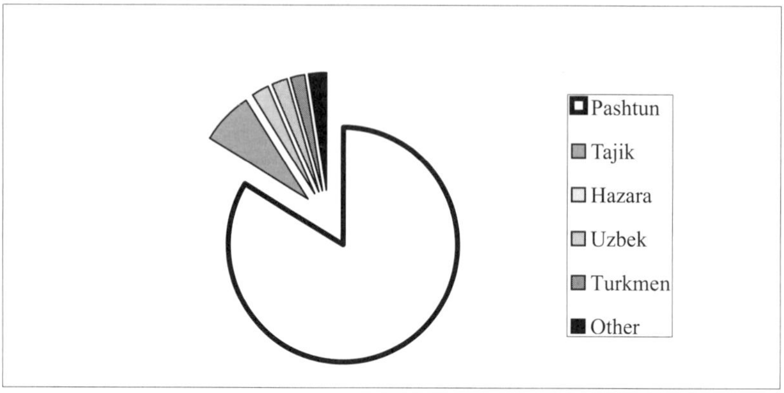

Figure 6.2 Documented Afghans in Pakistan by ethnicity (2007)
Source: Government of Pakistan (2007).

Afghan refugees in Iran

Afghans who migrated to Iran and settled there during the nineteenth and early twentieth centuries 'were naturalised as Iranian citizens and came to be classified as an ethnic group known as *Khawari* or *Barbari*' (Adelkhah and Olszewska 2007, 140). Later on Afghan migrant workers came to Iran after the 1960s, 'particularly during the terrible famine of 1971–1972' (Adelkhah and Olszewska 2007, 141). While Iran, as noted earlier, did ratify the 1951 Refugee Convention and the 1967 Protocol, and while Iran's 1963 Regulations Relating to Refugees (1963 Regulations) provided that 'Refugees should not be forcibly returned to the country where their life or freedom is endangered for political, racial or religious reasons or for their membership in a particular social group', Iran maintained some reservations including the provision in the 1979 Constitution that disallowed granting asylum to applicants if 'they are regarded as traitors and saboteurs'.[20] In 1991, when the Afghan refugee population in Iran peaked, the government finally decided to grant refugees *prima facie* status, issuing them with 'blue cards' (Adelkhah and Olszewska 2007, 141). This, however, did not mean that Iran gave

20 <http://www.refugees.org/countryreports.aspx?id=2001>, accessed 24 January 2008.

refugees many rights[21] (see also Centlivres 1989, 12 regarding labour restrictions of Afghan refugees).

A majority of the refugees lived in big cities or surrounding rural areas (Adelkhah and Olszewska 2007), although some resided along the border with western Afghanistan (Turton and Marsden 2002). According to Wilkinson (1997, 14), this absorption of the refugees 'into local communities [is] in sharp contrast to other regions', but also puts the burden for finding a place to stay on refugees, who tended to concentrate in urban areas in enclaves where other Afghans lived (Abbasi-Shavazi and Glazebrook 2006).

The lack of refugee camps and a refusal to register refugees who arrived after 1997 (Turton and Marsden 2002) makes the counting of refugees very difficult: according to Abbasi-Shavazi and Glazebrook (2006, 2), there are 'no official published statistics on the substantial number of Afghans in Iran who are neither registered nor counted as labour migrants'. A recent (late 2005/early 2006) government registration exercise (Amayesh-II), which 'aimed to ascertain the number of Afghans living in Iran', put the number of officially registered Afghan refugees in Iran at 920,000 (UNHCR 2007b, i). This, however, only included re-registered refugees who had arrived and registered prior to 2001, not counting new arrivals or those that never had been registered (Margesson 2007). UNHCR estimates another half a million Afghans among undocumented refugees and labour migrants (Abbasi-Shavazi and Glazebrook 2006, 2), while Iranian media sources estimate the number of illegal Afghans in Iran at one million (IRIN, 17 February 2008).[22]

Figure 6.3 provides an overview of Afghans in Iran by ethnicity, showing that, in contrast to Pakistan, there are very few Pashtun refugees while the Hazara (a minority in Afghanistan) and Persian speakers (Tajiks) make up the bulk (47 and 30 per cent respectively: Schetter 2003, 386).[23] This reflects the kinds of cultural–geographical 'pools' from which the refugee population was drawn. In contrast

21 'According to Iranian law, property ownership of foreigners is illegal, and such ownership by Afghans is uncommon. The exception to this is Mashad, where a system of informal property ownership has evolved that allows Afghans to informally purchase houses' (Abbasi-Shavazi and Glazebrook 2006, 4). Furthermore, 'Afghans are restricted to certain types of manual labour in Iran' (Abbasi-Shavazi and Glazebrook 2006, 7; see also Adelkhah and Olszewska 2007, 143). However, they were still able to find work, 'not least because so many Iranian men were conscripted to fight in the war against Iraq which began in September 1980' (UNHCR 2000, 116).

22 'Afghanistan mass deportation from Iran may cause crisis, official warns', 17 February 2008 (IRIN), available at <http://www.irinnews.org:80/Report.aspx?ReportId=76790>, accessed 21 May 2008.

23 The Ameyesh-II exercise shows that half of all Afghan refugees in Iran are from the northern provinces of Samangan, Faryab, Balkh and Badakhshan (26 per cent) and central provinces of Parwan, Kabul and Ghazni (24 per cent) (UNHCR 2007b). The remainder are from the western region (13 per cent, Herat and Farah) and south (8 per cent, Kandahar, Uruzgan), with another 8 per cent having fled the Central Highland region, which is the

to Afghan refugees in Pakistan who came from the Pashtun-dominated south, east or southeast, those in Iran originated largely from the northern (26 per cent), central (24 per cent) and western provinces (13 per cent) (UNHCR 2007b). 'The proportion of Hazaras in the ethnic breakdown had risen by 6 per cent since the beginning of 2004, suggesting that they are the ethnic group that is most reluctant to repatriate' (Adelkhah and Olszewska 2007, 143).

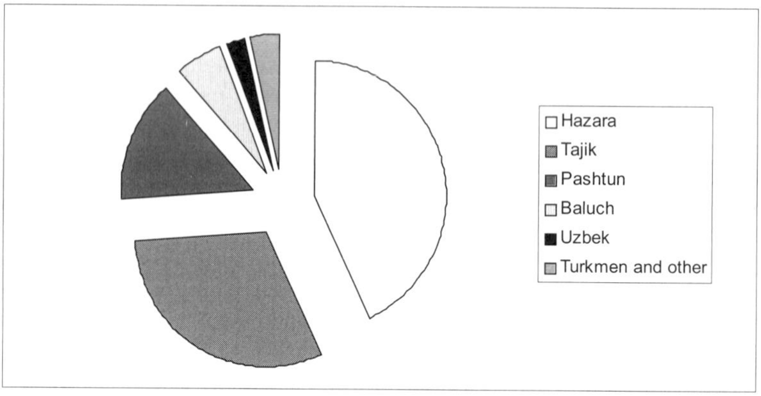

Figure 6.3 Documented Afghans in Iran by ethnicity (2005)
Source: AMAYESH-II registration exercise (Iran 2005/6).

In contrast to Pakistan, less than half (40 per cent) arrived by 1985, with 36 per cent having entered Iran after 1996 (Adelkhah and Olszewska 2007, 143). There are more men (56 per cent) than women (44 per cent) corresponding with earlier figures that put the percentage of adult men among Afghan refugees in Iran at over 60 per cent in the 1980s (Centlivres 1993). 'The Amayesh statistics indicate that the vast majority of registered refugees were living as families (89 percent), with a mean family size of 4.7 persons' (Adelkhah and Olszewska 2007, 143), which stands in contrast to the single male domination of unregistered refugees and migrants. As in Pakistan, political parties had an influence among the Afghan refugees in Iran, mainly the Hezb-e Wahdat (Unity Party) targeting mostly Shia refugees (such as the Hazara). Education levels among Afghans in Iran seem higher than those in Pakistan (see Adelkhah and Olszewska 2007) with 90 per cent of all refugee families in Mashad being literate (Abbasi-Shavazi et al. 2005).

As noted earlier, Iran has pursued a strong policy of pushing Afghan refugees back home since the fall of the Taliban in late 2001. This may be for political reasons as much as fears of rising unemployment and has been done through

traditional territory for the Hazara population. Refugees from the east and southeast are in the minority (2 per cent).

various measures, such as 'restricting employment and freedom of movement, levying taxes, launching mass roundups of unregistered Afghans, and revoking the refugee cards of Afghans arrested for petty offences'.[24] While in the past Afghans had equal access to education and health care, they are now forced to pay the same rates as other foreigners, and the Iranian government closed informal schools used by Afghan refugees (Monsutti et al. 2006). Worst of all, however, is physical deportation (nearly 1 million over the past five years (UNHCR 2007a)), including 'some 250,000 illegal Afghan migrants', mainly single males (UNHCR 2007c, 257). This has made life in Iran difficult for Afghans, who had few rights to begin with and have been exploited for cheap labour (sometimes not receiving proper wages) and face high rental prices for property. That said, labour migration between Afghanistan and Iran, clandestine or not, was and still is very active, because job opportunities and salaries are nevertheless higher than in Pakistan.

Overview of internal displacement

In its *Global Appeal 2008–2009*, UNHCR defined assistance to internally displaced persons (IDPs) in Afghanistan as one of its major priorities. Internal displacement has been part of the Afghan wars as much as refugee movement, but, even more than in other parts of the world, has been poorly documented. Since 2002, UNHCR has assisted about half a million IDPs to return home (UNHCR 2007b, iv).[25]

---

24 <http://www.refugees.org/countryreports.aspx?id=2001>, accessed 24 January 2008. Furthermore, 'Iranian women who marry Afghan men lose their Iranian citizenship' (Strand and Suhrke 2004, 3).

25 There are various reasons why documenting IDPs in Afghanistan is difficult:

- Due to frequent displacement in Afghanistan, IDPs may not consider smaller movements over short distances as worth acknowledging, especially if displacement is of short duration and accommodation is with relatives.
- IDP figures often fluctuate greatly as it is not uncommon that families flee during fighting, but return during the cultivation season to tend to their land or poppy harvest or to work and tend the fields. For example, persons displaced during fighting between the Taliban and NATO in Musa Qala, Helmand, in 2006 returned home after violence ceased. Similarly, while the battle of Chora in Uruzgan (15–19 June 2007) created extensive displacement in the area, many were able to return to their villages a few months later.
- Humanitarian access to the area with the majority of internal displacement (the south) is currently extremely limited. There are only a few IDP camps in existence, such as in the capitals of the three southern provinces of Helmand (Lashkar Gah), Uruzgan (Tirin Kot), and Kandahar. Often IDPs live in poor conditions (with respect to health, sanitation, nutrition, education) due to lack of assistance. Lack of assistance also forces many IDPs to settle with relatives, with the more affluent ones renting houses, thus falling outside most estimations.
- Fourth, prospects of assistance to IDPs may have also contributed to exaggerated figures in Helmand. For example, while a local Afghan NGO working with IDPs in Lashkar Gah estimates that there are about 3,000 IDP families from Nawzad, Musa

According to UNHCR, at the end of 2007, about 130,000 individuals were still displaced within Afghanistan, mainly (86 per cent) in the south 'living in camps (particularly in the Southern region [mainly Kandahar and Helmand] in Maiwand, Mukhtar, Zahir Dasht and Panjwayi Camps) and camp-like situations … [where they] are in need of assistance and/or protection' (UNHCR 2007b, iii). The Afghan Red Crescent Society (ARCS) recently described conflict-induced displacement in southern Afghanistan as a 'major' humanitarian challenge (IRIN, 20 November 2007).[26] The Internal Displacement Monitoring Centre (2007) estimates IDPs in Afghanistan to be around 300,000, including the following groups:

- IDPs due to ethnic oppression, such as Pashtuns from the north who were forced to leave due to systematic persecution, though not all are in the caseload of UNHCR. There are 3,285 IDPs in the northern region (Gujur Afghans, an ethnic minority in the north of Afghanistan, originally from Takhar) who cannot return home due to protection problems (Rahjo 2007). Far less documented are those displaced by tribal (or factional) disputes in the south and elsewhere.
- Recent and ongoing displacements from insecurity and escalation of conflict in the south (insurgency) and east. Violence and fighting between NATO and Afghan National Army forces and the insurgency had displaced about 20,000 families (about 100,000 individuals) in the provinces of Helmand, Kandahar and Uruzgan by the end of 2006.[27] This figure increased drastically in 2007 when the UN estimated in August 2007 that some 80,000 people had been displaced by insecurity, predominantly in the south, southwest and east of the country (IRIN, 16 August 2007)[28] and displacement is continuing.[29] UNHCR has raised its concern with both the Afghan government and international military forces about the protection

Qala, Garamsir and Sangin districts, government officials have raised the number to 7,000 families in order to receive refugee ID cards (and associated assistance and benefits) for their families and tribes. A local NGO reports that a Ministry of Rural Reconstruction and Development driver was caught with 50 refugee cards that he wanted to distribute to friends and family, causing WFP to refuse to accept new applications, which in the end harmed IDPs with legitimate claims.

26 'Afghanistan: Conflict-affected displacement "major" humanitarian challenge – Afghan Red Crescent', 20 November 2007 (IRIN), available at <http://www.irinnews.org/Report.aspx?ReportId=75399>, accessed 1 March 2008.

27 <http://www.internal-displacement.org/8025708F004CE90B/(httpCountries)/DFADB5842F9262BF802570A7004BA6F0?OpenDocument>.

28 'Afghanistan: UN highlights conflict's impact on civilians', 16 August 2007 (IRIN), available at <http://www.irinnews.org/Report.aspx?ReportId=73759>, accessed 1 March 2008.

29 'Afghanistan: Hundreds flee fighting in Helmand Province', 6 December 2007 (IRIN), available at <http://www.irinnews.org/Report.aspx?ReportId=75722>, accessed 1 March 2008.

of these individuals. They are generally unassisted due to lack of access. Two groups can be differentiated:

  - Political IDPs consisting of families related to pro-government strongmen who flee out of fear of persecution from the Taliban insurgency in their native district.
  - Those who flee more generally from existing or anticipated violence and fighting in districts of Taliban insurgency. Many flee proactively, fearing NATO/US bombardment in areas where the Taliban has taken control; many do not return out of the same fears. [30]

- Returning refugees/migrants unable (or unwilling) to return back to their province/district of origin such as deportees from Iran having to settle in IDP camps in Herat.[31] This may be due to a general lack of the rule of law, widespread landmines and a dearth of livelihoods (see Afghanistan Independent Human Rights Commission 2007). This also includes urban IDPs in Kabul – mainly refugees from other areas in Afghanistan who have returned to the capital for lack of employment, shelter or economic survival elsewhere (Koser 2007). UNHCR has knowledge of 3,600 IDPs in the Kabul region, but there could be many more considering that the population of Kabul has grown drastically since 2001 (Rahjo 2007).
- IDPs who have been forced to move due to drought and lack of economic opportunities in their native provinces or districts. Food security is a major issue in Afghanistan, especially in the west (for example Ghor), which is often exacerbated during hard winter months. Pressure on poor rural areas by returning refugees creates a situation of competition for scarce resources.
- There is also a new form of 'development-induced displacement' affecting mainly poor urban dwellers living on 'borrowed' land. The most publicized displacement was the forced displacement of urban dwellers from a squatter settlement close to one of Kabul's most prominent neighbourhoods (Sherpur) after the Ministry of Defence reclaimed its land to distribute it among politicians. Other displacement is caused by the rising prices of land in urban areas and illegal land-grabbing, again mainly affecting poor urban dwellers.

30 For example, insurgency activities and international bombardments of insurgents as well as heavy fighting in certain areas have caused internal displacement in Uruzgan, mainly from Chora, Deh Rawud, Shahidi Hassas and the Taliban stronghold areas of Mehrabad and Darafshan in Tirin Kot. In Helmand this includes displacement in Musa Qala, Sangin, Girishk, and Nawzad.

31 'Afghanistan–Iran: Afghan deportees complain of lack of aid', 14 August 2007 (IRIN), available at <http://irinnews.org:80/Report.aspx?ReportId=73721>, accessed 1 March 2008.

- The hardest form of displacement to assess might be that of Kuchis as they are nomadic people constantly on the move. More recently, however, ethnic tensions (for example in Wardak), increased poppy cultivation, and illegal land seizures have infringed upon their traditional grazing land, forcing them to go elsewhere. There are no figures available on this problem.

All-inclusive solutions for IDPs in Afghanistan do not exist at present: 'There is lack of a comprehensive strategy with different instruments in place that can meet the needs of IDPs.'[32] The two entities working on assistance are the Directorate for Refugees of the Afghan government, and UNHCR, with the former lacking resources and the latter lacking humanitarian access, mainly working through local non-government organizations or the Afghan government.[33] Governmental assistance to IDPs overall has been very poor. A local Afghan NGO has alleged, for example, that IDPs in Helmand were exploited as many of the government departments distributed food ration cards meant for the displaced population among the their own staff and clientele.[34] A recent policy discussion centred on the use of IDP camps, as there is hope that people will return faster when living in non-camp environments.[35]

Protection challenges

About 14 per cent of all refugees in Pakistan cited special needs during the registration process conducted by the government of Pakistan with 58 per cent citing legal and physical protection needs with special medical conditions also being noted (AREU 2007, 3). Furthermore, female-headed households, children and youth are added to the risk categories (AREU 2007, 3). More crucial, however, is the current situation in Afghanistan, which makes for a very difficult protection environment. There has been overall a lack of concerted reconstruction

32 Walter Kalin, UN Representative for IDPs as cited in IRIN 'Afghanistan: UN highlights conflict's impact on civilians', 16 August 2007 (IRIN), available at <http://www.irinnews.org/Report.aspx?ReportId=73759>, accessed 1 March 2008.

33 Even in traditional areas known for assistance to IDPs, things have changed. Many IDPs, for example, moved to Helmand as it is known as a province where the government has traditionally distributed land to landless communities since the 1950s. The government of Helmand, however, has not taken any initiative in regard to the current displaced communities in the province. The director of the Refugee/Immigration Department argued that the former governor, Engineer Daoud, did not want to allocate a specific location for displaced families because this would encourage other communities to move to the IDP camp in Lashkar Gah.

34 Interview with local Afghan NGO. Furthermore, teachers' salaries were less than originally assigned by the Ministry of Education.

35 'Afghanistan: Should conflict-displaced IDPs go into camps?', 28 November 2007 (IRIN Radio), available at <http://www.irinnews.org/Report.aspx?ReportId=75542>, accessed 1 March 2008.

efforts, keeping Afghanistan at the bottom of the Human Development Index.[36] A great number of landmines remain uncleared; farmers lacking other livelihoods are turning increasingly to poppy production. Returnees to Afghanistan have to cope with insufficient services in the areas of health care, education, and basic infrastructure. This makes it especially difficult for women, children, elderly, sick and handicapped individuals. The new Afghan state is in no position to offer short-term solutions to these problems: the substantial collapse of the Afghan state during years of war means that, to this day, much of the activity of the new post-Taliban state is funded from external sources, with Afghans consequently subjected to the policy priorities of donors (Maley 2006).

According to a recent report by the Afghanistan Independent Human Rights Commission (AIHRC 2007)[37] on economic and social rights in Afghanistan, based on interviews with over 11,000 people (focusing, among others, on returnees), the following key challenges exist for those living in and returning to Afghanistan:

- Livelihood: 62.3 per cent of all interviewees reported no stable income within their households, with more than 60 per cent living below the poverty line, earning less than US$1 per day. UNHCR (2004a, 15) also identified landlessness or access to agricultural land as a key challenge, as about 70 per cent of returnees claimed to have no land. This is especially a problem for the Kuchis, the Afghan nomadic pastoralists, whose access to grazing lands has been diminishing due to drought and conflict (UNHCR 2004a).
- Shelter: 67.1 per cent of interviewed returnees chose not to return to their places of origin due to lack of shelter; and 67.3 per cent left their places of origin for the same reason after returning there. Similarly 43.4 per cent of IDPs claimed lack of shelter as a reason for displacement. There are also problems with supportive infrastructure, such as potable water, sanitation, roads, transportation and irrigation canals that impact on livelihood (UNHCR 2004a).
- Adequate health care: although over 80 per cent had access to governmental/NGO health care services, about 40 per cent either had no access or felt the service provided and staff skills were of poor quality.
- Access to (primary) education: one-third of all interviewees stated that their primary school age children (mainly girls) did not attend school regularly, either because of lack of school buildings (girls) or the need for child labour (boys).

36 About one-quarter of all Afghans live at the fringes of poverty; in some provinces this is as high as 50–90 per cent.

37 The research, based on field monitoring activity, was conducted over the period of one year (January–December 2006) in 32 of Afghanistan's 35 provinces, in partnership with UNHCR.

The human rights context also needs careful consideration. Many rights only exist on paper, especially for women who are still subject to discrimination at the hands of traditional conflict resolution mechanisms in the Afghan justice system. A majority of all Afghans still rely on traditional justice mechanisms (AIHRC 2007), which are considered 'a common source of violation of rights' (for example, lack of due process) (Stapleton 2007b, 19).[38]

The last two years have seen an increase in insurgent activity and violent incidents in Afghanistan. UNHCR (2004a, 14) also raised a concern about the 'ethnicisation' of the Afghan conflict and the presence of 'controversial figures in Afghanistan's ongoing political process'. The year 2007 witnessed 20–30 per cent more attacks than in 2006 and in 2008 another increase is expected (Oxfam 2007). Intensified warfare by the insurgents has been met very forcefully by the ANA and ISAF/NATO, raising many concerns about civilian casualties during aerial bombing. According to an Oxfam report (2007), 'there are four times as many air-strikes by international forces in Afghanistan as in Iraq' (Oxfam 2007, 16).

The strategy of the insurgency builds on asymmetric and psychological warfare,[39] while at the same time exploiting the mistakes made by the Afghan National Army (ANA) and its international supporters. The insurgents' approach that 'if you are not with us, then you are against us' makes it difficult for anybody to stay neutral. Teachers in particular, but also health workers, and recently anybody seen as associated with international forces and what are considered pro-government clergy, are targeted. Added to this are systematic acts of intimidation by regional warlords, militia commanders, criminal groups and narcotics dealers, many with links to the Afghan government. This includes illegal land occupation, which is fuelling land disputes all over Afghanistan. Competition for resources (mainly land and water), but also ruthless government officials abusing their power, have caused an increase in tribal conflicts, including blood feuds. The increasing war economy has also resulted in entire areas being under the control of drug mafias and smuggling networks, which tend to work in a mutually beneficial relationship with the insurgency.

As a result, the local population, especially in the volatile south, but increasingly also in the east and southeast and elsewhere, are caught between a rock and a hard place. On the one hand, they have to deal with a malfunctioning, and often highly corrupt, Afghan government that is unable to provide basic security, protection and even a semblance of the rule of law. On the other hand, they are confronted by

38 There is no justice for converts and homosexuals. For example, a number of successful asylum claims by Afghans in Australia have been based on the feared consequences of either conversion or homosexuality. While freedom of speech is guaranteed and Afghanistan has one of the most progressive media laws in the region, there are questions about the scope of this freedom, with media coming frequently under attack or practising self-censorship.

39 This section draws from unpublished research in the south of Afghanistan by a local Afghan NGO during 2007.

a growing insurgency that is supported internationally by Pakistan and *al-Qaeda*. The latter has led to cross-border infiltrations of 'foreign' Taliban into Afghanistan (such as Urdu, Punjabi and Arabic-speaking militants). As security has become a scarce commodity, communities increasingly accommodate the insurgency.

Last but not least, the lack of access for UNHCR and other international agencies in many parts of Afghanistan makes protection, and especially the monitoring of returnees, difficult (Amnesty International 2003, 28) and the space for humanitarian action is diminishing every day, especially as the insurgency has made the kidnapping of aid workers part of their psychological warfare. In addition to this overall difficult protection environment in Afghanistan, UNHCR (2006d, 1) divides

> extremely vulnerable cases … into two broad categories:
>
> (1) Individuals whose vulnerability is the result of a lack of effectively functioning family – and/or community support mechanisms and who cannot cope, in the absence of such structures.
>
> (2) Individuals who cannot cope, either because such support structures are not available or because Afghanistan lacks the necessary public support mechanisms and treatment opportunities.

This includes the following population groups (UNHCR 2006d; Rahjo 2007; Stapleton 2007b):

- Deportees: 'Deportations from the Islamic Republic of Iran and the return of unregistered Afghans from Pakistan highlighted the need to address population movements outside the refugee framework' (UNHCR 2007c, 257).
- Women: (especially if victims of serious trauma), for example female-headed households (unaccompanied females), widows, and young girls (at risk of forced marriage, or use as bounty for settling community disputes and trafficking). This can also include women with foreign spouses or trying to live a 'Western life-style'.
- Children: (at risk of forced labour and trafficking), especially if un-accompanied and victims of serious trauma.
- Those born in exile who lack social networks at home.
- The elderly and the sick, especially if unaccompanied, as well as physically and intellectually disabled persons.
- Families of 'Communists', who may be persecuted upon return.[40]

40 This depends on the positions held in the Communist government, as some ex-Communists have returned to take up government posts in the current regime, while others have been elected to serve in the lower house of the Parliament.

- Afghans in areas where they constitute an ethnic minority (for example, Pashtuns in the north).
- Individuals (for example journalists, human rights activists) voicing critiques of power figures or thought to be associated with internationals (in Taliban-dominated areas).
- Landowners (due to land-grabbing and land disputes).

The politicization of durable solutions for Afghan refugees

The previous sections in this chapter have highlighted that Afghanistan, the Afghan wars and resulting refugees have all been subject to politicization by multiple players. Such politicization is not uncommon, but 'perhaps more clearly than in other refugee situations, the humanitarian and political dimensions of the Afghan refugee situation were mutually reinforcing' (Zolberg et al. 1989, 154) with refugees, and humanitarian aid, becoming 'pawns in the larger geopolitical struggle' for regional and international domination (Loescher 1993, 89; see also Schöch 2008).

In such an environment, the likelihood of also politicizing durable solutions is very high, with political considerations of host and donor countries overriding the welfare of refugees. Thus, repatriation was always a preferred durable solution for the Afghan refugee population. Muslim countries were able to provide assistance in support of their religious brothers and Pakistan could exploit the situation to bolster its influence in the region. Pursuing other kinds of durable solution would have simply sent a wrong message at this time. Furthermore, Western countries did not have to open their borders in order to resettle a very large refugee population.

Local integration hindered by political developments

While refugees found ways to settle down in their host countries through intermarriage, obtaining local ID cards, or simply blending in with the local population in areas with a similar ethnic background, neither Iran nor Pakistan encouraged local integration officially (Turton and Marsden 2002), 'especially in view of the large numbers involved' (UNHCR 2006d, 144). Pursuing an official integration policy would have contradicted political stances of both Iran and Pakistan linked to regional politics, the resentment among the local population (mainly out of competition for jobs and housing) and refugees being easy scapegoats for many social ills, particularly growing terrorism in Pakistan. Nevertheless,

> it is highly likely … that a significant number of Afghans will seek to remain in Pakistan and Iran, both as family groups and as single wage earners, and that they will find increasingly inventive methods to circumvent any attempts at stricter border control and policy scrutiny inside the country. (Turton and Marsden 2002, 52)

Adelkhah and Olszewska (2007, 148) argue that 'by turning its back on its traditional welcoming policy towards Afghans, Iran [but also Pakistan] is undoubtedly closing itself into a trap of impossible choices'. Afghans in Iran and Pakistan are part of a long migration history predating forced migration, with strong communal ties in border areas. Complete expulsion would attempt to reverse a historical trend, leave both economies without the benefits of cheap Afghan labour and neglect the symbiosis between cities and economies in the border regions of all three countries. This is compounded by a border that is, if not impossible, still difficult to control and where Afghans have managed to blend into the local population, given that 'a significant portion of the population of border regions [is] ... of "uncertain identity"' (Adelkhah and Olszewska 2007, 154).

In sum, by driving a stringent return policy instead of looking for alternative solutions, both countries situate themselves 'in the same kind of schizophrenia as western European societies ... as its [Iran's] economy depends on travellers and immigrant labour, whether or not they are legal' (Adelkhah and Olszewska 2007, 157), something which is very true as well for Pakistan. Still, all this inconsistency (at times tolerating Afghan refugees/migrants and other times harassing and expelling them) may actually all be part of a strategy that allows both countries to benefit from the cheap labour of Afghans while not committing to local integration or permanent settlement (Monsutti 2005, 129–30).

Resettlement

Even though resettlement did occur, and still does, there never was a concerted and significant resettlement programme (in terms of numbers), as it would have been impossible to resettle such vast numbers of refugees all together. The majority of all Afghan refugees were resettled during the beginnings of the refugee crisis, when the refugees still fitted the 'Cold War mould'. Figures are hard to obtain, as resettlement was mainly based on individual applications for asylum and later family reunification schemes; but the total was likely under half a million (well under ten percent of the total Afghan refugee population).

Access to resettlement is still difficult; as with the fall of the Taliban many Western countries started '"incentive programmes" in order to induce the "voluntary repatriation"' of Afghan refugees, especially for those with pending asylum claims (Amnesty International 2003, 11), with several halting the judgement of new incoming asylum claims. In the 2006 UNHCR Projected Global Resettlement Needs Report (UNHCR 2006e), UNHCR did not project resettlement needs for the majority of refugees in Pakistan and Iran, due to little willingness among potential countries of resettlement to take in more refugees, clinging to the belief that the situation in Afghanistan had changed for the better. UNHCR found only Afghan refugees residing in Central Asia to have urgent resettlement needs, due to their having served in the past Communist regime, or having fled more recently from sectarian violence and persecution. Similarly, the remaining Afghan population in India, being mainly of Hindu or Sikh origin, and some Ismailis, may also be unable to return to Afghanistan.

This is consistent with UNHCR Pakistan stating that resettlement is available only for 'a limited number of Afghan refugees [a tiny minority] for whom neither staying in Pakistan nor returning to their homeland is a safe option, such as women at risk or security cases'.[41] They go on to argue that 'the number of refugees UNHCR resettles from Pakistan remains among the highest of any country, despite the obstacles created by much more stringent security checks since the 11 September 2001 attacks on the United States'.[42] This leaves family reunification or marriage with refugees who hold legal documents in Western countries as a last option to 'resettle'. Smuggling is also still attempted, but cannot be considered a durable solution, at least not officially.

The fact that most Afghan refugees have integrated well into their countries of resettlement could be a consideration favouring resettlement in the future. However, the profile of refugees resettled in the late 1980s and early 1990s differs from the ones that currently remain. The bulk of resettlement prior to 1996 was provided to Afghans from an elite background, well educated and aspiring to a Western lifestyle. Many of the refugees still in Iran and Pakistan do not fit this description.

According to UNHCR statistics, 1,829 refugees of Afghan origin were resettled from their first country of asylum in India, the Islamic Republic of Iran, Kazakhstan, Pakistan, the Russian Federation, the Syrian Arab Republic and Tajikistan in 2006 (UNHCR 2006b). Prior to this, for the period 1996–2005, UNHCR assisted in the resettlement of 26,846 Afghan refugees from Azerbaijan, India, the Islamic Republic of Iran, Kyrgyzstan, Pakistan, the Russian Federation, Tajikistan, Turkmenistan and Uzbekistan (UNHCR 2005b). This results in a global figure of less than 30,000 Afghan refugees being resettled over the past ten years.

Given the deteriorating security situation in Afghanistan, the unwillingness of major host countries to integrate refugees locally, and increasing political instability in the biggest host country, Pakistan, circumstances may force the international community to reconsider its stance on resettlement. Especially in Central Asian countries such as Tajikistan and Turkmenistan, the relatively small remaining numbers of Afghan refugees seem to consider resettlement as their preferred durable solution (see IRIN 2003, 2004). Some members of the Afghan refugee population in India, albeit in small numbers, are also in dire straits as they are currently not allowed to work and thus are reliant on subsistence allowances from UNHCR, illegal work, or remittances.

41 <http://www.unhcr.org.pk/about.html>, accessed 4 January 2008.

42 <http://www.unhcr.org.pk/about.html>, accessed 4 January 2008.

Repatriation – preferred durable solution?

'The Governments of Pakistan and Iran, the two countries most affected by the presence of Afghan refugees, have long insisted on repatriation as the preferred solution' (UNHCR 2006d, 144). One small and two major waves of repatriation can be identified over the past years (see Figure 6.4), with ad hoc and trickle movements occurring throughout. The first peak in repatriation occurred when the *Mujahideen* fighters finally captured Kabul in 1992 (even though the departure of the Soviet Army in 1989 had already initiated tentative return into an ongoing conflict). After smaller movements totalling about 200,000 (1989–1991), the year 1992 saw 'a huge surge of collective optimism which resulted in no fewer than 1.2 million Afghans returning from Pakistan in six months … assisted by an extremely stretched UNHCR' (Colville 1997, 6); nearly another million moved home in 1993 (see Figure 6.4). Afterwards repatriation began to trickle off as the Afghan population watched different political groups struggle for control of Kabul.

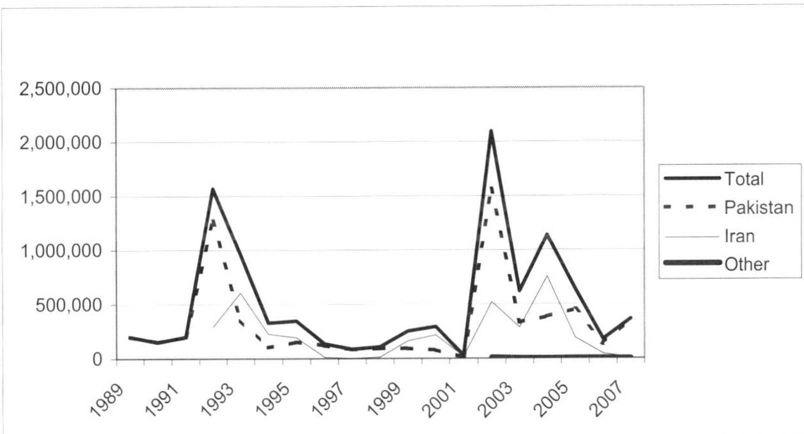

Figure 6.4 Return to Afghanistan, 1989–2007
Source: UNHCR (Statistics of Population of Concern, various years) and UNHCR (2007b).

A second wave of return to Afghanistan, albeit much smaller in numbers, occurred after 1996 when the Taliban captured Kabul, and some Afghans were initially overjoyed to be rid of what they saw as warmongering *Mujahideen* fighters. However, having already had one bad experience with return and renewed displacement, Afghan refugees did not react as swiftly as before. As the Taliban soon began to impose strict constraints on everyday life (including the banning of movies, music and photography), return remained well under one million between 1996 and 2001. However, the 'subsequent fall of the Taliban government and the establishment of the AIA [Afghan Interim Administration] by the Bonn Agreement of 5 December 2001 led, in turn, to the largest and most rapid return movement of Afghan refugees ever, and the largest UNHCR assisted repatriation programme in almost 30 years' (Turton and Marsden 2002, 17). As noted earlier, according to UNHCR (2007b), nearly five million refugees returned to Afghanistan after 2002 in this third wave, out of which nearly 3.8 million were assisted (see Figure 6.5). Of these refugees, the majority returned from Pakistan (over 3 million), 90 per cent of whom were assisted in their return, and in the first year of return 61 per cent were recent refugees who had been in exile for five years or less (Lumpp et al. 2004, 150). Exact figures on unassisted return are difficult to gauge and hence less reliable.

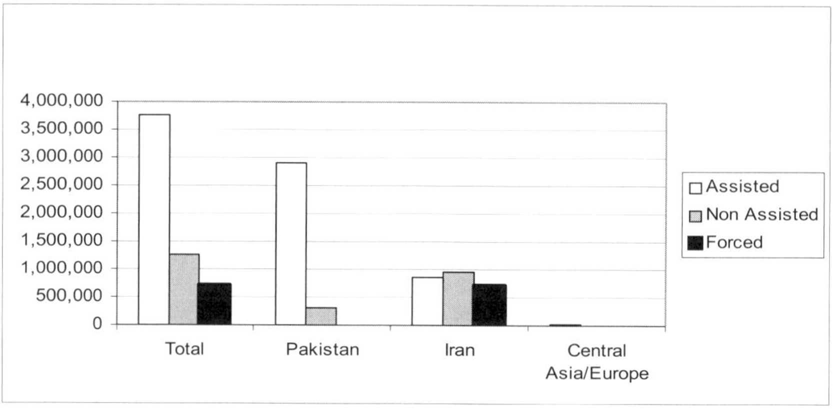

Figure 6.5 Assisted vs. non-assisted (voluntary and forced) return to Afghanistan (2002–2007)
Source: UNHCR 2007b.

The return of Afghan refugees was *facilitated* through various measures, which clearly had an impact on the massive return figures in the first years (see Lumpp et al. 2004 for a detailed discussion), although Turton and Marsden (2002, 33) conclude that return was mainly linked to assistance packages offered (having both a symbolic and material value), to 'great, but misplaced, expectations about the level and early impact of international assistance', and to push factors from host states:

- First, return was organized through a 'tripartite repatriation framework' in the region that was negotiated by UNHCR, the first agreement being signed between Afghanistan, Iran and Pakistan in 2002. Non-neighbouring countries that also signed such agreements were France, the UK and the Netherlands.

- Second, UNHCR launched massive information campaigns and arranged 'Go and See' visits for elders and representatives of Afghan refugees and 'Come and Talk' visits for community representatives and authorities to refugee camps.
- Third, the Afghan government issued a 'decree of dignified return' that assured 'exemption from prosecution, irrespective of political affiliation, for criminal offences against the internal and external security of Afghanistan … except crimes against peace or humanity or war crimes' (Lumpp et al. 2004, 157).
- Fourth, the Bonn agreement allowed Afghan refugee populations to participate in the state-building exercise by reserving seats for representatives of refugee communities in the 2002 Emergency Loya Jirga that decided on the transitional administration, and by allowing refugees to vote in the 2004 presidential elections. Furthermore, the National Solidarity Programme (NSP), aimed at rebuilding rural communities, prioritized those districts with high return figures, and NSP community development councils were asked to incorporate returnees into their ranks.

In contrast to Pakistan, and more in line with other refugee repatriations, the majority (66 per cent) of refugees returning from Iran did so without assistance. This again mirrors the long-standing discrepancy in assistance to Afghan refugees hosted by Pakistan as opposed to those hosted by Iran. More interesting, however, might be that nearly as many refugees were forcibly deported from Iran (700,000) as those that were assisted to return (UNHCR 2007b). This makes the return from Iran nearly evenly distributed between assisted, spontaneous and forced (see Figure 6.5).[43]

Official reports put the forced return (deportation for security reasons) from Pakistan at a much lower figure (about 6,000 refugees). However, it is important to recall, as noted earlier, that at least in the case of the closure of the South Waziristan camps in Pakistan, UNHCR accepted the official story from Pakistan claiming that return was voluntary in order to be able to assist the refugees, despite the refugees' telling a story of threats and military bulldozing down of camps by force, and UNHCR's suspecting that the return was forced.[44] Thus, some of the spontaneous unassisted (but also some of the assisted) return from Pakistan may very well have been of a forced nature.

Finally, as noted earlier, several Western countries have initiated an active encouragement of 'voluntary' return. Several of them (for example Germany, Switzerland and the United Kingdom) have set up programmes in collaboration

43 In addition to refugees returning home, UNHCR also assisted nearly half a million internally displaced persons (IDPs) to return to their homes (UNHCR 2007b).

44 Informal discussions by one of the authors (Schmeidl) with UNHCR in 2004 while working with a local organization, which helped UNHCR with receiving the returning refugees in Paktika province.

with the International Organization for Migration (IOM) while others even deported Afghans from their territory who enjoyed only so-called 'complementary protection'[45] (see McAdam 2007) rather than full refugee status. According to UNHCR (2007b), between 2002 and 2007, over 2,000 Afghan refugees were deported from Western countries such as the United Kingdom (1,959), Germany (236), Norway (199), and the Netherlands (76) (UNHCR 2007b, iii). Returns from Central Asia and Europe did not figure much in the overall return statistics, partially due to the small number of refugees residing there.

As UNHCR assisted the majority of the returns from Pakistan, it has been rather well documented (UNHCR 2007b; Monsutti et al. 2006), with more scant information on those returning from Iran:

- A majority of returnees from both Pakistan and Iran had only lived for a short time in exile (five years or less).
- A majority of refugees from Pakistan and Iran returned to urban destinations (about 40 per cent), with one-third (29 per cent) of all refugees from Pakistan returning to Kabul province alone, and it is likely that most of the refugees from Iran went to the western city of Herat.
- Ethnicity of refugees in Pakistan shows Pashtuns proportionately more numerous (56 per cent) due to living in the border areas, followed by Tajiks (25 per cent) and Hazara (8 per cent). Even though many Hazara (Shia) refugees sought refuge in Iran (about 43 per cent of documented Afghans in Iran), 'their returns are only 25.6 percent of the total UNHCR-assisted return figures up to August 2005. The imbalance is due both to greater economic opportunities in Iran for Hazaras, and perceptions of continued prejudice against Shias in Afghanistan' (Abbasi-Shavazi and Glazebrook 2006, 7).
- Only slightly fewer women (5 per cent difference) than men repatriate; this figure shows a slight increase in the last year of repatriation.
- The majority of all returnees are families, with only 19 per cent being single individuals. For Afghan refugees in Iran, this is different, with single men making up the majority of the refugees that repatriated outside the UNHCR voluntary return process or were deported (the latter indicating links between refugees and labour migration among Afghans in Iran, see Monsutti 2006, 14).
- It is important to consider the education and skill level of returning refugees from Pakistan, as according to UNHCR, a majority (63 per cent) were non-

45 In order to provide an alternative basis for eligibility for protection for individuals who fall outside the specificity of the 1951 Refugee Convention framework, a variety of complementary protection mechanisms have evolved drawing on human rights treaties (for example the International Covenant on Civil and Political Rights, the Convention against Torture, the Convention on the Rights of the Child) or international protection standards (for example, providing assistance to persons fleeing from generalized violence). These mechanisms are not as binding as the Refugee Convention.

literate (UNHCR 2007b). Of the 19 per cent with education, the majority (56 per cent) only completed primary education and another 20 per cent secondary (18 per cent are under the age of five, and hence not of school age). This is somewhat puzzling given that both UNHCR and Afghan political parties actually had set up schools inside the Afghan Refugee Villages.
- Similarly, 67 per cent of returning refugees claim to have no skills, with the remaining 33 per cent being split between domestic workers (48 per cent), agricultural workers (12 per cent), private sector workers (8 per cent), carpet weavers (7 per cent) and construction workers (5 per cent). This highlights a long-term neglect in providing adequate education and skills development to one of the biggest and longest-standing refugee populations in the world.

Conclusion: Sustainability of return and other solutions

Very few observers would disagree that the future of return to Afghanistan for the remaining refugee populations in Iran and Pakistan (but also elsewhere) is questionable at this moment. Monsutti (2008, 19) states the obvious, namely that 'full repatriation is neither feasible nor desirable', a sentiment which UNHCR is also coming to accept. Nevertheless, while the vast numbers of refugees who have returned tend to be used to demonstrate success, less attention has been given to the entire question of 'sustainability of return' leading to internal displacement after return, the 'recycling' of refugees, or returning refugees changing status to migrant workers (legal or illegal). How otherwise, for example, is it possible that '500,000 more refugees returned to Afghanistan in the first four years of repatriation than we thought to exist in the first place' (Kronenfeld 2008, 2), with 3.5 million still remaining? Figure 6.6 illustrates the seemingly 'bottomless pit', the unlimited supply, of Afghan refugees.

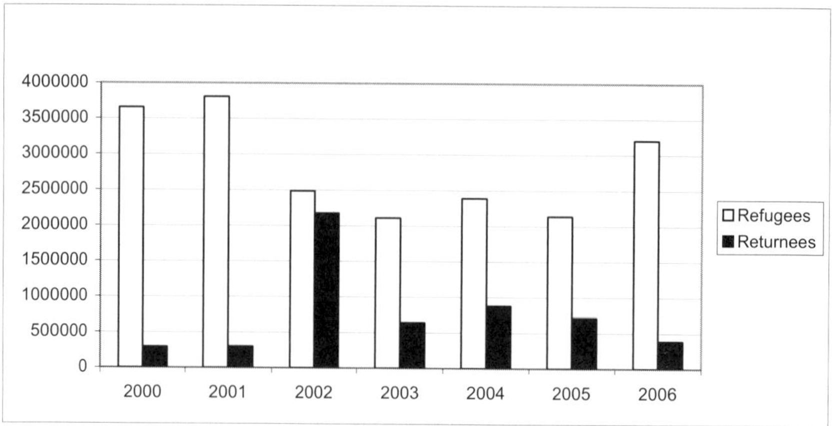

Figure 6.6 Afghan return movements to Afghanistan
Source: UNHCR 2007b.

There are several issues that are worth considering in the search for durable solutions for Afghanistan's displaced population. First, the pull factors influencing the return of Afghan refugees to Afghanistan currently are, and will remain, extremely modest (UNHCR 2007a). In a 2004 report, UNHCR (2004a, 1) already found 'a clear correlation between willingness to return and length of exile'. Those who had left during the Taliban years or shortly prior have returned home, those who left ten years or more prior, remain. Thus, a clear distinction needs to be made between those who have repatriated until now and those who remain. For UNHCR, 'natural repatriation' has come to a halt, and future repatriation may depend entirely on push factors linked to asylum country policies, treatment of refugees by host societies and states, as well as forced removal.[46] 'Encouraging Afghans who have lived for two and a half decades outside their country – some of whom, in fact, may never have even set foot in Afghanistan – to repatriate may be a distinct challenge in the coming months and years' (Margesson 2007, 4). A refugee who has lived long in exile often lacks necessary ties and networks at home that tend to facilitate return. This explains why most (about 82 per cent) of all refugees in Pakistan may have no desire or intention to return home. Similarly, 'most Afghans in Iran – refugees and labour migrants – do not intend to return to Afghanistan in the medium term' (Abbasi-Shavazi and Glazebrook 2006, 2).

Second, the absorptive capacity[47] of Afghanistan, a country that so far has not succeeded in rebuilding its state and rule of law, needs to be carefully considered, as it is linked to sustainable return (see also Amnesty International 2003; Monsutti 2008). While return can legitimize a new government (Turton and Marsden 2002),

46 Email exchange with UNHCR official in Afghanistan, 27 January 2008.
47 The authors acknowledge that absorption capacity is difficult to quantify.

which explains why Afghanistan was very open to refugee return, it can also place an undue burden on the stability of a country that has not yet dealt with justice and reconciliation issues. One needs to ask the very basic question of how well Afghanistan is able to care for its current population, let alone returning refugees, when it is largely dependent on external donor support (Maley 2007).

The problems for those refugees that have already returned home were discussed earlier and include issues such as lack of livelihoods, unemployment and underemployment, lack of access to land or shelter, low living standards, but also rights issues such as unresolved community conflicts or fear of persecution of minorities (for example, Hazara, who are often more reluctant to return, or Pashtuns, who were persecuted in the north). Security is also increasingly becoming an obstacle, especially in the south where fighting has prevented refugees from returning to their homes. The deteriorating security situation in Afghanistan 'has already had an impact on repatriation trends, which have declined notably since 2005' making the maintenance of sustainable repatriation increasingly difficult (UNHCR 2007c, 256), and also more expensive (Margesson 2007).

Many refugees who are unable or unwilling to return to their original homes due to lack of livelihoods, security and de-mining move to Kabul and other big cities already stretched beyond capacity in terms of infrastructure support. All this has already caused renewed internal displacement as we explored earlier[48] and a 'recycling' of refugees who were forced to return to Iran and Pakistan (mostly illegally) to rejoin family members (in refugee camps) or re-enter as new migrant labourers.[49] Some returnees have complained bitterly that their expectations of integration assistance in Afghanistan were disappointed, leading to their decision to return to Pakistan or Iran (Turton and Marsden 2002). This return to renewed displacement needs to be seriously addressed when considering durable solutions for remaining Afghan refugees. As UNHCR sees return as depending on 'Afghanistan's overall progress toward political stability and security' (UNHCR 2007a, 260), the outlook is not promising.

This leads to a third point: whose interests does finding a durable solution serve – refugees' or host countries' – and what does this say about the definition of 'sustainability' of return? As noted earlier, return in a post-conflict context is frequently treated as a priority, often less for the benefit of refugees than for the messages it sends about the change at home (Black and Gent 2004, Turton and Marsden 2002). A recent briefing paper by the Development Research Centre on Migration, Globalisation and Poverty (2005, see also Black et al. 2004) asks the question – what makes return sustainable? While living conditions (and accessing

48 For example, several refugees returning from Iran (about 11,000 in the western region, mainly Maslakh camp in Herat) are currently hosted in makeshift IDP camps around Herat or simple squatter settlements in urban slums (for example Kabul).

49 While some Afghan refugees leave permanently due to a lack of livelihood, some tend to leave temporarily only, such as during cold winter months, as survival may not be possible in poor neighbourhoods with a lack of electricity and heating.

rights) may not be ideal in the country to which refugees return, they may be sufficient if they are better than in the host countries that they left. This can make the return of some Afghans sustainable, while not that of others, especially those who still remain at this point. The impact of refugees on the areas to which they return also needs to be part of the assessment. In Afghanistan, this is a mixed picture with many refugees contributing positively to the reconstruction process, while, as discussed earlier, the sheer number does put a strain on the Afghan state. Similarly, 'staying put', may not be the best way to understand sustainability either, especially in the Afghan context (Monsutti et al. 2006). The briefing paper concludes that two factors crucially influence sustainability of return – voluntariness and the return environment. This should discourage host states from forcefully removing or deporting refugees, as they are likely to come back (under whatever status). Greater support of returnees once they have returned home should be emphasized, something for which UNHCR has tried to gain support (Turton and Marsden 2002).

Fourth, the psychological and personal reasons why a majority of refugees in both Pakistan and Iran (but also abroad) do not show a strong desire to return home need to be better understood. As just discussed, we tend to focus on the situation in Afghanistan rather than looking at the experience abroad (Monsutti et al. 2006), especially the exposure to a semi-urban lifestyle, higher standards of living, better public services (health, education) and employment opportunities, all making refugees more reluctant to go home (Turton and Marsden 2002; Grare 2003; UNHCR 2006d). Long-term exile also tends to impact on the notion of what 'home' means to many Afghans. Those who have lived a long time abroad (or were born there) may consider their host countries as 'home', while also having a nostalgic feeling for their country of origin (*watan*) – Afghanistan (Turton and Marsden 2002). Thus, while the Afghan identity of refugees may still be strong in theory, it may be much weaker in practice and many second generation Afghans, especially, may prefer to live in Pakistan, Iran or abroad due to feeling excluded when returning home. 'Instead of asking who is a refugee and who is not, a better question might be: what is best for Afghans and their neighbours? … as it is unrealistic, considering the extent of economic interdependence, to expect that every last Afghan will permanently return' (Kronenfeld 2008, 4).

Fifth, solutions for the remaining refugee population need to be seen within a wider framework than protracted displacement only (see UNHCR 2004a; Monsutti 2008). Mobility has long been part of life for Afghanistan and its people for a variety of reasons (economic, political and cultural: UNHCR 2004a; Adelkhah and Olszewska 2007; Monsutti 2008). The Afghan wars only added to the magnitude and urgency of the issue, making migration (forced or voluntary) part of an Afghan survival strategy. Afghans have learned to spread risk through strategic mobility (Monsutti et al. 2006; Monsutti 2008), which is a reason why many families tend to have some members in Afghanistan, some in Iran and/or Pakistan, some in the Gulf States, and yet others abroad in Western countries. One could argue that Afghans never put all their eggs into the durable solutions basket and thus can benefit from economic remittances and existing networks abroad. Hence, 'we should give up any idea that "sustainability" equates to immobility – that it ideally involves "anchoring" people to their places of origin' (Turton and Marsden 2002, 52). As noted earlier, although the identity of Afghan refugees is often still strong, and some may even still have strong links to their original *watan*, strategic considerations result in a preference to stay put or engage in a more translational lifestyle such as moving between Afghanistan and Iran/Pakistan. Thus, it is best to treat refugees as rational decision-makers that calculate, within existing circumstances, the cost and benefits of return, possibly more than initial exit (Turton and Marsden 2002; Monsutti et al. 2006).

In light of the above, solving the Afghan puzzle of protracted displacement may not lie with the traditional durable solutions approach within the UNHCR framework, but with greater attention to economic and migration complexities. According to Monsutti (2008), the traditional framework is too simple for the complex nature of the Afghan situation of which UNHCR (2004a) has been aware. This led UNHCR (2004a, 4) to suggest that 'the nature of cross border movements to and from Pakistan and Iran should be studied more closely to identify patterns and modalities', specifically the multi-directionality of population movements (Monsutti et al. 2006). Given the current scapegoating of refugees in Iran and Pakistan, such analysis should also include an assessment of the contribution of Afghan refugees and migrants to both countries as well as the challenges of 'mixed population' flows (refugees and migrants) to host states (Turton and Marsden 2002). The 'push factors' in the form of the refugee policies of the two major countries of first asylum (Pakistan and Iran), but also countries of resettlement that currently dominate the 'voluntary return' to Afghanistan, especially need to be addressed. As Crisp (2004) notes, local integration does not necessarily mean the awarding of citizenship in host countries. Afghanistan, Iran and Pakistan should be encouraged and supported 'to work out the terms of any such agreement on their own' assisted by outside actors open to non-traditional solutions to protracted refugee situations (Kronenfeld 2008, 17). This may include a transnational model that allows for more permanent and flexible labour migration agreements between Afghanistan and its neighbours (but also countries of resettlement), which can benefit the country of origin (through remittances) as much as the host countries (through access to labour). If no alternative solutions are found, Afghans will adapt and find their own, as they have done in the past. This may include continued (illegal) labour migration to both Iran and Pakistan and Afghan refugees blending with local populations in Pakistan and Iran.

Last but not least, in addition to 'managing the flow of persons who are moving back and forward for economic and social reasons; and … responding to the wishes of those Afghans with legitimate reasons for remaining in the asylum countries, and identifying those with genuine needs for continuing international protection' (UNHCR 2004b, 14), the return environment in Afghanistan should also not be neglected. This includes overcoming poverty, dealing with the absence of security and rule of law, and working on reintegration programmes. If 'problems' inside

Afghanistan as well as in the main host countries are not addressed, a worst-case scenario could be greater regional destabilization. It may be easier and cheaper, however, to prevent this, by seriously addressing the issue of protracted Afghan displacement now.

Bibliography

Abbasi-Shavazi, M.J. and Glazebrook, D. (2006), *Continued Protection, Sustainable Reintegration: Afghan Refugees and Migrants in Iran* (Kabul: Afghanistan Research and Evaluation Unit).

Abbasi-Shavazi, M.J., Glazebrook, G., Jamshidiha, H., Mahmoudian, M. and Sadeghi, R. (2005), *Return to Afghanistan? A Study of Afghans Living in Mashad, Islamic Republic of Iran* (Kabul: Afghanistan Research and Evaluation Unit (AREU)).

Adelkhah, F. and Olszewska, Z. (2007), 'The Iranian Afghans', *Iranian Studies* 49: 2, 137–65.

Afghanistan Independent Human Rights Commission (AIHRC) (2007), 'Economic and Social Rights in Afghanistan II', Report released 1 August 2007, available at <http://www.unhcr.org/cgi-bin/texis/vtx/refworld/rwmain?docid=471f4a5b0>, accessed 1 January 2008.

Amnesty International (2003), 'Afghanistan: Out of sight, Out of Mind: The Fate of the Afghan Returnees', Report published 23 June 2003, Index No. ASA 11/014/2003, available at <http://www.unhcr.org/cgi-bin/texis/vtx/refworld/rwmain?docid=3f12f8a92>, accessed 22 February 2008.

AREU (2007), 'Feature: Registration of Afghans in Pakistan', *Afghanistan Research Newsletter* 14, 2–3 (Kabul: Afghanistan Research and Evaluation Unit).

Azarbaijani-Moghadam, S., Schetter, C. and Schmeidl, S. (2002), 'The Transition from Relief to Development from a Human Security Perspective: Afghanistan', Unpublished Report to the UN Commission on Human Security (New York: United Nations).

Baitenmann, H. (1990), 'NGOs and the Afghan War: The Politicisation of Humanitarian Aid', *Third World Quarterly* 12: 1, 62–85.

Benard, C. and Khalilzad, Z. (1984), *'The Government of God': Iran's Islamic Republic* (New York: Columbia University Press).

Black, R. and Gent, S. (2004), 'Defining, Measuring and Influencing Sustainable Return: The Case of the Balkans', Working Paper No. T7 (Brighton: Development Research Centre on Migration, Globalisation and Poverty).

Black, R., Koser, K., Munk, K., Atfield, G., D'Onofrio, L. and Tiemoko, R. (2004), 'Understanding Voluntary Return', Home Office Online Report 50/04, available at <http://www.homeoffice.gov.uk/rds/pdfs04/rdsolr5004.pdf>, accessed 2 July 2008.

Boesen, I. W. (1988), 'What Happens to Honour in Exile? Continuity and Change Among Afghan Refugees', in B. Huldt and E. Jansson (eds), *The Tragedy of*

Afghanistan: The Social, Cultural and Political Impact of the Soviet Invasion (London: Croom Helm), 219–39.
Centlivres, P. (1987), 'Gestion administrative et organisation politique des camps', in É. Gille (ed.), *Les Réfugiés afghans* (Paris: Amitié Franco-Afghane), 18–23.
Centlivres, P. (1989), 'L'Iran, l'autre pays d'accueil', *Afghanistan Info* 24, 12.
Centlivres, P. (1993), 'A State of the Art Review of Research on Internally Displaced, Refugees and Returnees from and in Afghanistan', Report prepared for the Planning Committee of the Fourth International Research and Advisory Panel Conference on Forced Migration (IRAP), Oxford, January 1994.
Centlivres, P. and Centlivres-Demont, M. (1988a), 'Hommes d'influence et hommes de partis: L'organisation politique dans les villages de réfugiés afghans au Pakistan', in E. Grötzbach (ed.), *Neue Beiträge zur Afghanistanforschung* (Liestal: Stiftung Bibliotheca Afghanica), 29–43.
Centlivres, P. and Centlivres-Demont, M. (1988b), 'The Afghan Refugees in Pakistan: A Nation in Exile', *Current Sociology* 36: 2, 71–92.
Centlivres, P. and Centlivres-Demont, M. (1988c), 'The Afghan Refugees in Pakistan: An Ambiguous Identity', *Journal of Refugee Studies* 1: 2, 141–52.
Centlivres, P. and Centlivres-Demont, M. (2000), 'State, National Awareness and Levels of Identity in Afghanistan from Monarchy to Islamic State', *Central Asian Survey* 19: 3/4, 419–28.
Centlivres-Demont, M. (1993), 'Afghan Women in Peace, War and Exile', in M. Weiner and A. Banuazizi (eds), *The State and Social Transformation in Afghanistan, Iran and Pakistan* (Syracuse, NY: Syracuse University Press).
Cheema, P.I. (1988), 'Impact of the Afghan War on Pakistan', *Pakistan Horizon* 41: 1, 23–45.
Collective for Social Science Research (2006), *Afghans in Pakistan: Broadening the Focus* (Kabul: Afghanistan Research and Evaluation Unit).
Colville, R. (1997), 'The Biggest Case Load in the World', *Refugees* 108, 3–9.
Connor, K.M. (1987), 'Rationales for the Movement of Afghan Refugees to Peshawar', in G.M. Farr and J.G. Merriam (eds), *Afghan Resistance: The Politics of Survival* (Boulder: Westview Press), 151–90.
Crisp, J. (2004), 'The Local Integration and Local Settlement of Refugees: A Conceptual and Historical Analysis', New Issues in Refugee Research, UNHCR Working Paper No. 102 (Geneva:UNHCR Evaluation and Policy Analysis Unit).
Development Research Centre on Migration, Globalisation and Poverty (2005), 'Defining, Measuring and Influencing Sustainable Return', Briefing Paper No. 3 (Brighton: Development Research Centre on Migration, Globalisation and Poverty).
Dupree, N.H. (1987), 'The Demography of Afghan Refugees in Pakistan', in H. Malik (ed.), *Soviet-American Relations with Pakistan, Iran and Afghanistan* (London: Macmillan), 366–94.
Dupree, N.H. (1988), 'Demographic Reporting on Afghan Refugees in Pakistan', *Modern Asian Studies* 22: 4, 845–65.

Dupree, N.H. (1992), 'The Present Role of Afghan Women and Children', Studies and Evaluation Papers No. 7 (The Hague: Bernard van Leer Foundation).
Edwards, D.B. (1986), 'Marginality and Migration: Cultural Dimensions of the Afghan Refugee Problem', *International Migration Review* 20: 2, 313–25.
Eighmy, T.H. (1990), 'Afghanistan's Population Inside and Out', Report (Islamabad: Office of the AID Representative for Afghanistan).
Farr, G.M. (1985), 'The Effect of the Afghan Refugees on Pakistan', in C. Baxter (ed.), *Zia's Pakistan: Politics and Stability in a Frontline State* (Boulder: Westview Press), 93–110.
Glatzer, B. (1998), 'Being Pashtun – Being Muslim: Concepts of Person and War in Afghanistan', in B. Glatzer (ed.), 'Essays on South Asian Society: Culture and Politics II', Arbeitshefte/Working Paper No. 9 (Berlin: Zentrum Moderner Orient), 83–94.
Glatzer, B. (1998), 'Is Afghanistan on the Brink of Ethnic and Tribal Disintegration?', in W. Maley (ed.), *Funamentalism Reborn? Afghanistan and the Taliban* (London: Hurst and Co.; New York: New York University Press), 167–81.
Glatzer, B. (2001), 'War and Boundaries in Afghanistan: Significance and Relativity of Local and Social Boundaries', *International Journal for the Study of Modern Islam* 3, 379–99.
Glatzer, B. (2002), 'The Pashtun Tribal System', in G. Pfeffer and D.K. Behera (eds), *Concept of Tribal Society* (New Delhi: Concept Publisher), 265–82.
Goodson, L.P. (1998), 'Periodicity and Intensity in the Afghan War', *Central Asian Survey* 17: 3, 471–88.
Government of Pakistan (2007), 'Registration of Afghans in Pakistan', Report (Islamabad, Pakistan: Ministry of States and Frontier Regions, National Database and Registration Authority (NADRA) and United Nations High Commissioner for Refugees).
Grare, F. (2003), 'The Geopolitics of Afghan Refugees in Pakistan', in S.J. Stedman and F. Tanner (eds), *Refugee Manipulation: War, Politics, and the Abuse of Human Suffering* (Washington, DC: Brookings Institution Press), 57–95.
Guillo, A., Puig, J.-J. and Roy, O. (1983), 'La guerre en Afghanistan. Modifications des déplacements traditionnels et émergence de nouveaux types de circulations', in M. Centlivres-Demont (ed.), *Migrations en Asie* (Berne: Société Suisse d'ethnologie), 139–53.
Gutman, R. (2008), *How We Missed the Story: Osama Bin Laden, the Taliban, and the Hijacking of Afghanistan* (Washington, DC: United States Institute of Peace Press).
Hanifi, M.J. (2000), 'Anthropology and the Representations of Recent Migrations from Afghanistan', in E.M. Gozdziak and D.J. Shandy (eds), *Rethinking Refuge and Displacement: Selected Papers on Refugees and Immigrants*, Vol. 8 (Arlington: American Anthropological Association), 291–321.
Hussain, R. (2005), *Pakistan and the Emergence of Islamic Militancy in Afghanistan* (Aldershot: Ashgate).

Internal Displacement Monitoring Centre (IDMC) (2007), 'Afghanistan: Fighting in the South Sets Off New Wave of Displacement', 22 December 2006, available at <http://www.internal-displacement.org/8025708F004BE3B1/(httpInfoFiles)/33F6037E738F686DC125724C0037AFF1/$file/Afghanistan_overview_dec06.pdf>, accessed 3 July 2008.

International Crisis Group (2003), 'Afghanistan: The Problem of Pashtun Alienation', Asia Report No. 62 (Brussels: ICG).

IRIN (2003), 'Turkmenistan: Afghan Refugees Want Third-country Resettlement', 30 July, available at <http://www.irinnews.org/report.aspx?reportid=20566>, accessed 23 July 2008.

IRIN (2004), 'Tajikistan: Focus on Afghan Refugees', 16 February, available at <http://www.irinnews.org/report.aspx?reportid=40399>, accessed 23 July 2008.

Jawad, N. (1992), *Afghanistan: A Nation of Minorities* (London: Minority Rights Group).

Khalidi, N.A. (1991), 'Afghanistan: Demographic Consequences of War, 1978–1987', *Central Asian Survey* 10: 3, 101–26.

Koser, K. (2007), 'Internal Displacement in Afghanistan', presentation at seminar on Internal Displacement in South Asia, Brookings Institution, 8 November, available at <http://www.brookings.edu/speeches/2007/1108_afghanistan_koser.aspx>, accessed 1 January 2008.

Kronenfeld, D.A. (2008), 'Afghan Refugees in Pakistan: Not All Refugees, Not Always in Pakistan, Not Necessarily Afghan?', *Journal of Refugee Studies* 21, 1–21.

Kunz, E.F. (1973), 'The Refugee in Flight: Kinetic Models and Forms of Displacement', *International Migration Review* 7: 2, 125–46.

Lischer, S.K. (2005), *Dangerous Sanctuaries: Refugee Camps, Civil War, and the Dilemmas of Humanitarian Aid* (Ithaca: Cornell University Press).

Loescher, G. (1993), *Beyond Charity: International Cooperation and the Global Refugee Crisis* (New York: Oxford University Press).

Loescher, G. (2001), *The UNHCR and World Politics: A Perilous Path* (Oxford: Oxford University Press).

Lumpp, K., Shimozawa, S. and Stromberg, P. (2004), 'Voluntary Repatriation to Afghanistan: Key Features', *Refugee Survey Quarterly* 23, 149–73.

McAdam, J. (2007), *Complementary Protection in International Refugee Law* (Oxford: Oxford University Press).

Maley, W. (1998), 'Introduction: Interpreting the Taliban', in W. Maley (ed.), *Fundamentalism Reborn? Afghanistan and the Taliban* (New York: New York University Press), 1–28.

Maley, W. (2001), 'Security, People-Smuggling, and Australia's New Afghan Refugees', *Australian Journal of International Affairs* 55: 3, 351–70.

Maley, W. (2002), *The Afghanistan Wars* (New York: Palgrave Macmillan).

Maley, W. (2003), 'A New Tower of Babel? Reappraising the Architecture of Refugee Protection', in E. Newman and J. Van Selm (eds), *Refugees and*

Forced Displacement: International Security, Human Vulnerability, and the State (Tokyo: United Nations University Press), 306–29.

Maley, W. (2006), *Rescuing Afghanistan* (London: Hurst & Co.).

Maley, W. (2007), 'Talking to the Taliban', *The World Today* 63: 11, 4–6.

Mansfield, D. (2007), '"Economical with the Truth": The Limits of Price and Profitability in both Explaining Opium Poppy Cultivation in Afghanistan and in Designing Effective Responses', in A. Pain and J. Sutton (eds), *Reconstructing Agriculture in Afghanistan* (Rugby: Practical Action Publishing), 213–234.

Margesson, R. (2007), 'Afghan Refugees: Current Status and Future Prospects, 26 January 2007', Report for Congress (Washington, DC: Congressional Research Service (CRS)), available at <http://fpc.state.gov/documents/organization/80250.pdf>, accessed 1 January 2008.

McAdam, J. (2007), *Complementary Protection in International Refugee Law* (Oxford: Oxford University Press).

Monsutti, A. (2005), *War and Migration: Social Networks and Economic Strategies of the Hazaras of Afghanistan* (New York: Routledge).

Monsutti A. (2006), *Transnational Networks: Recognising a Regional Reality* (Kabul: Afghanistan Research and Evaluation Unit).

Monsutti, A. (2008), 'Afghan Migratory Strategies and the Three Solutions to the Refugee Problem', *Refugee Survey Quarterly* 27: 1.

Monsutti, A., Abbasi-Shavazi, M., Glazebrook, D., Jamshidiha, G., Mahmoudian, H. and Sadeghi, R. (2006), *Afghan Translational Networks: Looking Beyond Repatriation* (Kabul: Afghanistan Research and Evaluation Unit).

Orywal, E. (ed.) (1986), *Die ethnischen Gruppen Afghanistans: Fallstudien zu Gruppenidentität und Intergruppenbeziehungen* (Wiesbaden: Dr Ludwig Reichert Verlag).

Orywal, E. (1993–94), 'Afghanen in Deutschland: Eine Statistische Notiz zur Migrationssituation', *Afghanistan Info* 34, 17–19.

Oxfam (2007) Submission to the House of Commons International Development Committee Inquiry 'Development Assistance in Insecure Environments: Afghanistan,' Overview of Priorities, December 2007, available at <http://www.oxfam.org.uk/resources/policy/conflict_disasters/downloads/071212_idc.pdf>, accessed 23 July 2008.

Qassem, A.S. (2007), 'Afghanistan–Pakistan Relations: Border Controversies as Counter-Terrorist Impediments', *Australian Journal of International Affairs* 61: 1, 65–80.

Rahjo, M.A. (2007), 'Afghanistan: UNHCR Considerations for Specific Groups Relevant to the Determination of Refugee Status', in Austrian Centre for Country of Origin and Asylum Research and Documentation (ACCORD) (ed.), *Country Report Afghanistan, 11th European Country of Origin Information Seminar* (Vienna, 21–22 June 2007), 23–54, available at <http://www.unhcr.org/cgi-bin/texis/vtx/refworld/rwmain?docid=473451a31e>, accessed 1 January 2008.

Rashid, A. (2000), *Taliban: Islam, Oil and the New Great Game in Central Asia* (London: I.B. Tauris).

Rogers, T. (1987), 'Afghan Refugees and the Stability of Pakistan', *Survival* (September/October), 416–29.
Rubin, B.R. (1997), 'Arab Islamists in Afghanistan', in J.L. Esposito (ed.), *Political Islam: Revolution, Radicalism, or Reform?* (Boulder, CO: Lynne Rienner), 179–206.
Rubin, B.R. (2000), 'The Political Economy of War and Peace in Afghanistan', *World Development* 28: 10, 1789–803.
Rubin, B.R., Ghani, A., Maley, W., Rashid, A. and Roy, O. (2001), *Afghanistan: Reconstruction and Peacebuilding in a Regional Framework*, KOFF Peacebuilding Report 1/2001 (Bern: Swiss Peace Foundation).
Ruiz, H.A. (2001), 'Afghan Refugees in Pakistan at Risk', *Refugee Reports* 22: 7, 1–8.
Saikal, A. and Maley, W. (1991), *Regime Change in Afghanistan: Foreign Intervention and the Politics of Legitimacy* (Boulder: Westview Press).
Saikal, F.H., and Maley, W. (1986), 'Afghan Refugee Relief in Pakistan: Political Context and Practical Problems', Department of Politics Working Paper (Canberra: University College, University of New South Wales).
Schetter, C. (2003), *Ethnizität und ethnische Konflikte in Afghanistan* (Berlin: Dietrick Reimer Verlag).
Schmeidl, S. (1994), 'Ethnic Dynamics in Forced Migration: A Comparison of Afghan and Palestinian Refugees', *International Journal of Group Tensions* 24: 4, 333–60.
Schmeidl, S. (2002), '(Human) Security Dilemmas: Long-term Implications of the Afghan Refugee Crisis', *Third World Quarterly* 23: 1, 7–29.
Schmeidl, S. (2007), The Emperor's New Clothes: The Unravelling of Peacebuilding in Afghanistan', *Friedens-Warte – Journal of International Peace and Organizations* 1–2, 69–86.
Schöch, R. (2008), 'UNHCR and the Afghan Refugees in the Early 1980s: Between Humanitarian Action and Cold War Politics', *Refugee Survey Quarterly* 27: 1.
Shahrani, N. (1995), 'Afghanistan's Muhajirin (Muslim "Refugee Warriors"): Politics of Mistrust or Mistrust of Politics', in E.V. Daniel and J.C. Knudsen (eds), *Mistrusting Refugees* (Berkeley: University of California Press), 187–206.
Sliwinski, M. (1989a), 'On the Routes of "Hijrat"', *Central Asian Survey* 8: 4, 63–93.
Sliwinski, M. (1989b), 'Afghanistan: The Decimation of a People', *Orbis* 33: 1, 39–56.
Stapleton, B.J. (2007a), 'A Means to What End? Why PRTs are Peripheral to the Bigger Political Challenges in Afghanistan', *Journal of Military and Strategic Studies* 10: 1, 1–49, available at <http://www.jmss.org/2007/2007fall/articles/stapleton.pdf>, accessed 29 February 2008.
Stapleton, B.J. (2007b), 'Afghanistan at the Cross Roads' in Austrian Centre for Country of Origin and Asylum Research and Documentation (ACCORD) (ed.), *Country Report Afghanistan, 11th European Country of Origin Information*

Seminar (Vienna, 21–22 June 2007), 7–23, available at <http://www.unhcr.org/cgi-bin/texis/vtx/refworld/rwmain?docid=473451a31e>, accessed 1 January 2008.

Strand, A. and Suhrke, A. (2004), 'Afghan Refugees in Iran: From Refugee Emergency to Migration Management', CMI/PRIO Policy Brief, 16 June 2004 (Norway: CMI/PRIO), available at <http://www.cmi.no/afghanistan/peacebuilding/docs/CMI-PRIO-AfghanRefugeesInIran.pdf>, accessed 1 January 2008.

Tapper, N. (1983), 'Abd Al-Rahman's North-West Frontier: The Pashtun Colonisation of Afghan Turkistan', in R. Tapper (ed.), *The Conflict of Tribe and State in Iran and Afghanistan* (London: Croom Helm), 233–61.

Terry, F. (2002), *Condemned to Repeat? The Paradox of Humanitarian Action* (Ithaca: Cornell University Press).

Turton, D. and Marsden, P. (2002), *Taking Refugees for a Ride? The Politics of Refugee Return in Afghanistan* (Kabul: Afghanistan Research and Evaluation Unit).

UNHCR (2000), *The State of the World's Refugees: Fifty Years of Humanitarian Action* (New York: Oxford University Press).

UNHCR (2004a), 'Afghanistan: Challenges to Return', Report published March 2004, available at <http://www.unhcr.org/cgi-bin/texis/vtx/refworld/rwmain?docid=4231bc0d4>, accessed 22 February 2008.

UNHCR (2004b), 'Protracted Refugee Situations', Executive Committee of the High Commissioner's Programme, Standing Committee, 30th Meeting (EC/54/SC/CRP.14, 10 June 2004), available at <http://www.unhcr.org/excom/EXCOM/40c982172.pdf>, accessed 4 January 2008.

UNHCR (2005a), *Statistical Yearbook 2005: Trends in Displacement, Protection and Solutions, Statistical Annex II* (Geneva: UNHCR), available at <http://www.unhcr.org/statistics/STATISTICS/464478a72.html>, accessed 4 January 2008.

UNHCR (2005b), 'Afghan Refugee Statistics February 2005', available at <http://www.unhcr.org/cgi-bin/texis/vtx/home/opendoc.pdf?tbl=SUBSITES&id=421316072>, accessed 15 February 2008.

UNHCR (2006a), 'Refugees By Numbers' (UNHCR/MRPI/B•1/ENG 1, September 2006), <http://www.unhcr.org/basics/BASICS/4523b0bb2.pdf>, accessed 28 July 2008.

UNHCR (2006b), *UNHCR Statistical Yearbook 2006: Trends in Displacement, Protection and Solutions, Statistical Annex* (Geneva: UNHCR), available at <http://www.unhcr.org/statistics/STATISTICS/478cda572.html>, accessed 29 February 2008.

UNHCR (2006c), 'Rethinking Durable Solutions' in *The State of the World's Refugees 2006* (New York: Oxford University Press), 129–99.

UNHCR (2006d), 'Humanitarian Consideration With Regard to Return to Afghanistan', Report published May 2006, available at <http://www.unhcr.org/cgi-bin/texis/vtx/refworld/rwmain?docid=4561c4094>, accessed 22 February 2008.

UNHCR (2006e), 'UNHCR Projected Global Resettlement Needs 2006', Annual Tripartite Consultations on Resettlement; Geneva, 14–15 June 2005, available at <http://www.unhcr.org/refworld/docid/43f5d1a62.html>, accessed 23 July 2008.

UNHCR (2007a), 'Afghanistan', in *UNHCR Global Appeal 2008–2009* (Geneva: UNHCR), available at <http://www.unhcr.org/publ/PUBL/474ac8e00.pdf>, accessed 4 January 2008, 260–63.

UNHCR (2007b), 'Statistical Overview of Afghan Refugee Population in Pakistan, Iran and Other Countries, Returned Afghan Refugees from Pakistan, Iran and Non-Neighboring Countries, IDP Population Movements, Reintegration Activities and Extremely Vulnerable Individuals (EVIs) Program' (2 January–31 October 2007), Operational Information Monthly Summary Report – October 2007 (Kabul: Operational Information Unit), available at <http://www.aims.org.af/services/sectoral/emergency_assistance/refugee/unhcr_summaries/oct_07/summary1.pdf>, accessed 3 January 2008.

UNHCR (2007c), 'South-West Asia', in *UNHCR Global Appeal 2008–2009* (Geneva: UNHCR), 256–60, available at <http://www.unhcr.org/publ/PUBL/474ac8df11.pdf>, accessed 24 January 2008.

UNODC (2007), 'Afghanistan Opium Survey 2007', Report of United Nations Office on Drugs and Crime, 16 November 2007, available at <http://www.unodc.org/pdf/research/Afghanistan_Opium_Survey_2007.pdf>, accessed 3 July 2008.

Westad, O.A. (2005), *The Global Cold War: Third World Interventions and the Making of Our Times* (Cambridge: Cambridge University Press).

Wilkinson, R. (1997), 'An Iranian Surprise', *Refugees* (Focus Afghanistan) 108, 14–15.

Zolberg, A., Suhrke, A. and Aguayo, S. (1989), *Escape from Violence: Conflict and the Refugee Crisis in the Developing World* (New York: Oxford University Press).

Chapter 7
The Refugee and IDP Problem in Iraq

Howard Adelman

Summary

After depicting the past and current state and size of forced migration within and from Iraq, this chapter looks into the ethnic and religious origins of these refugees as a crucial component of the analysis, paying particular attention to minorities other than the dominant Sunni, Shiite and Kurd communities (UNHCR 2006b). Specifically, the plight of the Assyrians and Palestinians will be highlighted, though passing attention will be paid to the Turkoman (Turkmen), Syrian, Iranian, Sabean-Madean, Yazidi and Armenian minorities. The primary focus will be on refugee and IDP flows as an indicator of an inability to repatriate minorities.

Introduction

In a United States House of Representatives hearing on the Iraq War on 11 March 2008, the discussion focused on US obligations to 4.5 million Iraqi refugees and IDPs. The Democrats insisted that the US had a duty to provide aid for their survival in Jordan and Syria and even allow a few into the US since the proximate cause of 'this human tragedy is the invasion of Iraq and its aftermath' and the consequences of neglect could be terrorism targeting the US (Hinnebusch 2007). The Democrats also complained that the contribution of $25 million by the Nouri al-Maliki government was far too little. In contrast, the Republicans wanted the refugees to 'return home'. As the Republican Senator from California, Dana Rohrabacher noted, 'It is not the job of the people of the United States to subsidize the existence and living standards of refugees in Jordan or anywhere else if they have the option of going home' even though, for 70 per cent of those refugees, their homes had been destroyed in sectarian violence. Nevertheless, the Bush administration authorized 12,000 admissions for Iraqis for 2008, a number which included the 500 translators that had worked for the US.[1] Rohrabacher did not criticize the administration for its minimal initiative given the size of the problem, but insisted that, 'They're wonderful people who'd like to live here, especially the

1 'Fact Sheet: Iraqi Refugee Processing', release date 11 March 2008, US Department of Homeland Security (DHS) and US State Department (DOS), available at <http//:www.dhs.gov/xnews/releases/pr_1205327590498.shtm>.

ones who have helped us, but the last thing we want to do is to have people who are friendly to democracy … moving here in large numbers at a time when they're needed to build a new, thriving Iraq' (Pincus 2008).

The Democrats wanted more aid provided. The Republicans wanted the refugees to return. Neither party recognized the desire, need or responsibility of the US to resettle large numbers of Iraqi refugees since large numbers of minorities are unlikely to be able to return home given the pervasive ethnic and religious cleansing that has been rampant in Iraq.

The US was not alone in this attitude even though Iraqis in 2007, as they did in 2006, topped the list of asylum seekers in Western countries, doubling to 45,200 for the year. In Canada, which had not even participated in the US-led invasion of Iraq and which originally had dealt generously with Iraqi refugees seeking asylum from Damascus, where acceptance rates had risen significantly in 2006, they suddenly spiraled downward, as documented by the Canadian Council for Refugees' (CCR) analysis of negative decisions submitted in December 2006.[2] As an email from Janet Dench, the chief executive officer of the CCR, noted,

> there was a shift in attitude towards Iraqis seeking resettlement … we have heard of some disturbing cases where it seems that the visa officer is determined to reject the applicants. In particular, there is a trend – apparently unique to Canada – of arguing that Iraqis of Armenian ethnicity can go to Armenia and therefore are not eligible for resettlement to another country.

However, Canada's Minister of Citizenship and Immigration, Diane Finley, on 19 March 2008 announced that it would double the number of Convention Refugees from 900 to 1800 that it would take from Iraq, one-third of Canada's overseas intake. If the need for resettlement of Iraqi refugees totals one-quarter of a million (just the estimated number of minorities in Syria alone who are unlikely to want or be able to return), then Canada would be expected to take at least 25,000, not 1,800.

On 5 January 2008, a headline article appeared in the *Washington Post Foreign Service* entitled '46,000 Iraqi have left Syria'.[3] The article was subtitled, 'Returns reflect security gains' but that was not what the content of the article said. As Said Hakki, President of the Iraqi Red Crescent Organization was quoted, 'Security has definitely improved, and improved by far … yet the return is really not that dramatic, when you consider that there are almost two million Iraqi refugees out

---

2 See <http://www.ccrweb.ca/IraqiPSRrefusals.pdf>.

3 The Red Crescent report estimated that, '45,913 refugees returned to Iraq from Syria between 15 September and 27 December Most of them came to Baghdad, with only 7,177 returning to provinces in the rest of the country' (*Washington Post Foreign Service* 2008). See <http://www.unhcr.org>.

of the country' and most of those are in Syria.[4] The current phase of the problem of refugees in Iraq is much greater than any previous refugee crisis from Iraq or anywhere else in the Middle East, dwarfing previous refugee crises in that area, including those of the Armenians and the Palestinians. Further, rather than stressing improved security, attention should be paid to the long-term insecurity within Iraq and in the surrounding region as a consequence of the large number of refugees and IDPs (Ferris 2007b)[5] as well as the political implications of the forced displacement.

The figure of 46,000 represented the return movement in the last quarter of 2007, but the explanation suggesting the main reason was increased security begins to smack of propaganda when Iraqi government officials start touting figures like 50,000 returnees a month. Hakki had another explanation. 'People are coming because they are desperate.[6] The majority of them are broke or their visas have expired. That is the bottom line'.[7] The UNHCR survey cited concluded that only 14 per cent of returnees returned because of improved security; 72 per cent had run out of funds or their visas had expired. What Hakki could also have added is that they are returning to areas, overwhelmingly in Baghdad, where their group is in the majority and then only when subsidized with $800 by the Iraqi government to facilitate re-establishing themselves. They are not returning to minority areas,[8]

4 In mid-2006, UNHCR estimated that there were 700,000 Iraqis in Jordan and from 600,000 to 1.5 million in Syria. Later figures suggested from 500,000–750,000 in Jordan but 1.2–1.4 million in Syria, giving a total of about two million. Cf. UNHCR (2007), 'Statistics on Displaced Iraqis around the World', September, available at <http://www.unhcr.org/cgi-bin/texts/vtx/home/opendoc.pdf?tbl=SUBSITESandid=470387fc2>. An earlier Norwegian Fafo research foundation study surveying Iraqis in Jordan concluded that there were between 450,000 and 500,000 Iraqis living in Jordan.

5 Ferris deals with the security impacts of the refugees and IDPs both within Iraq and in the surrounding region.

6 Three research studies conducted at the end of 2007 provide some insights into the situation of Iraqi refugees in Syria, Lebanon and Jordan. 'In Syria, UNHCR and IPSOS Market Research have just finished a second round of research – a follow up to a survey in May. A total of 754 families, comprising 3,553 people, were surveyed. The results show that Iraqi refugees are running out of financial resources – 33 percent say their financial resources will last for three months or less, while 24 percent are relying on remittances from family abroad to survive. Ten percent of the children of families surveyed are working. Iraqi children continue to fall behind in education with 46 percent of those surveyed reporting their children have dropped out of school. The study also highlighted that 17 percent of those surveyed suffer from chronic illnesses with 19 percent unable to take medication due to financial constraints. The research highlights the well-educated profile of the refugee population with 31 percent having a university degree.'

7 As of early December 2007, 536 Iraqis were in detention for illegal entry or for overstaying their visas.

8 'A number of those returning are not going back to their homes and communities, but rather are living in areas where they feel safe, and particularly where they are not a sectarian minority' (Ferris 2007c, 5).

leaving the issue of property reclamation and rights as a further destabilizing area of continuing conflict.

Some scholars emphasize the class nature of the crisis since Iraq is losing its middle class (Ferris 2007c; Lochhead 2007; Watenpaugh 2007).[9] As Michael Messing so pithily described the situation of Iraqis 'expressing anger and gloom, exasperation and despair':

> The overwhelming sense is that of a society undergoing a catastrophic breakdown from the never-ending waves of violence, criminality, and brutality inflicted on it by insurgents, militias, jihadis, terrorists, soldiers, policemen, bodyguards, mercenaries, armed gangs, warlords, kidnappers and everyday thugs. 'Inside Iraq' [the name of the Iraqi blog he is describing] suggests how the relentless and cumulative effects of these various vicious crimes have degraded virtually every aspect of the nation's social, economic, professional, and personal life. (Messing 2008, 18)

Massing went on to describe 'the huge exodus out of Iraq, a stampede that has deprived the country of many of its most competent citizens' (Massing 2008, 19). While this emphasis on middle class suffering and cleansing is both important and accurate, and since the absence of professions creates further incentives to flee because one cannot get access to services, particularly health services, this chapter stresses the process of *ethnic* rather than professional purification since our concern is more with the possibility of reconstruction of Iraq as a pluralistic society rather than its economic reconstruction.[10]

On 28 February 2008, Elizabeth Ferris, Senior Fellow in the Brookings-Bern Project on Internal Displacement, issued an open letter to US presidential candidates entitled, 'Prepare for the Iraqi Humanitarian Crisis'. Ferris is absolutely correct in offering the warning and in insisting on a multilateral effort. She is correct that the property issue is a ticking time bomb that can and should be made far less onerous. What is needed is an implementation scheme along the lines of that used in Bosnia-Herzegovina in 2000, which itself should have been introduced in 1996. However, Ferris fell short in just insisting that a humanitarian response was the priority *or* 'resettle 20,000 refugees this year'. Her own colleagues, Ashraf

9 Ferris cites an Oxfam report – Oxfam and NGO Coordination Committee in Iraq (2007) 'Rising to the Humanitarian Challenge in Iraq', July, pp. 12, 15, for the data that '40 percent of the country's professional class has left the country since 2003' and that the Iraqi Medical Association reported that, '50 per cent of the 34,000 doctors registered in 2003 have left the country'.

10 Other reports are concerned with the lack of an adequate humanitarian response. 'I think everyone at this point is in denial about the human consequences of the war', said Kathleen Newland, director of the Migration Policy Institute, who is familiar with the State Department's views.

al-Khalidi,[11] Sophia Hoffmann and Victor Tanner in their Brookings-Bern paper, 'Iraqi Refugees in the Syrian Arab Republic: A Field-Based Snapshot' (al-Khalidi et al. 2007), noted that Christians 'are over-represented as refugees in Syria compared to their numbers in Iraq' (2007, 1).[12] Further, the authors noted that, 'the overwhelming majority of Iraqis in Syria do not think that it will be safe enough to return in the near future and many believe it will never be safe enough'. Though Sunni Iraqis from Anbar and Salah ad-Din are the largest group (2007, 11), and they will likely return when the security situation is settled, very large numbers of refugees will not be going home. The resettlement plans must be far greater as the US leads a massive interim humanitarian aid effort for both the refugees in Jordan and Syria (Fagen 2007) and for the IDPs. Ferris advocated 'a robust resettlement program as both an expression of US commitment to the humanitarian burden and as a way of protecting the most vulnerable Iraqi refugees'. Resettling 20,000 is far from the robust programme needed not just for the most vulnerable but for the vast number of refugees (estimated to total at least a quarter of a million in Syria alone) who will not be returning home even if much greater security is established in Iraq: for the non-Sunni and non-Shiite refugees will most likely not be able or willing to return and this will significantly diminish the massive repatriation Ferris expects.

Background

The current Iraqi refugee and IDP crisis can be dated specifically to the attacks by al-Qaeda on the World Trade Center and the Pentagon on 11 September 2001 (9/11). In response, George W. Bush launched the Global War on Terror, first by dislodging the Taliban from power in Afghanistan and then instigating a war to overthrow the tyrannical regime of Saddam Hussein in Iraq on what were soon revealed to be false allegations, namely that the regime had weapons of mass

11 Ashraf al-Khalidi is the pseudonym of an Iraqi researcher who previously co-authored with Victor Tanner 'Sectarian Violence: Radical Groups Drive Internal Displacement in Iraq' (al-Khalidi and Tanner 2006).

12 As the authors note, 'After the 2003 invasion, pressure mounted on Christian communities. Many Christians had been government employees under Saddam, which gave them an (undeserved) reputation as servants of the regime. Christians were also associated with the international presence, and many did indeed work for foreign organizations and even the MNF. Radicals also targeted a typically Christian livelihood, the sale of alcohol, and Christian women for not wearing full Islamic dress. Hard-line Islamic groups began referring to Christians as *nasaara* [Christians with a pejorative connotation], which was perceived as threatening ... radical Sunni insurgents are asking local Christians to pay a monthly $100 *jizya* (a head-tax that non-Muslims historically paid in Muslim states) to the "Mosque". Or leave ... Moreover, Christians don't have the tribal structures that can help protect them in times of high insecurity' (2007, 13). See also al-Atraqchi 2007; Amnesty International 2007a; IRIN 2007a; Margesson et al. 2007.

destruction (WMD) and was also aiding and abetting (or was in a position to aid and abet) terrorists and could supply them with WMDs.[13] In addition to the criminality and thuggery, the invasion set off a four-dimensional domestic violent conflict.

Of course, preceding the civil conflict was the dramatic fight between the American-led forces and the Iraqi army. The US was prepared to deliver humanitarian relief for the 100,000 to 150,000 internally displaced persons expected to be produced (Loescher 2002), though the UN and others had anticipated as many as 600,000 would be forcefully displaced. In fact, there were virtually no refugees or IDPs produced by the first phase of the war and many of the 500,000 in exile from the Saddam Hussein regime began to return. After the Iraqi army's speedy defeat and the dismantling of the armed forces, this conflict morphed into a strong insurgency, largely led and conducted by Sunni Iraqis who had been dislodged from power (Zeidel 2008). Second, an even more dramatic inter-communal religious violence erupted between Shia and Sunni.

> Since Shi'a restraint ended in February following the bombing of the holy Shi'a shrine in Samarra, Shi'a and Sunni armed groups have been driving 50,000 people from their homes each month. To date, more than a half a million have been forced out, with Sunni and Shi'a as well as Christians, Kurds and other religious and ethnic groups fleeing to areas where their own group is in the majority. Not only is this changing the social and demographic makeup of many Iraqi cities and undermining any potential for a multiethnic/religious democratic state. It is also causing a grave humanitarian crisis. (al-Khalidi and Cohen 2007)

Cohen and al-Khalidi went on to report:

> The newest and fastest growing number of displaced people is from sectarian violence.[14] Hundreds of thousands more Iraqis are teetering on the brink of displacement, sleeping in different homes at night, and fearing to go to work or to school during the day. Both the Sunni and Shi'a armed groups regularly use threats and intimidation followed by kidnappings and murders to force people out. To make sure they do not return, they frequently rely on brutality, including the beheading of children and the use of electric drills to kill people. They have two goals – to consolidate their territory and to serve as provider and protector, thereby usurping the government's authority. Indeed, people are increasingly turning to armed groups for security rather than the government because they are the ones that protect neighborhoods and provide relief. Moqtada al-Sadr's

13 There are still a few commentators who believe that Saddam Hussein was supplying significant aid to Islamist terrorists. Cf. Irving Kristol's column in *The Australian*, 13 March 2008, arguing that the contents of a recent Pentagon study show that such support existed, even though the study concludes that it did not.

14 Some estimate the exiles to number a million rather than half a million. 'One million Iraqis displaced under the Saddam Hussein regime (the old displaced) remained displaced after the US-led invasion in March 2003.' Cf. Ferris 2007c.

Mahdi army at present is driving most Sunni families out of eastern Baghdad. In the Hurriyeh district, which is only about 3 miles from the Green Zone, the government is doing little to protect the Sunnis from expulsion. The armed groups are connected to political parties, which use them to maximize their own power. Members of government security forces and police often assist the Mahdi army, while Prime Minister Nouri al-Maliki must rely on al-Sadr who controls 30 seats in the parliament. (*Washington Post*, 5 January 2008, A11)[15]

Third, *intra*-communal conflict broke out within both the Shia and Sunni communities. In the Shia religious community, militias led by Moqtada al-Sadr,[16] who leads the Mahdi 'army', were engaged in a struggle with 'moderates' led by Grand Ayatollah Ali al-Sustani.[17] The Sadrs declared a truce in 2007 after they had consolidated their control of Sadr City in Baghdad, on which it imposed religious law in addition to hunting down Palestinians (see later) and Sunnis with ties to Saddam Hussein's Baath Party.

Though not of the scale, intensity or viciousness of the Shia/Sunni inter-religious violence, the fourth and least known record of ethnic cleansing is being conducted largely by Kurds against Arabs, many of whom were forced or subsidized to move to Kirkuk by Saddam Hussein, who repressed the Kurds mercilessly[18] to diminish the Kurdish majority in the oil-rich Kirkuk region and reduce the historical aspirations of Kurds for independence.[19] The Kurdish National Movement (KNM)

15 The change in this pattern was indicated following the increased security that resulted from the surge of American troops when Iraqi troops arrested the commander of the Mahdi Army militia for the southern province of Qadisiyah, Kefah al-Qreeti, at the beginning of January 2008. Al-Qreeti was accused of kidnapping and killing Iraqi military officials (*Washington Post Foreign Service* 2008).

16 Cf. International Crisis Group 2006, 5. The Baker/Hamilton Report estimated the militia strength of the Mahdi army to be as much as 60,000 fighters.

17 The Shiite Soldiers of Heaven, for example, launched a large attack against Najaf, the holy city for Shiites, to occupy the sacred shrine and massacre the religious leadership there, including Ayatollah al-Sistani on Ashura, on the tenth day of Muharram on the Muslim calendar (29 January 2007). They were repelled only because US forces and air power intervened to reinforce the Iraqi army. Reporting from Baghdad, see Santora (2007), 'Militia nearly overran Iraqi troops'.

18 Saddam Hussein was not the only Iraqi ruler to have oppressed the Kurds. Consecutive Iraqi governments used various oppressive policies for assimilating Kurds. Hussein distinguished himself by using chemical weapons to induce those who survived his attacks to integrate fully. In the notorious Anfal campaign between 1980 and 1988, Saddam Hussein killed about 200,000 Kurds. Even after the no-fly zone introduced by the Americans allowed Kurds to control *most* of their own area, Hussein retained control of Kirkuk, Makhmoor, Shingar and Khanaqeen until finally overthrown by the Americans in 2003. From 1991–2003, Saddam forcibly displaced over 300,000 Kurds, Turkomans and Assyrians; 300,000 Arabs from southern Iraq were resettled into these areas.

19 Cf. Human Rights Watch (1993) 'Genocide in Iraq – The Anfal Campaign Against the Kurds', July. In an act of ethnic targeted murder, the report documents the systematic and deliberate murder of up to 100,000 Kurds between February and September 1988.

came into being after the collapse of the Ottoman Empire when modern Iraq was created by Britain, and included Southern Kurdistan[20] following the division of Greater Kurdistan (GK)[21] in the 1920s.[22] As a result, the Kurds have effectively been warring either for independence or greater autonomy until they finally gained their highest degree of autonomy ever[23] over most of their traditional homeland when the US established the no-fly zone over the area in 1991.

Kurds want control over the rest of their traditional lands. They feel justified in asking for the return of their property and the repatriation of the 300,000 Kurds expelled by Saddam Hussein (Gunter 1999). However, more is at stake than simply return. The Kurds also want to regain hegemony in Kirkuk.[24] Unlike the Sadrs,

At the time of the American-led invasion in 2003, of the one million existing internally displaced from the Saddam Hussein regime, 800,000 were Kurds living in the northern governorates. Cf. Ferris 2007c.

20 In response to the revolt of the Kurds against rule from Baghdad, in 1924 the British sent the Royal Air Force (RAF) to bomb Kirkuk. The British captured Kirkuk and sent the leader of the revolt, Shaikh Mahmood, who controlled the Sulaymani province, into exile in India. The first 7000 refugees from Iraq were produced.

21 Greater Kurdistan includes southeastern Turkey, northwestern Iran, northeastern Iraq and northeastern Syria, where Kurds constitute the majority of the population. In that area of 230,000 square miles, there are 25–35 million Kurds, the largest nation without their own state.

22 The Treaty of Sèvres of 10 August 1920 between the Allied Powers and Ottoman Turkey abolished the Ottoman Empire. Turkey was required to renounce its control over Arab areas in Asia and North Africa. The treaty provided for an independent Armenia, an autonomous Kurdistan, and Greek control over the Aegean islands commanding the Dardanelles. However, when the young Turks rebelled at these terms, the imperial ambitions of Britain and France, reinforced by an increasingly isolationist US, led to concessions. The Treaty of Lausanne replaced the Treaty of Sèvres and the promises of independence for the Armenians and autonomy for the Kurds based on Wilson's principles of national self-determination were abrogated.

23 During the protracted civil war between Kurds and Arabs from 1919 until the American invasion in 2003, hundreds of thousands of Kurds were killed or forcefully displaced as IDPs or refugees. Only once in that period did the Kurds come close to independence when they declared a Kurdistan Republic in January 1946. When their main backers, the Soviets, agreed to evacuate Iran in the agreements among the superpowers, the Kurdistan Republic collapsed in six weeks as the British assisted the Shah of Iran to crush the revolt. Barzani, who had joined the revolt, fled Iraq with 600 followers and sought refuge in the Soviet Union. However, over the last 75 years Iran has been the main sanctuary for Kurds fleeing Iraq, including 500,000 between 1975 and 1988, except for the over million Kurdish refugees who tried to flee into Turkey in 1991. Cf. Laizer 1996; MacDowall 2000.

24 In April 2003, the Kurds liberated Kirkuk before the US forces arrived. The interim constitution (Transitional Administrative Law (TAL)) of March 2004 made provision for KRI as a self-rule region leaving its ultimate territorial status in abeyance. The inclusion of Kirkuk within the KRI was left undetermined. Cf. Wong (2004): 'recent protests by Arab and Turkmen residents against Kurdish claims have already ended in gunfire and death;

Iraqi Kurds have largely relied on politics and diplomacy to achieve their ends.[25] Originally there was a great deal of good news to support hope for a peaceful outcome including the election of a Kurdish mayor in Kirkuk on 29 May 2003. The Transitional Administrative Law, after the creation of the first appointed Iraqi Governing Council following the fall of Saddam Hussein, in March 2004 agreed on self-rule for the Kurdistan Region of Iraq but ominously failed to agree on the border of that region. Kurdish was recognized as an official Iraqi language. Article 58 even provided for the return of the 100,000 Kurds to Kirkuk,[26] but issues of compensation or property reinstatement were left unresolved. Jalal al-Talbani, a separatist Kurdish leader, even became President of Iraq; and the new constitution guaranteed Kurds self-rule and the power to legislate in key areas, control over the Kurdish militia, the *Peshmarga*, and the right to determine oil and gas policy in the Kurdish territory. The constitution provides for a referendum to determine whether Kirkuk would be included within the Kurdistan Region of Iraq (KRI) but strenuous efforts were made to postpone the vote that was promised by the end of 2007.[27] Further, following the replacement of a Kurdish figure as Prime Minister and the re-inclusion of Sunnis in the political process, Kurdish representatives in the central government have been increasingly marginalized and the timetable for resolving property issues and returning displaced Kurds to their homes keeps being delayed. Should their autonomy be threatened, Kurds fear the loss of the oil-rich province of Kirkuk (the region produces 40 per cent of Iraq's oil and 70 per cent of Iraq's gas) especially if the Americans withdraw precipitously as they did from Lebanon and Somalia. Kurds fear the creation of a strong central government in Iraq that would threaten their hard won autonomy since 1991.[28]

However, in addition to the ominous notes cited above, there are more serious indications pointing to a future failure, such as the continuing resistance and objections to Kurdish demands from the Shiite followers of Sadr. Sistani at first also opposed the Kurdish demands and only gave in at the prospect of the failure of forming an Iraqi government. There were also efforts to dissolve the *Peshmarga* and integrate it into the Iraqi army. However, Kurds regard their militias as the key

---

Arabs paid to move to Kirkuk under Hussein's campaign to make region Arab fear that Kurds will exact vengeance; many have fled'. See also Wong 2005.

25 For a discussion of the role of the US in supporting the Kurds, see Kfir 2008.

26 After protracted negotiations with the Americans, in January 2005, 100,000 of the 300,000 exiles were allowed to return and vote in the Iraqi elections.

27 A referendum was supposed to have been held by 31 December 2007 for the inclusion of Kirkuk within the KRI, but the Iraq Study Group led by the former Secretary of State James Baker and the Democrat Congressman Lee Hamilton) recommended postponing the referendum on Kirkuk (Baker and Hamilton 2006).

28 Kurds had proposed autonomy before, instead of seeking independence. When the KNM revolted again in the 1930s in Barzan district in Arbil (Hewlair) province under Mustafa Barzani, Barzani was prepared, in 1943, to accept administrative, cultural and political autonomy for the Kurdish region consisting of Kirkuk, Hewlair (Arbil), Sulaymani, and several other Kurdish districts in Mosul and Diyala.

safeguard in preventing a recurrence of the past betrayals of Kurdish ambitions for self-rule from the 1920s, 1945 and 1975. One of the side effects of the Kurdish/ Arab struggle for control of Kirkuk has not only been the concerted effort to expel Arabs resettled in Kirkuk by Saddam Hussein, but also, though to a much lesser extent, attempts to drive out Turkmen (Associated Press 2007c)[29] as well as Christian Armenians and Assyrian-Chaldeans.[30]

Even more portentous signs than the policy decisions from the top are coming from what Iraqis are doing with their feet. They are fleeing minority areas in droves. UNHCR figures on the refugees and IDPs in Iraq are quoted but not really discussed in the Baker/Hamilton Iraq Report,[31] which mentions the figures of those forcibly displaced. Baker ignores any analysis of the refugees and IDPs. Of course, ignoring these indicators undermines the prognosis required. This is a huge mistake. For what has happened to the refugees and IDPs is a major early warning signal (Adelman 1998) of whether the struggle for a pluralist democratic Iraq can be salvaged. Further, when refugees and IDPs are left as a continuing festering sore on the body politic, IDPs are vulnerable to recruitment by military organizations in order to recover lost property and because they personally lack sources of income or security. Refugees go on to either finance such struggles if they successfully settle abroad or become a militant diaspora community with the object of return. Since the bulk of the refugees from Iraq are minorities who

29 'When Abdul-Karim Wadi, a Shiite Arab, got what amounted to thousands of dollars cash and a free apartment to move to Kirkuk from Baghdad 18 years ago, he says he didn't know he was a tool of Saddam Hussein's campaign to flood the ethnically mixed, oil-rich city with Arabs. Now, Wadi says, Kirkuk is home and he has no plans to leave. He's trying to ride out the increasing outbreaks of ethnic tension, a symptom of a deeper struggle for the city's future – a complex tangle of ancient ethnic antagonism and hardball twenty-first century struggle for oil resources. The Arab and Turkmen population in Kirkuk are fighting Kurdish efforts to join the city – they call it the 'Jerusalem of the Kurds' – to their semiautonomous region just to the north. Thrown into that ethnic cauldron are Armenian and Assyrian-Chaldean Christian minorities' (Associated Press 2007c).

30 For a broader perspective in the current context, see International Crisis Group (2006b), 'Iraq and the Kurds: The Brewing Battle of Kirkuk'. The report documents the struggle over oil and identity among Kurdish, Turkoman, Arab and Assyrian-Chaldean communities.

31 'Exile of Kurds from Kirkuk in late 1980s planted seeds for bitter ethnic antagonism that has grown into most incendiary issue outside of Sunni-led insurgency, and one that more than any other is delaying formation of a new government; when Kurds were relocated, Arabs were settled there to exploit vast oil reserves and solidify control of region; fear is that growing struggle over Kirkuk and efforts to restore Kurds to jobs and property without disenfranchsing Arabs could ignite civil war; debate has so inflamed passions that any real decision on Kirkuk's future may be delayed; Kurdish leaders say their claim to region has historical basis; while many realize that Arabs brought into region are also victims of Saddam Hussein, there is disagreement on how to rectify situation' (Baker and Hamilton 2006).

cannot and will not go back, this source of continuing insecurity is unlikely to be a major problem.

At the beginning of 2008, borders have largely been closed to refugees fleeing Iraq. But in 2006, figures of those forcefully displaced ranged up to 1.8 million Iraqi refugees[32] and 2.25 million IDPs. 12.7 per cent of the population had been displaced. Of the refugees, in mid-2006 UNHCR estimated that there were 700,000 Iraqis in Jordan; from 600,000 to 1.5 million in Syria; at least 100,000 in Egypt; 20,000–40,000 in Lebanon; 54,000 in Iran; 100,000 in Turkey and 200,000 in the Gulf.[33] As we noted earlier in this chapter, later figures suggested from 500,000–750,000 in Jordan but 1.2–1.4 million in Syria, giving a total of about two million. Forty thousand Iraqis applied for asylum during 2006 – mostly in Europe as the war and its fallout caused a new displacement of tens of thousands of Iraqis and long-term refugee residents in the country. By 1 January 2007, there were 36,200 Iraqis in Germany, 22,000 in the UK, 21,800 in the Netherlands and 23,600 in Sweden with smaller numbers spread throughout the rest of Europe. As neighbouring countries close their borders, refugees are often deported back to Iraq as their visas expire, thereby increasing the IDP population and reducing the refugee numbers. Many of the initial refugees were professionals – doctors, teachers, computer technicians – so crucial to the stability and the well-being of a country. Even more significantly, a very large and very disproportionate number of the refugees were made up of minorities from Iraq. Of the IDPs, 80 per cent were from Baghdad, and fled from neighbourhoods where they were in a minority to other neighbourhoods where they were in a majority (Ferris 2007c). [34] At the same time, of 18 governorates in Iraq, ten have closed their borders to IDPs.[35]

Media coverage

There were many UNHCR bulletins about the Palestinians from Iraq, and they received scant attention in the media.[36] Before 2008, the public heard virtually

32 The Washington-based United States Committee for Refugees provided a figure of only 889,000 refugees in mid-2006. USCR 14 June 2006. Elizabeth Ferris, a renowned expert on Iraqi refugees and IDPs, in a January 2007 speech cited figures of 2.25 million IDPs and 1.5 million refugees. 'The best estimates today are that there are some 2.25 million internally displaced Iraqis and over 1.5 million Iraqis in Syria, 500–750,000 in Jordan, 150,000 in Egypt, 55,000 in Iran, 40,000 in Lebanon, 10,000 in Turkey and 200,000 in the Gulf (including Saudi Arabia)' (Ferris 2007a).

33 If maximum figures are used, the total comes to 2.7 million refugees.

34 'Some 80% of the IDPs in the country are from Baghdad, many of whom have moved to other neighborhoods in the capital city.' (Ferris 2007c).

35 Only Anbar, Baghdad, Diyala, Ninewa, Salah al-Din, Missan, Thi-Qar, and Wassit allow entry for IDPs. Cf. International Organization for Migration 2007.

36 The situation has changed little since the publication of a paper by Spiegel and Qassim (2003), 'Forgotten Refugees and Other Displaced Populations', in *The Lancet*. If

nothing about the other minorities.[37] Elizabeth Ferris, in an address at the beginning of 2007, said that, 'I find it shocking that there has been so little media attention to Iraqi displacement and that it has been so invisible in the current political debates about the "surge"' (Ferris 2007a). At the end of 2007, she began an address with the statement that Iraqi IDPs have largely been 'absent from mainstream media coverage of the war' (Ferris 2007a).[38] Referring to the Christian refugees, William Warda[39] noted that, 'Western sources seem uninterested in writing about their number or situation'. We read a great deal about the struggle between the Sunni and the Shiites and certainly between the Americans and the insurgents. We certainly read a great deal in the early phases of the war about the international diplomatic struggles – France and Germany versus the US – often fought out in the Security Council (Malone 2006) and the US versus Iran and Syria. We also read of the domestic conflicts between dissident Republicans and Democrats against the administration policies. But there has been relatively little coverage of the refugee and IDP situation of Iraqis.

The reason was not because the region was being ignored. As American news services noted, the Middle East shaped much of how Americans viewed 2006. Only one of the top ten news stories of 2006 had nothing to do with the Middle East. Iraq was the number one Middle East story. But the focus has been on deaths, the American commitment to keep troops in Iraq, and the structural, operational, organizational and normative challenges posed by Iraq. In 2007, attention turned to the surge and the subsequent reduction in violence, as much a by-product of the reincorporation of Iraqi tribal Sunnis into the political and military efforts to challenge the insurgency as from the increase in American troops. There has

one looks at the academic journals, one finds a generally blissful ignoring of the refugee issue. For example, see the 2008 special issue of *Survival: Global Politics and Strategy* 50: 1, focusing on Iraq, with articles by McMaster; Strachan; Nye; Wehner; Pickering; and Yamani, available at <http://www.informaworld.com>.

37 UNHCR issued many advisories over the last year. In response to one recent advisory on the protection needs of Iraqis outside Iraq, UNHCR received very few calls from media around Europe. In general, in the coverage of the Iraqi war, the refugee and IDP issue received relatively scant coverage. Cf. Murray et al. 2008. More recently, there has been some change, given the Brookings-Bern project's focus on the DPs and the appearance of some articles in the *Wall Street Journal* (*Wall Street Journal* 2008) and those papers that pick up Associated Press reports (Associated Press 2008).

38 As Ferris pointed out, 'the security and humanitarian communities have largely talked past one another. Those concerned with humanitarian issues haven't seriously considered security concerns of host governments and those concerned with security have rarely addressed refugee and displaced issues, except occasionally in terms of the need to 'contain' the spillover of Iraq's problems in the region and to prevent the de-stabilization of host countries by the presence of refugees' (Ferris 2007a). See also Ferris (2007b) and Byman and Pollack (2007).

39 William Warda is an Assyrian researcher and webmaster of Christians of Iraq, a website that monitors news and information on the community.

been little attention to the refugees and IDPs. The trajectory of increased numbers in both categories year after year since the invasion of Iraq adumbrates a poor prognosis for the future of Iraq since the displaced include a large number of the middle class who are needed for recovery and for ensuring stability.

Ignoring the refugee and IDP situation was surprising in a way since Jay Garner, the first proconsul America sent to Iraq, was a military man steeped in dealing with humanitarian crises and well prepared to deal with the anticipated humanitarian crisis of refugees and IDPs expected in light of the American-led assault on Iraq.[40] However, there was no real problem of any significance with refugees or IDPs in the immediate aftermath of the American invasion and the unexpectedly speedy initial victory.

There is an explanation for the little coverage of this aspect of the conflict up until 2007. It was too dangerous for journalists to cover the domestic violence, even for Iraqi journalists. At least 80 of them have been killed. The domestic violence and the purging of minorities were not the only subjects ignored. It is not that certain problems were overlooked. The aggressive behaviour of the mercenaries was also ignored and only became a matter of public debate when Blackwater private security contractors killed 17 unarmed civilians in al-Nossor Square in September 2006. This lack of coverage was not because the mercenaries were disguised or hidden. 'Indeed, with their wraparound sunglasses, assault rifles, and menacing manner, they were hard to miss. Yet with few exceptions … this major aspect of the US presence in Iraq remained until very recently hidden from American view' (Massing 2008, 18). Americans had other priorities.

This subsequently changed, and changed dramatically, as did the coverage of refugees and IDPs, though not quite as dramatically. Perhaps the most ominous sign of all of the perilous ones is that, after a long period of ignoring the refugee and IDP issue, the international media have woken up. At the end of January 2007, a number of stories began appearing in the press on the Iraq refugee and IDP crisis. *The New York Times* even ran an editorial on the issue.[41] If the American media have latched onto the story, then the symptoms of systematic ethnic cleansing have become very apparent.

40 As UNHCR has noted, in preparation for an expected exodus of up to 600,000 refugees in 2002–2003, UNHCR had a budget of $154 million. For a caseload of six times that number, UNHCR has one-sixth of the budget, only $29 million, and even that miniscule sum is only about 60 per cent funded. Billions of dollars in reconstruction have not been able to be spent because of poor security. Nevertheless, humanitarian programmes inside Iraq and in neighbouring states remain neglected.

41 *The New York Times* 2007: 'To calculate the price that Iraqis have paid for the American misadventure in their country, you have to deal in big, round, horrifying numbers. Civilians killed last year: 34,000. Driven from their homes within Iraq: 1.8 million. Fled to other countries: an additional 2 million, and growing. The number of Iraqis who have found refuge in the United States is easier to pin down. This country has admitted a grand total of 466 Iraqi refugees since 2003.' The emphasis of the editorial was on the US admitting more Iraqi refugees.

After reading about the incessant violence before the surge, most observers became pessimistic about the outcome of the various struggles and could only envision more and more violence and the possible dissolution of Iraq.[42] The recent diminution in violence, however, has not reduced the pessimistic outlook for Iraq. After all, where is there evidence of trust between the various communities? Certainly, Kurdish voices have been insisting on northern autonomy if not outright independence since they probably fear the Shiite majority even more than the Sunni minority.[43] What we read of is people fleeing their homes and neighbourhoods to escape Iraq or fleeing their homes to neighbourhoods dominated by their own ethnic or religious group. Further, there is a lot at stake. However, while the cities of Mosul and Falluja are considered Sunni safe havens and Karbala and Najaf are Shia safe havens, and the north is safe for Kurds, there are no safe havens where Christians (and others such as Sabean-Madeans) or Palestinians are a majority.

Economics exacerbates the problem (Looney 2008). The north has 40 per cent of the nation's oil. The south has 60 per cent, and it is dominated by Shiites.[44] And extremist Shiites are gaining in strength. In the middle, where Sunnis are predominant, there is evidently no oil. Now that Shiites control the political levers of power, the merger of power, oil and demographic strength gives them a powerful status and little reason to be trusted by other groups. I believe that the situation in Iraq has passed the tipping point and ethnic cleansing is being driven by radicals from each of the different dominant communities (al-Khalidi and Victor 2006).[45]

---

42 Cf. the story on Stephen Hadley, President Bush's National Security Adviser, and his pessimistic worries: 'Top Bush adviser paints dark Iraq picture: Ending strife may not be possible: Hadley' (Powell 2007).

43 'Demographically, the threads that make up the fabric of the Iraqi population are a very powerful force working against unity in Iraq, making Iraq's territorial integrity questionable and unjustifiable. Iraq's population is made up mainly of Arabs and Kurds, two different nationalities each with their own distinct and unique national attributes. Iraq has been ruled by Arabs since its formation as a republic. Kurds as a distinct nation have fought their subjugation to the Arabs, and rightly demanded their statehood since the inception of Iraq. Kurds have been tortured and genocide has been committed against them by Iraqi Arabs, resulting in the Kurds' resentment of any forced union as a nation with the Arabs. Arabs themselves are divided; the majority in Iraq are Shiites and they feel closer to their fellow Shiites in Iran than the Sunni Arabs in Iraq. They too have suffered under Saddam and never had their fair share of political power. The Sunni Arabs have been dominant in Iraq, and now, as their last man, Saddam, has been ousted they are not willing to share power with the rest of the Iraqis. Therefore, they are behind the insurgencies and thus the progress of peace and stability in Iraq is not only barred by the differences of its people groups alone, but also by the outright actions of some of its own people to sabotage it' (Naqishbendi 2005).

44 Of the course the fight over oil involves not only Kurds, Sunnis and Shia but external actors as well, especially the US. Cf. Mahdi 2007.

45 The Brookings Institution paper builds on four weeks of field research by Iraqi researchers across the country to present a bottom-up view of the sectarian violence in Iraq and the ensuing displacement. Radical groups drive the agenda and there are few voices

Prior to the surge the accelerated rate of killing served as testimony to the trend line. The UN reported that 34,452 Iraqis were killed in 2006 as American deaths[46] in Iraq by 30 January reached a total of 3,084 since March 2003.[47] Kim Gamel achieved fame as a journalist by becoming the reporter of record for the Grim Reaper in Iraq.[48] In March and April of 2006, there were 3,500 *reported* Iraqi deaths, that is an average of over 50 per day, and it is generally believed that the death toll was actually much higher. During the same period, according to the Iraqi Red Crescent, 'more than 89,000 Iraqis became refugees', a ratio of 26 refugees for every death, though in wars of ethnic cleansing the usual rule of thumb is a ratio of 100 refugees for every person killed (Kaufmann 2006). Nevertheless, using the lower ratio, that would mean that almost a million Iraqis became refugees in 2006 alone.

The prestigious medical journal, *The Lancet*, published a report (Burnham et al. 2006) claiming that 601,000 Iraqis had been killed violently since the invasion, and 54,000 died non-violent deaths over and above the numbers that might have been expected to die. The additional numbers probably died as a result of the difficulties of accessing medical facilities or the deteriorated quality of those facilities. Assuming the accuracy of the report, and using a ratio of only 26:1 (26 refugees and IDPs for every violent death), that would yield a figure of 17 million refugees and IDPs, which would mean that 65 per cent of the population had been displaced. This figure seems enormous and not credible, so either the estimate of 601,000 violent deaths is far too high or the ratio of forced migrants to violent deaths is exaggerated. A much lower ratio of about five forcibly displaced for every violent death would yield a total of at least 3.4 million forcibly displaced, the figure cited by UNHCR at the time. Clearly, the international community has an

---

of moderation. The hot spots are the mixed cities in which one ethnic group has a clear opportunity to not only dominate but exclude others. They include: Baghdad, Mosul, Basra, Salah ad-Din Province (Balad, Dujeil, Samarra), Dyala Province (Baquba, Muqdadiya), and northern Babil, where there is faultline between Sunnis and Shiites. In Anbar, where there are no minorities and the city is exclusively Sunni, there is no violence.

46 In addition to Americans, 130 Britons, 13 Bulgarians, six Danes, two Dutch, two Estonians, one Fijian, one Hungarian, 32 Italians, one Kazakh, three Latvians, 18 Poles, two Romanians, five Salvadoran, four Slovaks, 11 Spaniards, two Thai and 18 Ukrainians have died in Iraq as of 26 January 2007. CNN, 'Forces: US and Coalition Casualties', as at 30 January 2007 <http://www.cnn.com/SPECIALS/2003/iraq/forces/casualties/>.

47 *The Boston Globe* has taken up the responsibility not only for counting the numbers but naming each of the persons who were killed. Cf. *The Boston Globe* 2007.

48 '137 killed or found dead across Iraq' (Associated Press 2007b), 'Suicide car bomb in Baghdad kills 17' (Associated Press 2007a), piled on top of story after story: 'A bomb hidden in a box of pigeons exploded Friday as shoppers gathered around;' 'American killed in Iraq was set to marry'; 'Security helicopter shot down in Iraq'; 'The deaths of three more US troops also were announced'; 'Bombs, shootings kill at least 137 in Iraq'; 'US military deaths in Iraq Hit 3069'; 'Iraq's government also began its own investigation of the deaths in Haditha'; 'Bomb attacks kill 2, wound 9 in Iraq'; 'A bomb hidden in a box'.

enormous crisis on its hands of massive forced displacement. The recent increased attention by UNHCR has been welcomed by those bearing the burden of housing the refugees (Jansen 2007).[49]

UNHCR

For 2007, UNHCR launched a $60 million general appeal to deal with Iraqi refugees and IDPs, an appeal which will only deal with hundreds of thousands of the most vulnerable forcibly displaced Iraqis. The appeal included not only those displaced within Iraq,[50] but those who fled to five other countries in the region – Syria, Jordan, Lebanon, Egypt and Turkey, which had received the largest number of Iraqis. The appeal did not include any provision for those who fled elsewhere, mainly to Europe.[51] In the West, there had been a 70 per cent increase in Iraqi asylum claims in 2006 in comparison to the previous year. In light of the widespread and targeted violence by one group against another and the dire security situation, UNHCR advised governments to look favourably on Iraqi asylum seekers, but only specified favouritism for those fleeing violence in southern and central Iraq because the security situation was relatively good in Kurdish controlled areas. UNHCR recommended that, 'no Iraqi from Southern or Central Iraq should be forcibly returned to Iraq until such time as there is substantial improvement in the security and human rights situation in the country'. On the other hand, in the resolution providing the mandate for the UN mission in Iraq, the UN Assistance Mission for Iraq (UNAMI) not only is required to coordinate the delivery of humanitarian assistance, but must enable 'the safe, orderly, and voluntary return, as appropriate, of refugees and displaced persons'.[52] However, with respect to those fleeing the north, UNHCR recommended that those *not* originally from the north be treated the same as those fleeing the south and central regions, and that

49 Though he could not avoid misrepresentation and exaggeration when arbitrarily linking the Palestinian exodus in 1948 to the current crisis while gratuitously chiding UNHCR that, incidentally, it paid inordinate attention to the Palestinian refugees from Iraq, Jansen's concern, like that of *The New York Times*, was on the failure of the US to provide resettlement for the refugees and its support for a Shiite dominated government.

50 Unfortunately, since most humanitarian agencies fled Iraq after the bombing of UNHCR headquarters in 2003, and those remaining are subject to great security risks with very restricted mobility, the distribution of aid within Iraq has been controlled overwhelmingly by sectarian organizations that just as often use relief to increase influence and power. Cf. Wong and Cave 2007; UN-IRIN 2007b; UN-IRIN 2007a; Cave 2007; all cited by Ferris 2007c. See also IRIN 2007b.

51 Of some 40 nationalities seeking asylum in European countries in the first half of 2006, for example, Iraqis ranked first with more than 8,100 applications (UNHCR 2007c).

52 UN Security Council Resolution 1770, 10 August 2007, <http://www.un.org/News/Press/docs/2007/sc9095.doc.htm>.

those originating from the north but who had fled from there be assessed on the individual merits of the case.

Assyrians

I begin with the Assyrians because, as Jonathan Lewis noted, they are the barometer of pluralism in Iraq (Lewis 2003)[53] and trace their heritage back to the ancient Assyrians and Babylonians. Assyrians suffered three major disasters in the twentieth century. In 1915, 'up to two-thirds of the Assyrian community of southeastern Turkey and northern Iran was physically decimated in a matter of months' (Lewis 2003). An estimated 750,000 were slaughtered. Secondly, in late summer of 1933 when an armed group of some 800 Assyrians crossed from Iraq into Syria and were pushed back again, they were attacked and crushed by the Iraqi military and slaughtered in the massacre at Simele. The Assyrian villages around Simele were destroyed by the Iraqi army and Kurdish irregulars. Under Saddam Hussein, Assyrian national and even cultural life was severely repressed. In the Iran–Iraq war, many Assyrians were drafted and sent as cannon fodder to the front lines, resulting in very high casualty rates. Denied their rights,[54] hundreds of thousands emigrated.

The vast majority of the 1.2 million Christians in Iraq at the time of the American invasion were Assyrians, though a very small minority of Assyrians were and remain Muslim rather than Christian.[55] Of the vast majority of Assyrians, 90 per cent are Chaldeans and ten per cent are not. Of the non-Chaldean Assyrians, two-thirds are Nestorians who date back to ancient churches of Persia and one-third follow the Syriac rite. Assyrians are proud of their Christian heritage as well as the fact that they speak the language of Jesus, namely Aramaic. They also resent being

53 'The future of Iraq now hangs in the balance. Should a postwar Iraq blossom into a democratic or quasi-democratic state, no one would welcome this more than the Assyrians. It would allow them to assert their cultural and religious rights within the context of the new Iraqi polity and relieve them of the fear of being persecuted as Christians or non-Arabs. This means assuring that Assyrians have a place in a post-Saddam Iraqi state and that their concerns about the role of Islam in the new polity are addressed. While Assyrians have demonstrated their willingness and desire for an Iraq for all Iraqis, they would not fare well in a state constitutionally influenced by shari'a (Islamic law).'

54 The United Nations Oil-for-Food programme stipulated that only 'Arab Christians', not Assyrians, could use ration cards.

55 There are Arabic-speaking Muslims who identify themselves as Assyrians. For example, the Mhalmoye or Mhallami can be found in the Tur Abdin area; it is believed that they were converted to Islam in the sixteenth century. The Barzani Kurds, the Tagritoye, the Tay and the Shammar are Arab tribes that believe themselves to be descended from Assyrian stock.

identified as Arab.[56] However, some Assyrians accepted assimilation. Tariq Aziz, the Iraqi deputy prime minister under Saddam Hussein, was an Assyrian-Chaldean Christian. To identify as an Arab, he changed his surname from Youkhana to Aziz when he joined the Baath party.

Fifteen years before the Kuwait invasion, Christian Assyrians constituted as much as ten per cent of the population or almost 2.5 million. After the 1991 Kuwait war, Iraqi Assyrians left in droves for Australia, Canada, and the United States, and in 2003, approximately 400,000 Assyrians were living in North America, concentrated in Detroit, Phoenix and San José as well as Toronto and Windsor. The Catholic Relief Agency (CARITAS) reported that it was sheltering refugees in Turkey, mostly Chaldean Christian women.[57] Today, the 1.2 million total Christian population at the start of the Bush war can be cut in half again. The half-life of the Assyrian Iraq population accelerates and the length of time to reduce to one-half again takes half the time of the previous reduction. At the beginning of 2008, reputable authorities estimate that only 150,000–200,000 Christians remain in Iraq, less than ten per cent of the total in 1990 (La Civita 2008).[58]

In the immediate aftermath of both the Kuwait war and the success of the initial invasion, many Assyrians made plans to return to their ancestral homeland to rebuild their churches and their community as well as to institute legal claims to recover their land and assets. Such hopes were quickly shattered and bear out the pessimistic prophecies of the great American writer, William Saroyan, who foresaw only a dismal fate for the Assyrian community after the 1933 pogroms (Sayoran 1934).

Though Assyrians made up five per cent of the population of Iraq before the US invasion, giving a total of perhaps up to 1.5 million, by 2008 they constituted less than one per cent of that population. The Assyrians live in Baghdad, Mosul, and villages in northwest Iraq. Half of the asylum seekers in Europe from Iraq are Christians. In some of the highest estimates, they make up one-third of the Iraqi refugees in just one country, Syria. These Christians fled the general violence as well as the specific attacks on Christians and the chronic abuse of human rights often targeting Christians.[59] Although the exodus began when civil order broke

56 In 2001, a coalition of Assyrian, Assyrian-Chaldean and Maronite organizations reprimanded the Arab American Institute for classifying Assyrians and Maronites as Arab and requested that the Arab American Institute 'cease and desist from portraying Assyrians and Maronites of past and present as Arabs, and from speaking on behalf of Assyrians and Maronites'.

57 <http://www.zenit.org>, 1 December 2007.

58 La Civita claimed that these figures come from the Holy See.

59 In a statement released by a Catholic Commission of Bishops headed by Bishop Thomas G. Wenski of Orlando, Florida, dated Remembrance Day (11 November) of 2006, pleading for help for the Iraqi Assyrian Christians, while documenting Christian persecution, such as the targeting of Christian shop owners and the firebombing of their shops for selling alcohol or music tapes and CDs because the Christians were 'corrupting Islamic society', the Bishops also claimed that the community faced beheadings, rapes, crucifixions and other

down in areas of Iraq after the invasion, the evacuation accelerated in August 2004 after Islamic terrorists bombed five churches in Baghdad and Mosul, killing seven and injuring more than 40. The exodus became a panic, however, after six churches were bombed in Baghdad and the northern city of Kirkuk on 29 January 2006 after protests swept through the Middle East over the cartoons depicting the Prophet Muhammad published in a Danish newspaper, and in February 2006 after the destruction of the Shia al-Askari Golden Mosque in Samarra.[60]

Though the US State Department made reconstruction projects a priority in areas with a dominant Chaldean-Assyrian population, relatively small amounts were actually taken up by the Chaldeans.[61] Within a very few years, Christian Assyrians, once the masters of the whole region, will likely be reduced to a rump in total disregard of the resolutions of indignant righteousness passed by the European

torture. The plea specifically itemized very recent atrocities including a car bombing on 4 October 2006 with a dozen fatalities, a priest kidnapped on 9 October 2006 and beheaded in Mosel, and a teenager crucified in Albasra. The most gruesome case was that of a 14-year-old boy in Baquba on 21 October 2006 when a group of veiled Muslims attacked Ayad Tariq, after asking to see his identity card and insisting that he was a 'dirty Christian sinner', and, screaming 'Allahu, Akbar! Allahu, Akbar!' then decapitated him. The Catholic Bishops had given up on urging that the Iraqi government provide protection for Christians. Instead, they addressed their plea to the United States government. They requested a full resettlement and asylum programme for the persecuted minority, arguing that the community members were victims of targeted violence. They were not just fleeing because of general insecurity as the Iraqi government insisted. A *Zinda* report on Iraqi Christians has proven to be very prophetic. 'The days of officially preached religious tolerance during Saddam's rule are gone and freedom to worship now gives way to fear about an impending Islamisation of Iraq.' (al-Atraqchi 2006) Though Michael La Civita, assistant secretary for communications for the Pontifical Mission, the Vatican development agency working in the Middle East, denied any 'outright' persecution of the Christian community, in May 2006 (cited by al-Atraqchi 2006, 4), the United States Commission on International Religious Freedom (USCIRF) also warned that religiously motivated attacks would result in 'an exodus that may mean the end of the presence in Iraq of ancient Christian and other communities that have lived on those same lands for 2,000 years'. See also UNHCR's '2006 Country Operations plan: Iraq', Planning Year 2006, revised September 2005, available at <http://www.unhcr.org/protect/PROTECTION/43327a8f2.pdf>.

60 Since the bombing of the al-Askari mosque in February 2006, sectarian violence has become the leading cause of displacement (Ferris 2007c). See also al-Khalidi and Tanner 2006.

61 Of $1.2 billion allocated for projects in the province of Nineveh, only $33 million have been utilized by the Chaldean-Assyrian population who are preponderant in that area.

Parliament.[62] What was started with the Muslim invasions of Mesopotamia and took off in the eleventh century, when Muslims became the majority in what is now Iraq, will have likely been completed by the end of this decade. The Assyrians are experiencing their fourth and likely ultimate disaster.

Palestinians

One group that UNHCR has focused upon in an extraordinary way has been the Palestinians. In 2003, before the American-led invasion, Iraq hosted more than 130,000 refugees – including up to 100,000 Palestinians (Human Rights Watch, 'Refugees and Other Non-Nationals in Iraq', <http://www.hrw.org/reports/2003/iraqjordan/Iraqjordan0503-03.htm>.[63] In the immediate aftermath of the war, most of the Palestinians were evicted by their landlords and the majority left Iraq.[64] On 14 December 2006, the UNHCR made a special appeal to countries to provide a

62 After the bombing of the six churches, the European Parliament passed a resolution of strong condemnation with respect to the Assyrians (Chaldeans, Syriacs and other Christian minorities) urging Iraq to protect its Christian minorities. The resolution began with the following preamble that ended with an ironic adumbration of the final outcome.

A. 'whereas on 29 January 2006 four churches and the offices of the Vatican's representative in Baghdad, as well as two churches in Kirkuk, were attacked, killing three people (including a fourteen-year-old child) and injuring several others;
B. whereas the Assyrians (Chaldeans, Syriacs and other Christian minorities) have increasingly become the victims of targeted violence such as destruction of property, kidnapping, attacks on churches, harassment, extortion, and torture of persons perceived as not respecting Islam;
C. recognising that there has also been a rise in attacks on Christian students in Iraqi universities, especially in Mosul, and that Christian citizens of Mosul are being told to move out of the area;
D. noting the dire situation of Christians who have fled from Iraq and are refugees in neighbouring countries, mainly Syria and Jordan, where, according to a report by the UN Refugee Agency (UNHCR), they receive no international aid;
E. whereas the Assyrians (Chaldeans, Syriacs and other Christian minorities) constitute an ancient and indigenous people who are very vulnerable as a result of persecution and forced emigration, and whereas *there is a danger of their culture becoming extinct*' [emphasis added].

63 There were also 14,500 Iranians, 13,000 Kurds from Turkey, and about 4,000 Syrians.

64 'Palestinians – up to 100,000 residing mostly in Baghdad – found themselves displaced anew when their Iraqi landlords demanded exorbitant rents or evicted them outright, resenting the subsidized housing and special privileges that Saddam Hussein had extended to Palestinians' (US Committee for Refugees and Immigrants 2004). After the UN pullback following the bombing of its headquarters in Baghdad in August of 2003, which killed 23 people including the UN Special Representative for Iraq, Sergio Vieira de Mello, the Palestinians felt extremely vulnerable without UN protection and fled in droves.

humanitarian solution for Palestinians fleeing Iraq, and sent out a press release that stated that,

> The UN refugee agency is alarmed by a violent attack by armed militia on a Palestinian neighbourhood in Baghdad which left at least nine people dead, and is appealing to countries to provide a humanitarian solution for Palestinians attempting to flee Iraq. Local militia on Wednesday reportedly shelled the Al Baladiya area for three hours with no attempt by the Iraqi police or multinational forces to halt the attack. The militia also blocked ambulances from taking the dead and wounded to hospital. At least nine people were reportedly killed, including several children, and many injured during the attack.

Why the special focus on Palestinians? Does UNHCR have a Palestinian mole that makes sure their plight is known? Possibly, but not likely! The real reason is the one the UNHCR gives: the Palestinians, once favoured by Saddam Hussein, are now persecuted by all sides, but particularly by the Shiites since the Shia Golden Mosque in Samarra was bombed in February of 2006.[65] Further, they have nowhere to go.[66] However, beside the push factor of persecution and the absence of a place to pull them, there are other reasons for emphasizing the Palestinian cause. Since a very vocal minority of Palestinians were outspoken supporters of Saddam Hussein, all Palestinians became suspect. Further, given that the Hamas leadership won the election and came to power in Palestine, though they retained that power only in Gaza, there is less inclination than ever by the West to support what might be a hive of supporters of terrorism and the elimination of Israel. Even Syria, so open to other refugees from Iraq, has been closed to the Palestinians.

In 2006, 'Syria continues to deny access to all Palestinians who are now stranded in two makeshift camps. A group of 356 has been in the no-man's land between Iraq and Syria since May, while the second group, which has now expanded to some 340, is stuck in El Waleed on the Iraqi side of the border'. The

---

65 The rise in sectarian attacks, abductions and killings not only applied to Palestinians after the bombing of the holy Shia shrine in Samarra's Golden Mosque in February 2006; all inter-communal violence increased. Many viewed this as the date on which Humpty Dumpty could no longer be put together again. UNHCR estimates that some 425,000 Iraqis fled their homes for other areas inside Iraq in 2006, largely due to sectarian violence sparked by the Samarra bombings in February. Internal displacement since then continued at a rate of 50,000 a month.

66 Human Rights Watch (2006), 'Nowhere to Flee: The Perilous Situation of Palestinians in Iraq'. The report documents the deterioration in the security of the estimated 34,000 Palestinian refugees in Iraq since the fall of Baghdad in April 2003 as militant groups targeted and evicted the Palestinians. The report attributes the actions as revenge for the benefits these refugees received from Saddam Hussein's government, but the early evictions motivated for these reasons were carried out by the landlords. Subsequent actions involved kidnapping, targeted killings and sending mortars into Palestinian areas. They were much more clearly bent on ethnic cleansing, in common with the attacks on other minorities where there was little foundation for any feelings of revenge.

conditions there are atrocious.[67] Syria at least admitted 287 in May 2005 before it closed its doors. No other Arab country has been willing to take any Palestinians. Pushed by the dire situation of the Palestinians, UNHCR asked Israel to allow the Palestinians to be relocated to the West Bank and Gaza. As UNHCR pleaded: 'We again urge the international community, including neighbouring and resettlement countries, to help find a humane solution for these refugees who are persecuted inside Iraq and have nowhere to go. UNHCR estimates that some 15,000 of an original group of 34,000 Palestinians remain inside Iraq'. Only Canada opened its doors in 2006 in response to this plea and took 64 Palestinians who had been stuck in the Jordanian desert for years.[68]

The Palestinians trapped in Iraq have received death threats. Leaflets have been distributed to their homes warning them that they had better leave or else. The Palestinian Al Baladiya area has come under repeated mortar attacks. Palestinians do not dare risk even taking their wounded to hospitals.[69] Kidnappings and targeted killings[70] of Palestinians have increased. Palestinians have been evicted from their rental accommodations and housed in quarters rented by UNHCR. But even there they have been unsafe. In mid-January 2007, UNHCR received a report that, '17 male Palestinians accommodated in a Baghdad apartment building rented by UNHCR in the Hay El Nidal neighborhood were taken away by men dressed in Iraqi security force uniforms and driving security vehicles'.[71] In response to the abductions, 90 Palestinian men, women and children fled Baghdad in two rented buses.

The Iraqi government have a responsibility to protect *all* the residents of Iraq. However, the police and military have shown no interest in providing that

67 'It's cold. Clean water has to be trucked in. There is limited access to food. Tents are crowded and unhygienic. Tensions are high. The refugees feel very insecure and some report having been victimized by security officials near the border. The group is in a very vulnerable situation with no solution in sight'. UNHCR (2006), 'Iraq: UN agency raises third alarm in week at "unrelenting violence" against Palestinians', UN News Service, 26 January, available at <http://www.un.org/apps/news/story.asp?NewsID=21348&Cr=palestin&Cr1=>.

68 Fifty-three of the 150 Palestinian refugees from Ruwayshed camp in Jordan have received medical and security clearance for Canada and were scheduled to travel before the end of 2006. Another ten were in the process of obtaining security and medical clearances.

69 'Local militia on Wednesday reportedly shelled the Al Baladiya area for three hours with no attempt by the Iraqi police or multinational forces to halt the attack' (UNHCR 2006a).

70 In December 2006, the Palestinian embassy in Baghdad provided UNHCR with a list of 161 Palestinians killed in Baghdad since 2003. However, in a 20 January 2007 statement, the PLO Head of Refugee Affairs claimed that 520 Palestinians had been killed, and another 140 wounded by militias inside Iraq since March 2003. In December 2006 and January 2007, UNHCR received reports of at least 34 Palestinians killed and five kidnapped.

71 UNHCR 2008.

protection. When UNHCR 'confronted' the government of Iraq, UNHCR officials found 'little room for optimism that anything can be done to improve protection for this population' (UNHCR 2007b).

Dealing with the refugee and IDP problem

One way of dealing with the problem is ending the crisis and violence in Iraq. Baker, Hamilton and the International Crisis Group have recommended cooperating with Iran and Syria to stop the violence. ICG President Gareth Evans warned,

> We are looking at Iraq's complete disintegration into failed-state chaos, threatening to drag down much of the region with it[72] ... More troops in – or out – are not going to solve this. What is needed above all is a new multinational effort to achieve a new political compact between all relevant Iraqi players.[73]

According to this scenario, all states and stakeholders who, one way or another, are involved in the country's internecine violence, must be brought to the negotiating table.

It appears that James Baker, Lee Hamilton, the ICG and many others are as deluded as George W. Bush. At least UNHCR came to recognize that it had previously based its policies on an illusion.

> Much of our work in the three years since the fall of the previous regime was based on the assumption that the domestic situation would stabilize and hundreds of thousands of previously displaced Iraqis would be able to go home. Now, however, we are seeing more and more displacement linked to the continuing violence. This has necessitated a reassessment of UNHCR's work and our priorities throughout the region – from assisting returns and aiding some 50,000 non-Iraqi refugees in Iraq, to providing more help to the tens of thousands who are fleeing every month (UNHCR 2007).[74]

If one adopts the very pessimistic, but I believe realistic, scenario of former Yugoslavia redux, then we are simply watching the separation of populations within Iraq, whatever the eventual structural solution, with no place for Turkoman, Palestinians, Sabean-Madeans, Assyrian-Chaldeans and Armenians. Others may be able to await repatriation to an enclave where their community retains a majority status. But there is no such escape for the Iraqi minorities. The end for them, I fear, is very near. In Iraq, we are not facing a protracted refugee crisis

72 The countries around Iraq closed their borders but only after very large intakes. They reacted to the increased pressures on their social and educational services and long-term instability, with the precedent of the Palestinian refugees.

73 Cf. International Crisis Group 2006c.

74 UNHCR 2008.

but a doomsday crisis for the minorities as Iraq splinters into de facto ethnic and religious enclaves.

Bibliography

Adelman, H. (1998), 'Early Warning and Prevention: The Case of Rwanda', in F. Nicholson and P. Twomey (eds), *Refugee Rights and Realities: Evolving International Concepts* (Oxford: Oxford Univesity Press).

Al-Atraqchi, F. (2006), 'Violence Robs Iraq of Christian Heritage', *Zinda Magazine* XII: 10, 4, available at <www.zindamagazine.com/html/archives/2006/05.13.06/index_sat.php>.

Al-Atraqchi, F. (2007), 'Fighting Robs Iraq of Christian Heritage', *Al Jazeera*, 8 June.

Al-Khalidi, A. and Cohen, R (2007), 'Time for the United States to Recognize Iraq's Humanitarian Crisis', Opinion, 4 January (Washington: Brookings Institution), available at <http://www.brookings.edu/opinions/2007/0104iraq_cohen.aspx>.

Al-Khalidi, A. and Tanner, V. (2006), 'Sectarian Violence: Radical Groups Drive Internal Displacement in Iraq', Occasional Paper, Brookings Institution-University of Bern Project on Internal Displacement (Washington: Brookings Institution).

Al-Khalidi, A., Hoffmann, S. and Tanner, V. (2007), 'Iraqi Refugees in the Syrian Arab Republic: A Field-Based Snapshot', Occasional Paper, Brookings Institution-University of Bern Project on Internal Displacement (Washington: Brookings Institution), available at <http://www3.brookings.edu/fp/projects/idp/200706iraq.pdf>.

Amnesty International (2007a), 'Iraq: The Situation of Iraqi refugees in Syria, Jordan and Egypt', Briefing, available at <http://asiapacific.amnesty.org/library/Index/ENGMDE140362007?open&of=ENG-IRQ>, accessed 4 July 2008.

Amnesty International (2007b), 'Iraq: Carnage and Despair: Iraq Five Years On', Report, 17 March, available at <http://www.amnesty.org/en/library/info/MDE14/001/2008/en>.

Amnesty International (2007c) 'Iraq: The Situation of Iraqi Refugees in Syria', Report, 26 July, available at <http://www.amnesty.org/en/library/info/MDE14/036/2007/en>.

Amnesty International (2008) 'Iraq: Human Rights Abuses against Palestinian Refugees', Report, 1 October, available at <http://www.amnesty.org/en/library/info/MDE14/030/2007>.

Associated Press (2007a), 'Suicide car bomb in Baghdad kills 17', 17 January.

Associated Press (2007b), '137 killed or found dead across Iraq', 22 January.

Associated Press (2007c), 'Tension on the rise between Kurds, Turkmen and Arabs over Kirkuk's fate', 28 January.

Associated Press (2008), 'Displacement of Iraqis takes heavy toll', 3 March.

Baker, J.A. and Hamilton, L.H. (2006), *Iraq Study Group Report* (New York: Random House, Vintage Books).

Burnham, G., Doocy, S., Dzeng, E., Lafta, R. and Roberts, L. (2006), 'The Human Cost of War in Iraq: A Mortality Study, 2002–2006'(Baltimore, MA: Bloomberg School of Public Health, Johns Hopkins University and Baghdad: School of Medicine, Ak Mustansiriya University).

Byman, D.L. and Pollack, K.M. (2007), 'Things Fall Apart: Containing the Spillover from an Iraqi Civil War', Analysis Paper No. 11, The Brookings Institution, available at <http://www.brookings.edu/papers/2007/01iraq_byman.aspx>.

Cave, D. (2007), 'In Baghdad, sectarian lines too deadly to cross', *The New York Times*, 4 March.

Cohen, R. and al-Khalidi, A. (2007), 'Time for the United States to Recognize Iraq's Humanitarian Crisis', Opinion, 4 January (Washington: The Brookings Institution), available at <http://www.brookings.edu/opinions/2007/0104iraq_cohen.aspx?rssid=idp>.

Fagen, P.W. (2007), 'Iraqi Refugees: Seeking Stability in Syria and Jordan', Paper (Georgetown, DC: Institute for the Study of International Migration, Georgetown University).

Ferris, E. (2007a), 'Regional Dimensions to the Iraqi Displacement Crisis and the Role of the United Nations', available at <http://www.brookings.edu/speeches/2007/1025_iraq_ferris.aspx>.

Ferris, E. (2007b), 'Security, Displacement and Iraq: A Deadly Combination', Paper presented at the University of Bern, 27 August, available at <http://www3.brookings.edu/views/papers/ferris/20070827.pdf>, accessed 4 July 2008.

Ferris, E. (2007c), 'The Real Challenge of Internal Displacement in Iraq: The Future', address to the Brookings Institution, 6 December 2007, 5, available at <http://www.brookings.edu/speeches/2007/1206_iraq_ferris.aspx?p=1>, accessed 3 July 2008.

Gunter, M.M. (1999), *The Kurdish Predicament in Iraq: A Political Analysis* (New York: St Martin's Press).

Hinnebusch, R. (2007), 'The US Invasion of Iraq: Explanations and Implications', *Critique: Critical Middle Eastern Studies* Fall 16: 3, 209–28, <http://www.tandf.co.uk/journals/journal.asp?issn=1066-9922andsubcategory=SS180000>.

Human Rights Watch (1993), *Genocide in Iraq – The Anfal Campaign Against the Kurds* (New York: Human Rights Watch).

Human Rights Watch (2006), 'Nowhere to Flee: The Perilous Situation of Palestinians in Iraq', Report (Washington, DC: Human Rights Watch) September.

International Crisis Group (2006a), 'Iraq's Muqtada al-Sadr: Spoiler or Stabilizer', Middle East Report No. 55 (Brussels: ICG), 11 July.

International Crisis Group (2006b), 'Iraq and the Kurds: The Brewing Battle of Kirkuk', Middle East Report No. 56, 18 July.

International Crisis Group (2006c), 'After Baker-Hamilton: What to Do in Iraq', Middle East Report No. 60 (Baghdad, Amman, Damascus and Brussels: ICG), 19 December.

International Organization for Migration (2007), 'Iraq Displacement: 2007 Year in Review', available at http://www.iom.int/jahia/webdav/shared/shared/mainsite/media/docs/reports/2007_year_in_review.pdf >.

IRIN (2007a), 'Baghdad Christians Flee as Violence Against Them Mounts', 3 May, available at <http://www.irinnews.org/Report.aspx?ReportId=71925>.

IRIN (2007b), 'Iraq: Aid work becoming more risky in Baghdad', 22 August, available at <http://www.alertnet.org/thenews/newsdesk/IRIN/5d3472e807f9397c54bc4c1978e690d0.htm>.

Jansen, M. (2007), 'The worst option for Iraq', *The Jordan Times*, 11 January.

Kaufmann, C. (2006), 'What to do in Iraq: A Roundtable', *Foreign Affairs* 85: 4, 157.

Kfir, I. (2008), 'US-Kurdish Relations in Post-Invasion Iraq' *MERIA*, 12: 1, March, <http://meria.idc.ac.il/journal>.

La Civita, M. (2008), 'Iraq's Endangered Christians', *Maryknoll Magazine*, 30 April.

Laizer, S. (1996), *Martyrs, Traitors and Patriots: Kurdistan after the Gulf War* (London: Zed Books Ltd).

Lewis, J.E. (2003), 'Iraqi Assyrians: Barometer of Pluralism', *Middle East Quarterly* X: 3, Summer.

Lochhead, C. (2007), 'Iraq Refugee Crisis Exploding: 40 per cent of Middle Class Believed to Have Fled Crumbling Nation', *San Francisco Chronicle*, 16 January.

Loescher , G. (2002), 'War in Iraq: an Impending Refugee Crisis? Uncertain Risks, Inadequate Preparation and Coordination', Working Paper No. 67 (San Diego: University of California, The Center for Comparative Immigration Studies), December, available at <http://repositories.cdlib.org/ccis/papers/wrkg67>.

Looney, R. (2008), 'Impediments to Stability in Iraq: The Illusive Economic Dimension', *MERIA*, 12: 1, March, <http://meria.idc.ac.il/journal>.

MacDowall, D. (2000), *A Modern History of the Kurds* (London: I.B. Tauris Publishers).

Mahdi, K. (2007), 'Neoliberalism, Conflict and an Oil Economy: The Case of Iraq', *Arab Studies Quarterly* 29: 1, 233–65.

Malone, D. (2006), *The International Struggle Over Iraq: Politics in the UN Security Council, 1980–2005* (Oxford: Oxford University Press).

Margesson, M., Sharp, J. and Bruno, A. (2007), 'Iraqi Refugees and Internally Displaced Persons: A Deepening Humanitarian Crisis', CRS Report for Congress (Washington, DC: Congressional Report Service) 23 March.

Massing, M. (2008), 'As Iraqis See It', *New York Review of Books* LV: 1, 17 January, 17–19, 18.

McMaster, H.R. (2008), 'On War: Lessons to be Learned', *Survival: Global Politics and Strategy* 50: 1, 19–30.

Murray, C., Parry, K., Robinson, P. and Goddard, P. (2008), 'Reporting Dissent in Wartime: British Press, the Anti-War Movement and the 2003 Iraq War', *European Journal of Communications* 23: 1, 7–27.

Naqishbendi, R. (2005), 'Iraq: Its Demography and Geography as Impediments to Peace and Stability', *KurdMedia.com* [website], 3 November.

Nye, J.S., Jr (2008), 'Recovering American Leadership', *Survival: Global Politics and Strategy* 50: 1, 55–68.

Oxfam and NGO Coordination Committee (2007), 'Rising to the Humanitarian Challenge in Iraq', Briefing Paper, July, 12, 15.

Pickering, T.R. (2008), 'Does the UN Have a Role in Iraq?', *Survival: Global Politics and Strategy* 50: 1, 133–42.

Pincus, W. (2008), 'A House hearing last Tuesday', *Washington Post*, 17 March, A15.

Powell, S. (2007), 'Top Bush Adviser Paints Dark Iraq Picture: Ending Strife May Not be Possible: Hadley', *The Globe and Mail*, 3 February 2007, A21.

Santora, M. (2007), 'Militia Nearly Overran Iraqi Troops', New York Times News Service, *The Globe and Mail*, 30 January, A15.

Saroyan, W. (1934), 'Seventy Thousand Assyrians', in W. Saroyan, *The Daring Young Man on the Flying Trapeze and Other Stories* (New York: New Directions).

Spiegel, P. and Oassim, M. (2003), 'Forgotten Refugees and Other Displaced Populations', *The Lancet* 362: 9377, 72–74.

Strachan, H. (2008), 'Strategy and the Limitation of War', *Survival: Global Politics and Strategy* 50: 1, 31–54.

The Boston Globe (2007), 'American Deaths in Iraq', 30 January 2007.

The New York Times (2007), 'Iraq's Refugees', 31 January 2007.

UNHCR (2006a), 'UNHCR Condemns Baghdad Attack; Urges Countries to Help Fleeing Palestinians', Geneva, 14 December, available at <http://www.unhcr.org/cgi-bin/texis/vtx/iraq?page=news&id=4581863b4>.

UNHCR (2006b), 'UN Assistance Mission for Iraq Human Rights Report', 1 November–31 December, available at <http://www.uniraq.org/FileLib/misc/HR%20Report%20Nov%20Dec%202006%20EN.pdf>.

UNHCR (2007a), 'Statistics on Displaced Iraqis Around the World', September 2007, available at <http://www.unhcr.org/cgi-bin/texis/vtx/home/opendoc.pdf?tbl=SUBSITES&id=461f7cb92>, accessed 4 July 2008.

UNHCR (2007b), 'Iraq: UN Agency Raises Third Alarm in Week at "Unrelenting Violence" Against Palestinians', *UN News Centre* [website], 14 December.

UNHCR (2007c), 'Asylum Levels and Trends in Industrialized Countries, 2006', Report (Geneva: UNHCR), 23 March, available at <www.unhcr.org/statistics/STATISTICS/460150272.pdf>, p. 7.

UNHCR (2008), 'Iraq Situation Update' (Geneva: UNHCR), 23 January, available at <http://www.rcusa.org/uploads///word%20documents/UNHCR,%20Iraq%20Situation%20Update,%201-23-08.doc>.

UN-IRIN (2007a), 'Iraq: Armed Groups Occupying Hospitals and Kidnapping Doctors', 13 February.

UN-IRIN (2007b), 'Iraq: Fighters Fill Humanitarian Vacuum', 14 February.

US Committee for Refugees and Immigrants (2004), *World Refugee Survey 2004 Country Report, Iraq*, available at <http://www.refugees.org/countryreports.aspx?__VIEWSTATE=dDwtOTMxNDcwOTk7O2w8Q291bnRyeUREOkdvQnV0dG9uOz4%2BUwqzZxIYLI0SfZCZue2XtA0UFEQ%3D&cid=119&subm=&ssm=&map=&searchtext>.

US Committee for Refugees and Immigrants (2006), *World Refugee Survey 2006 – Risks and Rights* (Washington, DC: US Committee on Refugees and Immigrants), Summary, p. 1.

US Government (2008), 'Iraqi Refugee Processing', 'Fact Sheet', 11 March 2008, US Department of Homeland Security (DHS) and US State Department (DOS), available at <http://www.dhs.gov/xnews/releases/pr_1205327590498.shtm>.

Wall Street Journal (2008), 'Iraq, 5 Years on, a Nation of Refugees', 17 March, available at <http://online.wsj.com/article/SB120553610561238057.html>.

Washington Post Foreign Service (2008), '46000 Iraqi Have Left Syria', 5 January, A11.

Watenpaugh, K.D. (2007), 'The Death of Iraq's Middle Class', *History News Network* [website], 22 January, available at <http://hnn.us/articles/34133.html>.

Wehner, P. (2008), 'Debating Bush's Wars', *Survival: Global Politics and Strategy* 50: 1, 69–90.

Wong, E. (2004), 'The Struggle for Iraq – Northern Iraq; Back from Exile, Kurds Demand Political Power and Reparations for Seized Property', *The New York Times*, 19 January.

Wong, E. (2005), 'Kurds' Return to City Shakes Politics in Iraq', *The New York Times*, 14 March.

Wong, E. and Cave, D. (2007), 'Baghdad District is a Model, but Only for Shiites', *The New York Times*, 22 May.

Yamani, M. (2008), 'The Two Faces of Saudi Arabia', *Survival: Global Politics and Strategy* 50: 1, 143–56.

Zeidel, R. (2008), 'Harsh Readjustment: The Sunnis and the Political Process in Contemporary Iraq', *MERIA*, 12: 1, March, <http://meria.idc.ac.il/journal>.

Chapter 8
Better Approaches to Protracted Displacement?

Michael G. Smith

> ... it is only through the utopian exercise of imagining other worlds that we can begin to see how a better world might be built. (Maley 2003, 308)

Introduction

This book is the product of a three-year collaborative research project through the Australian Research Council (ARC) between the Institute of Ethics, Governance and Law at Griffith University; the Asia-Pacific College of Diplomacy at the Australian National University; and the Australian non-government organization (NGO) Austcare. The Centre for Refugee Research at the University of New South Wales, which has a close working relationship with Austcare, provided excellent assistance to the project team. The aim of the study was to draw attention to significant cases of protracted displacement in Asia. The study did not aim to examine in detail the root causes of these displacements, but rather to understand through action research[1] the reasons for the *protracted* character of their flight. In particular, Austcare wanted to understand if more could be done to resolve situations of protracted displacement in Asia, and whether its own actions might be a contributing factor in perpetuating the problem. Austcare considered that action research might reveal practical measures beyond the much-quoted 'durable solutions' framework of the United Nations High Commissioner for Refugees (UNHCR): viz., voluntary repatriation, local integration and resettlement. Austcare wanted to examine whether any of the durable solutions were adequate when refugees and internally displaced persons (IDPs) remained in protracted situations. Were there other measures available to enhance the protection of displaced communities and empower them to achieve greater human security?

The ARC research project considered five cases of protracted displacement in Asia: the Bhutanese Lhotsampas in Nepal; Burmese communities along the

---

1 'Action research' is described as the effort to use research as a catalyst for change at the same time as a process of change and transformation is instigated through critical reflection on actions undertaken. Generally, action research is based on a partnership of practitioners and researchers.

Thailand–Burma border; Rohingyas from Burma in Bangladesh; Sri Lankan IDPs in Trincomalee; and Afghan IDPs and refugees, principally in Pakistan and Iran. In addition, a desk-based study of one potential future protracted displacement in Asia considered the situation of Iraqi refugees, mainly in Jordan and Syria.[2] Underpinning the displacement in all cases were significant political differences between those displaced and national governments in the country of origin. In the majority of cases these political differences were characterized by ethnic conflict or ethno-religious discrimination and accompanied by the acquiescence of the international community (or its impotence) to take preventative or timely remedial action. This concluding chapter captures lessons learned from the case studies and draws on these findings to inform how humanitarian agencies may respond more effectively to protracted displacement to enhance the protection of populations living in prolonged limbo. While the focus is on particular situations in Asia, the conclusions may be relevant for protracted displacement more globally, and raise key issues relevant for future research.

Protracted displacement in Asia

Not including over four million Palestinian refugees, the total number of displaced and stateless persons around the world in 2007, as a result of conflict and persecution, totalled about 33 million (UNHCR 2008). Over the previous decade the number of refugees and asylum seekers had been declining, but in 2007 the *World Refugee Survey* reported a total of 13.9 million refugees worldwide, an increase of two million refugees since 2005, while the number of IDPs – largely resulting from war and internal conflict – had grown remarkably to at least 25 million in over 52 countries[3] (IDMC 2007; see also, generally, Brookings-Bern Project on Internal Displacement).

In 2005, Asia hosted about 40 per cent of the displaced people of concern to UNHCR, with numbers having increased from 7,230,000 the previous year to 8,603,000. A significant change was the drop in the number of refugees in the Asia-Pacific region which hosted only ten per cent of the world's refugees, but the IDP population increased at a faster rate. Well over 50 per cent of IDPs were in the Asia-Pacific region (UNHCR 2006b).

UNHCR categorizes a 'protracted situation' as one that has existed for at least five years where refugees or IDPs of more than 25,000 people have been kept in

2 Iraq was chosen because it is located in Asia and has significant numbers of refugees with a potential impact on regional and international security. The desk-based study did not address the situation of Iraqi IDPs in detail.

3 IDP numbers have proved difficult to estimate. The figure of 25 million is considered by UNHCR/OCHA to be conservative. The Internal Displacement Monitoring Centre (IDMC) in Oslo, Norway, which tracks IDPs, estimated a figure of 24,500,000 IDPs in April 2007.

restricted areas and are denied their rights to work or move freely (UNHCR 2006a). UNHCR does not include the estimated over 4 million Palestinians refugees in this category. These refugees constitute those who fled or were forced to flee from that part of Palestine that became Israel in 1948, or who have fled or been expelled from the West Bank and Gaza since 1967, as well as their descendents. The Palestinian refugees from 1948 and their descendents fall under the mandate of the UN Relief and Works Agency for Palestine Refugees in the Near East (UNRWA), and represent the world's oldest protracted refugee situation. By 2007, the estimate of the average duration of refugees in protracted situations (not including Palestinians) had grown from nine years in 1993 to 17 years in 2003, with 7.7 million refugees in protracted situations (Betts 2007, 509–14; Loescher et al. 2007). Earlier, in 2004, this phenomenon of protracted displacement had been labelled by the US Committee for Refugees (USCR) as 'warehousing', a term denoting that people had been placed in 'storage' for at least ten years without resolution to their plight (Chen 2004; USCR 2004).

If protracted displacement in Asia has increased, then the corollary is that the 'durable solutions' framework has proved to be imperfect. Does this demand new thinking to resolve situations of protracted displacement in Asia? While IDPs suffer the same problems of homelessness and poverty as refugees, IDPs do not have the same legal rights of protection as refugees covered under the 1951 Convention. Moreover, the international community has been slow to address the specific protection needs of IDPs[4] (Feller 2006; Cohen 2008). The UN Guiding Principles on Internal Displacement were not promulgated until 1998 (UNGPID 1998), but they are not legally binding and have frequently been ignored or abused. Unlike many refugee communities, fewer IDPs live in the same camps or areas for protracted periods. Instead, they may be repeatedly forced to move to different locations, but nonetheless remain in a state of protracted displacement. The resolution of IDP situations requires a different political path than for refugees, because IDPs remain the sole responsibility of their governments who may be complicit in causing and perpetuating the displacement. Where this responsibility is not invoked by the state, the UN Security Council may mandate an international intervention under the Responsibility to Protect (R2P). R2P was unanimously agreed upon at the UN World Leaders' Summit in 2005 (UN Summit 2005).

Since commencement of the war in Iraq in 2003, more than four million Iraqis have been added to the displacement rolls comprising around 2.2 million IDPs and two million refugees. This movement has been too recent to yet classify as a protracted situation, but it has many of the hallmarks of other long-term displacements caused by intractable conflict. These Iraqis now constitute more than ten per cent of the global population of refugees and IDPs.

With around 5 million refugees in 20 protracted displacement situations globally, and increasing numbers of IDPs equally affected, many displaced

4 UNHCR's limited involvement with IDPs was initially set out in UNGA Resolution 53/125 of December 1998, but was subsequently extended.

communities face little or no likelihood of return. This trend to protracted displacement underwrites the value of exploring current political, legal and humanitarian approaches.[5] Improving the protection of refugees and IDPs (UNHCR 2002; UNHCR/WFP 2006) and applying durable solutions to situations of protracted displacement has for some years been a continuing theme in annual UNHCR Executive Committee Meetings and NGO Consultations (UNHCR 2004; 2007). But despite this attention, only limited progress has been made in resolving ongoing situations. It has been easy for the international community to highlight political barriers preventing resolution, but more difficult to acknowledge for whom the durable solutions are sought – the sending states, the receiving states, the international donor community or the displaced population.

Addressing protracted displacement

Conflict is the source of most protracted displacement. Modern conflict is often fuelled by ethnic, tribal or religious divisions amongst people. Often, minority groups struggle for recognition with weak or oppressive governments, or become the pawns of international intervention. Displacement is both a consequence and often a tacit strategy of conflict. If conflict could be prevented or managed better, then displacement would not be the problem that it is. But this is not a research project about peacemaking and conflict resolution: it is about dealing with the reality of protracted displacement. At the root of protracted displacement are the conflict-prone states from which displaced populations emerge. Building a coherent and locally contextualized understanding of these states and the conflicts in which they are engaged is critical to developing any kind of a strategy – for advocacy or for programming – to work towards resolution of displacement. Nor will the world's complex conflicts be resolved just because states, international agencies and NGOs understand them better. Humanitarian stakeholders must recognize the limits of their reach, employing a careful mix of lobbying and programme assistance to continue to improve the lives of the displaced. Condoning situations where people are forced to live in protracted displacement for years is a betrayal of human rights, and the international community should not be conditioned to consider such situations as legitimate or the norm. The negative consequences of displacement on people and host/donor states have been documented in numerous reports and publications. UNHCR has highlighted that protracted displacement wastes lives by perpetuating poverty and 'squanders precious resources of host countries, donors and refugees' (UNHCR 2004, 3). The case studies in this ARC research project confirm that efforts to resolve protracted displacement in Asia have been inadequate and/or slow to implement, though resettlement efforts are finally underway to potentially resolve the plight of the majority of the Bhutanese refugees in Nepal, and ease the pressure of refugees from Burma along the Thailand

5 See Preface.

border. The other four case studies show little likelihood of easy resolution, with the potential prospect of continuing displacement for many years.

States and relevant international agencies should be prepared to act more decisively if situations of protracted displacement and human suffering are to be resolved. The default position of 'durable solutions' is really no position at all if people are to be left in limbo for many years. Where necessary, states and UNHCR should be agile and prepared to consider solutions outside the durable solutions box. But UNHCR, the agency most responsible for decisive action, is often limited in what it can do. Not only is it the advocate for durable solutions, it has limited autonomy because it is captive to funding from states, and it is expected to perform the sometimes contradictory functions of *relief* and *protection*: contradictory because relief can cause dependency, thereby prolonging displacement and making protection all the more difficult (Maley 2003, 318–22). But can situations of protracted displacement be resolved more quickly or, better still, avoided? If the international community has been unable to prevent all wars and conflicts, and if the incidence of protracted displacement has been rising, then there would seem little point in examining this matter further. Have valiant efforts crashed against a brick wall? One could have made similar comments about the futility of early attempts to abolish slavery, prevent the use of mustard gas, or ban the production and use of landmines, and yet these efforts (and many others) have come to pass with outstanding results for the betterment of humankind. If situations of protracted displacement are increasing – caused principally by political circumstances and ethno-religious divisions – then the international community should work harder to prevent or resolve them. The warehousing of people should not blindly be accepted; international actors with the ability to resolve and/or prevent protracted displacement should feel a stronger commitment to act decisively. Moreover, while humanitarian assistance to displaced populations is essential and warranted, care is required to ensure that such support is not institutionalized to perpetuate dependency if/when other options are more appropriate.

The case studies in this ARC research project confirm that each displacement situation is unique, making it difficult to devise universal solutions to resolve situations of protracted displacement (in addition to the causes of displacement). Numerous factors may influence the resolution of conflicts and the design of practical solutions: size, duration, degree of hardship, cost to host countries, political circumstances, resources expended by UNHCR and the broader international community, and problems experienced by neighbouring and/or third countries as a result of secondary movements. Understanding each situation and devising sensible policy options would seem the best way to begin the process of resolving protracted displacement. Such initiatives, however, would need to involve the key stakeholders and be developed collaboratively with prime and early input from the affected populations and governments. The reality is, however, that in most situations of protracted displacement, negotiated political settlements are difficult to achieve quickly. Moreover, those displaced usually lack power or influence and are the pawns of more powerful governments and agencies, or of controlling elements within displacement camp management structures.

The dilemmas of protracted displacement

The resolution of intractable displacement requires specific policies, strategies and comprehensive plans of action. These can be better determined by understanding the dilemmas that confront decision makers and the displaced. Understanding these dilemmas may assist key stakeholders and decision makers in taking positive steps to achieve an acceptable outcome at the earliest possible opportunity. But acceptable to whom? While humanitarians focus solely on the plight of the displaced, states and some non-state protagonists often pursue different objectives and priorities. This may help explain why in each of the six case studies, positive action was slow in coming and each situation was allowed to develop and then persist.

Situations of protracted displacement reflect a number of dilemmas. For example, most refugees and IDPs may genuinely want to return home, but political and economic (livelihood) barriers and fears of insecurity or persecution may prevent them. Also, host states may actively work to prevent those displaced from settling permanently in their new (temporary) location, while only a small number of states are prepared to offer a more permanent home through resettlement in a third country. Such resettlement, although sometimes welcome, benefits a small percentage of the global population of refugees, and even fewer IDPs. Displaced people are entitled to emergency humanitarian assistance, but with nowhere to go this may easily evolve into a situation of dependency, particularly for those living in camp situations where children can be educated and have access to health services, and where men can recuperate to continue their struggle as 'refugee warriors'.[6]

Perhaps the biggest dilemma is the inherent tension between humanitarianism and realpolitik: the former seeks to provide displaced communities with life-saving assistance regardless of ethnicity, gender, religion, or political association; the latter is pragmatism based on national self-interest, reflecting the political realities of what states will allow and who they will support, primarily for their own perceived self-interest rather than for ideological notions. As William Maley has cautioned, '*all* refugee assistance has political implications, and that to believe in a "pure" humanitarianism divorced from politics is profoundly naive' (Maley 2003, 308).

Three additional dilemmas are identified below: 1) state sovereignty versus human security; 2) national self-interest versus universal morality; and 3)

6 The concept of 'refugee warrior' is generally credited to Zolberg et al. (1989), and explored further in Adelman (1998), and Terry (2002); Terry credits Jean-Christophe Rufin (1986) with the origin of the phrase.

durable versus enduring solutions. These dilemmas are mutually inclusive and overlapping, and they help explain the intricacies inherent in addressing situations of protracted displacement. In complex circumstances there are rarely easy solutions. The humanitarian's quest to 'do no harm' will seldom be achievable in a universal and absolute sense, just as states' rhetoric for political resolution will seldom be fully realized. When realpolitik and morality come face to face it is likely that compromises will need to be made if reasonable solutions are to be developed and implemented. Understanding this complexity is a first step in negotiating settlements for and with displaced people. The desire to achieve a timely resolution in the best interests of the displaced needs to be balanced against what the state system will tolerate politically.

Several interrelated factors loom large in the achievement of durable solutions. The political underpinnings of displacement are magnified by the willingness of the international community to achieve resolution. Generally, the larger and more violent the displacement, the less likely remedial intervention will be. The situation might be capped, but it is unlikely to be resolved without a substantial comprehensive plan of action or innovative and voluntary forms of labour migration. History suggests that such solutions have been rare in international politics. In addition, where displacement has occurred based on persecution along ethno-religious divisions, the likelihood of return is low. Unless people have reasonable political representation and their physical security can be assured, they are not likely to return home voluntarily, nor is it advisable to expect them to do so. Realpolitik plays an important role in achieving durable solutions but is often problematic, as discussed in the three dilemmas below.

State sovereignty or human security?

The first dilemma is perhaps the most obvious yet difficult to resolve. State sovereignty is based on the central importance and authority of the state's existence, where territorial sovereignty is sacrosanct and all states are independent, and legally and diplomatically equal in status. In matters of state sovereignty, the individual is subordinate to the existence of the state. Human security, on the other hand, is based on the principle that individuals and communities are entitled to live in freedom from fear and freedom from want. When human security exists, people are *protected* from threats and *empowered* to make their own decisions and be accountable for them. State sovereignty and human security converge to the extent that it is the responsibility of a state to ensure the human security of its citizens and, when the state fails to do so, the international community is able to intervene in accordance with R2P. By virtue of their circumstances, however, displaced people are denied an adequate level of human security. In protracted displacement situations, people have access to fewer rights; they experience physical and sexual abuse, malnutrition and poor health, unemployment, a lack of property ownership, poor education and training, and disempowerment. And they are kept in this state of limbo for years, as shown clearly in the case studies.

The concept of human rights is central to a concern with human security; if rights are breached then human security cannot properly exist. When human rights are breached the principle of state sovereignty may be challenged, but the outcome is often large numbers of refugees and IDPs forced to live in a situation of statelessness and/or neglect. In most of the case studies covered in this ARC research project, displacement occurred either because the home government took action against some of its people, or was too weak or unwilling to prevent action against them. In the cases of Afghanistan, Iraq and Sri Lanka, foreign intervention made the displacement situation more complicated or contributed to it. When human rights are threatened, a question arises: should the international community intervene to ensure that human rights are maintained? Conversely, when a state, or coalition of states, intervenes without international legitimacy and invades another state (even for the proclaimed purpose of self-defence), significant internal and external displacement may occur, as witnessed by events in Afghanistan following the Soviet occupation in late 1979,[7] and in Iraq following the US-led intervention in 2003. By contrast, the failure of the international community to intervene effectively in Rwanda and Darfur (to name but two instances) witnessed massive dislocation, suffering and human rights abuses.

It is worthwhile considering this dilemma in relation to the six case studies addressed in this ARC research project. In the case of the Bhutanese Lhotshampa refugees in Nepal, little action was taken (or appears even to have been contemplated) by the international community to intervene directly to prevent or halt the displacement from Bhutan, a small and weak state, or to assure the safeguarding of the human rights of all its citizens. Greater attention was given to providing for the needs of the Bhutanese once they had arrived in Nepal. Generally, a similar situation applies in the case of Burmese refugees in Thailand. But although several Western countries tried to pressure the Burmese regime to move towards a more democratic system, the international discourse rarely mentioned the ethnic Karen refugees, and failed to mention the Rohingyas in Bangladesh who suffered human rights violations on both sides of the border. Pressure put on Burma to accept the return of Rohingya refugees led to their 'forced' return (*refoulement*), and their plight was made even worse. In Sri Lanka, the intervention by India, in part to stop the flow of refugees across the straits, resulted in more refugees and IDPs and helped intensify extremist actions by both sides in the civil war[8] (Piffenberger 1988, 137–47). India's intervention failed to secure human rights or alleviate the plight of displaced Sri Lankans, yet it cost India some 1,255 lives as well as several thousand wounded without resolving the conflict. In Afghanistan the refugees were

---

7 According to Schloch (2005), the Soviet invasion of Afghanistan exacerbated refugee flows, which had commenced due to the series of internal military coups in 1973, 1978 and 1979.

8 This is not to suggest that Indian intervention was the cause of conflict and displacement in Sri Lanka, but rather that India's brief intervention was ineffective in resolving the displacement, and contributed to its entrenchment.

never the key issue for the intervening powers. The Soviet Union invaded not to stop refugee flows, but to support its proxy government, and the response by the US and other states to support insurgents was the product of a Cold War mentality to fight against the Soviet Union through all means necessary, but had little to do with resolving the refugee crisis. This contest created more refugees and IDPs: a classic case of states' strategic and political interests having higher priority than the human security of affected populations. A similar story was repeated in Iraq by the US-led coalition almost 25 years later. This intervention, ostensibly a preventative act of self defence as well as intending to create democracy in Iraq, resulted in the largest case of displacement to date in the twenty-first century.

The case studies also demonstrate that governments conducted, promoted or condoned discrimination of communities within their own population, or were impotent to prevent divisions by militant ethnic or religious groups. This makes the 2005 unanimous agreement on R2P at the UN Leaders' Summit all the more relevant. In the case of Burma, ethnic discrimination against the Rohingyas and Karen (among others) continues to cause displacement (to the Bangladesh and Thailand border regions respectively), raising the question as to whether the international community should invoke R2P against the country producing refugee flows. But as the case studies of Afghanistan and Iraq also show in counterpoint, interventions by states without UN legitimacy can also cause massive displacements of populations (Chesterman 2001).[9] The displacement from Iraq was a consequence of foreign invasion and occupation by the US-led coalition. Yet in this case no action was taken by the occupiers in a timely way to prevent the flow of refugees or adequately provide for those displaced. R2P envisions intervention under the authority of the Security Council. However, if Darfur offers any insight at this moment in history, R2P intervention may not be timely or restorative, or be of much comfort to the displaced. In Darfur, intervention has been continuously plagued by requiring the consent of the Sudanese regime in Khartoum at each step of the way, a pattern totally at odds with the idea of intervening in the domestic affairs of a state that fails to prevent the persecution of its population.

So what conclusions can be drawn from this dilemma? The most important would seem to be the need to elevate the importance of human security and align it more closely with national self-interest. More countries are taking this approach, at least rhetorically, but displaced communities are yet to reap the benefits. Nor is the adoption of a human security approach likely to prevent future displacement or resolve current long-standing situations. In the cases of Sri Lanka and Burma it can be seen that human insecurity largely (but not entirely) results from the actions of the respective governments. In the former case, the international community

9 The UN did not endorse the US-led invasion of Iraq in 2003. The UN role was more equivocal with respect to the US-led invasion of Afghanistan in 2001 since the UN did not endorse the initiation of the war but did authorize the International Security Assistance Force (ISAF), an international stabilization force, by means of a United Nations Security Council resolution on 20 December 2001.

has generally sided with the Sri Lanka government against the Tamil Tigers as the lesser of two evils, whilst in the latter the international community has failed to intervene at all. Afghanistan provides a clear case where human security improved for some Afghans after the fall of the Taliban regime, yet almost two million refugees have not yet been convinced that it is safe to return, and some studies indicate that improvements are shallow with questionable long-term impact.[10] These situations suggest that human security in and of itself is not the answer to resolving displacement, but that it can be an important contributor in the right political circumstances.

The case studies suggest four other conclusions worthy of consideration. First, the primacy of state sovereignty has consistently trumped human security, and the case studies do not offer any optimism that this situation is likely to change. R2P may mitigate against this, but only to the extent that R2P is perceived to be in the intervening states' interests. In each of the case studies, human rights were relegated to a lower priority until after displacement had occurred, and then attended to inconsistently. Either the international community reacted to the outcome of displacement by accepting the principle of state sovereignty ahead of the assurance of human rights, or tacitly accepted the breach of state sovereignty without ensuring human rights protections. Second, and related, the political interests of states have consistently been placed ahead of the rights of the displaced. If this was not the case then states would not have accepted and enabled situations of protracted displacement to continue. Rather than preventing or resolving human rights abuses, protracted displacement has been perceived by states as a social and humanitarian problem to be contained and managed in order to avoid or minimize the chances of future conflict. In such situations, UNHCR has found itself 'caught' between the sometimes contradictory requirements of providing long-term relief (which has helped maintain the status quo), and providing adequate protection mechanisms aimed at resolving protracted displacement. Third, far from assuring human rights, state intervention has sometimes caused human rights breaches, with massive displacement occurring, for example, as a result of the Soviet invasion of Afghanistan in 1979, and the more recent US-led interventions in Afghanistan in 2001 and Iraq in 2003. Fourth, the principle of R2P is yet to be tested in preventing or halting human rights abuses of displaced populations. Having acceded to

10 According to figures provided by the government of Afghanistan in January 2008, significant development occurred following the fall of the Taliban regime. For example, schools had increased from 1,000 to 9,000; access to health care had increased from eight per cent to 78 per cent of the population; infant mortality had been reduced by 25 per cent; electricity production had increased from 430 to 754 megawatts; and the road network had increased from 21,000 km of damaged roads to 34,782 km of repaired and upgraded roads (Wilkinson 2008). Despite this progress large parts of the country remained insecure, the country near the bottom of the human development index, and lacking in human rights for much of the population (AIHRC 2007).

R2P in 2005, states have been slow to apply it meaningfully to prevent or halt displacement and human rights abuses.[11]

National self-interest or universal morality?

A second and related dilemma of protracted displacement is the competing priorities between national self-interest and universal morality. Simply put, do states and communal groupings exist and behave primarily to further their own perceived vital interests, or do they act ethically under international laws and conventions to promote universal morality? E.H. Carr suggests that the 'harmony of interests' between these two extremes is elusive and that, on balance, national self-interest is the prime mover (Carr 1964). If this was not so then it would be hard to imagine millions of displaced people being encamped in protracted situations for indeterminate periods.

The primacy of national self-interest is evident from the case studies. India's refusal to allow the Bhutanese Lhotshampa refugees to return to Bhutan by transiting Indian territory or to resettle in India fundamentally consigned the Bhutanese refugees to a situation of forced displacement in Nepal. This outcome was condoned by the international community as much by its muteness as by the unwillingness of states to intervene or to offer resettlement. In this case, India's national interests were to contain the problem within a geographic locality outside India, yet enable relations to be maintained with both Bhutan and Nepal. The question of morality hardly seems to have been a determining factor, other than perhaps the avoidance of a possible bloody ethnic conflict within Bhutan had the Lhotshampas been allowed to return. Nor has the plight of more than 100,000 Bhutanese refugees been of significant interest or importance to the broader international community. With no possibility of repatriation to Bhutan, UNHCR and major donors' efforts for more than a decade focused on the provision of humanitarian assistance and encouraging the Nepalese government to permit local integration. Not until 2006 did serious efforts begin by the international community to develop a structured plan of resettlement to third countries.

On the Thailand–Burma border, as in Nepal, resettlement emerged as a way forward not because of moral compunction to assist refugees (in which case a

11 To try to ensure that the R2P doctrine is translated into action, the Global Centre for the Responsibility to Protect (GCR2P) was launched in New York at the Ralph Bunche Institute at the City University of New York on 14 February 2008, funded by the governments of Australia, Belgium, Canada, the Netherlands, Norway, Rwanda, the United Kingdom, and private donors. The objectives of the GCR2P include advancing and consolidating the global consensus on R2P, protecting the integrity of the R2P concept, clarifying when non-consensual military force can and cannot be used, building capacity on R2P with international institutions, governments and regional organizations, and developing mechanisms and strategies to generate an effective political response as new R2P situations arise.

durable solution would have been promised to all refugees), but as a result of pressures flowing from realist behaviour based primarily on US self-interest.[12] In the case of the Rohingyas in Bangladesh, the international community has shown almost no compassion or morality. These 200,000 stateless people have been forced to live in abject poverty for 30 years, having suffered considerable human rights abuses even with the knowledge of UNHCR and donor states. Their situation remains deplorable with little chance of peaceful return to Burma, and limited prospects for proper local integration or resettlement to a third country.

The subordination of morality to the self-interest of states has already been partially explained in relation to the interventions in Afghanistan. Further, it is also notable that the encampment of Afghan refugees in Pakistan initially served the interests of the US and Pakistan. Keeping refugees in Pakistan was a good way to blame the Soviet Union during the Cold War and to provide Pakistan with political leverage. It may seem ironic that some of these same camps have a long tradition of links to insurgent groups in Afghanistan: first the Mujahideen, then the Taliban, and probably to al-Qaeda more globally.

Can we draw an additional conclusion from this dilemma? Perhaps unsurprisingly for political realists it seems that only rarely will international morality be more important than national (or regional) self-interest. Like those in protracted displacement, the extent to which R2P may alter this equation remains in limbo. In principle at least, R2P places national self-interest and morality on an equal footing because R2P is based on the premise that it is in a state's best interest to intervene to prevent or halt atrocities. R2P provides hope for the future, but it remains an untested concept and in all likelihood may not be used to prevent or stop many situations of displacement.

Durable or enduring solutions?

A third dilemma concerns the search for durable solutions, while at the same time requiring displaced communities to endure their situation for years without resolution. In other words, when a durable solution cannot be found then displaced people are compelled to live with an 'enduring solution'. This enduring solution approach is no solution at all, but it reflects the reality for those in protracted displacement, as well as testimony to the impotence of the international community to act decisively to prevent or resolve the situation.

Agencies have been dealing with the symptoms and effects of protracted displacement for many years, using a combination of strategies. During the 'enduring solution' period, UNHCR has highlighted the need for the international

---

12 The international community initially focused on the durable solution of repatriation in the late 1990s, but circumstances in Burma did not permit repatriation. Resettlement came onto the agenda seriously in 2005–2006. See Lang (2001). A comprehensive plan for assistance to Burmese refugees was developed in 2006 and began to be implemented in 2007.

community to move away from a 'care and maintenance' approach so as not to create dependencies or divert attention from implementing the durable solutions. But in reality few alternative options have presented themselves. When people are at risk they are entitled to protection. When people are hungry they deserve to eat. When people are sick they require medical attention. When people have nowhere to live they deserve a roof over their heads. When there are no schools children still require education. When there are no jobs people are entitled to training. When people have no resolution to their displacement they are entitled to hope for the future. When people are in abject poverty through no fault of their own they are entitled to be empowered to emancipate themselves, in line with the Millennium Development Goals unanimously agreed upon by states and championed relentlessly by development agencies.

Persecution, generalized violence and violations of human rights continue in protracted displacement within and beyond national borders. Far from being a place of safety, often refugees and IDPs continue to be subjected to murder, armed attack, sexual and gender-based violence, forced military recruitment, separation of families, violations of or threats to their personal security and other fundamental rights for prolonged periods. In most of the case studies in this ARC research project the overwhelming majority of displaced people have been sequestered in camps, although a minority have economically integrated within local communities. People naturally prefer to congregate in their communities, in part to cope with the threats they face. But fundamental questions also need to be asked: should camps be encouraged during extensive periods of an 'enduring solution'; does the structural management of camps encourage dependency, and work against the implementation of durable solutions; do camps help prolong the conflict by providing a safe place for refugee warriors? Such questions have not been specifically addressed in this study and are worthy of future research.

It is particularly difficult to draw meaningful conclusions from this dilemma, but perhaps more attention needs to be given by the international community to resolving displacement before it becomes protracted, and less on institutionalizing the management of camps. But this is easier said than done, mainly because the two durable solutions of local integration and resettlement will seldom impact on the vast majority of those displaced, and the preferred solution of voluntary and safe repatriation will not be a viable option. Thus, when displaced populations are left in limbo, when the enduring solution is the only option, there may be little alternative to camp regimes.

Common lessons from the case studies

The aforementioned dilemmas work against drawing universal lessons that would enable humanitarian agencies to resolve situations of protracted displacement. It is necessary, first, to disaggregate the various displaced populations in order to differentiate solutions according to the needs of specific groups. Second, in many cases, solutions to protracted situations cannot be solved by humanitarianism alone. Humanitarian agencies are certainly unable to prevent the causes of protracted displacement. But neither can they guarantee a cure. Third, humanitarians need to think beyond the delivery of aid as well as outside the traditional UNHCR framework of 'durable solutions'. As Milner and Loescher have noted, 'humanitarian agencies – like UNHCR and humanitarian NGOs – cannot single-handedly resolve protracted refugee situations. Comprehensive solutions to long-term displacement require the sustained engagement of a wide range of political, strategic, development and humanitarian actors' (Milner and Loescher 2006).

Each of the case studies reflects the circumstances of a specific displacement, but all, to some degree and in different ways, have been politicized. Displacement in Afghanistan, Iraq and Sri Lanka reflect situations of civil war and foreign intervention, whereas the Bhutanese, Karen and Rohingya refugee populations reflect the actions of repressive governments. Only for Afghanistan and Iraq do the studies provide a generic overview of displacement, while the other studies provide a snapshot of particular refugee or IDP communities. Afghanistan and Iraq represent the largest number of displaced people and perhaps the best prospects for some refugee return, although not for some population groupings. Both the Sri Lanka and Afghanistan studies consider IDPs, with Sri Lanka focusing on communities in a specific geographic area, but both studies are cautious of a peaceful outcome. Nepal and Thailand are cases where resettlement is finally underway, but with a number of negative impacts on the remaining refugee populations. By contrast, the numbers of Rohingyas in Bangladesh would provide a manageable caseload for resettlement, but plans for this are not currently in preparation.

Humanitarian agencies might accept the truism that resolution is beyond their remit and dependent on political factors. Equally, they may see a legitimate need to advocate for political resolution, refusing to accept the unjust practice of 'warehousing' and working hard to keep displacement in the consciousness of the United Nations and its member states. But, most importantly, humanitarian agencies involved in service delivery are required to grapple with the fundamental question of what actions, if any, they can and will take to alleviate the suffering of the displaced, and whether or not their actions may inadvertently contribute to the situation remaining unresolved. To this end, four important and related lessons may be inferred from the case studies: first, the need for action research to better understand the dynamics of protracted displacement and possible solutions outside the traditional UNHCR framework; second, the critical importance of assuring human security for those displaced; third, the need to rethink the traditional concept of 'humanitarian space' in displacement situations, particularly given its juxtaposition with governance and the rule of law; and finally, the importance of improved communication and coordination among agencies and actors.

Action research

Effective humanitarian agencies are able to react quickly to help alleviate the immediate suffering of displaced communities. But often they are not sufficiently aware of the causes of the displacement or of the impact of their actions in resolving or perpetuating a longer-term problem. Moreover, most humanitarian agencies are 'outsiders', with the risk of imposing themselves to assist local communities with policies and procedures often devised by donor countries. An analysis of the case studies in this ARC research project suggests that more emphasis needs to be given to action research, to understand both the causes of displacement and the early application of appropriate and alternative solutions, especially if they fall outside the traditional UNHCR framework. For example, research that uncovers the conditions under which a particular humanitarian intervention is most likely to be effective can help inform the operational design of an aid programme.

Action research enables agencies to understand and disaggregate displaced populations in order to differentiate solutions according to the needs of specific groups, rather than attempting to apply broad durable solutions more universally. What might work for one group might not work for another, particularly when comparing refugees and IDPs, or specific ethnic or religious sects. It may be possible for certain groups to return but not others. Alternatively, when voluntary repatriation or local integration is not possible, then more lateral thinking can be given to migration and resettlement options, rather than to protracted camp management. The duration of the displacement impacts on solutions and can distort expectations. A person's understanding of 'home' may bear little resemblance to the actual situation in the home location, particularly after years of protracted displacement. This suggests that it may be possible or preferable for people to return to a different location, but regardless, it is important to act quickly and avoid generations of displacement and resentment.

Action research can also assist in devising practical solutions for local integration. Providing greater assistance for host countries and facilitating community acceptance and understanding of local conditions goes beyond political agreement: in such situations the host government and population must be able to see the benefits from local integration. Another important aspect for action research could be to determine the effectiveness of establishing regional early warning and management systems. Such a system has been operating with some success in the Horn of Africa since 2001, yet no comparable system has been evident for any of the case studies in this ARC research project (CEWARN 2001; Keyserlingk and Kopfmuller 2006). While such a system might not currently be feasible for Burma, it might be more applicable for the other case studies.

Gaining a better understanding of the actual circumstances on the ground through action research should enable evidence-based policies and programmes to be adopted by humanitarian agencies, hopefully mobilizing political and donor support. Action research rests on reciprocity, with humanitarian agencies affirming their practical commitment to assistance and advocating for and implementing more productive and relevant approaches to the difficulties of displacement. Through action research, humanitarian agencies, having considered the positions of various stakeholders and having implemented programmes beyond the need merely to provide immediate assistance to displaced recipients, should be able to design more appropriate programmes that have increased levels of local ownership.

A research-led approach will also assist humanitarian agencies to determine the effectiveness of their interventions. When crises occur and donor funding becomes available, it is not uncommon for a flood of humanitarian actors to become engaged, often with little understanding of the specific circumstances and with no long-term strategy. A commitment to ongoing research might help to avoid such circumstances.

Human security

The cornerstones of human security are protection and empowerment. In all of the case studies, protection and empowerment of the displaced were a challenge. In situations of protracted displacement humanitarian agencies need to work collaboratively to provide better and more consistent levels of protection while growing local capacity among the displaced populations.

A major difficulty in the provision of humanitarian protection occurs when access is denied to displaced communities because of the very insecurity that protection seeks to avoid. In such situations there seems little option but to invoke the principle of R2P, or to authorize UN mandates short of R2P that specify the protection of displaced communities. In such circumstances humanitarian and military protection mechanisms will be required to work in unison if they are to be effective.[13]

Agencies uncomfortable with the military and political agendas of government actors should attempt to build more productive relationships and coordination with government administrators to improve negotiation space and the possibility for influence. More effective coordination and communication between agencies enables a multiplier effect and allows displaced communities to benefit from agencies with greater access and influence. When political divisions manifest at the community level, threatening the effectiveness of traditional protection mechanisms, humanitarian agencies should develop their approach to support the building of community networks and capacity, utilizing community capital.

All of the case studies suggest that there is greater need for protection at a local level. Building community resilience and creating shared mechanisms and interests in contexts of ethnically and politically fractured communities are important. In such situations, humanitarian agencies can bring longer-term commitments to particular village-level interventions. This enables them to better

13 In the last decade the UN Security Council has authorized seven UN missions in Africa with a mandate to protect civilians, short of R2P. For a discussion on the effectiveness of protection see Holt and Berkman (2006).

understand threats, vulnerabilities and capacities of communities in order to build local approaches. Genuine and lasting partnerships with community-based organizations can help develop long-term commitment to the community. Longer-term engagement is necessary to ensure that humanitarian agencies can address entrenched features of the protection environment. In this way, community-based organizations will be better able to develop their specific protection regime, so crucial to longer-term peace building.

As with action research, human security can be more effective if protection needs are disaggregated. Different refugee and IDP communities have specific needs. Dealing with specific groups on specific issues, such as gender and religious requirements, and the protection requirements for safe return or resettlement, may help to devise solutions that go beyond the traditional UNHCR framework.

Humanitarian space and the rule of law

The case studies imply that the traditional understanding of humanitarian space seldom applies in situations of protracted displacement. This finding is consistent with other studies regarding humanitarian space (Wheeler and Harmer 2006; Meharg 2007, 1–7, 211–24). The traditional humanitarian principles of the International Committee of the Red Cross (ICRC) – humanity, independence, impartiality and neutrality – have proved difficult to apply in contested environments. Humanitarian agencies have increasingly worked in contexts where refugee and IDP situations have become deeply rooted and where political, military and institutional factors have coalesced to bring into question the ability or willingness of all humanitarian agencies to follow the ICRC humanitarian principles. In some situations UNHCR and other humanitarian agencies have been compelled by their donors to make decisions that were far from independent, neutral or impartial; increasingly NGOs have turned their backs on neutrality to actively champion the rights of displaced people.

The Sri Lanka study suggests that it is particularly difficult to implement protection mechanisms and work in a safe humanitarian space within a country where the government is at least part of the source of insecurity. This case suggests that protection-mandated agencies need to work transparently and confidently according to their principles, and ensure the government is held accountable for its responsibilities and does not stagnate in the face of over-reliance on international agencies. Also, non-mandated protection agencies need to work collaboratively with local communities to enhance protection through more non-traditional means.

The acceptance of R2P and an increasing number of UN missions mandated to protect civilian communities has meant that military forces and humanitarian agencies are working in the same space. Indeed, humanitarians and military forces (foreign and/or local) are required to coexist, often in an ill-defined and uneasy relationship. If situations of protracted displacement are to be resolved, or at least managed more effectively, then greater collaboration between civil and military actors will be required. Moreover, this will have increasing relevance to the standards of governance and rule-of-law modalities within displaced communities. Much more research is required to understand and develop better approaches to these critical issues.

Communication and coordination

A common lesson implied from the case studies is the scope for improved communication and coordination among agencies and actors, and closer collaboration with affected communities. The United Nations is giving increased emphasis to this in its policies and procedures, just as governments are emphasizing 'whole of government' approaches to complex emergencies. While more integrated approaches are welcome, improved communication and coordination with and for displaced communities has some way to go. The Sri Lanka case study shows the benefits of a protection multiplier effect if agencies could work more collaboratively; the study of Rohingyas in Bangladesh highlights the need for a more coordinated advocacy approach; the Nepal study alerts us to the benefits of interlinking refugee plans with national development strategies; the Afghanistan study raises the importance of better coordinated return and reintegration programmes; the Burma–Thailand border study indicates the importance of coordinated mechanisms to enhance refugee governance; and the Iraq study highlights the critical need for integrated planning around displacement before and after intervention.

Specific lessons from the case studies

This section of the chapter aims to highlight a few key lessons for humanitarian agencies from each of the case studies in the preceding chapters.

Iraqi refugees

Although not yet classified as a protracted displacement situation, the large number of displaced Iraqis demands attention from the international community. This displacement is the result of foreign military intervention, with little consideration given to the displacement impact on millions of individuals and neighbouring countries. The lasting impact on international security is yet to be determined, but in all likelihood could rival the situation with Palestinian refugees.

Some important lessons for humanitarian agencies include:

- Intervention, even for supposedly just causes such as democratization and ridding states of tyrants, can result in what many would consider greater harm, including the production of enormous numbers of refugees and IDPs.

- Refugee and IDP populations must be disaggregated to formulate solutions.
- IDP populations may be able to return, but to areas where their ethnic or religious group is predominant rather than to their original homes.
- Many of the minorities displaced – particularly the Palestinians and the Christians – will be unlikely to be able to return in the foreseeable future and alternative solutions, such as resettlement, should be promoted.

Afghan refugees

As with Iraq, the displacement from and within Afghanistan is the product of conflict and foreign intervention. Afghanistan is the longest protracted displacement of the case studies and provides an example of a complex and confusing situation over several decades in changing political circumstances. Despite significant improvements in some areas of human security since the fall of the Taliban regime in 2001, other areas have seen little or no improvement, and security has deteriorated drastically in parts of the country. Thus, despite one of the biggest repatriations in UNHCR's history (nearly five million), large numbers of refugees have decided not to return voluntarily from Pakistan and Iran (as well as Western countries abroad), with incidences of 'recycling' and subsequent internal displacement. Continuing insecurity and conflict, coupled with corruption and limited absorption capacity of the Afghan state (infrastructure, service delivery, governance, employment, etc.), are creating new or repeated incidents of internal and external displacement.

The Afghan refugee situation may be the most blatantly politicized case discussed in this ARC research project. For Pakistan, the Afghan refugees were initially convenient leverage for regional domination and attention by the US and other international actors. Now they have become an easy scapegoat for social ills, terrorism and insecurity. Similarly, Iran has increasingly used refugees as a political bargaining chip in the region, as well as a scapegoat for internal problems. Internationally, the Afghan refugees were an excuse to criticize the Soviet Union during the Cold War; resolving protracted displacement at this time would have sent the wrong message, as it would have excused Soviet actions. Here the goals of the Afghan resistance converged with those of others for whom the refugee community was a source of support and justification for action, as well as a fertile recruitment ground. Later on, the rapid repatriation in a politically unstable environment became a classic justification to demonstrate change (obtained through an international intervention, maybe even justifying it in retrospect) and improvement in Afghanistan to provide support for a fledgling state (a common occurrence in post-conflict situations where refugee return has symbolic importance).

The lack of coordinated civil–military planning in Afghanistan, with different national objectives and priorities, continues to cause divisions between the national government, intervening coalitions, the United Nations, humanitarian agencies, and, of course, the people of Afghanistan. One might also argue that this situation has provided a fertile recruiting ground for an insurgency that exploits to its own advantage every mistake made by the Afghan government and the international community. UNHCR in all this has been forced to work in a difficult political environment trying to balance strategic protection needs with the wishes of host and donor countries.

Humanitarian agencies working in Afghanistan are able to reflect on a number of important lessons, including:

- From a strategic perspective, the politicization of refugee situations is dangerous and can backfire, as seen for example in the re-emergence of the Taliban and the survival of al-Qaeda aided by a protracted refugee situation.
- Total repatriation of Afghans at this point is neither feasible nor desirable. Humanitarian actors and states need to distinguish and disaggregate the needs of those who remain from those who have returned.
- Returnees need to be considered as rational actors, who decide to return after a careful calculation of costs and benefits, including not simply the situation at home, but also the experience abroad (the latter being often overlooked). For example, the notion of 'home' is often transformed during long-term displacement. It is important for both refugees and involved humanitarian actors to distinguish between a nostalgic longing for what once was home, and a more rational understanding of what the actual conditions may be.
- Refugees and returnees are a diverse group with diverse needs. It is necessary to understand and differentiate and disaggregate refugees' needs depending on their reasons for displacement, their actual circumstances and the length of time they have been displaced. Usually those displaced for a longer period are more reluctant to return (often lacking networks to do so). Similarly, those who may fear persecution or are lacking protection may also be reluctant to return. Solutions for the remaining refugee population need to be seen within a wider framework than protracted displacement and the traditional UNHCR durable solutions framework, to include greater economic and migration considerations. For example, local integration does not necessarily have to mean awarding of citizenship, but possibly temporary labour agreements allowing a transitional and transnational lifestyle. Assistance to host states should be a major consideration in working out arrangements of how to deal with long-standing refugee situations.
- Immobility is not the solution for Afghan refugees as migration is a strategic survival tool of many Afghan families, by spreading their risks. Hence it is advisable to reject any idea that 'sustainability' equates to immobility – that it ideally involves 'anchoring people to their places of origin' (Turton and Marsden 2002, 52). Mixed population movements are common, and both politics and discourse should reflect this.

- Forced return should not be tolerated as it does not only violate people's rights, but also provides only for a short-term solution, given that there is a high likelihood that many may try to find alternative ways to leave Afghanistan in the future.
- The reality of conditions in Afghanistan should not be neglected. This includes the challenges of overcoming poverty, dealing with the absence of security and rule of law, and the practical difficulties of effective reintegration. Many returnees have expressed that their expectation of assistance upon return was not adequately met, and if they had known this they would not have returned. This is particularly important if renewed displacement is to be avoided after return. The linkage between return and internal displacement needs further research.

Sri Lankan IDPs

Sri Lanka provides the primary example of local internal displacement considered in these case studies, although broader consideration of IDPs is also covered in the Afghanistan case study. Since 1983, displacement in Sri Lanka has been caused by intractable conflict. Many IDPs have experienced repeated and ongoing cycles of displacement whilst some IDPs have stayed temporarily in the same place for more than ten years. Durable solutions and proper protection for IDPs have been elusive due to threats, risks and vulnerabilities that continue to exist in a militarized environment without political resolution to the conflict. Unlike the situation in Aceh, Indonesia, the devastation caused by the tsunami in December 2004 did not lead to a negotiated settlement of the conflict.

The key operational challenges for humanitarian agencies relate to negotiating the politically sensitive relationships with the government, while operating in a militarized environment and with deeply divided and traumatized communities.

Some important lessons for humanitarian agencies from this case study include:

- Highly politicized durable solutions and a deteriorating security situation create a particular challenge to protection approaches in an internally displaced context. Agencies constantly need to develop and implement humanitarian action that is informed by political understanding of the context, and consistently take a principled and protection-sensitive approach.
- For protection-mandated agencies it is important to work transparently and confidently, not compromising the principles of the agency.
- In the current state of conflict, non-mandated protection agencies need to maintain a low profile in implementing protection mechanisms. NGOs should be careful about advocating protection if they are involved in service delivery, lest retribution be taken on those whom they are trying to empower and protect. At present, this requires publicly avoiding the 'protection' label in favour of building a protection-sensitive orientation

in their service delivery programmes. In this environment, protection is as much an orientation as a set of activities.

- More effective communication and coordination between agencies is desirable. This enables a 'protection multiplier' effect, bringing together agencies with their different mandates, expertise, resources and networks to meet commonly identified protection needs. Long-term engagement enables agencies to utilize non-controversial entry points that are perceived as less political. As the local conflict dynamics are in flux, agencies need to remain vigilant regarding how communities and the authorities perceive their protection work.
- Strengthening community protection capacity is particularly important in an environment in which political divisions manifest themselves at a community level and dismantle traditional community/collective coping mechanisms. Building community resilience to safeguard against the breakdown in community protection strategies is necessary in the context of political factionalism and fractured communities. Creating shared mechanisms and interests between and within communities should be incorporated into approaches to build opportunities for resilience in divided communities.
- Approaching protection as a process requires long-term engagement and ownership by the local community, consistent with cultural sensitivity. Protection mechanisms are likely to work when they are owned by the community and not imposed.

Bangladesh – Rohingya refugees from Burma

The protracted displacement of Rohingya refugees in Bangladesh is arguably the most depressing of all the case studies in this ARC research project. Largely abused, forgotten and ignored, the Rohingyas are the innocent victims of contested colonial borders and international inaction to rein in the anti-ethnic actions of the Burma government. Not until recently has UNHCR given this matter the attention it deserves, and the international community has much work ahead. While intervention in Burma under R2P would seem justified based on its continuing discrimination of minority groups like the Rohingyas, there seems little inclination for this by regional countries and the broader international community.

At least four key lessons for humanitarian agencies emerge from this study:

- Advocacy based on sound research is a critical tool for putting issues on the international agenda. Moreover, the more coordinated the advocacy, the more attention it is likely to attract. More so than the other displaced populations in this ARC research project, the Rohingyas have largely gone unnoticed by the international community. Humanitarian agencies need to mobilize support and advocate greater attention for the Rohingyas. Also,

a regime of continued research and project evaluation is required, with continued leadership from UNHCR.
- More effective communication on the Rohingya problem is required between UNHCR, UN agencies, NGOs and the donor community if improvement and viable solutions are to be achieved. UN agencies must be faithful to their humanitarian mandates, despite the political challenges. In particular, international NGOs should become more active in assisting the Rohingyas to meet their humanitarian needs.
- Assistance to the Rohingyas in Bangladesh should be considered in tandem with the needs of the local Bangladesh communities. Failure to do this will jeopardize prospects for local integration and risk enmity arising between the two groups. A comprehensive and integrated approach is required.
- The number of Rohingyas in Bangladesh represents a relatively small caseload in comparison to many other protracted refugee populations. Immediate attention should be given to commencement of a resettlement programme.

Thailand – Burmese refugees

The mix of different types of displaced populations in Thailand makes this protracted situation a particular challenge. The interaction between durable solutions, protection efforts and humanitarian assistance programmes on refugees, migrants, camp residents, urban refugees, IDPs and other groups demonstrates that there is no simple 'quick fix' solution for all populations. Even so, Burmese refugees in Thailand are afforded better treatment than the Rohingyas in Bangladesh. This may be due to the significant presence of humanitarian agencies on the Thailand–Burma border. As resettlement moves forward in an accelerated fashion, it is important to keep in mind that it will not resolve the root causes of displacement from Burma. Voluntary repatriation to Burma, once considered the only acceptable solution for the Burmese, is now fading as a possibility, at least in the short term.

At least three important lessons for humanitarian agencies can be gleaned from this case study:

- The behaviours and actions of one group of displaced people influence the choices and actions of other groups. Humanitarian agencies should heed this relationship when designing humanitarian programmes.
- Similarly, it is critical that humanitarian agencies carefully consider all possible populations with whom they want to work. While camp residents and 'refugees' as defined by UNHCR are often the easiest populations to access, they are not necessarily the most vulnerable.
- In order to ensure that protection is practised throughout an agency's programmes, all possible target groups should be considered as well as their effect on one another. This is relevant not only for different types

of displaced, but for programmes that target one group over another: one ethnicity over another, one gender over another, one age group over another, etc.

Nepal – Bhutanese refugees

If the Rohingyas represent the most depressing of the case studies, the Bhutanese case study may be presented as the most frustrating. After 17 years the international community has finally implemented a voluntary resettlement programme, when it should have been obvious that voluntary repatriation was unlikely to be politically achievable, and local integration only partially so. While the prospects of resettlement may satisfy many of the Lhotshampas, it has also led to deep divisions in the camps, where some refugees are loathe to turn in a new direction, fearing that any chance for future repatriation will be lost. On the other hand, the alternative is no better: if the option of resettlement were to be taken away, the Lhotshampas would only be harmed again, as they would forego the first chance in 17 years for legal rights and a release from their present state of limbo. Apart from the obvious lesson of the need to pursue solutions that are politically achievable, humanitarian agencies working in Nepal can learn two primary lessons from recent events in the Bhutanese camps:

- Home and host governments do not function in a vacuum. Understanding their interaction with other stakeholders, such as international agencies, regional powers, and the refugees themselves, is critical not only to awareness of how durable solutions will play out in the long term, but how enduring solutions will manifest themselves in the short and intermediate term.
- Country strategies developed by humanitarian agencies are a valuable means by which to plan funding drives and design specific programmes, but they should be sufficiently flexible to adapt to changing circumstances in a refugee context. A country strategy that assumes the repatriation of its recipients, for example, should have a 'Plan B' in the instance that refugees do not repatriate.

Conclusion

This ARC research project was initiated because an Australian NGO, Austcare, wanted to better understand the nature of protracted displacement in Asia. By enhancing its knowledge of protracted displacement, Austcare considered that it would be better placed to assist the displaced and prioritize its efforts. The preliminary research findings informed Austcare's programming decisions, identifying priority areas for engagement and enabling Austcare to better understand and respond to the changing dynamics of these cases. In the course of the life of this ARC research project, resettlement of Burmese and Bhutanese refugees became a reality on the international agenda. The research findings provided evidence for Austcare to design programmes that more effectively addressed the evolving situation and developed humanitarian responses situated within the broader causes, symptoms and consequences of the context. The research provided evidence to mobilize donor support for programmes that addressed new and emerging protection issues. The credibility of evidence-based proposals proved successful in enrolling donor support, allowing Austcare to affirm its commitment to the case study countries and develop more productive and relevant programmes. Furthermore, the research involved collaboration with a range of actors in the case study countries that established new relationships and networks for Austcare, enabling the agency to tap into and benefit from broader knowledge and experience.

This ARC research project provided a useful vehicle for Austcare to give higher priority to research and to link this with more integrated programming and assign priorities for the allocation of limited financial resources. Research recommendations confront organizational goals and donor dependencies, but action research is not simply an end product. Research is also about ensuring that Austcare staff and local partners are involved in and benefit from the research methodology and outcomes. Action research encourages critical reflection on the part of practitioners and facilitates critical analysis to reflect operational realities.

More specifically, the preliminary findings of this ARC research project influenced Austcare in submitting major proposals to donors for funding to support Iraqi refugees in Jordan and Syria, Rohingya refugees in Bangladesh, and Burmese refugees on the Thailand–Burma border. The study also enabled Austcare to explore possibilities of protection of Sri Lankan IDPs through local partners rather than establishing a more permanent Austcare presence. Importantly, this study also assisted Austcare in giving higher priority to research, knowledge management and advocacy, in addition to service delivery projects through local partners.

NGOs like Austcare are committed to working with people affected by conflict and natural disaster to help them build their human security. In seeking to identify opportunities at the community level to protect and empower displaced communities, NGOs, in collaboration with local community-based partners and UNHCR, are well placed to listen to and understand the needs of refugees and IDPs, and to work with them over extended periods of time. Refugees and IDPs should not be *outside* efforts to understand protracted displacement contexts.

This study suggests that humanitarian agencies are seldom able to resolve situations of protracted displacement, but that they can make a significant contribution to enhancing the human security of the displaced and raising the consciousness of states to take remedial action, as belated and unsatisfactory as this might be. The study also suggests that humanitarian agencies must be careful not to institutionalize protracted displacement and create a culture of dependency through their eagerness to assist, and to constantly adapt their approach to each situation. Of increasing importance for humanitarian agencies is the need to enhance protection mechanisms, to better coordinate these with other relevant actors, to move beyond the traditional acceptance of humanitarian space, and to enhance the effectiveness of civil–military coordination where it is warranted. In pursuing these ends, NGOs in particular must continue to influence policymakers as well as delivering humanitarian relief. Above all, humanitarian agencies must continually question their own actions lest they become part of the problem of protracted displacement rather than the cure.

It is too easy for humanitarian agencies to accept the political impasse that bedevils the achievement of the durable solutions framework. But it is much more important for these same agencies to be prepared to think laterally and, where necessary, to beat the drum. William Maley is correct: ‘it is only through the utopian exercise of imagining other worlds that we can begin to see how a better world might be built’ (Maley 2003).

Bibliography

Adelman, H. (1998), ‘Why Refugee Warriors Are Threats’, *The Journal of Conflict Studies* xviii: 3, 49–69.

Afghanistan Independent Human Rights Commission (AIHRC) (2007), ‘Economic and Social Rights in Afghanistan II’, Report published 1 August 2007, available at <http://www.unhcr.org/cgi-bin/texis/vtx/refworld/rwmain?docid=471f4a5b0>, accessed 1 January 2008.

Betts, A. (2007), ‘Conference Report: The Politics, Human Rights and Security Implications of Protracted Refugee Situations’, 19–20 September, St Antony’s College, University of Oxford, *Journal of Refugee Studies* 19: 4, 509–14.

Brookings-Bern Project on Internal Displacement (ongoing) (Washington DC: Brookings Institution), website and resources available at <http://www.brookings.edu/projects/idp.aspx>.

Carr, E.H. (1947), *International Relations between the Two World Wars* (London: Macmillan).

Carr, E.H. (1964), *The Twenty Years Crisis, 1919–1939: An Introduction to the Study of International Relations* (New York: Harper and Row).

CEWARN (2001), ‘Report of the High Level Meeting on the Development of a Conflict Early Warning and Response Mechanism for IGAD Member States’, Nairobi, 3–4 May.

Chen, G. (2004), ‘A Global Campaign To End Refugee Warehousing’, *World Refugee Survey 2004 – Warehousing Issue* (Washington, DC: US Committee on Refugees), available at <http://www.refugees.org/data/wrs/04/pdf/21.pdf>.

Chesterman, S. (2001), *Walking Softly in Afghanistan: the Future of UN State-Building* (Boulder: Lynne Rienner).

Cohen, R. (2008), *UNHCR: Expanding its Role with IDPs* (Washington, DC: Brookings Instittion).

Feller, E. (2006), 'UNHCR's Role in IDP Protection: Opportunities and Challenges', *Forced Migration Review*, Brookings-Bern Special Issue, December.

Holt, V.K. and Berkman, T.C. (2006), *The Impossible Mandate? Military Preparedness, the Responsibility to Protect and Modern Peace Operations* (Washington, DC: Henry L. Stimson Center).

Internal Displacement Monitoring Centre (IDMC) (2007), 'Global Overview of Trends and Developments in 2006', Report published April 2007 (Geneva: IDMC and Norwegian Refugee Council) available at <http://www.internal-displacement.org/8025708F004BE3B1/(httpInfoFiles)/9251510E3E5B6FC3C12572BF0029C267/$file/Global_Overview_2006.pdf>.

Keyserlingk, N. von and Kopfmüller, S. (2006), *Lessons Learned from Establishing a Conflict Early Warning and Response Mechanism (CEWARN) in the Horn of Africa* (Addis Ababa: CEWARN).

Lang, H. (2001), 'The Repatriation Predicament of Burmese Refugees in Thailand: A Preliminary Analysis', UNHCR Working Paper No. 46 (Geneva: UNHCR).

Loescher, G., Milner, J., Newman, E. and Troeller, G. (2007), 'Protracted Refugee Situations and Peacebuilding', Policy Brief No. 1 (Tokyo: United Nations University), available at <http://www.unu.edu/publications/briefs/policy-briefs/2007/PB01-07.pdf>.

Maley, W. (2003), 'A New Tower of Babel? Reappraising the Architecture of Refugee Protection', in E. Newman and J. van Selm (eds), *Refugees and Forced Displacement: International Security, Human Vulnerability, and the State* (Tokyo: United Nations University Press).

Meharg, S. (ed.) (2007), *Helping Hands and Loaded Arms: Navigating the Military and Humanitarian Space* (Nova Scotia: Canadian Peacekeeping Press).

Milner, J. and Loescher, G. (2006), 'Protracted Refugee Situation in Thailand: Towards Solutions', presentation to the Foreign Correspondents' Club of Thailand, 1 February.

Newman, E. and van Selm, J. (eds) (2003), *Refugees and Forced Displacement: International Security, Human Vulnerability, and the State* (Tokyo: United Nations University Press).

Piffenberger, B. (1988), 'Sri Lanka in 1987: Indian Intervention and Resurgence of the JVP', *Asian Survey* 28: 2, 137–47.

Rufin, J.-C. (1986), *Le piége: Quand l'aide humanitaire remplace la guerre* (Paris: Jean-Claude Lattès).

Schloch, R. (2005), 'UNHCR and the Afghan Refugees in the Early 1980s: Between Humanitarian Action and the Cold War', Paper for the research project on 'UNHCR and the Global Cold War' (Geneva: Graduate Institute of International Studies, and the Geneva Centre for Security Policy).

Terry, F. (2002), *Condemned to Repeat? The Paradox of Humanitarian Action* (Ithaca and London: Cornell University Press).

Turton, D. and Marsden, P. (2002), 'Taking Refugees for a Ride: The Politics of Refugee Return to Afghanistan', Issues Paper (Kabul and Islamabad: Afghanistan Research and Evaluation Unit).

UN Summit (2005), 'UN World Summit: High-Level Plenary Meeting of the 60th Session of the General Assembly 14–16 September 2005: An Overview', available at <http://www.un.org/summit2005/>.

UNGPID (1998), 'UN Guiding Principles on Internal Displacement', available at <http://www.unhchr.ch/html/menu2/7/b/principles.htm>, accessed 23 January 2008.

UNHCR (2002), 'Agenda for Protection', Executive Committee of the High Commissioner's Programme, Standing Committee 24th Meeting, 26 June (EC/52/SC/CRP.9/Rev.1) (Geneva: UNHCR).

UNHCR (2004), 'Protracted Refugee Situations', Executive Committee of the High Commissioner's Programme, Standing Committee 30th Meeting, 10 June (EC/54/SC/CRP.14) (Geneva: UNHCR), available at <www.refugees.org/data/warehousing/docs/sc_prs.pdf>.

UNHCR (2006a), *The State of the World's Refugees 2006* (New York: Oxford University Press).

UNHCR (2006b), 'Refugees by Numbers', 2006 edition (UNHCR/MRPI/B•1/ENG 1, September 2006) (Geneva: UNHCR).

UNHCR (2007), 'Informal Consultative Meeting', 16 January.

UNHCR (2008), 'Protecting Refugees and the Role of the UNHCR 2007–08' (Geneva, UNHCR) available at <http://www.unhcr.org/basics/BASICS/4034b6a34.pdf>.

UNHCR/WFP (2006), 'Acute Malnutrition in Protracted Refugee Situations: A Global Strategy', UNHCR/World Food Programme Joint Report, January.

US Committee for Refugees and Immigrants (2004), *World Refugee Survey 2004 – Warehousing Issue* (Washington, DC: US Committee on Refugees and Immigrants).

US Committee for Refugees and Immigrants (USCRI 2007), *World Refugee Survey 2007* (Washington, DC: US Committee on Refugees and Immigrants), <http://www.refugees.org/article.aspx?id=1941>, accessed 25 July 2008.

Wheeler, V. and Harmer, A. (eds) (2006), 'Resetting the Rules of Engagement: Trends and Issues in Military–Humanitarian Relations', Research Report No. 21 (London: Humanitarian Policy Group, Overseas Development Institute), March.

Wilkinson, P. (2008), 'Insurgency Concerns and Vulnerabilities: Progress in Afghanistan as of 1 Jan 08', distributed as part of a Roundtable presentation, Toronto, Canada, 11 February.

Zolberg, A., Suhrke, A.and Aguayo, S. (1989), *Escape from Violence: Conflict and the Refugee Crisis in the Developing World* (New York: Oxford University Press).

Index

Page numbers in **bold** indicate figures, *italics* indicate tables.